Green Practices and Business Augmentation

Hosting the Green Card

Green Practices and Business Augmentation

Hosting the Green Card

Editors

Professor (Dr.) Manodip Ray Chaudhuri

Professor of Management in HR & OB and Former Dean
DRC PhD Convener in Management
Xavier Business School
St. Xavier's University, Kolkata, India
Graduate Alumnus, University of Guelph, Ontario, Canada

Professor (Dr.) Soma Sur

Professor of Management in Marketing and Former Dean
Xavier Business School
Director of LCERI and PhD Coordinator
St. Xavier's University, Kolkata, India

ALLIED PUBLISHERS PVT. LTD.

Noida • Mumbai • Kolkata • Chennai • Bangalore

ALLIED PUBLISHERS PRIVATE LIMITED

D-5, Sector-2, **Noida**–201 301
Ph. Nos.: 0120-4320295/2542557/4352866 • E-mail: delhi.books@alliedpublishers.com

17 Chittaranjan Avenue, **Kolkata**–700072
Ph.: 033-22129618 • E-mail: cal.books@alliedpublishers.com

15 J.N. Heredia Marg, Ballard Estate, **Mumbai**–400001
Ph.: 022-42126969 • E-mail: mumbai.books@alliedpublishers.com

No. 25/10, Commander-in-Chief Road, Ethiraj Lane (Next to Post Office)
Egmore, **Chennai**–600008
Ph.: 044-28223938 • E-mail: chennai.books@alliedpublishers.com

P.B. No. 9932, No. 15, 3rd Floor (Next to Vijaya Bank), 5th Cross, Gandhinagar,
Karnataka, **Bangalore**–560009, Ph.: 080-41530285 / 22386239
E-mail: bngl.books@alliedpublishers.com

Website: www.alliedpublishers.com

ISBN: 978-93-89934-67-0

Published by Sunil Sachdev and printed by Ravi Sachdev at Allied Publishers Pvt. Ltd.,
D-5, Sector-2, Noida–201 301

Dedicated

With Love and Reverence

To

Our
Respective Family Members

From

Professor (Dr.) Manodip Ray Chaudhuri
Professor (Dr.) Soma Sur

Foreword

It gives me a deep sense of pleasance and satisfaction to pen a foreword for this book. The editors, Professor (Dr.) Manodip Ray Chaudhuri, whom I personally know as a brilliant academician and a vivacious learner and Professor (Dr.) Soma Sur, have honestly put in their best of effort to integrate, and assimilate 24 out-of-the-ordinary chapters from various chapter authors internationally across the globe to draft this book in its present form.

The distinctive feature of this book is that it attempts to bring to light the issue of *Green Practices in relation to Business Process Augmentation* in real terms through conceptual papers and case studies all through the chapters of the book. The work has been meticulously dealt with to highlight the significance, appositeness, and pertinence of the notion of *Green Business Practices* in the corporate world today.

The presentation of the domain in the chapters have an appropriate flow and runs smoothly across the platform of a holistic discussion of *Green Initiatives* in the workplace and how it accelerates organizational growth and development in the long term. The detailing out of the book has a plethora of considerations and concerns in the fields of *Green Practices and Business Augmentation* viz. Green Business Practices and Law; Green Academics using AI; Green Coding; Entrepreneurial Orientation and Social Seal; HR Sustainability; Green Technology Innovation; Green Practices to Attract Customers; Transition between Shopper Types; Green Marketing and Consumers; Sustainability and Success in Home-based Business; Green Packaging; Corporate Social Responsibility and Green Practices; Case Study on Big Basket; Green HRM; Concept of Business Augmentation through Implementation of Green Practices; Green Finance; Case Study on Tata Power; Learning Organization and Green Practices; Green Hospitals; Green HRM Post Pandemic; Green Packaging and Purchase Decision of Customers; Stakeholders' Influence on Green Practices in Firms; Sustainable Development Goals Seven and Thirteen; and Holistic Notion of Sustainable Green Business for Bharat.

An interested reader would find this book as a thorough reflection of the dynamism of the view of *Green Initiatives* from various focal and crucial angles. The crux of the book is to hold up to the reader the backbone, roadblocks, and turnarounds of initiating *Green Practices* at work with an eye to Business Development and Processual Augmentation. On the one hand the book is a theoretical journey of the underlying concepts, while on the other hand it is an adaptation and accommodation of case-specific application-oriented discussions as well.

I have no inhibitions to say that this book would be a lucid and an easy-access reference reading for learners, scholars, researchers, and academicians in the field of

Green Business Practices in Corporations aiming at *Business Process Augmentation.* The opulent and translucent presentation of the 24 chapters of the book, coupled with the masterpiece of the editors have made this book a real good treasure for enthusiasts in this concerned filed of studies in Business Management.

Cheers and Happy Reading!

James Edward Joseph '83 EdD '23
Vice President,
Advancement & Innovation,
Le Moyne College,
Dean,
Madden College of Business and Economics
Syracuse, New York, USA
&
Ignatian Carroll School Global Fellow at Boston Collège,
Chestnut Hill,
Boston, Massachusetts, USA

Preface

This book moves along 24 meticulously selected chapters in the field of *Green Practices and Business Augmentation.* The focus of the book is on a wide range of understanding of the concept of Green Initiatives in corporations and their relationship with the holistic growth and development of the firm in the true sense of the term. The book is an anthology, useful to the learners, researchers, and academicians in Sustainability, Green Practices and Organizational Development. The thrust of this book is to identify and analyze pertinent and a wide range of concepts and applications within the purview of Green Interventions in organizations and business process escalation and environmental sustainability.

As a research reference book, it delves deep into quite a handful of related clusters in some 24 identifications as chapters in the book viz.

1. Green Business Management and the Law
2. Impact of Green Academics using AI and its Applicability in Enriching Educational
3. Green Coding
4. Entrepreneurial Orientation and Organizational Performance in Companies Certified by The Social Seal
5. Human Resources and Sustainability: The Present and The Future
6. Green Technology Innovation in Indonesia: Analysis of the Current Leading Green Practices
7. Instigating the Discourse of "Green Practices": A Persuasive Strategy to Attract Customers
8. Transition between Shopper Types: A Study of Food Buying by Indian Professionals
9. Effect of Green Marketing on Consumers' Purchase Behaviour: A Review
10. Balancing Sustainability and Success: An In-depth Analysis of Home-Based Businesses in India
11 Impact of Green Packaging and Labelling on Consumers' Evaluation and Choice: A Study Based in Kolkata
12. Leveraging Sustainability through Green Practices in CSR
13. Playing the Green Game: The case of Big Basket's Environmental Stewardship.
14. Green Human Resource Management in Indian Organisations
15. Green Practices and Business Augmentation: Reality or an Illusion
16. Green Finance: Prerequisite Towards Sustainability
17. 'Sustainability is Attainable' - Tata Power's Transition to Green Energy
18. Learning Organisation and Green Practices

19. Green Hospitals: Future of Sustainable Healthcare
20. A Study of Green HRM Post Pandemic: An Emerging Trend in the New Era
21. Influence of Green Packaging on Consumers' Purchase Decision: An Exploratory Study.
22. A Study on Stakeholders' influence on Green Practices by Firms
23. Linkage between Sustainable Development Goal 7 &13: Challenges and Way Forward
24. Building Sustainable Green Businesses for Bharat

The book, with this valued set of selected works, in the form of an anthology, would rightfully articulate and bring in coherence towards paving the way for further investigation, probing, understanding and study of Green Initiatives and Business Augmentation in reality. Budding researchers and academicians would be genuinely benefitted reading this book.

Professor (Dr.) Manodip Ray Chaudhuri
Professor of Management in HR & OB and Former Dean
DRC-PhD Convener in Management
Xavier Business School
St. Xavier's University, Kolkata, India
Graduate Alumnus, University of Guelph, Ontario, Canada

&

Professor (Dr.) Soma Sur
Professor of Management in Marketing and Former Dean
Xavier Business School
Director of LCERI and PhD Coordinator
St. Xavier's University, Kolkata, India

Acknowledgments

Our deepest sense of appreciativeness and acknowledgement towards all those who have supported us in preparation of this book.

As this book is an incorporation of 24 chapters in the form of an anthology, we are genuinely thankful and overtly grateful to all the chapter-authors of the various chapters integrated in this book.

Our sincere thankfulness is to the publisher, Allied Publishers Private Limited, Noida, Kolkata, Mumbai, Chennai, Bangalore, Hyderabad for taking care and offering the necessary help towards publication of this book in this present form.

Our respect to Father John Felix Raj, S.J., Vice Chancellor, St. Xavier's University, Kolkata and Prof. Ashis Mitra, Registrar, St. Xavier's University, Kolkata for their encouragement.

Our wholehearted adulation and appreciation to James Edward Joseph, '83 EdD '23, Vice President, Advancement & Innovation, Le Moyne College and Dean of Madden College of Business and Economics, Syracuse, New York, USA & Ignatian Carroll School Global Fellow at Boston Collège, Chestnut Hill, Boston, Massachusetts, USA for writing the Foreword for this book.

With veneration and reverence, we shower our gratitude to our respective family members without whose support the book would not have seen the light of the day.

We thank the Almighty for His Kindness and Blessings on us for preparation of this book.

We acknowledge one and all who were by us for preparation of this book in this present form.

Thank you all.

Professor (Dr.) Manodip Ray Chaudhuri
Professor of Management in HR & OB and Former Dean
DRC-PhD Convener in Management
Xavier Business School
St. Xavier's University, Kolkata, India
Graduate Alumnus, University of Guelph, Ontario, Canada

&

Professor (Dr.) Soma Sur
Professor of Management in Marketing and Former Dean
Xavier Business School
Director of LCERI and PhD Coordinator
St. Xavier's University, Kolkata, India

Contents

Greening Corporate Governmentality: A Juridical Tryst with Sustainability

Dr. Debasis Poddar[1]

ABSTRACT: With clandestine contribution of commercial enterprises, so called Anthropocene has made a mark of its own toward global climate change in the contemporary times. The insignia of Anthropocene are apparent, also, omnipresent, on the face of record; not without reasoning that the clarion call for green business management, followed by adherence to the Sustainable Development Goals, appears on its rise worldwide. Despite being a fast-emerging economy, the State and its Inc. taken together, India extends responsible response to the call of international community for climate action by means of adherence (read compliance) to demonstrate its climate discipline. Thus, as the maiden of its kind, the Companies Act of 2013 introduces a unique provision vis-à-vis corporate social responsibility as a legal obligation for commercial enterprises in India. Afterwords, a potential space for their corporate environment responsibility is initiated by means of delegated legislation, Office Memorandum of 2018, superseded by another subsequent Office Memorandum of 2020; issued by Ministry of Environment, Forest and Climate Change, Government of India.

Accordingly, there is a synergy—if not merger—of corporate social responsibility with corporate environmental responsibility to be done by the commercial enterprises in India. For instance, the inventory includes infrastructure creation for drinking water supply, sanitation, health, education, skill development, roads, cross drains, electrification including solar power, solid waste management facilities, scientific support, and awareness to local farmers to increase yield of crop and fodder, rainwater harvesting, soil moisture conservation works, avenue plantation, plantation in community areas, etc. Taken social and natural variants of human environment together, in a nutshell, the statutory ideation of corporate responsibility but reiterates a progressive ideation of environment with inclusive imagination, including local public good, toward more humane environment.

Keywords: *Corporate Social Responsibility, Corporate Environment Responsibility, Corporate Good Governance, Boardroom Meeting, Conversation Vis-à-vis Conservation, Independent Directorate, Corporate Environmentality, Greenwashing to Greening, etc.*

---

[1] Professor of Law, National Law University and Judicial Academy, Assam.

"We need a new breed of corporate lawyers—including house counsels, lobbyists, and outside attorneys—with both the expertise in emerging regulatory regimes and the management skills to use that expertise. We need lawyers who use the law offensively rather than just defensively. The new corporate counsels must act as coach, adviser, and strategist, embracing their companies' most innovative plans. Law is the last great untapped source of competitive advantage. To extract it, the culture of business, not to mention the cultures of law schools and business schools, will have to evolve mighty fast."

—Downes (2004)[1]

INTRODUCTION

A decade back, the (new) Companies Act of 2013 has brought in a radical provision vis-à-vis corporate social responsibility (hereafter CSR), the first of its kind worldwide, for all commercial enterprises; with statutory qualifiers under section 135 of the Act.[2-3] Here lies the threshold of such transformative legislation to understand and appreciate contemporary jurisprudence in the wake a paradigm shift in corporate governmentality. In a nutshell, social responsibility- of natural and juristic personae alike- is a matter left to morality, rather than to legality, in all major legal traditions worldwide and the same remains commonplace in course of corporate social responsibility; after global practice. With lived experience of earlier legislation- the Companies Act of 1956- for six decades (1956–2014), social responsibility remained a moral grandeur in the ambitious wish-list toward good corporate governance. Since the adoption of 'inclusive growth' by agenda of the Eleventh Five-year Plan in 2007, followed by so-called 'voluntary guidelines' on CSR in 2009, ideation of transformative corporate jurisprudence went initiated 2007 onward and culminated in the new Act of 2013 to push corporate social responsibility toward a paradigm shift (detailed in the Annexure); shift from the morality to the legality by means of the Act of 2013; something unprecedented in the chronicles of benevolent corporate governmentality and the consequent social responsibility so far.

---

[1] Downes, Larry (2004, December). First, Empower All the Lawyers, *Harvard Business Review, From the Magazine*. https://hbr.org/2004/12/first-empower-all-the-lawyers

[2] Every company having net worth of rupees five hundred crore or more, or turnover of rupees one thousand crore or more or a net profit of rupees five crore or more during any financial year shall constitute a Corporate Social Responsibility Committee of the Board consisting of three or more directors, out of which at least one director shall be an independent director.
The Companies Act, 2013, section 135(1).

[3] The Board of every company referred to in sub-section (1), shall ensure that the company spends, in every financial year, at least two per cent. of the average net profits of the company made during the three immediately preceding financial years, in pursuance of its Corporate Social Responsibility Policy.
The Companies Act, 2013, section 135(5).

Without entry to the nitty-gritty of larger juridical issues vis-à-vis corporate social irresponsibility, e.g., aggressive land acquisition in the name of development project- with recourse to regressive statutes- to gross detriment of Gramin Bharat, Tribal Bharat and the wildlife well within the forest coverage as its default habitat, the author limits research foci upon the character of CSR under the Companies Act of 2013 for a decade (2014–2024);[4] something in semblance with the window-dressing- either by colourwash[5] or otherwise- and detrimental to the very propriety of corporate good governance genre. The corporate governmentality vis-à-vis CSR, in particular, constitutes colloquial canon to decipher legisprudence behind the clause for CSR and corporate political economy played out to keep the ocular opulence subverted by means of its procedural nitty-gritty. For instance, the following are major criteria to net few- too few- commercial players: (i) not too many possess the financial strength stipulated by the statutory provision, (ii) Corporate Social Responsibility Committee of the Board has had functional autonomy toward formulation of the Corporate Social Responsibility Policy, followed by the power to recommend the amount of expenditure and monitor functioning of the policy regime (iii) two per cent (2%) of the average net profits of the company made during the three immediately preceding financial years is affordable to the company, (iv) under Entry (x) of Schedule VII to the Act, the Committee is empowered to prescribe the residual matters as its Policy to convenience of the company, (v) in the absence of adherence to CSR, impunity is apparent on the face of record, (vi) last yet not least, there lies the genesis of this effort, in the disguise of ensuring environmental sustainability under Entry (vi),[6] greenwash by the commercial enterprises proves a commonplace malpractice nowadays.

'CORPORATE ENVIRONMENT RESPONSIBILITY': THE GRANDEUR

With its genesis in the Act, the catchphrase, quoted above, has received restatement in the relevant rules,[7] followed by subsequent documentation by means of memorandum titled 'Corporate Environment Responsibility' (CER); issued by Government of India.[8] The corporate social responsibility thereby corresponded to environmental sustainability; thereby got transcended to newer discourse, named corporate environment responsibility. Thus, Janus-faced development-environment relations underwent a

[4] Mandatory provisions of CSR under section 135 of the Companies Act of 2013 became effective from 01.04.2014.

[5] Available at: https://www.sustainablefashionmatterz.com/what-is-colorwashing

[6] Entry (vi), Schedule VII to the Companies Act of 2013; read with section 135 of the Act.

[7] The Companies (Corporate Social Responsibility Policy) Rules, 2014; section 6(1).

[8] Office Memorandum: F No. 22-65/2017-1A.III, dated 1st May, 2018, Impact Assessment Division, Ministry of Environment, Forest and Climate Change, Government of India, Available at: https://environmentclearance.nic.in/writereaddata/public_display/circulars/OIEBZXVJ_CER%20OM%2001052018.pdf

paradigm shift to set themselves face-to-face toward mutual conversation vis-à-vis environmental conservation with one other; by means of CSR activities as a responsible juristic persona; something out of corporate environmentality, a catchphrase coined by the author toward theorization of corporate governmentality vis-à-vis environmental sustainability with the engagement of CSR committee, policy, activity, audit, and stocktaking, after the company law regime. The juristic personality thereby derives legitimacy by means of responsibility and here lies discursive space to explore corporate governmentality; thereby expose the endgame with the arguendo that, more than environment, legisprudence vis-à-vis corporate social responsibility is meant to secure a systemic legitimacy for sundry corporate government as an institution. This hypothesis stands validated by means of the following reasoning: had such a provision not been meant for the corporate government, the same could have been put to environmental legislation; rather than to a mainstream corporate legislation.

So far as etymological meaning of the technical term 'responsible' is concerned, meaning turns two-fold: (i) a-priori and (ii) a-posteriori. After the dictionary, verbatim:[9]

> *"With regard to the legal use of the word, two conceptions are often confused — namely, that of the potential condition of being bound to answer or respond in case a wrong should occur, and that of the actual condition of being bound to respond because a wrong has occurred. For the first of these responsible is properly used, and for the second liable."*

After literal construction of the statutory provision vis-à-vis corporate environment responsibility, and of the very phrase 'responsibility' in particular, section 135 of the Act refers to responsibility in generic sense of the term, rather than liability or accountability; something meant to cope with specific disaster to environmental cause, done meanwhile. Indeed, both precautionary principles and CSR are meant to engage usage before mankind suffers from loss of environment. Still, the precautionary principles under environmental jurisprudence differs from CSR policy. While the former proscribes activities out of caution to gross detriment of the environment, the latter prescribes activities out of care to protect the environment. The government as a political institution apart, responsibility to protect is thereby invoked by the mainstream corporate regime to keep commercial institutions duty bound by a legal responsibility to protect populations from environmental pollution; something otherwise left to political institutions worldwide as repository of public trust.[10] Also, after settled position of the Supreme Court of India since long back, a corporate

---

[9] *Vide* Century Dictionary. Available at: https://www.etymonline.com/word/responsibility

[10] Cf. 2005 World Summit Outcome. Resolution adopted by the General Assembly, 16 September 2005. Available at: https://www.un.org/en/development/desa/population/migration/generalassembly/docs/globalcompact/A_RES_60_1.pdf

institution- engaged either in public service or public sphere or both- is 'other institution' under inclusive constitutional definition of "the State";[11] thereby entrusted with corporate environment responsibility to protect populations from environmental pollution. Such an apparently unproblematic responsibility but appears pregnant with another corollary responsibility: not to indulge in environmental pollution to the detriment of populations on its own; something not expressed by letters of the provision, yet implied in its spirit.

The statutory provision for corporate social/environment responsibility, therefore, is a double-edged sword to get commercial institutions bound by means of commitment and restraint alike; not without reason that the CSR provision ought to get construed with due diligence vis-à-vis inclusive social/environment responsibility of commercial institutions- with coverage of commission and omission alike- to protect environment since the same supplements its responsibility to protect populations in circuitous routes.

CONVERSATION VIS-À-VIS CONSERVATION: TOWARD CAUCUS

The Office Memorandum of 2018 was the beginning of a systemic conversation vis-à-vis environmental conservation out of the corporate environment responsibility. With inbuilt limits of its own, the Memorandum of 2018 but suffered setback with the following consequences, e.g.: (i) the Ministry was in receipt of several representations regarding imposition of certain percentage of project cost or expansion cost as Corporate Environment Responsibility,[12] (ii) Further, the said OM was also challenged before the Hon'ble High Court at Delhi in WP(C) No. 13252/2019in the matter of CREDAI, NCR Versus Union of India and Ors.[13] In response to this case, the (new) Office Memorandum of 2020 has superseded the earlier Memorandum of 2018.

Accordingly, it is declared by the Memorandum of 2020 that henceforth the Expert Appraisal Committee shall deliberate on the commitments made by the project proponent to address the concerns raised during the public consultation and prescribe specific condition(s) in physical terms while recommending the proposal, for grant of prior environment clearance instead of allocation of funds under corporate environment responsibility.[14] Also, it is declared by the Memorandum that all the activities proposed by the project proponent or prescribed by the Expert

[11] Ramana Dayaram Shetty v. The International Airport Authority of India and Others, Supreme Court of India, 04/05/1979, 1979 SCR (3) 1014. Available at: https://main.sci.gov.in/jonew/judis/4802.pdf

[12] Office Memorandum, F. No. 22-65/2017-1A.III, dated 30th September, 2020, Impact Assessment Division, Ministry of Environment, Forest and Climate Change, Government of India, Available at: https://moef.gov.in/wp-content/uploads/2021/02/OM-dated-30092020-Revised-CER.pdf

[13] *Ibid.*

[14] *Ibid.*

Appraisal Committee or State Level Expert Appraisal Committee, as the case may be, shall be part of the Environment Management Plan.[15] All these Environment Management obligations as statutory responsibilities for commercial institutions, hitherto claimed as part of Corporate Environment Responsibility, are thereby taken out of the coverage to be accomplished under the CSR clause. Now onward, therefore, such a clandestine claim may be held corporate greenwash in a way or other.

The character of conversation on conservation under the CSR clause raises a moot point of concern since the same often than not stands reduced to commercial conservation; with core priority in commerce. Consequently, so-called conservation drive turns greenwash by means of ocular opulence; thereby showcases commercial institutions as compliant to the CSR clause while legislative intent behind the clause to minimize corporate contribution to environmental pollution remains stuck to status quo. What appears worse lies in legal exoneration of commercial institutions from responsibility and liability alike; by courtesy, compliance to the CSR clause by great grandeurs of their own while legality of the enterprises suffers from lack of legitimacy. In final count, by means of such greenwash, the statutory object and purpose behind CSR jurisprudence stand unattended, if not subverted, with impunity. Here lies rationale for the conversation vis-à-vis environmental conservation; something *sine qua non* for democratic governance by means of negotiation in quest of dialogic space in course of corporate environment responsibility discourse. The dialogic space ought to be charged with inclusivity to cover every sundry stakeholder, including public participation, and positivity toward public good as non-negotiable criteria for proactive protective coverage to safeguard the environment. The dialogic space ought to be understood as a two-fold course in its everyday praxis: (i) inter-institutional and (ii) intra-institutional discourse. Taken together, both facilitate negotiations succeed toward construction of consensus; at the least, functional space toward corporate contribution to environmental protection. In a nutshell, democratic governance has had potential to succeed corporate governance.

ENVIRONMENTALITY: A NEWER GENRE OF GOVERNMENTALITY

The genesis of environmentality lies in governmentality; the way it was theorized in course of its postmodern discourse.[16] Thus, environmentality is meant to supplement

---

[15] *Ibid.*

[16] The will to govern, and more specifically, the will to improve the welfare of the population, is expansive. In Foucault's definition it is concerned with "men in their relations, their links, their imbrication with ... wealth, resources, means of subsistence, the territory with all its specific qualities, climate, irrigation, fertility, et cetera; men in their relation to … customs, habits, ways of acting and thinking, et cetera; and lastly, men in their relation to … accidents and misfortunes such as famine, epidemics, death, etcetera" (Foucault).

governmentality; thereby implement social responsibility the statecraft is entrusted with as a major repository of public trust. As responsible stakeholders in market governance, commercial institutions ought to share the social responsibility on their own by default while lived experience of the public in everyday lifeworld proves to the contrary; albeit, rare exceptions apart. Rather, in lieu of environmentality, what commercial institutions often than not showcase is establishmentality; something contrary to governmentality, to uphold crude institutional interests by hook or by crook. And here lies the challenge in course of business management since the establishmentality of commercial institutions remains charged with advertisementality; thereby misuses corporate environment policy to carry forward its outreach to the public in the disguise of service to its environment. Thus, Janus-faced by default, environmentality and establishmentality posit themselves to juxtaposition with a dire consequence that *de jure* environmentality stands supplanted by *de facto* establishmentality to gross detriment of environmental interests of the public.

At the same time, however, lived experiences of the public lifeworld in the given time and space deserve care and caution of both commercial institutions and "the State" (under Article 12, read with Article 36, of the Constitution of India) alike. Rather than ritualistic compliance, responsibility but lies in reading in between the lines of the law:[17]

> *"It's neither practical nor logical for all companies to engage in the same types of CSR, since CSR programs are driven by diverse factors including the industry and the societal environments in which businesses operate and the motivations of the people who staff, run, and govern each company. For example, although a manufacturing company may have rich opportunities to reduce its environmental impact, a financial services company may be hard-pressed to do so— but it may be vastly more successful in the social sphere, with significant initiatives supporting financial inclusion and literacy. In a country lacking sufficient government funding for public health, a company's philanthropic funding for clean water and sanitation may be far more valuable to the community than carbon mitigation initiatives to reduce climate impact, while a society that enjoys robust government provision for social welfare services may place greater importance on environmental conservation programs."*

Tania Murray (2007), Li, Governmentality, *Anthropologica*, 49(2), 275-281. https://www.jstor.org/stable/pdf/25605363.pdf?casa_token=-OR2AIdm3FsAAAAA:3GZC8gAfn8hMPK1pBnYxCxFEz-yCZehLaiZnVzlWtk18VQManC1OXlH2OuiBXjpog3X3Bj724KBr1_uSRz29qwKH3zN6O-wLO-Vx3ryaWfD9yuHkkLLc

[17] V. Kasturi Rangan *et al* (2015, January-February), The Truth about CSR: Most of these programs are not strategic—and that's OK, *Harvard Business Review, from the Magazine*. https://hbr.org/2015/01/the-truth-about-csr

In the South-Asian subcontinent including India, therefore, basic socio-economic individual rights deserve priority over and above esoteric collective right to environment; albeit, without compromise with the corporate responsibility to protect the latter while getting the former served by commercial institutions out of their statutory responsibility.

So far as greenwash- through false description of commercial institutions as green (innocent to environment)- is concerned, such falsification may get construed as a ploy to mislead consumer by means of "misleading advertisement"[18] as unfair trade practice; something with potential to attract legal consequences for errant institutions concerned. Indeed, the statutory definition of "unfair trade practice" does not cover false description of either goods producer or service provider,[19] the same but may at ease be interpreted by the Judiciary in time ahead as inclusive enough to cover a misleading advertisement for falsification of character of either goods producer or service provider by greenwash.

FROM GREENWASHING TO GREENING: TOWARD PARADIGM SHIFT

The shift from greenwashing to greening corporate governance, therefore, requires a socio-systemic revolution; by means of review in the legal and policy analyses alike. First, commercial establishmentality ought to get set aside by societal environmentality, a social revolution. Second, conversation for environmental conservation ought to get initiated in and around commercial institutions toward environmental protection. Third, environmental education in course of everyday public discourse ought to get augmented across the board, corporate ecosystem and public sphere alike, including core principles of environmental jurisprudence, e.g., prior informed consent, precautionary principles, polluter pays, cost-benefit analysis between development and environment, etc., to name few among them; something non-negotiable for public discussion and debate to this end.

These three qualifiers, mentioned above, may bring in a socio-systemic revolution either way. With gradual rise of environmentality in course of commercial institutional discourse, conversation on environmental conservation ought to blossom into fruition, followed by environmental education to sustain and carry forward the social revolution. On reversal of the sequence, environmental education appears pregnant with potential to spearhead mutual conversation on environmental conservation; thereby sow the seed of environmentality toward the systemic revolution in time ahead. Also, course may get initiated with conversation for environmental conservation; followed by others either way.

---

[18] *Vide* the Consumer Protection Act, 2019; section 2(28)(iii)-(iv).

[19] *Vide* the Consumer Protection Act, 2019; section 2(47).

While environmentality received a review in course of the postmodernist discourse in earlier paragraphs, other institutions- conversation and education- deserve deliberation in the given context. With deontic indoctrination to the directorate under new company legislation, environmental protection is put to the core of the new company law regime by means of statutory duties of directors; in clear and unambiguous letters of the law.[20] The role of independent director attracts academic attention. To serve the given purpose of corporate environment responsibility, independent director ought to possess relevant expertise and experience, for instance, either in environment or in education or in both, for independent contribution to the commercial institution and to the community alike. Likewise, education serves the purpose of enlightenment and consequent empowerment toward conversation for environmental conservation with relevant information required for arrival at wisdom through public discussion and debate in the democratic governance.

So far as independent directorate is concerned, for the purpose of legislative intent to be served, the same ought not to remain too limited in its lower cap; for instance, one in the CSR Committee; as per statutory requirement.[21] Rare exceptions apart, one cannot possess equal expertise and experience in social issues and environmental issues alike while both deserve priority in course of corporate governance. The statutory provision, therefore, deserves amendment to include at least another in the independent directorate; one for social issues and another for environmental issues respectively. Since no society is capable to progress in the absence of pedagogy and institutional community constitutes a miniature society, institution cannot afford to keep pedagogy away from its ecosystem. The inclusion of educationist in the institutional ecosystem, therefore, ought to add value to the statutory wish list for better corporate governance in time ahead. Thus, inclusion of three personae, taken together, ought to bring in transformative corporate governance. The corporate environment ought to get committed to its conviction that, institutional intent toward gainful business apart, commerce is meant to extend service to the society; not vice versa. Earlier such wisdom stands upheld by institutions is better to the society. The knowhow for sustainability lies in balance between development and environment. More than social and/or environmental quotient, ethical quotient constitutes core corpus of responsible business; something reflected by means of the CSR chorus worldwide:[22]

---

[20] *Vide* the Companies Act, 2013; section 166(2).

[21] *Supra*, n. 2.

[22] Directors Institute (2023, December 21). *The Boardroom Business of Corporate Social Responsibility (CSR).* https://www.directors-institute.com/post/the-boardroom-business-of-corporate-social-respon sibility-csr

> *"Corporate Social Responsibility (CSR) represents the ethical and strategic commitment of businesses to contribute positively to society. Beyond profit-making, CSR encompasses initiatives that address environmental concerns, social issues, and ethical considerations. Companies engage in CSR to build a sustainable and responsible business model that goes beyond mere financial success."*

The corporate boardroom, an official venue for meeting of the Board of Directors in its headquarters, deserves deliberation. So far as public corporations are concerned, diversity in demography of the Board of Directors ought to facilitate progressive policy toward responsible business management; including social and environmental goodwill:[23]

> *"Board diversity and CSR have become two pressing issues for publicly held corporations. Regulators are urging companies to improve diversity in boardrooms, and contemporaneously, firm stakeholders and the public are demanding companies to be more socially responsible.*
>
> … … …
>
> *We find that overall board diversity measure is positively associated with CSR strengths and negatively associated with CSR concerns, supporting the stakeholder theory and consistent with the view that more diverse boards are more effective in monitoring social responsibility performance than less diverse boards".*

Even, core competence in professional knowledge domains apart, gender diversity in the Board of Directors may and does play critical qualifier toward better governance in commercial institutions. The professional workspace being often than not male space, inclusive public policy vis-à-vis gender diversity is pregnant with potential to bring in transformative corporate governance in course of everyday institutional discourse; also, in response to humanitarian calls toward mitigation of social and environmental pain, beyond commercial gain. With socio-cultural diversity in their boardroom demography, commercial institutions ought to carry forward more responsible corporate governance since the Board of Directors thereby get elevated to a trustee of institutional community in the miniature society of a commercial institution; incorporated as a juristic persona under the company legislation. The CSR clause sounds tautology toward characterization of commercial institutions as social institutions for public good in the economic sphere; something commonplace. All the public corporations are run as commercial institutions by "the State" while it is a political institution in itself; meant for basic public services.

---

[23] Maretno Harzoto *et al* (2015), Board Diversity and Corporate Social Responsibility, *Journal of Business Ethics*, 132(4), 641-660. https://www.jstor.org/stable/pdf/24703556.pdf?casa_token=Du3bgM1-QaYAAAAA:6LSWA_Sr1w RZWg2tIlNezIhL7VWhiiG8dT_2UYXrFdwvMlzCrod5TQCUiayj_jbxpE9ZUf0_sndR2B5zCpUH BiQ-ef9b8xlCIizbeoPbH2U1fsl7kGMa

CONCLUSION

While greening commercial institutions toward responsible corporate governance, after the given legislative intent via corporate social responsibility, Board of Directors ought to balance somewhere between poles-apart polemics (read choices) vis-à-vis corporate idealism and corporate realism. While the status-quoist greenwash approach hardly serves the purpose of environmental sustainability, progressive go-green approach is but ridden with hurdles of its own, for instance, commercial sustainability of the Inc.; something critical to survival of the institution. An otherwise great grandeur of greening corporate governmentality, therefore, lies in maintenance of functional balance between poles-apart poles of the pendulum, e.g., idealism and realism respectively. It resembles affirmative action toward compliance to corporate environmental obligations, to be done so far as possible (sic.); as per the given capability of commercial institution concerned.

So far as environment is concerned, in larger sense of the term, the CSR clause is meant to cover environment in a way or other: either social responsibility toward human environment or environmental responsibility toward natural environment; either is meant to complement and supplement other. While human environment appears major concern for the Global South, arguendo in favour of response to human environment alone ought to suffer from systemic setback,[24] more so in the wake of global climate change, since natural environment is no less vulnerable than otherwise vulnerable human environment. Therefore, environmental responsibility deserves due diligence of commercial institutions and delayed delivery ought to get too late to lament for the global commons. Besides, two variants of environment share corelations since human environment ought to influence natural environment and vice versa. None can afford to stay independent of other since both are interdependent to one other. Thus, exclusive response to human environment ought to defeat legislative intent behind the CSR clause since the social responsibility is inclusive enough to embrace the environmental responsibility in letters and spirit alike. Thus, social environment and natural environment, taken together, what matters most is responsible corporate governmentality in holistic sense of the term.

With scientific knowledge vis-à-vis lethal impact of the environmental pollution upon flora, fauna and natural resources as common concern of humankind, whether and how far corporate establishmentality to gross detriment of human, animal and plant life and health may get construed as treason against humanity is a moot point and the same ought to put commercial institutions to peril. Indeed, after the traditional indoctrination, *actus reas* sans *mens rea* constitutes a vacuum- if not void- toward commission of crime. In exceptional occasions, such as homicide out of negligent drive without guilty mind, crime is construed despite the absence of *mens*

[24] *Supra*, n. 17.

rea since *actus reas* with the knowledge of reasonable apprehension of the consequences vis-à-vis harm constitutes presumption of presence of *mens rea* despite the absence of guilty mind in technical sense of the term. In a prognostic reading of corporate environment responsibility, commercial institutions may be held culpable in time ahead as guilty for commission or omission of pollution- as the case may be- since the same involves indulgence with knowledge of consequence against carrying capacity of the sustainable environment in a morbid and mortal world. Treason against humanity appears appropriate since commercial institutions- registered under the company law regime- enjoy status of social institutions, and resemble trustees of public good, thus supplement "the State"; so far as social responsibility is concerned. Therefore. indulgence in environmental pollution- by either commission or omission- for commercial interest, to gross detriment of social interest, ought to prove inimical toward progressive development of the society; with knowledge of its consequence in advance.

REFERENCES

Primary Documents

Statutes:

1. The Companies Act, 2013 (Act No. 18 of 2013).
2. The Companies (Corporate Social Responsibility Policy) Rules, 2014.
3. The Consumer Protection Act, 2019.
4. Office Memorandum, 2018 (under the Companies Act, 2013).
5. Office Memorandum, 2020 (under the Companies Act, 2013).

Judgment:

1. Ramana Dayaram Shetty v. The International Airport Authority of India and Others, 1979 SCR (3) 1014.

Secondary documents

1. Directors Institute (2023, December 21). *The Boardroom Business of Corporate Social Responsibility (CSR).* https://www.directors-institute.com/post/the-boardroom-business-of-corporate-social-responsibility-csr
2. Downes, Larry (2004, December). First, Empower All the Lawyers, *Harvard Business Review, From the Magazine.* https://hbr.org/2004/12/first-empower-all-the-lawyers
3. Harzoto, Maretno *et al.* (2015), Board Diversity and Corporate Social Responsibility, *Journal of Business Ethics*, 132(4), 641-660. https://www.jstor.org/stable/pdf/24703556.pdf?casa_token=Du3bgM1-QaYAAAAA:6LSWA_Sr1wRZWg2tIlNezIhL7VWhiiG8dT_2UYXrFdwvMlzCrod5TQCUiayj_jbxpE9ZUf0_sndR2B5zCpUHBiQ-ef9b8xlCIizbeoPbH2U1fsl7kGMa

4. Murray, Tania (2007), Li, Governmentality, *Anthropologica*, 49(2), 275-281.https://www.jstor.org/stable/pdf/25605363.pdf?casa_token=-OR2AIdm3FsAAAAA:3GZC8gAfn8hMPK1pBnYxCxFEz-yCZehLaiZnVzlWtk18VQManC1OXlH2OuiBXjpog3X3Bj724KBr1_uSRz29qwKH3zN6O-wLO-Vx3ryaWfD9yuHkkLLc
5. Rangan, V. Kasturi, *et al.* (2015, January-February), The Truth about CSR: Most of these programs are not strategic—and that's OK, *Harvard Business Review, from the Magazine.* https://hbr.org/2015/01/the-truth-about-csr

ANNEXURE[25]

2007	2009	2010	2011	2012	2014
Adoption Of Inclusive Growth-11Th Five Year Plan	Voluntary Guidelines On Corporate Social Responsibility, 2009	Parliamentary Standing Committee On Finance-21St Report On Companies Bill, 2009	National Voluntary Guidelines(NVGs) On Social, Environmental & Economic Responsibilities Of Business, 2011	Business Responsibilities Reporting	Mandatory Provision Of CSR Under Section 135 Of The Companies Act, 2013 Coming Into Effect From 01/04/2014

Nota bene. The piece titled 'Green Corporate Governmentality: A Juridical Tryst with Sustainability', prepared by Debasis Poddar, is original work of his own. It is neither published nor submitted by the author for publication elsewhere so far.

[25]National CSR Portal, History (Timeline for evolution of Corporate Social Responsibility in India). Available at: https://www.csr.gov.in/content/csr/global/master/home/aboutcsr/history.html

2

Impact of Green Academics Using AI and Its Applicability in Enriching Educational Perspectives

Dr. Subrata Chattopadhyay[1]

ABSTRACT: VUCA, the covid pandemic resulted in a BANI world impacting sustainability in all aspects. Green academics and choice based self-paced learning as a supplement for self-development as well as virtual learning pedagogy is gradually gaining sustainable momentum. Artificial Intelligence (AI) is playing a pivotal role assessing one's personal and behavioral perspectives and creating customized learning experiences.

Access to the courses and learning materials of the world class Institutions and interface of the corporate needs and industry demands is changing the way the learners shape up to be equipped to a T.

The importance of AI in green academia development is paramount and the chapter focuses on the ways and means of enrichment towards holistic benefits and upliftment of the intended recipients.

Keywords: *Green Academia, AI, Sustainable Education, Sustainable Development Goals.*

INTRODUCTION

Green education can be found at various educational levels, from elementary schools to universities. It is driven by the need to raise awareness about environmental issues, promote sustainable living, and empower individuals to become environmentally responsible citizens. It plays a crucial role in addressing global environmental challenges and transitioning to a more sustainable and environmentally conscious society.

Green education and artificial intelligence (AI) can intersect in various ways to address environmental challenges and promote sustainability. Here are some key ways in which AI can be integrated into green education:

- **Environmental Monitoring and Data Analysis:** AI can be used to monitor and analyze environmental data more efficiently and accurately. For example, AI-powered sensors and drones can collect data on air quality, water quality, and

[1] Professor, Institute of Engineering and Management, Kolkata.

wildlife behavior. Students can learn how to use AI tools to interpret and visualize this data, gaining insights into environmental changes and trends.

- **Climate Modeling:** AI can enhance climate modeling and help students understand the complexities of climate change. By using AI models and simulations, students can explore the potential impacts of climate change on different regions and ecosystems.
- **Sustainable Agriculture:** AI technologies, such as precision agriculture and predictive analytics, can be incorporated into agricultural education to teach students about sustainable farming practices. This can include using AI for crop optimization, monitoring soil health, and reducing the environmental impact of agriculture.
- **Conservation Efforts:** AI-powered tools, like image recognition software, can assist in wildlife conservation efforts. Students can engage in projects that involve monitoring and protecting endangered species using AI technology.
- **Energy Efficiency:** AI can help students learn about energy efficiency and renewable energy sources. They can explore how AI is used to optimize energy consumption in smart buildings and the integration of solar and wind power through AI control systems.

  Waste Management: Students can explore how AI is used in waste management, such as waste sorting and recycling, to reduce the environmental impact of waste disposal.
- **Environmental Education Platforms:** AI can be used to create personalized and interactive educational platforms for students, tailoring the content to individual learning styles and interests. These platforms can provide information and resources related to environmental issues, sustainability, and conservation.

  Green Innovation and Entrepreneurship: AI can be used to inspire students to develop innovative solutions for environmental challenges. They can learn how AI-driven technologies can be applied to create sustainable startups or products that address ecological issues.
- **Green Career Development:** AI can help students explore career opportunities in the green sector by providing insights into the demand for various green jobs and the skills required. AI-powered career guidance tools can assist students in planning their educational paths.
- **Environmental Policy Analysis:** Students can use AI to analyze and understand environmental policies and their impact. AI can help process and interpret large volumes of legislative and regulatory text, allowing for more comprehensive analysis of environmental laws and regulations.

LITERATURE REVIEW

Changes in learning methods as a result of the COVID-19 pandemic in Indonesia are highly complained about by students because learning processes such as practicum, field studies, research and devotion cannot be done (Gong *et al.*, 2021). Moreover, the use of teleconference media among students has not been applied. As a result, students' motivation to study is dwindling. Many technical challenges make it difficult for students to receive educational materials from teachers. Students struggle to understand the materials provided, and access to the materials is extremely limited and difficult to comprehend (Sholahuddin *et al.*, 2021). Based on preliminary studies conducted on Biology students at the Hindu University of Indonesia related to the implementation of online learning during the COVID-19 pandemic showed that 91.7% (22 people) stated that with the application of online learning, students do not understand the materials provided, difficult internet access, lack of interaction with lecturers, and difficulty in using learning management systems. While, 8.3% (2 people) stated that online learning is more efficient in learning time, supporting the termination of the COVID-19 chain in the education sector, and the learning process is carried out anywhere and anytime (Ali *et al.*, 2021; Aryabkina *et al.*, 2021). Based on this phenomenon, it is necessary to find a solution to improve students' understanding of the online learning process and to improve learning skills along with the effectiveness of online learning during and after the COVID-19 at the college level, one of which is in the Biology Study Program, Hindu University of Indonesia. Efforts can be made to implement a green education-based blended learning model with the hope of improving the quality of learning in the time of COVID-19 (Charitas *et al.*, 2021; Huang, 2021). The adoption of green education-based blended learning models was formed concerning students' deteriorating knowledge, interests, and abilities to engage in, improve and conserve the environment, one of which is biology students (Tasman *et al.*, 2021; van den Bogerd *et al.*, 2020). It is envisaged that students will apply it to their own family and community environment by improving knowledge through the concept of green education incorporated into the blended learning model outside and within the network (Sholahuddin *et al.*, 2021; Tovar-Gálvez, 2021). This strategy has numerous advantages and strengths, ranging from reinforcing indigenous knowledge to integrating current efforts to manage, rejuvenate, and establish a green environment in all aspects of operations. The concept of green education is developing a learning model focused on the environment's management, alignment, and rescue. The application of this concept is initiated by stagnation of student response, especially biology students in environmental development, lack of sense of student participation in maintaining environmental sustainability, and decreased response and role of students to human activities resulting in decreased ecological quality and increasing global warming. Prior research of Ardoin *et al.* (2020) and Toomey *et al.*

(2017) stated that environmental education integration in the learning process could effectively improve ecological attitudes, values, and knowledge and build collaboratively in conservation efforts for learners. Blended learning and green education are two learning models expected to bring students into an effective, efficient, and targeted way of Learning while paying attention to the quality of learning outcomes and improving and training students' skills in facing, improving, and solving environmental problems in real life.

GREEN EDUCATION AND AI

Incorporating AI into green education can enhance students' understanding of environmental issues, empower them to take action, and prepare them for careers that contribute to sustainability and ecological conservation. It can also enable educators to keep pace with the rapidly evolving field of environmental science and technology.

"Green academics" generally refers to environmentally conscious practices within the field of education, particularly at academic institutions like universities and colleges. Online learning can play a significant role in promoting sustainability and reducing the environmental impact of traditional educational practices. Here are some ways in which online learning can align with "green academics":

- **Reduced Carbon Footprint:** Online learning eliminates the need for commuting, reducing the carbon emissions associated with travel to and from physical campuses. This can significantly contribute to a decrease in the carbon footprint of students, faculty, and staff.
- **Paperless Education:** Online learning materials are often digital, reducing the need for printed textbooks and handouts. This can save trees and energy and reduce the environmental impact of paper production and waste.
- **Energy Efficiency:** While online learning does require energy to power servers and devices, it can be more energy-efficient than traditional classroom setups. Institutions can use renewable energy sources to power servers and encourage students to use energy-efficient devices.
- **Reduced Facility Needs:** With online learning, there's less need for large physical facilities like classrooms, reducing the environmental impact of constructing and maintaining these buildings.
- **Global Access:** Online learning can provide access to education for people around the world, reducing the need for international students to travel to attend classes physically. This can contribute to a more sustainable global education system.
- **Digital Collaboration:** Online learning often promotes collaboration and communication through digital tools, reducing the need for travel and in-person meetings.

- **Sustainable Curriculum:** Some academic programs may include courses and research on sustainability and environmental issues, promoting a culture of environmental responsibility.

However, it's essential to note that online learning is not inherently environmentally friendly. There are environmental concerns associated with data centers, the production and disposal of electronic devices, and the energy required to power online platforms. Therefore, it's important for academic institutions to consider sustainable practices in their online learning initiatives, such as using green data centers, encouraging responsible device use, and reducing digital waste.

In summary, "green academics" in the context of online learning involves promoting sustainable practices within the education sector, taking advantage of the environmental benefits offered by digital education, and addressing the environmental challenges associated with online learning to create a more eco-friendly educational system.

"Green education" typically refers to educational programs and initiatives that focus on environmental sustainability, conservation, and the promotion of a more environmentally responsible and sustainable way of living. It encompasses a wide range of topics and approaches, including:

- **Environmental Science:** Green education often includes the study of environmental science, which explores the natural world and the impact of human activities on ecosystems. Students learn about topics like climate change, biodiversity, pollution, and conservation.
- **Sustainability:** Sustainable education emphasizes the importance of sustainable practices in various fields, such as agriculture, energy, architecture, and transportation. It encourages individuals and organizations to make choices that minimize their ecological footprint.
- **Conservation and Biodiversity:** This aspect of green education involves teaching about the importance of preserving biodiversity and protecting endangered species. It often includes field studies, habitat restoration, and wildlife conservation efforts.
- **Green Building and Design:** Education on green architecture and sustainable building practices focuses on reducing the environmental impact of construction and maintenance, including concepts like energy-efficient designs and materials.
- **Environmental Policy and Advocacy:** Many green education programs also address environmental policy and advocacy. Students learn how to influence policy decisions, raise awareness about environmental issues, and advocate for positive change.
- **Outdoor and Experiential Learning:** Outdoor and experiential learning can be a key component of green education. It involves hands-on experiences in nature, fostering a deeper connection with the environment.

- **Eco-friendly Practices:** Students often learn about everyday eco-friendly practices, including waste reduction, recycling, composting, and responsible consumption.
- **Green Business and Economics:** Some green education programs cover sustainable business practices, green entrepreneurship, and the economics of sustainability.
- **Climate Change Education:** Understanding and addressing climate change is a central aspect of green education. It includes climate science, mitigation strategies, and adaptation measures.

The United Nations Sustainable Development Goal 4 (SDG 4) is specifically related to education and is part of the broader Sustainable Development Goals established by the United Nations. SDG 4 is commonly known as "Quality Education" and is aimed at ensuring inclusive and equitable quality education for all. It encompasses various targets and indicators, with an emphasis on achieving universal access to education and improving the quality of education to foster lifelong learning opportunities for everyone.

GREEN ACADEMICS AND UN SDG-4

The concept of "green academics" can intersect with SDG 4 in the following ways:

- **Sustainable Education:** Green academics can promote education that focuses on environmental sustainability, including topics such as climate change, conservation, and sustainable practices. This aligns with the idea of incorporating sustainable development concepts into educational curricula.
- **Inclusive Education:** SDG 4 emphasizes inclusive education for all, regardless of gender, age, ability, or other factors. Green academics can contribute to making environmental education accessible and inclusive, ensuring that everyone has the opportunity to learn about and engage in sustainable practices.
- **Research and Innovation:** Academic institutions engaged in green academics can conduct research to develop innovative solutions for sustainability challenges. This research can inform educational content and contribute to achieving the goals of SDG 4 by improving the quality of education.
- **Collaboration and Partnerships:** Universities and academic institutions can collaborate with governments, non-governmental organizations, and other stakeholders to advance both green academics and SDG 4. Collaborative efforts can lead to better educational outcomes and more sustainable practices.
- **Advocacy and Awareness:** Green academics can also play a role in raising awareness about the importance of sustainable development and environmental conservation, which is a key aspect of SDG.

In summary, green academics can contribute to achieving SDG 4 by integrating sustainability concepts into education, conducting relevant research, fostering inclusive and accessible education, and advocating for quality education that addresses environmental and sustainability challenges. This intersection supports the broader goal of sustainable development as outlined by the United Nations.

CONCLUSION

Green education provides sustainability by equipping individuals with the knowledge, skills, and values needed to promote and practice sustainable behaviours and lifestyles. Builds the capacity of people to address global environmental change and associated challenges such as climate change, loss of biodiversity, and scarcity of resources in an effective and equitable way.

Green education, when combined with artificial intelligence (AI), has the potential to create a powerful force for effective sustainable development. AI can provide accurate predictions of future scenarios, monitor the environmental change, and increase the capacity of people to take timely decisions in favour of sustainability. It can help individuals to gain better understanding of complex environmental issues and to make decisions that enable sustainable use of resources. AI can also aid in the development of better methods for assessing environmental impacts, developing sustainable solutions, and providing feedback to stakeholders on their performance.

AI enables the development of more efficient and sustainable to many of the world's environmental problems through predictive and proactive action. It also has the potential to provide effective and tailored solutions to environmental challenges by utilizing data from multiple sources, including climate data, sensor data, environmental models, and more. AI can provide improved collaboration between stakeholders in order to facilitate more effective decision making and implementation of sustainable practices. Finally, AI can help to increase the understanding of natural processes and the impact of human activities on these processes, as well as providing valuable insights into how to promote sustainable development.

REFERENCES

Aggarwal, D. (2021). A Pragmatic Approach to the Usage of Digital Devices in Education in Developing Countries", *Turkish Journal of Computer and Mathematics Education,* Vol. 12, No. 13.

Aggarwal, D. (2023). Integration of Innovative Technological Developments and AI with Education for an Adaptive Learning Pedagogy. *China Petroleum Processing and Petrochemical Technology*, Volume 23, Issue 2.

Devesh Lowe, B.G., "AI Based Examination System: A Paradigm Shift in Education Sector", *IEEE 2022 International Conference on Machine Learning, Big Data, Cloud and Parallel Computing (COM-IT-CON),* 26–27 May 2022.

G.I. and Windarti, A. (2020). Impact of Corona Virus Outbreak Towards Teaching and Learning Activities in Indonesia. *Jurnal Sosial Dan Budaya Syar-I,* 7(3), 269282. DOI: https://doi.org/10.15408/sjsbs. v7i3.15104

Garcia-Ponce, E.E. and Mora-Pablo, I. (2020). Challenges of using a blended learning approach: A flipped classroom in an english teacher education program in mexico. *Higher Journal of Image Processing and Intelligent Remote Sensing*

Kurniawati, A.A., Wahyuni, S. and Putra, P.D. (2017). Utilizing of Comic and Jember's Local Wisdom as *Integrated Science Learning Materials International Journal of Social Science and Humanity*, 7 1 p. 47.

M., Yang, W., Peng, M., Wang, Z., Ouyang, L. and Yang, G. (2021). Application of blended learning approach in clinical skills to stimulate active learning attitudes and improve clinical practice among medical students. *PeerJ*, 9, e11690. DOI: https://doi.org/10.7717/peerj.11690 Green, M. J. and

Rosyida, A., Mustaji, M. and Subroto, W. (2018). The Development of Contextual Teaching and Learning-Based Comic as a Learning Media for Elementary School Students In *1st International Conference on Education Innovation (ICEI 2017),* Atlantis Press.

Shearer, A. (2012). Defining U.S. Indian ocean strategy. Washington Quarterly, 35(2), 175–189. DOI: 10.1080/0163660X. 2012.666925

Wardana, I.N. Gede. (2021). Effectiveness of Blended Learning in Human Anatomy Courses. *Jurnal Pendidikan Indonesia*, 2(2), 209–219. DOI: https://doi.org/10.36418/japendi.v2i2.102

Yapici, İ.Ü. (2016). Effectiveness of Blended Cooperative Learning Environment in Biology Teaching: Classroom Community Sense, Academic Achievement and Satisfaction. *Journal of Education and Training Studies*, 4(4), 269–280. DOI: https://doi.org/10.11114/jets.v4i4.1372 Zaharah, Z., Kirilova.

3

Green Computing and Green Coding: IBM Leads the Way

Rahul Bose[1]

ABSTRACT

Green Coding: Years ago, coding had boundaries. Bandwidth restrictions and limited processing power forced developers always to be mindful of the length and complexity of their code. As technology enabled greater innovation, programmers were no longer constrained by size.

For example, greater computing power allowed faster processing of large files and applications. Open-source libraries and frameworks allowed software engineers to reuse pieces of code in their projects, creating greater possibilities. This also led to programs with more lines of code—and more processing power required to parse it. The unintended consequence was greater energy usage and a higher global electricity demand.

As companies look to transform business and implement more sustainable practices, they are exploring established processes to find new efficiencies. This includes evaluating the building blocks of their business operations, from storing data more efficiently to examining how code is written.

In this article, we will explore how green coding helps organizations find innovative ways to prioritize sustainability and reach their energy reduction goals.

Green coding is an environmentally sustainable computing practice that seeks to minimize the energy involved in processing lines of code and, in turn, help organizations reduce overall energy consumption. Many organizations have set greenhouse emission reduction goals to respond to the climate change crisis and global regulations; green coding is one way to support these sustainability goals.

Green coding is a segment of green computing that seeks to limit technology's environmental impact, including reducing the carbon footprint in high-intensity operations, such as in manufacturing lines, data centers, and even the day-to-day operations of business teams. This larger green computing umbrella also includes green software—applications that have been built using green coding practices.

---

[1] CEO RB Consulting (ex-IBM).

Keywords: *Green, Coding, Energy, Infrastructure, Computing, Sustainability, Environment.*

IBM CASE STUDY

Green computing reduces energy consumption and lowers carbon emissions from the design, use, and disposal of technology products.

Green computing (also known as green IT or sustainable IT) is the design, manufacture, use, and disposal of computers, chips, other technology components, and peripherals in a way that limits the harmful impact on the environment, including reducing carbon emissions and the energy consumed by manufacturers, data centers and end-users. Green computing also encompasses choosing sustainably sourced raw materials, reducing electronic waste, and promoting sustainability using renewable resources.

The potential for green computing to have a positive impact on the environment is considerable. The information and communication technology (ICT) sector is responsible for between 1.8% and 3.9% of global greenhouse gas emissions. Moreover, data centers account for 3% of annual total energy consumption—an increase of 100% in the last decade.

"The energy demands and carbon output of computing and the entire ICT sector must be dramatically moderated if climate change is to be slowed in time to avoid catastrophic environmental damage," according to a report published by the Association for Computing Machinery.

Every aspect of modern information technology—from the smallest chip to the largest data center—carries a carbon price tag, and green computing seeks to reduce that carbon price tag. Technology makers play a role in green computing, as do the corporations, organizations, governments, and individuals that use technology. From massive data centres instituting policies to reduce energy consumption to individuals choosing to not use screen savers, green IT is multi-faceted and involves myriad decisions at every level.

WHAT MANUFACTURERS CAN DO

The decisions regarding going green begin long before products reach consumers. For example, product design and manufacturing are prime areas to lessen the impact of technology on the environment.

Chips that are more energy efficient—such as the chip designed by IBM and Samsung that can be stacked vertically or the IBM 2 nm chip—are examples of innovative design that improves sustainability in computing. The energy consumption of a single computer chip may seem negligible, but when you multiply that by millions, it is possible to make significant reductions.

IBM has also identified systems that can reduce energy usage. Heterogenous structures, for instance, bring together frameworks like CPUs and graphics processing units (GPUs) to optimize power and energy efficiency.

One example is a computer named AiMOS (which stands for Artificial Intelligence Multiprocessing Optimized System), developed as part of a collaboration between IBM, Empire State Development and NY CREATEs. AiMOS is one of the most energy-efficient computers in existence, and it is used to develop more advanced and efficient computing chips, along with many other initiatives.

When designers take steps to reduce the amount of energy each product uses in operation and reduce the amount of heat those products produce, the carbon price tag of computing gets lower. For instance, sleep mode is one of the earliest examples of designers applying the concept of green computing to conserve energy.

Material selection is crucial, as well. Design that avoids using hazardous materials keeps those materials out of landfills later. Generating less waste in manufacturing devices and components, too, lessens the burden created by technology on the environment. Green manufacturing is a separate, but related, category of green technology that governs how the factory itself operates.

Other green computing actions manufacturers can take include lengthening the lifespan of computing devices and components, so they don't need to be replaced as frequently, increasing users' ability to reuse products, and making devices recyclable when they do need to be replaced.

The largest gains in making IT more sustainable may be made by corporations, governments, and other large organizations. Data centers, server rooms, and data storage areas have a significant opportunity to run more efficiently.

In such areas, setting up hot and cold aisles is an important step toward greener computing because it reduces energy consumption and optimizes heating, ventilation, and cooling. When automated systems designed to control temperature and similar conditions are combined with hot and cold aisles, emissions are further lowered. Cost savings from reducing energy use may eventually be realized, as well.

One simple step toward efficiency is to make sure things are turned off. Central processing units (CPUs) and peripheral equipment such as printers should be powered down when not in use. Scheduling blocks of time for specific tasks like printing means peripherals are only in use when they are needed.

Purchasing departments have a role to play in green computing, too. Choosing equipment that will last and consume the least amount of energy necessary for the task to be performed are both ways to reduce the carbon footprint of IT. Notebooks use less energy than laptops, and laptops use less energy than desktop computers, for example.

What you can do

Green computing isn't only for large organizations; you can play an important part in improving sustainability in the world of IT, as well. When many individuals choose to use functions like hibernate or sleep mode, the impact can be huge.

Whatever the device, employing the power management features reduces energy consumption, as does adjusting the screen brightness. Other ways to use less energy include turning off computers at the end of the day and keeping peripherals like speakers or printers turned off unless they are being used.

Refilling printer cartridges rather than purchasing new ones produces less waste and buying refurbished equipment rather than buying new reduces environmental impact. Safe disposal of electronic equipment improves sustainability and has security advantages.

Just as purchasing departments should choose the most efficient equipment for the tasks to be performed, so should you. If a notebook or laptop can perform necessary tasks as well as a desktop computer, opt for the more efficient device. Energy Star ratings are a good guide for individuals purchasing new equipment.

THE EVOLUTION OF GREEN COMPUTING

In 1992, the Environmental Protection Agency (EPA) began the Energy Star Program in the United States, which aimed to promote and recognize energy efficiency. That program was the impetus for the adoption of the sleep mode function across the IT industry, and it brought about numerous other initiatives to increase efforts toward green computing. Energy Star-certified products must meet certain operation standards and have power management features that non-certified products may lack.

The program was furthered by a grant from the EPA to the Global Electronics Council, which resulted in the Electronic Product Environmental Assessment Tool (EPEAT). EPEAT is a product registry for products that are held to specific performance criteria, including materials used, greenhouse gas emissions from transportation, product longevity, energy use, and end-of-lifecycle management.

Multiple initiatives to improve green computing standards through the creation of industry metrics related to sustainability exist, as do various certifications. The Green500 is a sub-list of the Top500, which lists supercomputers and the applications for which those computing systems are used. The Green500 ranks the supercomputers by energy efficiency. The Transaction Processing Performance Council (TCP) is a nonprofit organization that develops benchmarks for performance in the transaction processing industry. SPECPower also creates benchmarks for the power and performance characteristics of single- and multi-node servers to improve efficiency.

CHALLENGES TO IMPLEMENTING GREEN COMPUTING

Perhaps one of the greatest barriers to advancing green computing is a lack of concern. Few people think of the IT industry when they think about climate change. Along with a general lack of concern, the IT market has developed in a way that prioritizes the development of smaller and faster components and devices rather than environmentally friendly ones.

The fact that technology evolves and changes very rapidly presents challenges in extending the lifecycle of products and requires technology makers to ensure each iteration continues to meet eco-friendly standards. Switching from a conventional set up in a factory, data center or corporate office to a green configuration requires an often-substantial up-front capital investment that represents an additional potential barrier.

Fragmented data and varying needs make decision-making difficult across the spectrum of IT end users. For example, speed and performance have a different value in a large data center than they do for a user at home.

At any given point in the lifecycle of a computing device, users must weigh various concerns. For a large organization, security may be a greater concern than environmental impact when it comes to servers. For a college student, a smaller device that is easier to carry may be more important than having one that is fully recyclable.

GREEN COMPUTING AND IBM

Green computing has the power to lessen the impact of computing on the environment. However, the ICT industry has an opportunity to do much more by using technology to benefit the environment through programs and systems designed to reduce power consumption, improve water management, and embrace virtualization as a way to conserve energy.

IBM is committed to green IT across the ecosystem of the business, including green design, operations, and the use of its technology. The company has received numerous awards for sustainable products, energy use, and environmental excellence. IBM's first corporate policy regarding environmental affairs was issued in 1971, and protecting the environment remains a key issue in worldwide operations.

As the tech industry expands and lines of code multiply, the emergence of "green coding" development is transforming software practices for a more sustainable future. This movement championed by The Green Software Foundation addresses energy consumption and environmental impact, aiming to create greener outcomes.

IMPACT OF INDUSTRY GROWTH

With the tech sector's growth, coding's increased presence impacts energy usage and overall processing power, prompting the need for more sustainable coding practices.

Understanding Green Coding

Green coding revolves around minimizing the environmental footprint of software development. It involves programming algorithms with minimal energy consumption, contributing to eco-friendly coding practices.

Inspired by 'Green Computing' which is concerned with responsible design, manufacturing, and disposal of physical computing systems. This concept extends green computing principles to the software development process.

Mitigating Carbon Footprint

Green coding's primary goal is to curb the carbon footprint of software development. By reducing non-renewable resource usage, energy consumption, and waste generation, this approach promotes sustainability.

Practical green coding explores energy-efficient development of resource-light software, and the integration of sustainable methodologies such as code reuse as valid implementations of green coding.

Green Coding in Action

Real-world examples of green coding, include energy-efficient data centers designed by industry giants like Google and Microsoft. Their commitment to sustainability is reflected in automatic server shutdowns for under-utilized servers and redistributing their workload to conserve energy. IBM is also pushing sustainability in its ecosystem.

Green coding extends beyond hardware efficiency to optimizing code performance, file size reduction, lower network usage, and efficient algorithm usage. These practices collectively minimize energy consumption and environmental impact.

Efficient Development Design

There are two types of considerations to make when developing a greener coding approach – behavioural and structural.

Structural relates to a lower levels such as the compilers and their abilities to create more efficient code blocks for the target platform.

Behavioural relates to evaluations of the application's main functionalities and that is where us developers can make more of an impact in the "green code" space.

Solution architecture also plays a role in green coding. Designing an application with just the optimum level of micro-services is a key aspect for consideration. Too often we end with hundreds of micro-services, especially to support versions of mobile app releases, and the excess services are not eventually deprecated resulting in energy wastage.

Sustainable Development Methods

Embrace agile development methodologies, focusing on collaboration, flexibility, and continuous improvement. Such practices create software that's not only efficient but also adaptive to changing user needs.

Legacy Transformation

With so much legacy code out there, application modernization is paramount. This will eliminate old hardware and will produce code that is optimized by the latest code interpreters and compilers and is virtualization-ready.

Digitize Everything

Green coding isn't just about code; it's about shaping a sustainable future. Removing manual processes and introducing efficient workflows that eliminate the consumption of paper is another aspect of the green code initiative.

REFERENCES

The Green Software Foundation.

The Green500.

Electronic Product Environmental Assessment Tool.

https://www.ibm.com/blog/green-coding/

IBM Cloud Education.

Brazil on the Path to Sustainability: A Study of Entrepreneurial Orientation in Companies Certified in the Social Seal Program

Robson Juscelino de Melo[1], Dr. Suzette Antonieta Lizote[2], Dr. Manodip Ray Chaudhuri[3], Dr. Sayonara de Fatima Teston[4] and Dr. Patrick Zawasdki[5]

ABSTRACT: Entrepreneurial orientation in companies certified with the social seal seeks to foster an organizational culture that not only promotes innovation and efficiency, but also contributes positively to sustainable development and social impact. In this sense, this study identified managers' perception of the dimensions of entrepreneurial orientation that are present in companies certified in the social seal program of Itajaí, Santa Catarina, Brazil. For a quantitative and descriptive analysis, the method was a survey, using already validated collection instruments. To measure entrepreneurial orientation, the Lumpkin and Dess (1996) model was used. The questionnaire was composed of closed questions using a seven-point Likert scale and data analyzes were carried out with descriptive analyses. The results showed that the proactivity dimension obtained the highest averages, with emphasis on the items "In general, when making decisions for your company, there is a strong tendency to be ahead of other competitors in the introduction of new ideas, products and/or services" and "In general, when dealing with your competitors, your firm is often the first company to introduce new products and services, administrative, technological, operational techniques". However, the competitive aggressiveness dimension presented the lowest averages with an emphasis on "In general, in your company, practices are implemented that prove to be efficient in successful competitors", "In general, in your company, advertisements and promotions are used intensively to win over customers" and "In general, your company has competitive prices to increase sales". It is concluded, therefore, that according to the managers' view, the five dimensions of entrepreneurial orientation are present in companies. The relevance of this work is

---

[1] Mestre em Administracao, Universidade do Vale do Itajia, Santa Catarina, Brazil.

[2] Doutora em Administracao e Turismo, Professora no Programa de Pos-Graduacao em Administracao, Universidade do Vale do Itajia, Santa Catarina, Brazil.

[3] Professor of Management in HR & OB and Former Dean, DRC-PhD Convener in Management, Xavier Business School, St. Xavier's University, Kolkata.

[4] Doutora em Administracao, Professora no Programa de Pos-Graduacao em Administracao, Universidade do Oeste Catarenense – Chapeco, Santa Catarina, Brazil.

[5] Doutora em Administracao, Professora no Programa de Pos-Graduacao em Administracao, Universidade do Oeste Catarenense – Chapeco, Santa Catarina, Brazil.

linked to the fundamental role that the social seal plays in the responsibility and sustainability of organizations, as well os its importance as an instrument of differentiation and creation of competitive advantage.

Keywords: *Entrepreneurial Orientation, Sustainability, Social Seal.*

INTRODUCTION

The 2030 agenda is an important instrument for overcoming development challenges. It is a global pact that has 193 countries as signatories, comprising 17 Sustainable Development Goals (SDGs), with their respective 169 targets that aim for global sustainable growth by 2030 (UN, 2015).

Brazil has positioned itself in a responsible and exemplary manner in the 2030 Agenda scenario, making the 17 SDGs official in all corners of the country, in a transparent and very encouraging way (Kronemberger, 2019). In this sense, several municipalities, with the wave of sustainable development, created, individually, their programs named as sociais seal, encouraging the fulfillment of the Sustainable Development Goals through the recognition of public and private organizations and individuals that allocate resources in benefit of society (Social Seal, 2023).

Companies certified in the social seal program of Itajaí, Santa Catarina, Brazil, have their "eyes" focused on generating social value, according to a vision of creating shared value, while they prosper economically to the extent that they also bring important contributions to people and the environment in which they are inserted through their projects. Understanding the entrepreneurial orientation of these companies from the perspective of their managers is the aim of this research.

It follows, therefore, that it is not enough for an organization to simply have economic prosperity; managers must be aware of the impacts caused by the actions developed from a perspective of respect for the environment and social causes. The current moment requires more than simply keeping accounts up to date and making a profit, Porter and Kramer (2011) already highlighted that organizations continue to be handcuffed in an outdated value creation perspective, seeing financial profit in the short term and failing to consider the real needs of its clients in the long term, such as the depletion of natural resources and economic problems of the communities in which they operate. Thinking about a solution would be to defend the use of the principle of shared value, simultaneously generating economic and social value. This is not about philanthropy, social responsibility or even sustainability, but about a new look at how to be economically successful.

Entrepreneurial orientation was initially seen as a personal quality of the manager or owner, being one who challenged the uncertainties of the environment, which Miller (1983) dismissed by saying that EO goes beyond the personal virtues of a single being, being a characteristic of organization. For Asemokha, *et al.* (2019) it is a decision that involves changes and strategic adjustments to the central elements of organizations, resulting in business model innovation and allowing the organization to stay ahead of its competition.

The dynamic environment has required proactiveness from companies in identifying opportunities, requiring them to also develop and maintain an entrepreneurial orientation capable of positively impacting organizational performance (Galbreath, 2020). The organizational context studied are companies certified in the Social Seal program of the Municipality of Itajaí/SC. The program aims to encourage compliance with the United Nations Sustainable Development Goals, through the recognition of public and private organizations and individuals who allocate resources for the benefit of society (Social Seal, 2023).

In view of the above, this research responds to the following problem: What are the dimensions of entrepreneurial orientation that are present in companies certified in the social seal program of Itajaí, Santa Catarina, Brazil, in the perception of their managers? To this end, the general objective was to identify managers' perception of the dimensions of entrepreneurial orientation that are present in companies certified in the social seal program of Itajaí, Santa Catarina, Brazil.

Discussions involving the topic of sustainability have become increasingly evident given the concern about the scarcity of natural resources and the need to enable actions that can reconcile development and sustainability. For Okado and Quinelli (2016), the SDGs call on governmental and non-governmental institutions and civil society, in general, to act in search of sustainability. The aforementioned author also highlights that sustainable development needs to be part of the strategic planning of organizations.

Organizations inserted in a constantly changing business environment tend to be more entrepreneurial and innovative and, to differentiate themselves from their competitors and create a sustainable position in the market, they seek competitive advantages (Shirokova, *et al.*, 2016). Therefore, a high EO is considered important for companies to seek new opportunities (Camozatto, *et al.* 2019).

The relevance of this study is also linked to the fundamental role that the social seal plays in the responsibility and sustainability of an organization. Currently, entrepreneurs must adapt to this reality and consider the profile of their employees together with their personal aspirations to increase the team's motivation and, consequently, achieve organizational goals, contributing to satisfying the needs of society. It is also important to highlight that social responsibility should not only be observed in companies, as all organizations must be aware of the impacts of their activities and respond appropriately to them.

THEORETICAL FOUNDATION

Entrepreneurial Orientation

The entrepreneurial orientation (EO) framework has emerged in the literature on entrepreneurship and organizational strategy in recent decades (Miller, 1983).

Initially, Mintzberg (1973) reported that organizational performance would be achieved through strategic decisions contaminated by the proactive action of the manager when learning about opportunities and threats and acting in the face of the uncertain environment in which he is inserted. Miller (1983), in turn, described EO as something that goes beyond understanding the entrepreneurial spirit solely of the owner or manager, as it should encompass the organization.

The definition of entrepreneurial orientation appears in the recognition of attitudes or behaviors that the organization has, providing greater or lesser capacity for entrepreneurship. According to Miller (1983), the definition of an entrepreneurial organization is given to the organization that is encouraged to innovate its products and services or markets, undertakes with deliberate risk and acts proactively towards its competitors and the market. For Rauch, *et al.* (2009), it can be described as the business strategy-making processes that top managers use to enact their company's organizational purpose, sustain its vision, and create a competitive advantage.

The process that involves decision-making and organizational strategies is impacted by the methods, practices and attitudes that make up EO, that is, EO is characterized by the organization's strategic behavior (Lumpkin & Dess, 1996). For Wiklund (1999), EO is associated with the manager's strategic behavior, which, according to Stevenson and Jarrilo (1990), is related to the styles, methods and processes performed to achieve the label of an entrepreneurial organization. Covin and Slevin (1991) use the term entrepreneurial posture as a synonym for Entrepreneurial Orientation, corroborating the three dimensions consolidated by Miller (1983), adding competitive aggressiveness as a synonym for proactivity.

For Miller (1983), entrepreneurial orientation is linked to three dimensions, i) innovativeness, which is the implementation of new products or services with the purpose of differentiating oneself in the market and achieving competitive advantage; ii) proactivity, which is the anticipation of market opportunities, seeking to meet a future need before the competitor does so; It is; iii) risk-taking is believing in what you cannot see, betting your chips (resources) on a supposed solution to a need or a problem, even knowing that there is a possibility of things going wrong, but doing so in a calculated way to achieve greater security and increase the chances of success. For the aforementioned author, these three dimensions have a unidimensional characteristic, being strictly intertwined, and to say whether an organization has EO, Miller's (1983) three dimensions must be present simultaneously, whatever the degree of presence of each dimension.

On the other hand, Lumpkin and Dess (1996) accept the dimensions proposed by Miller (1983) with the addition of two more dimensions to the EO construct: autonomy and competitive aggressiveness. The autonomy dimension concerns decision-making without any type of pressure, independently, cooperatively, and participatively. And competitive aggressiveness is facing competition in a combative and ambitious way with the aim of becoming number one in the market in which it operates and, if possible, eliminating the competitor.

Another aspect that differs from Miller's (1983) studies is the authors' understanding of the independence between the dimensions. According to Lumpkin and Dess (1996), the dimensions of EO are characterized by multidimensionality, that is, they can present themselves autonomously within an organization or even one appears and the other not, depending on the organizational context, which does not will prevent the characterization of an organization as holding an EO.

Strengthening this aspect is the research by Lizote, *et al.* (2014), which explored the perception of managers of companies in the underwear and beachwear segment, seeking to analyze the level of EO of these organizations from the perspective of the model of Miller (1983) and Lumpkin and Dess (1996). The study concluded, according to the managers' view, that five dimensions of EO are present in companies independently, perfectly meeting the multidimensionality requirement. It was suggested, for future research, the analysis of the relationship between OE and DO.

Begnini, Rossetto and Carvalho, (2023) conceptualize the entrepreneurial organization according to five dimensions established by Lumpikin and Dess (1996), that is, as that institution that seeks to innovate in products, services and processes; acts in a risky way from a strategic point of view; anticipates the opportunities and desires of your target audience even before your competitors act; giving space to its employees to act independently and autonomously, without any type of pressure; and, fighting a real fight against the competition, aiming to reach first place in its field of activity.

Miller (2011), when revisiting his 1983 research, recognizes the importance of the two dimensions added by Lumpkin and Dess (1996) to the EO construct, suggesting that new studies consider this contribution to better characterize EO and understand more broadly the entrepreneurship at the organizational level.

In this sense, Santos and Alves (2009) analyzed the influence of the 5 dimensions, by Miller (1983) and Lumpkin and Dess (1996) respectively, on the performance of technology incubators in southern Brazil. They concluded that the dimensions act independently (multidimensional perspective), that innovation is the significant dimension in the performance of these companies and that the risk-taking dimension has a negative impact on performance, indicating conservative behavior in an innovative context.

Bringing divergent results to the study by Santos and Alves (2009), Lazzarotti, *et al.* (2015) found that EO is established according to the unidimensional model in its relationship with the performance of graduated companies. They highlighted the dimensions of innovativeness, proactivity, autonomy and relationship networks as those with the greatest contribution to the existence of EO, corroborating the studies by Miller (1983) and Covin and Slevin (1989) that suggest the dependence of the dimensions. Therefore, multidimensionality was not supported in the hypothesis tests, given the unsatisfactory results of the risk-taking and competitive aggressiveness dimensions.

Martens and Freitas (2008) carried out research to introduce a conceptual model to diagnose EO considering its dimensions and elements. The study observed the three dimensions of Miller (1983) and the two of Lumpkin and Dess (1996), following the multidimensional perspective to compose the EO.

This research is based on the model of Lumpkin and Dess (1996) as it seeks to characterize the EO of companies certified in the Social Seal Program observing the five dimensions of the construct, namely: innovativeness, proactivity, risk taking, autonomy and competitive aggressiveness. Next, these dimensions will be individually described, based on different points of view of the authors.

METHODOLOGY

This is a descriptive, cross-sectional, and quantitative survey. The study was carried out with companies from Itajaí, state of Sant Catarina, Brazil, which were certified in the social seal program. The social seal certification for companies in Itajaí, according to the Selosocial website (2023), contributes to meeting the SDG goals. It represents a difference in creating links between brand, product, service, and social projects. Recognition for the program that the city council offers is a factor of respect that is increasingly recognized by consumers. Organizations, which need to be up to date with their taxes, are recognized when making and demonstrating internal investments for their employees and the community in which they operate.

The social seal program has a regulation that sets out all the rules governing the certification procedure. According to its art 5, paragraph 2, "[...] Investments made between the months of January and December of each year in the Municipality of Itajaí will be considered for certification purposes".

Individuals and legal entities are able to participate in the certification, as long as they are classified as I – Public Entities of Indirect Administration: Foundations, Local Authorities, Public Companies and Mixed Economy Companies; II – Private for-profit organizations: Micro, small, medium and large companies and individual entrepreneurs; III – Non-profit or non-profit Civil Society Organizations: NGOs, OSCIPs, Associations, Institutes, Parents and Teachers Associations, Private Education Units, Religious Institutions and others domiciled in the Municipality; IV – Individuals: Athletes, Writers, Musicians, Actors, Teachers and others domiciled in the Municipality (art. 7 of the Regulation).

However, participants must observe and fulfill the Municipal, State and Federal tax regularity requirements; as well as their projects must be registered with the necessary proof on the Social Seal Program website; and the requesting organization must promote investments to achieve the desired SDG (Art. 13 of the Regulation).

In addition to certification, among the registered organizations and individuals, the Commission will choose up to ten investments to receive the highlighted award, whose criteria are innovativeness and social impact achieved. The program website (http://selosocial.itajai.sc.gov.br) includes three important documents that help in the preparation of projects, a checklist for registering actions/projects and a booklet on its home page, in the Program link. of the Itajaí/SC/Brazil Social Seal Program, the latter presenting the goals of each SDG to be worked on by organizations interested in the Social Seal conferred by the Program, thus acting as a manual whose proposal is to facilitate the implementation of actions aimed at the 2030 Agenda, engaging and motivating participants in the development of their social projects.

The population was made up of 195 companies from Itajaí, state of Santa Catarina, Brazil, which have already been awarded in the social seal program between 2009 and 2022, which are available on the Social Seal Program website. The sample was characterized as non-probabilistic for convenience. To know the minimum sample size, the simple sample size of Barbeta (2002) was calculated. Therefore, a sampling error of 5% was defined, resulting in a 95% confidence level. Based on the calculations carried out, to analyze the sample, it would be necessary to obtain a minimum of 109 respondents. For this study, the sample obtained was 126. The respondents were the managers responsible for the social projects/investments developed by the organization in which they work, and who compete for the Social Seal of the Municipality of Itajaí, state of Santa Catarina, Brazil.

Data for this study were collected with a self-completed questionnaire, which was composed of three blocks. The first brought the presentation and the Free and Informed Consent Form. The second block had the function of collecting sociodemographic data, and no name or any data that could identify the respondent was requested.

The last block raised the managers' perception of entrepreneurial orientation and was based on that proposed by Lumpkin and Dess (1996), which was developed and validated by Martens *et al.* (2015). The instrument consists of 24 assertions divided into 5 dimensions – proactivity, innovativeness, risk taking, autonomy and competitive aggressiveness – and its quantification was carried out using a 7-point Likert scale, in which the value 1 represented completely disagree and 7 I totally agree.

The questionnaire was created on the Google Forms® platform. Initially, a pre-test was carried out. The link was sent to 3 professors in the area and 3 managers from companies in Itajaí, Santa Catarina, Brazil, which were awarded in the social seal program with the aim of verifying whether the questionnaire is appropriate for the respondents. After making the adjustments recommended by those who carried out the pre-test, an email was sent to the Secretariat for the Promotion of Citizenship

– Directorate of Thematic Relations on 05/08/2023 requesting that the link be sent to the companies that were awarded in the social seal program between 2009 and 2022. On 05/15/2023, the Secretariat resent the email. Verifying that the form was no longer receiving responses, on 05/19/2023 the deadline for filling it out was closed.

On 05/12/2023, the questionnaire was also administered personally by the researcher at a meeting of the Itajaí Business Association, to participating companies that were awarded in the social seal program in the defined period. Furthermore, contacts were made by telephone, via email and WhatsApp, with the aim of increasing the sample number.

To evaluate the distributions of variables, descriptive statistics were used, with tests of absolute frequency (n), relative frequency (%), mean (m), median (md), standard deviation (sd), asymmetry (a) and kurtosis (k). The adopted limit range of normality for asymmetry was [–2,+2] (George & Mallery, 2019) and for kurtosis considering it was [–3,+3] (Pearson, 1925).

RESULTS

A total of 126 participants made up the database. It was possible to observe that the average age of the participants was m = 27.90 (SD = 5.19) and length of service was m = 5.71 (SD = 2.76). Regarding gender, 65 (52%) of the participants declared themselves to be female and 61 (48%) male. Regarding marital status, 83 (66%) declared living with partner and 43 (34%) without a partner. And regarding the undergraduate level, 3 (2%) participants declare that they have a master's degree, 23 (18%) a specialization degree, 59 (47%) a higher education degree and 41 (33%) an incomplete higher education degree. The continuous variables age and length of service were categorized by their distribution tertiles to facilitate comparisons with the relationship between the study constructs.

The description of the items of the entrepreneurial orientation instrument can be seen in Table 01. It is observed that the highest means were found in items PR1 and PR3, and the lowest means in items AT2, AC2, AC3 and AC4. As for distributions, it is possible to observe that both asymmetry and kurtosis revealed values within the limits adopted as normal.

According to items PR1 (In general, when making decisions for your company, there is a strong tendency to be ahead of other competitors in introducing new ideas, products and/or services) and PR3 (In general, when dealing with your competitors, your firm is often the first company to introduce new products and services, administrative, technological, operational techniques, etc.), it is observed that the companies investigated have a strong propensity to develop anticipatory and pioneering behavior in the face of needs and demands of the target audience as well as taking advantage of opportunities, whether by opening new markets, creating products or remodeling processes capable of generating value and competitive advantage (Miller & Friesen, 1982; Lumpkin & Dess, 1996).

Table 1: Description of the Items of the Entrepreneurial Guidance Instrument

Dimension	*Itens*	*M*	*md*	*dp*	*a*	*k*
Proactivity	PR1	6.27	6	0.76	–0.50	–1.12
	PR2	5.21	5	1.28	–0.34	–0.45
	PR3	6.18	6	0.77	–0.33	–1.25
	PR4	5.57	5	0.98	0.23	–1.09
	PR5	5.88	6	0.94	–0.40	–0.78
Innovativeness	IN1	5.04	5	1.22	–0.10	–0.97
	IN2	5.04	5	1.24	0.10	–0.89
	IN3	4.81	4.5	1.21	0.07	–0.72
	IN4	5.41	6	1.21	–0.59	0.13
	IN5	5.29	6	1.41	–0.30	–1.23
	IN6	5.79	6	1.17	–1.06	0.94
Accept risks	AR1	5.25	5	1.34	–0.18	–0.94
	AR2	4.65	4.5	1.35	–0.16	–0.69
	AR3	5.52	6	1.34	–0.59	–0.89
	AR4	4.21	4	1.14	0.31	–0.18
	AR5	4.82	5	1.62	–0.27	–1.24
Autonomy	AT1	5.10	5	1.32	0.19	–1.24
	AT2	3.51	3	1.99	0.24	–1.30
	AT3	4.60	5	1.71	–0.22	–1.19
	AT4	4.52	5	1.48	–0.12	–0.88
Competitive aggressiveness	AC1	4.55	5	1.31	–0.27	–0.25
	AC2	3.48	3	1.50	0.38	–0.46
	AC3	3.23	3	1.67	0.10	–1.08
	AC4	3.52	4	1.75	0.13	–0.84

Note: m: average, md: median. dp: standard deviation. a: asymmetry. k: kurtosis.
Source: Prepared by the author (2023).

In this sense, Oliveira Junior (2009) investigated the impact of EO on the performance of Brazilian companies and found that the dimension of EO that proved to be most effective in relation to organizational performance was proactivity, in harmony with what was found in the present research.

And as mentioned previously, lower averages were identified in items AT2 (In general, in your company, employees pursue business opportunities, make decisions on their own, without constant reference from their superiors), AC2 (In general, in your company, practices are implemented that prove to be efficient in successful competitors), AC3 (In general, advertising and promotions are used intensively in your company), AC4 (In general, competitive prices are practiced in your company to increase sales). These findings demonstrate the weak interaction of employees in the search for new opportunities that depend on their own decisions, which is what the autonomy dimension prescribes. For Miller (1983), autonomous leadership is associated with companies with greater EO, with centralizing managers who are open to new technologies and emerging markets. The organizational culture must be based on promoting independent actions that enable the search for new opportunities without barriers, which will result in a strong presence of this dimension of EO (Lee & Peterson, 2000).

The research by Lazzarotti, *et al.* (2015) corroborates this perspective, as they proposed to evaluate EO in its six dimensions (innovativeness, proactivity, risk-taking, autonomy, competitive aggressiveness and networks) and its relationship with the performance of 128 graduated companies from Brazilian incubators and compare to the research by Santos and Alves (2009). Although the authors based the study on the multidimensional approach of the EO construct, the unidimensional approach outperformed, diverging from that found by Santos and Alves (2009) in incubated companies, concluding that the dimension with the greatest impact on the characterization of EO in the companies studied was the autonomy, which emphasizes the importance of this dimension in the composition of the EO construct.

Even though the average for item AT2 was low, the other items in the autonomy variable (AT1, AT3 and AT4) obtained a good score, demonstrating that the companies that make up the sample encourage their employees and teams to work autonomously in the selection process and implementation of pursued opportunities, seeking to develop a strategic, leadership and training vision.

The lower averages related to items AC2, AC3 and AC4 caused the competitive aggressiveness dimension to be disregarded in the formation of the EO of the companies studied. In other words, it was found that these companies do little to implement efficient practices used by the competition, they do not constantly use advertisements and promotions to win new customers and retain the ones they have.

Horz, *et al.* (2022) evaluated the effects of entrepreneurial orientation on the performance of credit cooperatives in the Brazilian market and their findings showed that the competitive aggressiveness dimension has a positive and significant association with organizational performance, making the important role of this dimension in the composition of the EO construct crystal clear. In the same sense, Lizote, *et al.* (2020), in turn, undertook research to identify the characteristics of entrepreneurial orientation present in social enterprises. Regarding the competitive aggressiveness dimension, they found that the four social enterprises studied enter a low-income market and position themselves in the market in which they compete through the development of quality products at low prices, emphasizing the role of marketing as a driver in fundraising, positioning of products and services provided to communities generating positive social impact.

FINAL CONSIDERATIONS

Economic profit and social impact are strong allies when it comes to the search for differentiation and competitive advantage. The market is dynamic and has presented numerous challenges that are demanding the remodeling of the way of doing business. Understanding the entrepreneurial spirit of organizations, strategic processes and performance is the scope of entrepreneurial orientation (Rauch, *et al.* 2009).

This study aimed to identify managers' perception of the dimensions of entrepreneurial orientation that are present in companies certified in the social seal program of Itajaí, Santa Catarina, Brazil. The results showed that the proactivity dimension obtained the highest averages, with emphasis on the items "In general, when making decisions for your company, there is a strong tendency to be ahead of other competitors in the introduction of new ideas, products and/or services" and "In general, when dealing with your competitors, your firm is often the first company to introduce new products and services, administrative, technological, operational techniques". However, the competitive aggressiveness dimension presented the lowest averages with an emphasis on "In general, in your company, practices are implemented that prove to be efficient in successful competitors", "In general, in your company, advertisements and promotions are used intensively to win over customers " and "In general, your company has competitive prices to increase sales". It is concluded, therefore, that according to the managers' view, the five dimensions of EO are present in companies independently, perfectly meeting the multidimensionality requirement.

The choice of the population made up of companies certified in the social seal program of Itajaí, Santa Catarina, Brazil was due to the fact that these organizations have their organizational practices focused on generating social value, as they seek to achieve economic success by impacting people and the environment in which they are inserted through their social projects, which is consistent with the creation of shared value.

It is not enough for an organization to simply have economic prosperity; managers must be aware of the impacts caused by the actions taken, from a perspective of respect for the environment and social causes. The current moment requires more than simply keeping accounts up to date and making a profit, Porter and Kramer (2011) already highlighted that organizations continue to be handcuffed in an outdated value creation perspective, seeing financial profit in the short term and failing to consider the real needs of its clients in the long term, such as the depletion of natural resources and economic problems of the communities in which they operate. Thinking about a solution would be to defend the use of the principle of shared value, simultaneously generating economic and social value. This is not about philanthropy, social responsibility or even sustainability, but about a new look at how to be economically successful.

Furthermore, future research may also include moderating variables in the analysis of the relationship between entrepreneurial orientation and organizational performance, such as organizational culture, organizational learning, strategic behavior, among others.

REFERENCES

Asemokha, A. *et al.* (2019). Business model innovation and entrepreneurial orientation relationships in SMEs: Implications for international performance. *Journal of International Entrepreneurship*, 17, 425–453.

Barbetta, P.A. (2002). *Estatística aplicada às ciências sociais.* Editora da UFSC, Florianópolis.

Begnini, S., Rossetto, C.R. and Carvalho, C.E. (2023). O impacto da capacidade de absorção do conhecimento na orientação empreendedora e na sustentabilidade no setor hoteleiro. ***Turismo: Visão e Ação***, 25(1), 22–50.

Camozzato, E.S.; *et al.* (2017). Orientação empreendedora, autoeficácia dos gestores e satisfação com o desempenho: um estudo em empresas incubadas. *Revista de Ciências da Administração*, 19(48), 68–83.

Covin, J.G. and Slevin, D.P. (1991). A conceptual model of entrepreneurship as firm behavior. *Entrepreneurship Theory and Practice*, 16(1), 7–26.

Dess, G.G. and Lumpkin, G.T. (2005). The role of entrepreneurial orientation in stimulating effective corporate entrepreneurship. *The Academy of Management Executive*, 19(1), 147–156.

Galbreath, J. *et al.* (2020). Entrepreneurial orientation and firm performance in Italian firms. *International Journal of Entrepreneurial Behavior and Research*, 26(4), 629–646.

George, D. and Mallery, P. (2019). *IBM SPSS Statistics 26 step by step:* a simple guide and reference (6. ed.), Routledge.

Horz, V. *et al.* (2022). Reflexos da orientação empreendedora no desempenho das cooperativas de crédito do mercado brasileiro. *Innovar*, 32(850, 7–82.

Kronemberger, D.M.P. (2019). Os desafios da construção dos indicadores ODS globais. *Ciência e Cultura*, 71(1), 40–45.

Lazzarotti, F. *et al.* (2015). Orientação empreendedora: um estudo das dimensões e sua relação com desempenho em empresas graduadas. *Revista de Administração Contemporâne*a, 19(1), 673–695.

Lee, S.M. and Peterson, S.J. (2000). Culture, entrepreneurial orientation, and global competitiveness. *Journal of World Business*, 35(4), 401–416.

Lizote, S.A. *et al.* (2021). Ambientes incertos com gestores proativos e pré-dispostos a riscos estão mais satisfeitos com desempenho: um estudo com pet shops. *Future Studies Research Journal: Trends and Strategies*, 113(3), 409–434.

Lizote, S.A. *et al.* (2014). Orientação empreendedora das empresas do seguimento de moda íntima e linha praia estabelecidas em Ilhota SC. *In:* XI Simpósio de Excelência em Gestão e Tecnologia, 2014. Tema: Gestão do Conhecimento para a Sociedade, 22, 23 e 24 de outubro.

Lizote, S.A. *et al.* (2020). Orientação empreendedora em organizações sociais. *In:* Congresso Internacional de Administração ADM 2020. As novas fronteiras da administração. 19 a 21 de outubro, Ponta Grossa, Paraná, Brasil.

Lumpkin, G.T. and Dess, G.G. (1996). Clarifying the entrepreneurial orientation construct and linking it to performance. *Academic of Management Review*, 21(1), 135–172.

Martens, C.D.P. *et al.* (2015). Relação entre orientação empreendedora e maturidade na gestão de projetos em empresas brasileiras de software. *Revista Ibero-americana de Estratégia*, 15(1), 14–32.

Martens, C.D.P. and Freitas, H. (2008). Orientação empreendedora nas organizações e a busca de sua facilitação. *Gestão. Org.* 6(1), 90–108.

Miller, D. (2011). Miller (1983) revisited: a reflection on EO research and some suggestions for the future. *Entrepreneurship Theory and Practice*, 35(5), 873–894.

Miller, D. (1983). The correlates of entrepreneurship in three types of firms. *Management Science*, 29(7), 770–791.

Miller; D. and Friesen, P. (1982). Innovation in conservative and entrepreneurial firms: two models of strategic momentum. *Strategic Management Journal*, 3(1), 1–25.

Mintzberg, H. (1973) *The Nature of managerial work.* New York, Harper & Row.

Okado, G.H.C. and Quinelli, L. (2016). Megatendências mundiais 2030 e os Objetivos de Desenvolvimento Sustentável (ODS): uma reflexão preliminar sobre a nova agenda das Nações Unidas. *Baru*, 2(2), 111–129.

Oliveira Junior, A.B. de. (2009). *O impacto da orientação empreendedora na performance das empresas brasileiras:* evidências de um estudo híbrido. Dissertação apresentada no Mestrado em Gestão Empresarial (Escola Brasileira de Administração Pública e de Empresas, Centro de Formação Acadêmica e de Pesquisa). Fundação Getúlio Vargas, Rio de Janeiro.

ONU, Organização das Nações Unidas (2015). *Cúpula das Nações Unidas sobre o Desenvolvimento Sustentável:* transformar nosso mundo para as pessoas e o planeta. Capturado de https://nacoesunidas.org/pos2015/cúpula.

Pearson, K. (1925). Das fehlergesetz und seine verallgemeiner-ungen durch fechner und pearson." a rejoinder. *Biometrika*, 4(2), 169–212.

Porter, M. and Kramer, M.R. (2011). *Criação de valor compartilhado.* Harvad Business Review.

Rauch, A. *et al.* (2009). Entrepreneurial orientation and business performance: an assessment of past research and suggestions for the future. *Entrepreneurship Theory and Practice*, 33(3), 761–787.

Santos, A.C.M.Z. and Alves, M.S.P.C. (2009). Dimensões da orientação empreendedora e seus diferentes impactos no desempenho de empresas instaladas em incubadoras tecnológicas da região sul do Brasil. *In:* Anais do Encontro Nacional da Associação Nacional de Pós-Graduação e Pesquisa em Administração, 2009.

Selo Social (2023). *Programa municipal selo social.* Capturado de https://selosocial.itajai.sc.gov.br/site/programa

Shirokova, G. *et al.* (2016). Entrepreneurial orientation and firm performance in different environmental settings: Contingency and configurational approaches. *Journal of Small Business and Enterprise Development*, 23(3), 703–727.

Stevenson, H.H. and Jarillo, J.C. (1990). A paradigm of entrepreneurship: entrepreneurial management. *Strategic Management Journal*, 11(5), 17–27.

Wiklund, J. (1999). The Sustainability of the entrepreneurial orientation-performance relationship. *Entrepreneurship Theory and Practice*, 24(10, 37–48.

Human Resources and Sustainability: The Present and the Future

Satatya Das[1]

ABSTRACT: With only approximately 6 years left till 2030, sustainability should clearly be our top priority. Despite unflagging and meticulous efforts towards sustainable development across the planet, meeting the SDG targets by 2030 seems challenging and frankly seems to be implausible across all levels through all sectors.

In today's world companies worldwide are becoming more aware of the momentousness of social, ethical, and ecological practices. In addition to financial profits, the companies are now clearly focusing on environmentally friendly performance and development. And the one discipline they are following to achieve the said objective is to promote the idea of Sustainable Human Resource Management (SHRM).

In this context, the fundamental task of SHRM is the supervision of human resources use and consumption, specifically, it is perceived as the managerial control of human capabilities and skills. This key role has a direct impact on attaining six of the UN's SDGs: 3 (health and wellbeing), 5 (gender equality), 8 (decent work and economic growth), 10 (reduction of inequality), 12 (responsible consumption and production), 16 (Peace, Justice and Strong Institution) and 17 (implementation and revitalization of global partnerships).

SDGs also help in mainstreaming the granular acceptance of ESG (Environmental, Social and Governance) based investment decisions while anchoring their wider reach in corporate circles.

The key points of discussion in this paper will be as follows:

- HR management can indeed contribute towards the achievement of SDGs.
- SHRM has indeed emerged as a way and means to contribute towards sustainable outcomes.
- SDGs and ESG—A pathway for a sustainable future.

INTRODUCTION

MBA students, faculty and professionals have heard the always repeated notion that employees are the most important asset of an organization. However actually developing the people and human capital is seldom done effectively.

---

[1] Senior Associate HR, ITC Integrated Business Services Limited.

For a company to be fully engaged in sustainability, human capital strategy is paramount. Employees need to have all the expertise and should be well-informed to carry out sustainability projects in their field of work.

According to Harvard Business Review, *human capital management* refers to a set of people-oriented capabilities including inclusive leadership practices, employee engagement, knowledge sharing, workforce optimization and learning capacity which together drive organizational performance. (McMurrer, 2007)

Sustainability as we know isn't only about vesting in the correct technologies or polishing the correct strategies, it is about creating an organizational culture which will be able to respond to social and ecological challenges.

The community now is realising the value of holding up and fulfilling the Sustainable Development Goals and in order to support this, Ivey Publishing in 2021 introduced the "Sustainability: ESG and SDG Collection" in order to enhance the amalgamation of sustainability into the thinking and decision-making capability of future leaders.

International Labour Organization (ILO), through its Twitter presence, impelled social media users by asking "How will you help achieve the Sustainable Development Goals at work?" People responded by tagging #Work4SDGs. (Chaudhary, 2023)

The HR or the Human Resource department is responsible for the management and development of an organization's human capital. It the same department that designs policies and framework for which increases the efficiency of the workforce and hence plays an important part in meeting the organizational goals. Its simple logic – if sustainability can be/is assimilated to HR programs, it can have a well built and constructive impact on the sustainable development of the company.

Today, organizations are becoming more mindful of the importance of social, ethical and ecological objectives. In addition to financial profit, organizations are setting themselves new goals, focusing on individual, communal, and environmental-friendly performance and development. One of the disciplines that is promoting "green" organizations is Sustainable Human Resource Management (SHRM). (García-Blandón, 2019)

SHRM has been evolving for more than two decades and central to this approach is the link between Human Resource Management (HRM) and Sustainability. Sustainable HRM aims to achieve positive economic, social, human and environmental outcomes concurrently, in the short and the long term.

WHAT DOES SUSTAINABILITY MEAN IN BUSINESS?

Sustainability in business refers to a company's strategy to reduce negative environmental impact resulting from their operations in a particular market. An organization's sustainability practices are typically analyzed against environmental, social, and governance (ESG) metrics. (IBM, n.d.)

We human as a species are now facing the consequences of the permanent changes which have been made in the Earth's system over the course of decades and it is time to accept that the commination of climate change has become too perilous to be oblivious to.

Over the past 20 years, the idea of corporate sustainability has become part of mainstream business discourse. Companies in many industries issue sustainability or corporate-social-responsibility reports; executives everywhere pledge allegiance to the idea. Even so, the concept still carries considerable baggage. In a recent report for the UN Global Compact, 84 percent of the 1,000 global CEOs surveyed agreed that business "should lead efforts to define and deliver new goals on global priority issues." But only a third said "that business is doing enough to address global sustainability challenges." (Swartz, 2014)

Even in the COVID-19 pandemic, organizations did continue to align to the UN's SDG goals intended to achieve by 2030. The SDGs if not anything, has been successful in laying the foundations of sustainability in business target areas like poverty, inequality, environmental degradation and climate change.

WHY IS SUSTAINABILITY IN BUSINESS IMPORTANT?

Simple reason being—Sustainability can drive business favourable results. Several venture capitalists and investors do use the ESG Matrix (Environmental, Social and

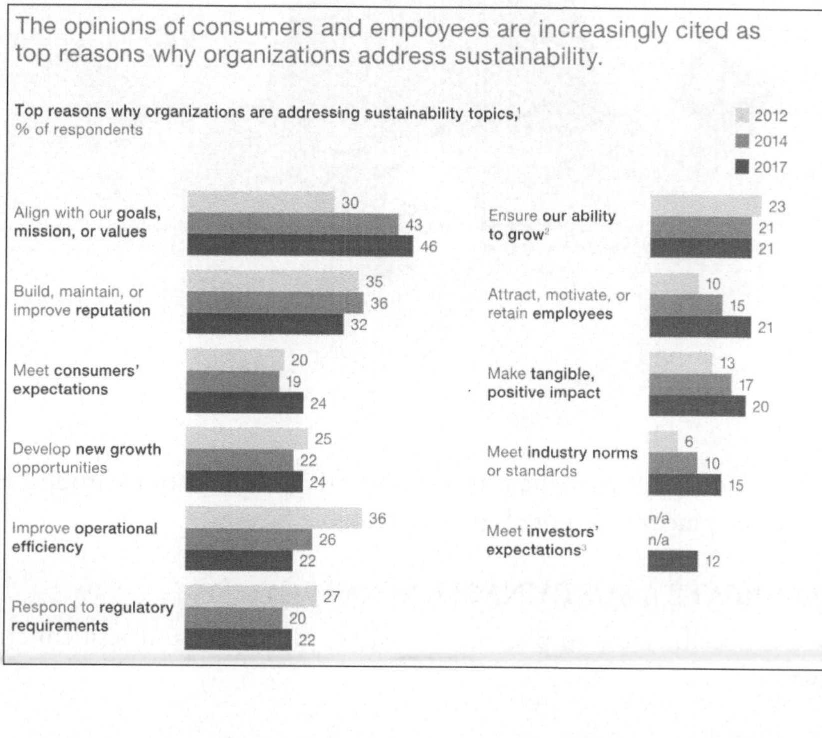

Governance) to scrutinize the company's ethical impact and sustainability practices. They investigate factors such as carbon footprint, electricity usage, water usage, board diversity and many other factors before putting their money on the table.

When McKinsey did a research which spanned over 5 years viz. 2012 to 2017, the reason as to why organizations addressed sustainability, the following results came forward:

The above results clearly shows that the strongest motivating factors to adopting a sustainable mindset back in 2017 were to align with a company's goals, missions, or values; build, maintain, or improve reputation; meet customer's expectations; and develop new growth opportunities.

This overlay of Business opportunities, social needs and Corporate assets and expertise is now known as the **"Shared Value Opportunity"**. The concept is fundamentally about the alignment of the organization's success with the success of the community it caters to.

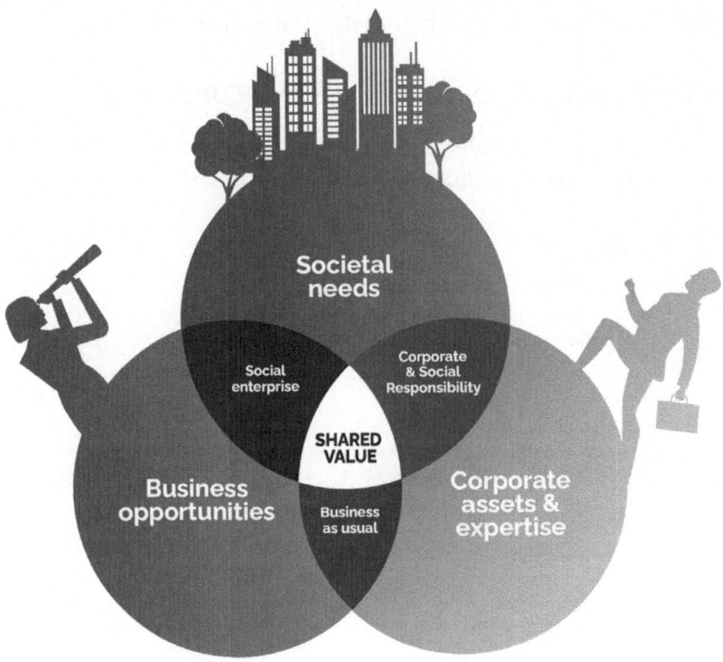

And, it is due to this particular opportunity that organizations around the globe have adopted the practices required for a sustainable future.

HOW TO CREATE A SUSTAINABLE STRATEGY?

There are five specific areas to plan a sustainable, profitable, and resilient strategy to move forward:

Climate Risk Management and ESG Reporting

The past two decades has been a witness to the largest number of natural disasters in the globe. Companies around the world now must take into account the effect of climate change, which is having an impact on their business's operations in a scalable and repeatable manner. Everything the organization now owns – from building infrastructure to their supply chains and their employees is now at risk from the growing toll which climate change has on the business.

In order to counter the problem, organizations need to consider geospatial data which comes from satellite monitoring of the planet. Plus, the companies need to add in the factor of global weather forecast data over and above the organization's data related to facilities and infrastructure. The result – cosmic and continually updated data sets that is too huge to pass.

Resilient Infrastructure and Intelligent Operations

The aim is simple i.e. to create more sustainable operations one asset at a time. A company's assets like buildings, energy grids, vehicles and industrial equipment are key benefactor to the sustainable challenges faced y organizations today.

Consider the number of assets a company needs to run their daily operations. Each of those assets has a finite lifecycle that includes regular maintenance and replacements of parts which are not the most eco-friendly activities out there.

One of the many ways to create more sustainable operations is by employing enterprise asset management through which an organization can reduce waste and gain operation efficiencies in its processes.

The prerequisite elements of sustainable business operations can be boiled down to lessening of labour force merged with enhanced products and quality of service.

The key to process optimization in every industry lies in understanding the root causes of failures and defects.

Sustainable Supply Chains and Circularity

Consumers of this day and age are becoming more involved about the traceability of the goods or services they are purchasing and the organization's supply chain leaders are currently looking into ways and means to invest in circular economies which invigorate reuse.

For organizations pursuing a sustainability agenda, the supply chain has to be a key area of focus. Why? Because up to 85% of environmental, social and governance (ESG)-related impacts occur in the supply chain—including over 90% of the emissions associated with providing an enterprise's products and services. Without supply chain transformation, there can be no sustainability transformation. (IBM, n.d.)

World Economic Forum defines Sustainable Supply Chain as one where ESG conditions are considered and embedded from production of raw materials to the means of delivery of the product to the end consumer.

Many organizations are now taking this definition up a notch and taking into consideration post purchase activities like returns and disposals. The conviction of a circular economy where products and materials follow the 3Rs (Reduce, Reuse and Recycle) rather than just throwing it away after usage is the crux of supply chain sustainability.

More sustainable supply chains are contemplated to help:

- Minimize greenhouse gas (GHG) emissions.
- Preserve resources by reducing, reusing and recycling.
- Meet customer expectations while mitigating climate impact.
- Tackle economic and social inequities through ethical and responsible sourcing.

Electrification, Energy and Emissions reduction aka. Decarbonization

Enabling decarbonization at a large scale will require leaders to collaborate and come together in new ways to rethink how the electrical system works and their part in a net zero Green House Gas emissions economy.

As organizations around the world and across industries push towards the target of net zero, one thing is for certain – in order to reach the desired milestone, new utilities partnerships, ecosystems and marketplaces will be desideratum.

The good news is that about 70% of today's global greenhouse gas emissions can be addressed by clean electrification. High-emitting sectors, like power generation and transportation, are investing heavily in in the process. US automakers, for example, committed to invest USD 250 billion in vehicle electrification by 2023. And despite the pandemic, 2020 was a record year for green energy, with more than 80% of all new electricity capacity coming from renewable sources.

Digital solutions that utilise AI, IoT and Blockchain technology are the key elements will support this objective.

Sustainability Strategy

Organizations must implant sustainability into the fabric of the business to get the relevant data needed to operationalize at scale. The hope is that this particular module will enable new business models to achieve the desired sustainable goals, increase their operational orderliness, will be compliant with the regulatory requirements which will in turn lead to increased customer experience and simultaneously create a competitive advantage.

DEVELOPING A SUSTAINABILITY MINDSET AND THE ROLE OF HR

A sustainability mindset can be defined as the way of thinking that comes from understanding how interconnected our environment is.

Isabel Rimoncozy says that there are three elements to develop a sustainable mindset:

- **The Knowing:** Becoming eco literate and using systematic thinking.
- **The Being:** Seeing oneself and your actions as a part of a wider eco system, reflecting on your habits and values.
- **The Doing:** Being connected with the community, developing social sensitivity and being innovative (Rimonoczy, n.d.).

To ensure that this change does happen, sustainable HR needs to operate by leveraging HR tools and processes to support sustainable business.

However, rather than HR being the 'voice of the employees' or the 'instrument of management', or both, the more precise role of HR is to enhance organisational capability, by understanding what the business needs and what people, knowledge, skills and culture need to be in place to deliver those needs. As increasingly companies adopt strategies for sustainable business, so too does HR's understanding of how their role, not only as a business partner, but as a sustainable business partner, need to evolve. (King, 2017)

> *"The SDGs provide a brilliantly helpful framework for professionals to assess their organisational performance and understand how they can contribute towards a more sustainable and fairer world. As HR professionals, we have a great opportunity to demonstrate our strategic capability and to raise these issues with our senior teams."*
>
> ***—Neil Morrison, HR Director at Severn Trent***

The SDGs address all the global challenges which are being faced by the planet Earth in this day and age—from poverty and climate change to economic growth and peace. The said goals calls to arms all the NGOs, private and government business houses as well as individuals to create, innovate and implement state of the art solutions to address the challenges faced to achieve the SDG goals.

For the private sector, SDG's market value opportunities are estimated to be at least US$12 trillion globally. (Business and Sustainable Development Commission, 2017)

So, what is the need of the hour one might ask. The answer to this question is actually quite simple—True Commitment. True commitment from business houses across the planet on SDGs is now absolutely essential, because their now primary stakeholder group aka. The Millennials are not entirely sure that the business houses will indeed put sustainability first.

Now that we have understood as to what sustainability means and why is it important in business, let us now look into the various ways in which the Human Resource Department of an organization can contribute to the sustainability goals of the organization and in broader aspect help in meeting the SDG goals of 2030.

SDG 5: Gender Equality

SDG 5 aims at achieving gender equality and empowering all women and girls across the globe.

> *"If HR isn't committed to gender diversity and isn't championing it, the needle won't move."*
>
> *—Ursula Mead, Founder of InHerSight*

The target here is simple—Ensuring women's full and effective participation and equal opportunities for leadership across all levels of decision making in political, economic and public life.

> *"Companies with the highest percentage of women in board positions outperformed in financial performance compared to companies least gender representative". (Catalyst, 2007)*

Evidence has been pretty conclusive that investing and promoting gender diversity is of paramount importance for economic growth, corporate development and productivity as well as the organization's financial performance and viability.

For any organization's HR department, gender diversity is predominant in order to retain the company's diverse abilities and backgrounds which are obligatory for having a highly skilled talent pool.

Ploughing in gender equality measures is not only principally non partisan but this will also lead to an enlargement in terms of employee productivity and satisfaction, and will give an entrance to the development of a highly proficient and skilled human capital for the organization.

To have gender equality in a business, all employees must be provided equal opportunities to develop and succeed in their roles regardless of their gender. Gender equality includes equal access to career development opportunities, fair pay, and a working environment without discrimination, bias, or harassment. Gender equality removes gender-based barriers, biases and gender stereotypes, guaranteeing everyone is provided equal opportunities and sources to be successful within society and the working environment. (BeyondHR, 2023)

SDG 8: Decent Work & Economic Growth

SDG 8 lays the groundwork for quality jobs for everyone inclusive of persons with disabilities, migrants and/or lower educated people.

The target here is simple—achieving higher levels of productivity through diversification, technological upgradation and innovation inclusive of a focus on high value added and labour-intensive industries and sectors.

The HR management practices prevalent in a company should ideally target work conditions that has an effect on an employee's physical, mental and social health as well. The organization policy needs to be framed in such a manner that work is not prioritized over family and community involvement and worsens the employee's social well-being.

On the continuum between bad jobs and good jobs, decent jobs are those that provide men and women with opportunities to obtain work that allows earning a decent income under conditions of freedom, equity, security and human dignity. (Burchell B., 2014)

In 1999, the ILO established four interdependent principles framing its Decent Work Agenda, which defines the broad parameters of decent work (ILO 2008). These principles include:

- Access to decent and productive work that ensures equity, security, and dignity.
- Human rights within the workplace that are both legislated and part of consensually agreed upon norms and value.
- Social dialogue that includes workers, employers, labour unions, and governments.
- Social protections, including safe working conditions, adequate time for rest, and other supports for workers and their families.

For "Decent Jobs" to be prevalent, a social dialogue needs to take place in three places:

- Between employers and employees to determine the terms and conditions of the said employment.
- Between the management and employees over the functioning of the organization.
- Between social partners and public authorities on social and economic policies.

For majority of the people around the globe, the social dialogue closest to them takes place in their workplace—amongst the employers and employees. In majority of the countries, this particular social dialogue takes place in the form of collective bargaining between the employee's unions and the employers.

From an HR perspective, employees' satisfaction is fostered when safety is provided.

The HR department needs to encourage development-oriented policies that supports creativity and innovation and encourage the formalization and growth of micro, small and medium scale enterprises.

SDG 10: Reduced Inequalities

While the coronavirus pandemic of 2020 has ravaged the entire job market, women are losing even more ground due to making up a larger percentage of employees in occupations with layoffs and reduction of hours. Women are also more likely to have childcare and eldercare duties fall on their shoulders, forcing them to voluntarily cut back their own working hours in some cases. And we've long known that any absence from the workforce for women results in them making even less pay when they return and diminished opportunities for career advancement. (Diversity Jobs, n.d.)

Growing disparities in income and wealth, as well as unequal opportunities, reinforce each other creating an "inequality trap" that disproportionately affects women and the most vulnerable members of society, including the poor, youth, persons with disabilities, older persons and migrants. (United Nations, 2015)

The target here is simple – Ensuring equal opportunity and to reduce inequalities of income via elimination of discriminatory laws, policies and practices and promoting appropriate legislation and taking appropriate actions and policies in this regard.

There are innumerable actionable items for the HR department in organizations to ameliorate inequalities:

- Base salary to be provided on company standards and not on previous salary for the new joiners.
- Barring employees to discuss their salaries with others.
- Being open for discussion with employees regarding salary ranges and how their current compensation has been decided.
- Allowing employees to measure their performance against expectations for each pay grade.
- Take charge of looking into inequalities within the same designation and job descriptions and pointing them out to the company management.
- Making rewardable accomplishments clear and attainable.
- Accepting the fact that unconditional bias does exist and will likely have an effect on salaries. The HR department needs to encourage the company management to discuss the same with employees and convince them to be open towards fixing the same.

SDG 12: Responsible Consumption and Production

Sustainable Development Goal (SDG) 12 calls for responsible consumption and production, essentially decoupling economic growth from unsustainable resource use and emissions and improving the management of hazardous substances and waste. In particular it calls for implementation of the 10-Year Framework of Programmes on Sustainable Consumption and Production (SCP), for efficient use of natural resources, for cutting food and other waste, for responsible management of chemicals, for sustainable public procurement and for companies to adopt more sustainable practices. (Stefanie Chan, 2018)

The target here is simple—to encourage organizations especially large transactional companies into adopting sustainable practices and integrating sustainability information into their reporting cycle.

Despite an astronomical economic growth and remarkable progress in terms of poverty reduction, inequality still persist and in some areas around the globe has intensified.

And, in order to achieve the said target the HR department needs to promote public procurement practices that are sustainable and comply with the country's policies and priorities the company is situated in.

SDG 16: Peace, Justice and Strong Institution

The adoption of SDG16 in the target for achieving within 2030 was not without controversy and debate about whether it was practicable or naive.

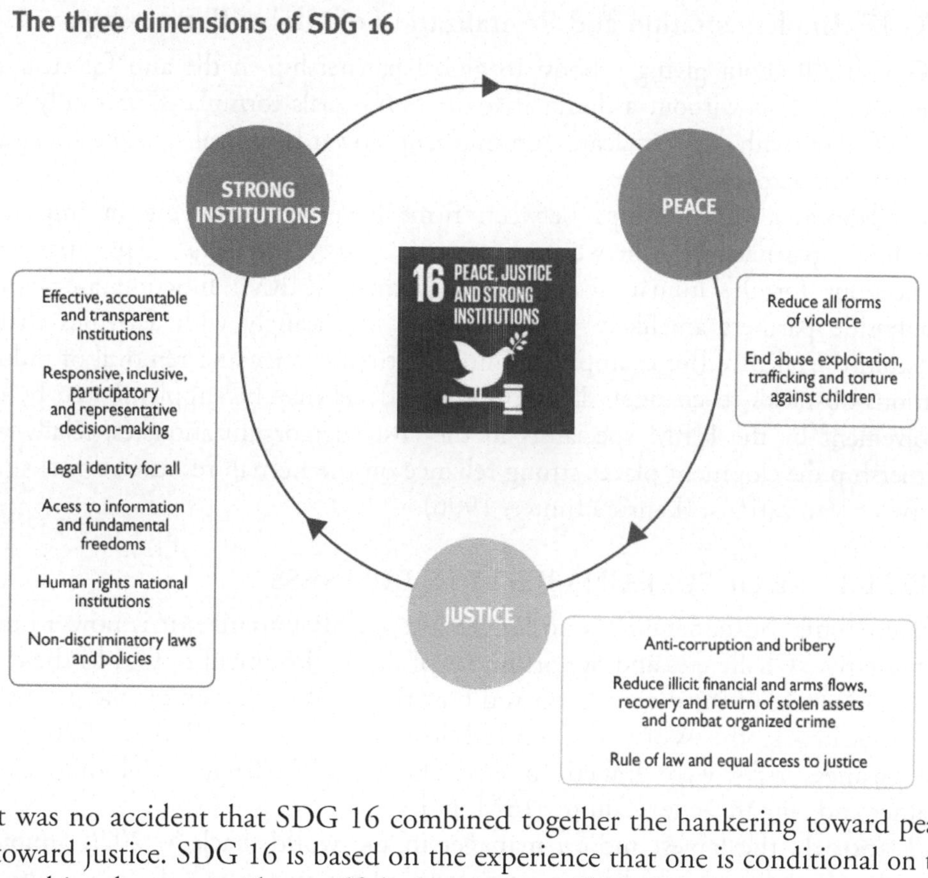

It was no accident that SDG 16 combined together the hankering toward peace and toward justice. SDG 16 is based on the experience that one is conditional on the other and it submerges within itself the best lessons of that long history of gradational progress.

The private sector has a catalytic role to play in SDG 16 at local and global levels. By being responsible partners throughout the chain of production, businesses can help the countries where they operate to meet the SDG 16 targets related to anti-corruption, labour rights, inclusive decision-making and community engagement. (Sustainable Development Goals Fund, 2017)

Organizations influence all aspects of public opinions through their products and services and the way they go about doing their business and making profits. And, that is the same reason as to why it is crucial to how they treat their employees.

The Human Resource department needs to champion the cause across all the levels of their organization. Firstly, they need to be advocate an honest and ethical business behaviour in which corruption in any form is not accepted. Corruption will eventually lead to financial losses, loss in brand image but above all will have a pessimistic effect on employee morale.

SDG 17: Implementation and Revitalization of Global Partnerships

SDG 17 is all about giving a boost to global partnership in the aim for sustainable development. It is without a doubt that the SDG goals formulated can only see the light of day with a herculean commitment towards global partnerships across organizations across the globe.

Collaborative relationships between firms have been growing in importance, including 'partnerships' between customers and suppliers. The partnership implications for the human resource management (HRM) function are explored. Supply-side partners are likely to be involved increasingly with activities that will underpin the alliance (for example, training, cultural change and removal of industrial relations obstacles to change). These indirect effects may be supplemented by direct involvement by the HRM specialists in the customer organization, especially where partnership development places strong reliance on the human resource dimensions of the two organizations. (Laurie Hunter, 1996)

THE FUTURE OF SUSTAINABILITY IN BUSINESS

Environmental Sustainability is no longer just a CSR initiative, it is now a business authoritative. Challenges and opportunities of the environment now risks the current operating model of the organization and how they do business and make profits.

According to the World Economic Forum's Global Risk Report 2020, the top five business risks were linked to environmental challenges, including extreme weather and climate action failure. (IBM, n.d.)

Blackrock, the largest money manager in the world, back in 2020 announced "that sustainability should be our new standard for investing". To raise capital for future growth, it will be of utmost importance that organizations need to align their business activities and objectives with the sustainability objectives.

The environmental agenda is quite simple – connecting forces make it a central feature of corporate strategy

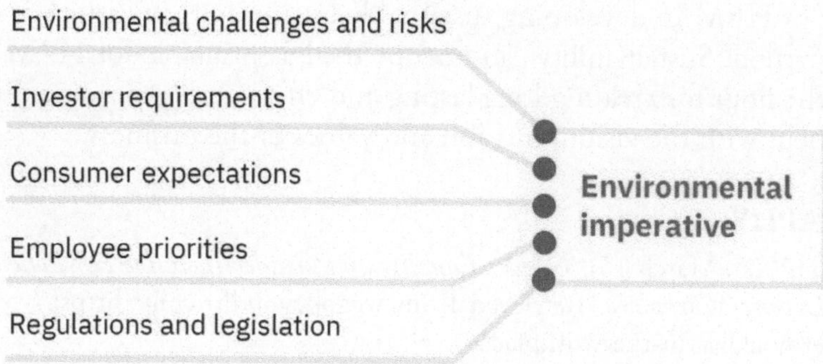

However it is to be noted that something like this is easier said than done and finding a path to successful action is another ball game all together. Growing innovations in technology like AI, 5G, IoT and Blockchain will accelerate the process in three ways:

- Capitalize on data to reveal new insights and suggest new solutions to existing problems.
- Change business policies and practices to drive the materializing of "Sustainable Enterprise".
- Can help in the construction of a new governance structure and model for environmental assertion.

CONCLUSION

With many goals, however, come many challenges: convincing employees their individual contribution is worthwhile, addressing some targets without diluting others, and avoiding the SDGs from becoming lip service.

However, to achieve optimal results, goals have to be broken down into meaningful and actionable outcomes for Human Resource personnel to pick up and engage with. Going through the 17 goals, there's something every company, no matter its size can turn into a meaningful plan of action.

In addition to these vertical inconsistencies, there is also horizontal inconsistency in which the knowledge and expertise of human resources do not match the demands of the labor market. Among university graduates, this horizontal inconsistency occurs when the employment rate is good in specific fields and majors but challenging in others. Parents and students themselves do not have much information on how the labor market demand will move in the future. They go to university with a vague idea of "I want to go to XX department and get a job in X" based on their acquaintances and their own experiences. However, in reality, the demand for human resources in a particular industry may already be heading in another direction. This is called information asymmetry between the labor market and job seekers. (Yamada, n.d.)

The role of HRM in developing sustainable business organizations is increasingly attracting attention. Sustainability can now be used as principle for HRM itself and is the need of the hour for creating long lasting and effective organizational plans which are in alignment with the vision, mission and values of the business.

BIBLIOGRAPHY

Beyond, H.R. (2023, March 15). *Gender Equality and Gender-Inclusive HR Policies: Creating a Fair and Diverse Workplace.* Retrieved from wegobeyondhr.com: https://wegobeyondhr.com/gender-equality-in-the-workplace/

Burchell, B., S.K. (2014). The quality of employment and decent work: Definitions, methodologies, and ongoing debates. *Cambridge Journal of Economics.*

Business and Sustainable Development Commission (2017). Better Business, Better World. 122.

Catalyst (2007). *The Bottom Line: Corporate performance and women's representation on boards.* Catalyst.

Chaudhary, S.S. (2023, March 22). *The (ab)sense of Sustainable Development Goals in HRM.* Retrieved from ET HR: https://hr.economictimes.indiatimes.com/news/industry/the-absense-of-sustainable-development-goals-in-hrm/98891378

David L. Blustein, E.I. (2023). Annual Review of Organizational Psychology and Organizational Behaviour: Understanding Decent Work and Meaningful Work. *Annual Reviews.*

David L. Blustein, E.I. (2023). *Understanding Decent Work and Meaningful Work.* Annual Reviews.

Diversity Jobs (n.d.). *How HR Leaders Can Eliminate Workplace Inequality.* Retrieved from diversityjobs.com: https://www.diversityjobs.com/career-advice/team-building/how-hr-leaders-can-eliminate-workplace-inequality/

García-Blandón, N.C. (2019, February). *On the importance of sustainable human resource management for the adoption of sustainable development goals.* Retrieved from Science Direct: https://www.sciencedirect.com/science/article/abs/pii/S0921344918303719

IBM (n.d.). *Build a more sustainable, resilient supply chain.* Retrieved from ibm.com: https://www.ibm.com/resources/business-operations/supply-chain-sustainability

IBM (n.d.). *Build a more sustainable, resilient supply chain.* Retrieved from ibm.com: https://www.ibm.com/resources/business-operations/supply-chain-sustainability

IBM (n.d.). *Build your strategic roadmap.* Retrieved from ibm.com: https://www.ibm.com/resources/guides/business-operations/strategic-roadmap

IBM (n.d.). *Sustainably fueling the future: accelerating decarbonization through clean electrification.* Retrieved from ibm.com: https://www.ibm.com/resources/guides/business-operations/sustainably-accelerating-decarbonization/

IBM (n.d.). *The Rise of Sustainable Enterprise.* Retrieved from ibm.com: https://www.ibm.com/thought-leadership/institute-business-value/report/sustainable-enterprise

IBM (n.d.). *What is sustainability in business?* Retrieved from ibm.com: https://www.ibm.com/topics/business-sustainability

King, E.C. (2017). Human resources management: developing sustainability mindset.

Laurie Hunter, P.B. (1996). A 'Partnership' Route to Human Resource Management? *Journal of Management Studies.*

McKinsey. (2017, December 11). *Sustainability's deepening imprint.* Retrieved from mckinsey.com: https://www.mckinsey.com/capabilities/sustainability-and-resource-productivity/our-insights/sustainabilitys-deepening-imprint

McMurrer, L.B. (2007, March). *Maximizing Your Return on People.* Retrieved from Harvard Business Review: https://hbr.org/2007/03/maximizing-your-return-on-people

Rimonoczy, I. (n.d.). *What is a Sustainability Mindset?* Retrieved from isabelrimanoczy.net: https://www.isabelrimanoczy.net/what-is-it/

Stefanie Chan, N.W. (2018). SDG 12: Responsible Consumption and Production. *Annex to the Formas report Forskning för Agenda 2030: Översikt av forskningsbehov och vägar framåt.*

Sustainable Development Goals Fund. (2017). Business and SDG 16: Contributing to Peaceful Just and Inclusive Societies.

Swartz, S.B. (2014, July). *Profits with purpose: How organizing for sustainability can benefit the bottom line.* Retrieved from mckinsey.com: https://www.mckinsey.com/~/media/McKinsey/Business%20Functions/Sustainability/Our%20Insights/Profits%20with%20purpose/Profits%20with%20Purpose.ashx

United Nations (2015). Time for Equality: The Role of Social Protection in Reducing Inequalities in Asia and the Pacific.

Yamada, S. (n.d.). *skillsfordevelopment.com.* Retrieved from Skills and Knowledge for Youth: https://skills-for-development.com/essay/fkgskm?en

Global Green Technology Initiatives: Analysis of the Current Leading Green Practices in Indonesia

Dyah Putri Puspitasari[1] and Dr. Farida Titik Kristanti[2]

ABSTRACT: The world continues to witness a growing awareness of environmental issues and a pressing need to address the challenges of sustainability. Indonesia's biodiversity hotspot and developing economic power put the nation in a position to become a focal point for green technology innovation. The unique geography and climate vulnerabilities underscore the pressing need for green solutions to address environmental degradation and climate change. In recent years, Indonesia has been taking an active part in answering the sustainability challenges by initiating green practices in various business activities. This study explores those initiatives in the dynamic landscapes of eight leading green companies as recognized by the Green Economic Forum in 2023. These companies have emerged as pioneers in developing and implementing innovative solutions to promote environmental sustainability, foster economic growth, and reshaping the country's economic landscape. The methodology employed in this research includes a comprehensive review of relevant literature and in-depth analysis of corporate reports, press releases, and published articles regarding the matter. Through this approach, we identify common themes and trends in green technology innovation across various sectors in Indonesia. This research is expected to provide valuable insights into the state of green technology innovation in Indonesia, showcasing the contributions of eight exemplary green companies as the pioneers of green practices in business and how they set a benchmark for environmentally conscious practices across industries. The findings of this study have practical implications for both policymakers and businesses seeking to accelerate the green transition in Indonesia, ultimately contributing to the broader global effort to combat climate change and promote a sustainable future.

Keywords: *Green Technology, Innovation, Sustainability, Green Business, Green Practices.*

WHAT IS "GREEN PRACTICE"?

The world is at a crossroads, facing pressing challenges related to environmental degradation, climate change, and resource depletion (Commoner, 2015; Ives, *et*

---

[1] S.T., MSM, Faculty of Economics and Business, Telkom University, Indonesia.

[2] Faculty of Economics and Business, Telkom University, Indonesia.

al., 2018; Marks, 2019; Vanapalli, *et al.*, 2021). In this era of unprecedented industrialization and technological advancement, the consequences of unsustainable practices have become increasingly evident (Thøgersen, 2014). In response to these challenges, the concept of "green practice" has emerged as a solution (Zaid, *et al.*, 2018). It is deemed as a way to navigate the path towards a more sustainable and ecologically responsible future.

Green practice embodies a set of principles and actions aimed at minimizing our ecological footprint while promoting the well-being of our planet and its inhabitants (Sánchez-Flores, *et al.*, 2020). It is a multifaceted approach that encompasses various aspects of human life, from individual choices to corporate strategies, and from community initiatives to global policy frameworks. The ultimate goal of green practice is to keep a harmonious balance between human needs and the health of the environment, conserving the planet's resources for current and future generations. One of the key pillars of green practice is sustainable consumption and responsible resource management (Murugesan, 2008; Lorek & Spaneberg, 2014). This involves making mindful choices about what we consume, how we produce goods and services, and how we manage waste. By reducing waste generation, conserving resources, and choosing eco-friendly products, individuals and organizations can significantly lessen their environmental impact.

Energy efficiency is another critical component of green practice (Mastelic, *et al.*, 2014). Our reliance on fossil fuels has led to greenhouse gas emissions and the subsequent warming of the planet (Ritchie, *et al.*, 2020). Green practices emphasize energy conservation, the use of renewable energy sources, and the adoption of energy-efficient technologies (Sánchez-Flores, *et al.*, 2020). Transitioning to sustainable energy systems not only mitigates climate change but also promotes energy security (Ang, *et al.*, 2015) and economic sustainability (Chu & Majumdar, 2012).

Agriculture and food production are examples of significant aspects of our daily lives, and they are also central to the green practice narrative (Koohafkan, *et al.*, 2012). Sustainable agriculture practices prioritize organic farming (Reganold & Watcher, 2016), reduced harsh pesticide use (Campos, *et al.*, 2019), and the conservation of biodiversity (Brooker, *et al.*, 2016). Moreover, they focus on minimizing food waste (Thyberg & Tonjes, 2016) and promoting local and seasonal food choices (Béné, 2020), reducing the carbon footprint associated with the food supply chain.

However, green practice extends beyond individual and corporate choices. Governments and policymakers play a pivotal role in driving sustainability on a broader scale (Sachs, *et al.*, 2019). The formulation and implementation of policies that promote green practices, such as carbon pricing, environmental regulations, and conservation programs, are crucial in shaping a sustainable future. International agreements, like the Paris Agreement on climate change, represent global efforts to unite nations in the pursuit of green practice at a planetary scale (Falkner, 2016).

Communities and individuals can also contribute to green practice through grassroots initiatives (Martinez-Alier, 2014). Community gardens, recycling programs, environmental education, and conservation efforts are a few programs that help empower people to take charge of their environmental footprint, fostering a sense of responsibility and belonging. Meanwhile in business and industry, green practice is not only an ethical choice but also a strategic advantage (Kuncoro & Suriani, 2018). Companies that adopt sustainable practices tend to be more resilient, attract environmentally conscious customers, and often realize cost savings through reduced resource consumption and increased efficiency. The principles of green practice can guide businesses in embracing sustainability as a core value (Papadas, *et al.*, 2019).

The urgency of embracing green practice has never been more apparent. Climate change, habitat loss, pollution, and resource depletion are global challenges that demand immediate action. Green practice provides a roadmap to address these issues, offering a holistic and interconnected approach to living sustainably and preserving our planet for future generations. It is a call to action, an invitation to reevaluate our choices, and a reminder of our shared responsibility to protect the Earth. Through conscious efforts, informed decisions, and a collective commitment to green practice, we can embark on a journey towards a more sustainable and harmonious world.

CURRENT GLOBAL STATE OF GREEN TECHNOLOGY INNOVATION

Due to the environmental challenges the world is facing, the global landscape is currently undergoing a transformative shift towards sustainable practices and the adoption of green technologies. Those technologies came about and were demanded by the need to address climate change, reduce environmental impact, and ensure a more resilient and sustainable future. In the light of the currently emerging issue of sustainability, this paper explores the state of the world in facing that global challenge. We will be discussing the current state of green technology, the real-life examples of initiatives that show key trends, and the potential developments that guide the global movement to achieve a more sustainable world.

We have been witnessing the undeniable issue of climate change that led to unprecedented awareness of environmental issues. High-profile events like the Intergovernmental Panel on Climate Change (IPCC) reports and climate strikes led by youth activists (Seyboth, 2013), exemplified by Greta Thunberg, have catalyzed a collective acknowledgment of the urgent need for action (Thunberg, 2019). The demand for transformative solutions, epitomized by the Green New Deal, underscores the imperative for governments and industries to prioritize sustainability in their policies and practices (Klein, 2020).

Economic considerations play a major role in driving the adoption of green technology, as nations and businesses increasingly recognize the value of environmentally conscious practices for long-term sustainability (Loiseau, *et al.*, 2016). Renewable energy sources, such as solar and wind, have become increasingly cost-competitive against traditional fossil fuels (Scheer, 2013). China, for instance, stands out as a leader in renewable energy adoption, investing heavily in solar and wind projects. South Korea also serves as a compelling example of a country strategically leveraging green technology for economic growth, strategically investing over $38 billion in renewable energy projects. Concurrently, European countries like Germany exemplify the economic benefits of transitioning to green technologies, with their robust renewable energy policies fostering innovation and job creation. India, in its ambitious efforts to increase renewable energy capacity, has implemented the world's largest renewable energy expansion program. By investing in solar and wind projects, India is not only reducing its carbon footprint but also addressing energy poverty and enhancing energy security for its growing population. Those commitments not only aim to curtail carbon emissions but also position the country as a frontrunner in the competitive landscape of green technology.

In the corporate setting, Apple Inc. emerges as a pioneer in integrating green practices into its operations. The tech giant has pledged to power its entire supply chain and product lifecycle with 100% renewable energy. Through investments in solar and wind projects, Apple not only mitigates its environmental impact but also sets a powerful precedent for corporate responsibility. This proactive stance not only aligns with growing consumer demands for sustainable products but also establishes a roadmap for other businesses to follow suit.

The transportation sector, a significant contributor to greenhouse gas emissions, is also undergoing a green revolution. Electric vehicles (EVs) have gained substantial popularity, supported by advancements in battery technology, government incentives, and a growing awareness of the environmental impact of traditional fossil fuel-powered vehicles (Rezvani, *et al.*, 2015). Major automotive manufacturers are investing heavily in the development of electric and hybrid vehicles, aiming to accelerate the transition towards sustainable transportation. Norway provides a compelling example, leading the world in the adoption of electric vehicles. Aggressive government incentives and a robust charging infrastructure have made Norway as the leading country in sustainable transportation. By offering tax breaks, toll exemptions, and free charging, the country has incentivized the easy adoption of EVs, demonstrating the transformative potential of green policies. In 2020, over 54% of new car sales in Norway were electric, marking a significant milestone on the path toward sustainable transportation (Klesty, 2021).

Netherlands also provides a compelling model for integrating sustainable practices into public transportation. The city of Utrecht has transformed its public transit system by introducing a fleet of electric buses charged through an innovative overhead wire system. This pioneering approach not only reduces air pollution and noise but also sets a precedent for other urban centers aiming to revolutionize their public transportation networks. China, as the largest market for electric vehicles, boasts a comprehensive approach, including aggressive government policies, subsidies, and investments in charging infrastructure. Chinese companies, such as BYD and NIO, are at the forefront of electric vehicle production, contributing significantly to the global shift towards sustainable transportation.

Green technology extends beyond energy and transportation to address the challenges of waste management and the transition to a circular economy (Pires & Martinho, 2019). Innovations in recycling, waste-to-energy technologies, and sustainable packaging solutions are gaining prominence. Sweden serves as a model for effective waste management through its waste-to-energy programs. By incinerating waste to generate heat and electricity, Sweden not only minimizes landfill use but also produces energy for its citizens. This exemplifies a holistic approach to waste management that combines environmental sustainability with energy production.

The rapid pace of urbanization presents both challenges and opportunities for sustainability. Smart city initiatives leverage green technology to enhance urban living by integrating innovative solutions for energy management, transportation, waste reduction, and efficient infrastructure (Viitanen & Kingston, 2014). Sustainable urban planning focuses on creating resilient, energy-efficient cities that prioritize environmental conservation while accommodating population growth. Singapore, renowned for its commitment to becoming a smart city, integrates green technology into urban planning.

Singapore also faces the issue of water scarcity and environmental conservation, which could also be critical global concerns. Singapore, a city-state with limited freshwater resources, has embraced environmental conservation through innovative water reclamation and purification technologies. The NEWater initiative, which purifies wastewater to meet drinking water standards, has significantly reduced Singapore's dependence on external water sources (Lee & Tan, 2016). This groundbreaking approach illustrates the potential of sustainable water management strategies in urban environments, where population density and limited resources pose unique challenges.

While the movement towards a green technology-driven future is promising, challenges are still inevitable (Surendra, *et al.*, 2014). Economic barriers, especially the initial costs of adopting green technologies, remain a challenge for some nations and businesses (Krass, *et al.*, 2013). Technological gaps and policy inconsistencies also underscore the need for concerted efforts to overcome these challenges (Song, *et al.*, 2019). It takes a collective and collaborative approach to be able to mitigate these challenges and successfully bring forth the green technology innovations to ensure a sustainable future (Fuso Nerini, *et al.*, 2019).

The landscape of green technology is dynamic, with continuous innovations shaping its trajectory. The current global state of green technology reflects a paradigm shift towards sustainability, driven by a confluence of environmental awareness, economic imperatives, and technological innovation. The real-world examples discussed above underscore that integrating green practices is not just an environmentally responsible choice; it is a strategic and economically advantageous imperative that can shape the future of industries and nations alike.

INDONESIAN LEADING GREEN COMPANIES

The current landscape of sustainable business in Indonesia reflects a dynamic shift towards environmental and social responsibility. The nation is witnessing a growing awareness among businesses of the need to balance economic growth with sustainable practices. Key sectors, including energy, mining, finance, and agriculture, are actively engaging in initiatives to mitigate environmental impact and foster community development. In this section we will be discussing eight leading green companies in Indonesia and their programs aimed at sustainable development.

The company ranked highest for their sustainability program comes from the energy sector, PT Perusahaan Listrik Negara (PT PLN). As an Indonesian state-owned electricity company, PT PLN plays a crucial role in the country's power generation and distribution (Budiarti, 2023). It has been actively involved in diversifying its energy mix by incorporating renewable sources, as announced in their press release (PT PLN, 2023). PLN has initiated projects to increase the share of renewable energy in its power generation portfolio, with a focus on solar, wind, and hydropower. These initiatives contribute to diversifying Indonesia's energy mix and reducing dependence on fossil fuels. PLN's sustainability programs align with Indonesia's broader commitment to reduce carbon emissions and transition towards sustainable energy sources. The company has also implemented energy efficiency measures in its operations and grid management, aiming to optimize energy use and reduce environmental impact. Ultimately, PLN engages in community outreach programs, focusing on educating the public about energy conservation and sustainable practices.

From the mining sector, PT Bayan Resources is a prominent player primarily involved in coal mining operations with quite a high regard in their sustainable practices (PT Bayan Resources, 2023). While the coal industry faces environmental scrutiny due to carbon emissions, Bayan Resources are increasingly adopting sustainable mining practices. This includes responsible land reclamation, community engagement programs, and efforts to minimize the environmental impact of mining activities. The company invests in advanced technologies to minimize environmental impact during coal extraction and processing. Bayan Resources places a strong emphasis on land reclamation efforts post-mining activities, demonstrating a commitment to environmental restoration. They also initiate community development programs that aim to improve the well-being of local communities, showcasing a commitment to social sustainability (Syahputra, 2023).

Similarly, PT Pertamina which comes from oil and gas sector also has their own sustainability programs considered as one of the best in Indonesia. Pertamina is also a state-owned company, and they have been actively exploring sustainable practices within the context of energy transition (PT Pertamina, 2023). Pertamina has ventured into bioenergy projects, such as biofuel production, to diversify its energy sources. The company is also exploring partnerships and investments in renewable energy projects, signaling a strategic shift towards a more sustainable energy future. The company is also exploring partnerships for renewable energy projects, demonstrating a commitment to transitioning away from traditional fossil fuels. Pertamina also focuses on research and development to enhance energy efficiency across its operations.

Comes from similar sector as companies discussed above, PT Adaro Energi Indonesia also ranks quite high based on their sustainability programs (PT Adaro Energi Indonesia, 2023). Adaro Energi Indonesia is a subsidiary of Adaro Energy, focusing on coal mining and power generation. Like other companies in the coal industry, Adaro faces challenges related to environmental impact. However, the company has expressed commitment to sustainable practices, including efforts to improve energy efficiency, reduce emissions, and contribute to community development in regions where it operates. Adaro Energi Indonesia invests in technology to improve the efficiency of its mining operations, reducing the environmental impact of coal extraction and processing. Adaro Energi Indonesia is committed to minimizing its environmental impact through responsible mining practices and adherence to sustainability principles. Adaro Energi Indonesia has undertaken community development initiatives in areas where it operates. These programs focus on education, healthcare, and infrastructure development, contributing to sustainable social development. The company also invests in technology to improve the efficiency of its mining operations, reducing the environmental impact.

Now moving away from the energy-related sectors, finance companies also play a big part in Indonesian movement towards green business practices. PT Bank Mandiri is one of Indonesia's largest banks, providing a wide range of financial services. In recent years, Mandiri has demonstrated a commitment to sustainability. The bank has implemented environmentally responsible practices in its operations, including initiatives to reduce its carbon footprint and enhance energy efficiency by incorporating energy-efficient technologies into its facilities (PT Bank Mandiri, 2023). Mandiri is also involved in supporting green financing, directing funds towards environmentally sustainable projects. The bank has initiated partnerships with businesses involved in renewable energy, energy efficiency, and eco-friendly practices. Mandiri's commitment to green financing aligns with global efforts to direct capital towards sustainable and environmentally responsible projects.

Still from the finance sector, PT Bank DBS Indonesia is also a prime example of a company that has implemented green practices as a part of their daily operations

(PT Bank DBS Indonesia, 2023). Bank DBS Indonesia is a subsidiary of DBS Bank based in Singapore, a multinational banking and financial services corporation which has also embraced sustainable finance. Like Bank Mandiri, DBS is also involved in green financing, supporting projects that contribute to environmental sustainability, one of them being the net zero transition in China. DBS Indonesia has incorporated environmental, social, and governance (ESG) criteria into its lending practices, aligning with global trends in responsible banking. The bank actively assesses the sustainability performance of its clients and incorporates ESG considerations into investment decisions. DBS Indonesia's commitment to responsible banking is reflected in its efforts to contribute to a more sustainable and socially responsible financial sector.

The final example from the banking industry, PT Bank Central Asia Tbk as one of the largest private banks in Indonesia has shown a growing awareness of environmental and social responsibility (PT Bank Central Asia, 2023). While specific sustainability initiatives may vary, the financial sector's overall commitment to green finance, ethical banking practices, and ESG considerations is becoming more prevalent. BCA has introduced environmentally responsible banking practices, including initiatives to reduce its carbon footprint. The bank is committed to sustainable business operations and has adopted energy-efficient technologies in its facilities.

Lastly, from agribusiness sector, PT Perkebunan Nusantara III's green practices serve as a great example of Indonesian movement toward more sustainable business (PT Perkebunan Nusantara III, 2023). PT Perkebunan Nusantara III is a state-owned agribusiness company engaged in the cultivation of crops, particularly in the palm oil sector. The palm oil industry faces sustainability challenges, such as deforestation and environmental impact. Companies in this sector, including PT Perkebunan Nusantara III, are under increasing pressure to adopt sustainable practices. Many are participating in certification programs and adopting responsible cultivation practices to address environmental concerns. The company adheres to responsible cultivation practices, including efforts to prevent deforestation and protect biodiversity. Community engagement programs by PT Perkebunan Nusantara III focus on enhancing the livelihoods of local communities in a sustainable manner.

MOVING FORWARD: WHAT HAPPENS AFTER THIS?

Indonesia, with its rich biodiversity and dynamic economic landscape, is at the crossroads of a sustainability revolution. As companies across various sectors embark on the journey towards environmental and social responsibility, the nation is poised to shape a more sustainable future. Examining the practices of key players like PT PLN, PT Bayan Resources, PT Pertamina, PT Adaro Energi Indonesia, PT Bank Mandiri, PT Bank DBS Indonesia, PT Bank Central Asia Tbk, and PT Perkebunan Nusantara III provides insights into the present and signals the path ahead.

The incorporation of renewable energy sources, responsible mining practices, sustainable finance, and community development programs showcase a burgeoning commitment to sustainability. Companies are increasingly recognizing that economic success and environmental stewardship can go hand in hand. This paradigm shift is crucial not only for the nation's environmental health, but also for its standing in the global sustainability arena.

While progress is evident, challenges remain. Economic constraints, regulatory uncertainties, and the need for widespread behavioral shifts pose hurdles. These are the steps that need to be taken to help ensure success in addressing those challenges and unlock the full potential of sustainability.

1. **Government Support:** Clear and consistent government policies, along with financial incentives, are paramount to encourage businesses to adopt sustainable practices.
2. **Investment in Innovation:** Research and development initiatives focused on sustainable technologies can drive innovation across industries, making green practices more accessible and affordable.
3. **Education and Awareness:** Promoting environmental literacy among businesses and the general population is crucial. Awareness campaigns can foster a culture of sustainability, encouraging responsible consumer behavior and corporate practices.
4. **Collaboration:** Cross-sector collaboration, involving government bodies, businesses, and civil society, is essential. Shared resources and knowledge can amplify the impact of sustainability initiatives.

As Indonesia navigates the future of its sustainability program, the blueprint lies in a collective commitment to balance economic growth with environmental responsibility. The strides made by key companies indicate a willingness to embrace change and contribute to a more sustainable and resilient nation. With strategic planning, collaboration, and a focus on innovation, Indonesia has the potential to lead the way in sustainable development, setting an inspiring example for the region and the world. The future is green, and Indonesia is poised to shape it.

CONCLUSION

The kaleidoscope of sustainable initiatives undertaken by key Indonesian companies paints a promising picture for the nation's future. From renewable energy to responsible mining, green finance, and community-centric sustainability, these endeavors signal a transformative shift towards a more conscientious and sustainable business landscape. Indonesia is recognizing the collaborative effort required to surmount the challenges that lie ahead as a part of this environmental evolution. Government support, continued investment in innovation, education, and cross-sector collaboration are pivotal elements in shaping a future where economic growth and environmental responsibility walk hand in hand.

The journey towards sustainability is not just an environmental burden but a collective responsibility to safeguard the nation's natural heritage and elevate the well-being of the communities. In these sustainable endeavors, Indonesia is not merely adapting to change but creating a harmonious future—one where progress is measured not only in economic gains but in the thriving ecosystems, resilient communities, and a legacy of responsible stewardship for generations to come. The journey has just begun, and Indonesia stands poised to lead the way into a truly sustainable tomorrow.

END NOTE

This article has not been published or submitted for publication elsewhere. The insights provided herein are original and intended for the purpose of informing and contributing to discussions on sustainability within the context of Indonesian businesses.

REFERENCES

Ang, B.W., Choong, W.L. and Ng, T.S. (2015). Energy security: Definitions, dimensions and indexes. *Renewable and sustainable energy reviews, 42*, 1077–1093.

Béné, C. (2020). Resilience of local food systems and links to food security–A review of some important concepts in the context of COVID-19 and other shocks. *Food security, 12*(4), 805–822.

Brooker, R.W., Karley, A.J., Newton, A.C., Pakeman, R.J. and Schöb, C. (2016). Facilitation and sustainable agriculture: a mechanistic approach to reconciling crop production and conservation. *Functional ecology, 30*(1), 98–107.

Budiarti, I. (2023, August 24). *PLN and just transition.* Advancing Trade Union rights in Indonesia. https://psisaskenergyprojectindonesia.org/2023/08/24/pln-and-just-transition/

Campos, E.V., Proença, P.L., Oliveira, J.L., Bakshi, M., Abhilash, P.C. and Fraceto, L.F. (2019). Use of botanical insecticides for sustainable agriculture: Future perspectives. *Ecological indicators, 105*, 483–495.

Chu, S. and Majumdar, A. (2012). Opportunities and challenges for a sustainable energy future. *nature, 488*(7411), 294–303.

Commoner, B. (2015). *Poverty of power: energy and the economic crisis.* Knopf.

Falkner, R. (2016). The Paris Agreement and the new logic of international climate politics. *International Affairs, 92*(5), 1107–1125.

Fuso Nerini, F., Sovacool, B., Hughes, N., Cozzi, L., Cosgrave, E., Howells, M., ... and Milligan, B. (2019). Connecting climate action with other Sustainable Development Goals. *Nature Sustainability, 2*(8), 674–680.

Ives, C.D., Abson, D.J., Von Wehrden, H., Dorninger, C., Klaniecki, K. and Fischer, J. (2018). Reconnecting with nature for sustainability. *Sustainability science, 13*, 1389–1397.

Klein, N. (2020). *On fire: The (burning) case for a green new deal.* Simon & Schuster.

Klesty, V. (2021, January 5). *Electric cars rise to record 54% market share in Norway in 2020.* Reuters. https://www.reuters.com/article/idUSKBN29A0ZK/#:~:text=So%2Dcalled%20battery%20electric%20vehicles,Road%20Federation%20(OFV)%20said.

Koohafkan, P., Altieri, M.A. and Gimenez, E.H. (2012). Green agriculture: foundations for biodiverse, resilient and productive agricultural systems. *International Journal of Agricultural Sustainability, 10*(1), 61–75.

Krass, D., Nedorezov, T. and Ovchinnikov, A. (2013). Environmental taxes and the choice of green technology. *Production and operations management, 22*(5), 1035–1055.

Kuncoro, W. and Suriani, W.O. (2018). Achieving sustainable competitive advantage through product innovation and market driving. *Asia pacific management review, 23*(3), 186–192.

Lee, H. and Tan, T.P. (2016). Singapore's experience with reclaimed water: NEWater. *International Journal of Water Resources Development, 32*(4), 611–621.

Loiseau, E., Saikku, L., Antikainen, R., Droste, N., Hansjürgens, B., Pitkänen, K., ... and Thomsen, M. (2016). Green economy and related concepts: An overview. *Journal of cleaner production, 139*, 361–371.

Lorek, S. and Spangenberg, J.H. (2014). Sustainable consumption within a sustainable economy–beyond green growth and green economies. *Journal of cleaner production, 63*, 33–44.

Marks, R.B. (2019). *The origins of the modern world: A global and environmental narrative from the fifteenth to the twenty-first century.* Rowman & Littlefield.

Martinez-Alier, J., Anguelovski, I., Bond, P., Del Bene, D., Demaria, F., Gerber, J.F., ... and Yánez, I. (2014). Between activism and science: grassroots concepts for sustainability coined by Environmental Justice Organizations. *Journal of Political Ecology, 21*(1), 19–60.

Mastelic, T., Oleksiak, A., Claussen, H., Brandic, I., Pierson, J.M. and Vasilakos, A.V. (2014). Cloud computing: Survey on energy efficiency. *Acm computing surveys (csur), 47*(2), 1–36.

Murugesan, S. (2008). Harnessing green IT: Principles and practices. *IT professional, 10*(1), 24–33.

Papadas, K.K., Avlonitis, G.J., Carrigan, M. and Piha, L. (2019). The interplay of strategic and internal green marketing orientation on competitive advantage. *Journal of Business Research, 104*, 632–643.

Pires, A. and Martinho, G. (2019). Waste hierarchy index for circular economy in waste management. *Waste Management, 95*, 298–305.

PT Adaro Energi Indonesia (2023, April 19). Adaro Energy Indonesia 2022 Sustainability Report. *Adaro.* Retrieved January 4, 2024, from https://www.adaro.com/pages/read/9/51/Sustainability%20Reports.

PT Bank Central Asia (2023, February). Laporan Keberlanjutan 2022: Live to Impact. *BCA.* Retrieved January 4, 2024, from https://www.bca.co.id/id/tentang-bca/Hubungan-Investor/laporan-presentasi/Laporan-Keberlanjutan.

PT Bank DBS Indonesia (2023, March 8). Sparking Change: A Different Kind of Bank. *Sustainability Report.* Retrieved January 4, 2024, from https://www.dbs.com/sustainability/reports-and-disclosures/sustainability-report.

PT Bank Mandiri (2023, February 10). Sustainability Report 2022: Transformasi Digital. *Mandiri*. Retrieved January 4, 2024, from https://bankmandiri.co.id/esg-report.

PT Bayan Resources, Tbk. (2023, April 3). Sustainability Report 2022. *PT Bayan Resources, Tbk*. Retrieved January 4, 2024, from https://www.bayan.com.sg/cfind/source/files/sr-2022-byan-final.pdf.

PT Perkebunan Nusantara III (2023, May 2). 2022 Sustainability Report: Creating Value for Sustainability. *Perkebunan Nusantara*. Retrieved January 4, 2024, from https://holding-perkebunan.com/sustainability/laporan-keberlanjutan/.

PT Pertamina (2023a, June 12). Sustainability Report. *Pertamina*. Retrieved January 4, 2024, from https://www.pertamina.com/en/dokumen/laporan-keberlanjutan.

PT PLN (2023, May 23). Buktikan Komitmen Bangun Energi Hijau, PLN Raih Predikat Green Ratings di Sektor Energi dan Pertambangan Pada Green Economic Forum 2023. *PLN*. Retrieved January 4, 2024, from https://web.pln.co.id/media/siaran-pers/2023/05/buktikan-komitmen-bangun-energi-hijau-pln-raih-predikat-green-ratings-di-sektor-energi-dan-pertambangan-pada-green-economic-forum-2023.

Rezvani, Z., Jansson, J. and Bodin, J. (2015). Advances in consumer electric vehicle adoption research: A review and research agenda. *Transportation research part D: transport and environment, 34*, 122–136.

Ritchie, H., Roser, M. and Rosado, P. (2020). CO_2 and greenhouse gas emissions. *Our world in data.*

Sachs, J., Schmidt-Traub, G., Mazzucato, M., Messner, D., Nakicenovic, N. and Rockström, J. (2019). Six transformations to achieve the sustainable development goals. *Nature sustainability, 2*(9), 805–814.

Sánchez-Flores, R., Cruz-Sotelo, S. and Ojeda-Benitez, S. (2020). Green practices in supply chain management to improve sustainable performance. In *Global Perspectives on Green Business Administration and Sustainable Supply Chain Management* (pp. 45–71). IGI Global.

Scheer, H. (2013). *The solar economy: Renewable energy for a sustainable global future.* Routledge.

Song, M., Fisher, R. and Kwoh, Y. (2019). Technological challenges of green innovation and sustainable resource management with large scale data. *Technological Forecasting and Social Change, 144*, 361–368.

Surendra, K., Takara, D., Hashimoto, A. and Khanal, S. (2014). Biogas as a sustainable energy source for developing countries: Opportunities and challenges. *Renewable and Sustainable Energy Reviews, 31*, 846–859.

Syahputra, E. (2023, August 4). *Komit Terapkan Prinsip ESG, Bayan Konsisten Bantu masyarakat.* CNBC Indonesia. https://www.cnbcindonesia.com/news/20230804144932-4-460292/komit-terapkan-prinsip-esg-bayan-konsisten-bantu-masyarakat

Thøgersen, J. (2014). Unsustainable consumption. *European Psychologist.*

Thunberg, G. (2019). *No one is too small to make a difference*. Penguin.

Thyberg, K. and Tonjes, D. (2016). Drivers of food waste and their implications for sustainable policy development. *Resources, Conservation and Recycling, 106*, 110–123.

Vanapalli, K., Sharma, H., Ranjan, V., Samal, B., Bhattacharya, J., Dubey, B. and Goel, S. (2021). Challenges and strategies for effective plastic waste management during and post COVID-19 pandemic. *Science of The Total Environment, 750*, 141514.

Viitanen, J. and Kingston, R. (2014). Smart cities and green growth: outsourcing democratic and environmental resilience to the global technology sector. *Environment and Planning A, 46*(4), 803–819.

Zaid, A., Jaaron, A. and Bon, A. (2018). The impact of green human resource management and green supply chain management practices on sustainable performance: An empirical study. *Journal of cleaner production, 204*, 965–979.

Instigating the Discourse of "Green Practices": A Persuasive Strategy to Attract Customers

Dr. Swati Singh[1]

ABSTRACT: Sustainable and green technology is paying attention to academics in the existing scenario. Studies in this area are increasing considerably in the last decades globally. Aptness of environmental initiation, the conversion of sustainable technologies and progressive environmental activities are the leading goals in business. Organizations put emphasis on the implementation of green practice as well as create awareness for the same. This study explores the use of discourse "Green Practices" by the companies as a marketing and persuasive strategy. Companies of Automobiles are specifically employing the term "Green Technology" to attract the customers. The study critically analyses the captions of cars that stresses on the features of sustainable and green technology. In order to analyse the web-content Approach-Avoidance model is used. The study will be beneficial in the field of marketing and advertising.

Keywords: Persuasive Discourse, Green Technology, Green Practice, Approach-Avoidance Model.

INTRODUCTION

Marketing discourse is essentially a communication enterprise that involves systematic and structured message coded in persuasive language. It is a specific kind of communication through well-defined medium that involves sharing of information with masses in order to persuade the target audience for purchasing particular products or services. In the current scenario of consumerism, consumption has representational and societal value added to it more than the actual need. Taking this stance, it can be easily understood why and how language of advertising is strategic, focused and structured communication. According to Kettemann, "Consumption, i.e. the purchase, possession and use of goods and services ... become the major signifier in today's society" (2013).

Marketing discourse is linked to the organizational discourse in the sense that various kinds of promotional content on the web is designed by organizations. It is, therefore, necessary to have a basic understanding of organizational discourse how the

[1] Assistant Professor, Department of English, Xavier Institute of Tribal Education (XITE), Gamharia, Jamshedpur, India.

way it interacts with the social realities and social structures. Text and communication strategies play a significant role in creating discourse of marketing.

This study enquirers how the select companies persuade their prospective customers through the web-content discourse and how uses of "Green practices" are employed to make the web-content persuasive. The study presents a comprehensive understanding of the techniques of persuasion used in the web-content of the select companies to advertise their products and promote their sales.

METHODOLOGY

The data is studied using Kurt Lewin's Approach-Avoidance Model. The Approach-Avoidance model works on the attitude and judgment of people by employing two different strategies for opinion modification. The two strategies are the alpha strategy and the omega strategy. While alpha strategy is widely acknowledged in the available research on persuasion, omega strategy is somewhat less talked about.

Kurt Lewin's Approach Avoidance Model proposes that the attempt of persuasion results in two types effects on the listener/audience—approach and avoidance. Lewin explained it effortlessly through a story of a child on a beach. A child's toy floated on the waves of an ocean and the child headed for the ocean to get the toy back. But once she got closer to the sea, the splattering high waves made her frightened. She stepped back and started thinking that if she went further, she could drown. She would not resist the temptation of getting the toy; at the same time, she was scared of the high waves. She was caught at that moment between approach and avoidance (Knowles and Linn, 2004). These two forces, namely approach force and avoidance force, simultaneously work on the listener's mind. A persuader's success will depend upon whether approach force is stronger than the avoidance force. Knowles and Linn proposed some alpha and omega strategies based on the past research on influence. They focused on the work of widely known social psychologists that extensively worked in the area of influence and persuasion, such as Cialdini, O'Keefe, Perloff, Pratkanis and Aronson, Wilson, etc.

ANALYSIS OF THE CAPTIONS OF SELECT COMPANIES

This study presents a systematic analysis of the web-content of products that includes cars of three brands namely, Maruti Suzuki, Hyundai and Toyota. Only the section "About the company" has been analyzed with the help of Lewin's Approach-Avoidance Model. An effort has been made to study how the strategies proposed in this model have been used in the web-content discourse of the companies and for what effect. The objective of this study is to examine the persuasive techniques that have been discursively crafted, interpreted and concluded on the grounds of the Sustainable and Green practices.

Table 1

Maruti Suzuki India	*Hyundai Motor India*	*Toyota Kirloskar Motor*
• *"Our Values: Customer obsession":* "Openness & Learning; Networking & Partnership; Fast, Flexible and First mover; Innovation & Creativity." • *"Technology":* "To improve driving experience and ensure a better future for the coming generations, Maruti Suzuki believes in green technology." • *"Experience":* "To make every journey an experience and every experience a memory, Maruti Suzuki puts people at the centre of everything it does." • *"Design":* "To give more than just a good-looking car, Maruti Suzuki ensures that every design element serves a purpose. More than design, it's design in technology."	• *"Our vision: Progress for Humanity":* "We are here to do the right thing for the humanity; Humanity unites us and makes us stronger; allowing us to strengthen our relationship feel connected and get more from life." • *"Connected mobility: Blue Link."* "The vision aims to provide a curated future lifestyle to customers in a society where all aspects of life are connected to mobility for a true Car-to-Life experience." "Hyundai is far outpacing the competition in the development of connected car technologies for the hyper-connected society of the future." "Our goal is to provide the widest possible variety of smart cars that can connect people seamlessly with their homes and offices, as well as with urban infrastructures." • *"Clean mobility: Driving with clean eco-friendly cars."* "We are leading the change for a cleaner tomorrow- one in which our planet and future generations can breathe more freely, vehicles use smarter, more sustainable technology, and mobility happens without emissions."	• *"Quality you can trust":* "At Toyota, we uphold the philosophy of continuous improvement (Kaizen) because we believe in always scope to do better." "It is this very philosophy that drives us towards quality, making it a way of life at Toyota." • *"Vision":* "Toyota India will continue to enrich the quality of life in India and help solve the societal problems by establishing high standards of safety, technology, quality & Corporate Social Responsibility." "With a spirit to constantly Learn, Teach, Improve and Innovate, all our stake holders and families will collaborate to help make India a better place." "We will strive for excellence in sustainability ensuring we are eco-friendly in our products, services and customers experiences."

Maruti Suzuki, as a part of alpha strategy, makes the message more persuasive by using strong arguments in the web-content. Their values are presented in the website with four clear points that grab the attention of the prospective customers and apparently influence them to explore the information further. The four points includes Value, Experience, Technology and Design as strong arguments increase the approach force in the prospective customers. The company addresses the resistance indirectly as a part of omega strategy. According to Pratkanis, "An influencer can disable a target's resistance by casting the resistor in the role of expert" (qtd. in Knowles and Linn 128). The company through the web-content establishes its image as an expert. The value focuses on the expertise of the company and the second line indicates the brand's efficiency. The second point of the content is presented to make maximum impact on the viewers. This part describes the company as influential, progressive and expert in their areas by using the head word Technology. So, this omega strategy certainly minimizes the inhibitions in customers regarding products and brands.

As a part of the alpha strategy of "increase source credibility" the company uses some techniques to make the brand look more attractive and trustworthy. The instance of this alpha strategy can be seen in the 'Technology', 'Innovation', and 'Design'. The company uses the sentences under this section to establish the brand as reliable and upright. Whereas the third part emphasizes the new-age technology, the later part describes the company's determination and commitment to give grand services to the customers and make their lives easier. These things encourage the customers towards the brand hence increases the approach forces in them. The company aims to protect the environment and future generations by using the green technology in their cars. The company claims to give priority to provide better driving experiences with sustainable technology. It shows its involvement by showing concern for the customers and the environment.

In advertising and marketing, companies present their enterprise by showing the "that's not all" technique. This strategy stresses the method through which companies show their products and offers by indicating something surprising for the customers. In doing so, companies offer great deals to the customers and present the bigger in the end. We can see this strategy in the web-content of Hyundai Motor India. Hyundai describes its enterprise by talking about the company's ventures, innovative products, details and services to the customers. Company shares incredible and futuristic things with the customers and declares that it is available in the present time, not tomorrow. This information affects the customers positively and increases the approach forces in them. The first message the company conveys to the audience is the bigger vision of progress for humanity. The company distinguishes itself from others by using this message in the web-content. The second message can be observed as a company's efficiency and capabilities by mentioning "future of mobility".

Company gives assurance to the audience that Hyundai is the brand that not only produces technologically efficient products but also offers other services. And the third message is used under the heading "Smart mobility solution provider". This third segment explains about the services that have been brought for the customer.

The company in order to persuade the customers employs alpha strategies in the web-content. The web-content is built to show the benefits to the customers claimed by the company. The alpha strategy of "Add Incentives" is used to increase the approach forces in customers. The section is structured skillfully to influence the wider audience. Hyundai systematically presents its venture as a part of omega strategy that reduces the resistance in customers. The products are made to look capable and efficient that decreases the resistance in customers and inspires them to choose the brand.

The Toyota company represents itself as a team that strives to contribute to better India, society and environment. For example, the company expresses its involvement by sharing its work philosophy with the customers. The company through its vision shares its spirit of collaboration with its stakeholders in making India a better place. In the sentence "we will strive for excellence in sustainability ensuring we are eco-friendly in our products, services and customer experiences" uses the pronoun 'we' to show team Toyota that includes employees, customers, investors, community and environment. Toyota CSR activity engages with multiple stakeholders of different significance and requirements. The company adopts the most comprehensive strategy to use corporate social responsibility to fulfill the interests of stakeholders. As linguistic markers of repetition, some words have been used by the company to show involvement such as quality, continuous improvement, CSR and so on. These words are repeatedly used in all the parts of the content to highlight the issue of quality, safety and sustainability.

CONCLUSION

The data were analyzed in terms of the Approach-Avoidance Model, it was found that the companies under this study used the alpha and the omega strategies to persuade the audience. Under the alpha strategy, the positives of the company and the products are highlighted, whereas the omega strategy is used to alleviate customers' fears and doubts about the product by giving a logical explanation, assurance of service, warranty etc. The web-content is presented by the companies so that it will have a positive impact on the customers. The most widely used alpha strategies are 'Add incentives', "Make message more persuasive", "Increase source credibility", "Provide consensus information", "Engage a norm of reciprocity", etc. The intention of the "About the company" section is to make users aware of the company's mission, values and determination. We have seen how the products have been depicted on the website and what persuasive strategies have been applied to influence the customers psychologically. This section stimulates the customers and molds their minds to buy the product.

So far, we have seen, companies of automobile extensively use "Green practices" and Sustainable technology in their web-content. The company builds a discourse that shows progressiveness so that customers can rely on the company's intent. As we know in today's scenario higher contributors of air pollution are motor vehicles. Companies shares the essential arguments that claim the products to be sustainable and environment friendly. This gives rational cause to the audience to believe in company's argument. Customers may feel motivated towards the brand as it claims to be sustainable and hence increases the approach forces in them. Similarly, companies highlight the global threats of emission, pollution and climate change as a part of omega strategy. Here companies address the resistance directly and provide solutions by showing the key features about the brand and products. This technique ultimately decreases the apprehensions of the customers and make them to take a favorable decision. The companies of cars use a variety of linguistic devices to show involvement in order to convey their point of view towards the customers. They show love, care and concern towards their employees, customers, and environment.

REFERENCES

Hyundai Motor India about Us. *Hyundai Motor India*, www.hyundai.com/in/en/hyundai-story/Accessed 12 Jan. 2021.

Knowles, S. Eric, and Jay. A. Linn. (2004). *Resistance and Persuasion.* Lawrence Erlbaum Associates.

Kettemann, Bernhard (2013). Semiotics of Advertising and the Discourse of Consumption. *AAA: Arbeiten Aus Anglistik Und Amerikanistik*, 38(1), 53–67. JSTOR, http://www.jstor.org/stable/43025841 Accessed 22 Oct. 2022.

Maruti Suzuki India Price, Features & Specification. *Maruti Suzuki India,* www.marutisuzuki.com Accessed 23 May. 2020.

Maruti Suzuki WagonR was the Top Performer in April 2021. *Cars 24.* www.cars24.com/blog/marutisuzuki. Accessed 17 Apr 2022.

McGuire, W.J. (1964). Inducing Resistance to Persuasion: Some Contemporary Approaches. *Advances in Experimental Social Psychology*, edited by L. Berkowitz, 1, 191-229.

Toyota about the Company, Products. *Toyota Kirloskar India*, www.toyotabharat.com/ Accessed 2 Apr 2020.

Transition between Shopper Types: A Study of Food Buying by Indian Professionals

Dr. Venugopal Pingali[1], Dr. Narasimham Rajkumar and Dr. Raghuram Tata

ABSTRACT: Indian food industry which is in a nascent stage is seeing both demand and supply side changes. On the demand side rising incomes and changing lifestyle are making consumers look for branded/packed food products perceived to be of better quality or organic foods which are perceived to be healthier. This coupled with the supply side changes, such as new retail formats, availability and cost are leading to the formation of different shopper types. The objective of the study is to understand the shopper types and identify the variables to upgrade the shopper type for food buying amongst Indian professionals. 1220 professional across India were interviewed to find out their attitudes and behavior for food purchases. The data was analyzed using hierarchical cluster analysis. Four shopper types and the linking variables to transit between them are identified. Implications for food retailing have been drawn.

Keywords: Food Buying, India, Hierarchical Clustering.

INTRODUCTION

The food market in India which is estimated to grow to $258 billion by 2015 (up from $181 billion in 2013) is getting increasingly complex both due to the supply side and demand side factors (Kathuria and Gill, 2013). On the demand side the changing lifestyles, increased disposable incomes and changing consumer tastes are modifying the food purchase behavior in India. On the supply side the Indian food industry is seeing a transition with the entry of organized sector into food retailing bringing along with-it branded food products, imported products and organic foods.

While the developed countries would have seen these changes over a longer period of time and in a phased manner, in India these changes are happening at one time. It is therefore important for the marketers to understand how all these changes would impact the food buying.

The objective of the paper is therefore to understand a) the shopper types for food buying in India and b) the linking variables for transition from one shopper

[1] XLRI, Jamshedpur.

type to another. The paper restricts itself to understanding the behavior of the professionals in India.

INDIAN FOOD INDUSTRY: DEMAND SIDE FACTORS

Indian Professionals

Opening up of the Indian economy and the increased job opportunities in the service industry has resulted in an increase per capita disposable income of the professionals in India (Ali *et al.*, 2010). In addition, the growth in the service sector has increased their interaction with their foreign counterparts leading to changing lifestyle and increasing health awareness (Gupta, 2009). Today they are willing to pay price premiums for quality products (Kathuria and Gill, 2013).

Food Buying

The middle class in urban India (mainly comprising of professionals) accounts for more than three-quarters of urban spending on food and this is expected to double by 2025 (McKinsey 2008).

Historically, Indian consumers preferred fresh food (Ling *et al.*, 2004). However now in addition to freshness, the consumers are becoming more discriminating in their food product choices and have started emphasizing more on convenience and quality of the products (Acebron *et al.*, 2000). Consumers have also started becoming more conscious in terms of nutritional diet, health and food safety issues (Rimal *et al.* 2001). This segment is expected to increase its spending on "higher-value" items in terms of variety and quality (Kathuria and Gill 2013). Ali *et al.*, (2010) also states that the middle-income group would spend a greater part of their income on upgrading and diversifying their diet (Ali *et al.*, 2010).

Indian Food Industry: Supply Side Factors

The supply side is mainly driven by three factors; viz., the change in the retail format, availability of branded food and the availability of organic food.

Change in Retail Format

Prior to the 1990s, India was a closed economy. The retail sector mainly consisted of small, privately owned single stores known as kirana stores (Saraogi, 2006). These kirana stores largely sold non-branded products (Mukerjee *et al.*, 2012). Around 2001, organized retailing started in the food industry in India. Though the penetration of the organized food retailing in India is only around one percent (Images F&R Research, 2007) it is playing an important role in influencing the purchase behavior.

Availability of Branded Food

Indian food industry is still at a nascent stage of development and only a third of the food processing and packaging industry is organized, and less than 10 per cent of the food market is branded (Kathuria and Gill 2013). Though the emergence of the supermarket and hypermarket brought in the packaged food products into the market (Wells *et al.*, 2007), today branded products are sold through both traditional and modern retail outlets (Mukerjee *et al.*, 2012).

Availability of Organic Food

India is one of the countries with the largest area under organic management (Chakraborti 2010). The size of organic agricultural land has reached 1.03 million hectares in India (Menon, 2009) producing 5,85,000 MT of certified organic products. However, since most of the organic produce is exported, organic food market in India is still at a nascent stage (Chakraborti, 2010). ACNielsen study states that the lack of availability of organic food products (ACNielsen, 2006) has been a concern for its adoption in India.

Food Purchasing Behavior

The interaction of the supply side and demand side factors is changing the food purchasing behavior. Researchers have tried to understand the changing perceptions and purchasing patterns of the Indian consumers.

While Kathuria and Gill (2013) found packaged food to be perceived to be hygienic and high quality and that the respondents are willing to purchase branded products despite being priced somewhat higher, Mukerjee *et al.* (2012) on the other hand found respondents perceive branded products as more expensive than non-branded products and that foreign brands are more expensive than Indian brands and these brands cater primarily to higher-income groups. Another study done across eight-cities in India as early as in 2006 indicated a potential demand to the tune of INR 5.6 billion for organic products in India (Mukerjee, 2008).

All these changes suggest that there is a transition happening in the food purchasing behavior and consumers are shifting from one shopper type to another.

METHODOLOGY

A total of 1220 professionals spread across the different metros in India were interviewed by the students of a premier management school in India during their summer internship during May-June.

About seventy percent of the respondents are male and the remaining are females. While a third of the respondents were in the age of 20-30 years, around 50 percent of the respondents were in the age of 30–40 years and the balance above 40 years.

Eighty percent of the respondents were graduates and the remaining were post graduates. Sixteen percent respondents were from Marketing department, 21 percent from Finance, 27 percent from HR department, eight percent from IT. Production and General Management had 5% each, Accounts and Project Management had 3% each and the balance were from other functions.

Twenty five percent of the respondents earn upto USD 20000 per year, 46 percent earn between USD 20000–40000 per year, 19 percent earn between USD 40000–60000 per year and the balance ten percent earn above USD 60000 per year.

The respondents were administered a questionnaire to understand their attitudes and behavior towards food purchases. The information was collected on a five point Likert type scale (refer exhibit 1 for instrument). Hierarchical clustering was done to group the variables. Using the distance at which the variables are joined, the shopper types are identified. The transition from one group to another is inferred by identifying the linking variables.

RESEARCH FINDINGS AND DISCUSSION

The cluster analysis output is given in figure 1. A cut off distance of 10 on the rescaled distance (40% of the total rescaled distance of 25) on the dendrogram (refer Figure 1) is used to differentiate the shopper types and the linking variables. Variables joining before the cut off are used to define the shopper types (shown by circles in the figure) and the variables combing clusters beyond the cut off are classified as the linking variables for transiting from one shopper type to another (linking variables are shown in bold in the figure).

Shopper Types

The study identified four shopper types within the professionals in India. They are: a) cost conscious, b) quality conscious, c) status conscious and d) health conscious.

The cost-conscious group may be aware of branded foods but they consider both branded and organic food to be costlier than unbranded food. The second group is the quality conscious group. The group accepts that branded food items are better and would be willing to buy them even if they are costly. The status conscious group prefers to buy imported brands even though they are costly. The fourth group is the health-conscious group which is interested in buying organic food and they consider organic food to taste better. The group would not mind paying more even if the organic food is costlier and the group is also willing to purchase organic food from the local grocery.

Cross tabulations using demographic variables did not suggest any distinct profile for the different groups. No distinct profile for the shopper types strengthened the earlier assumption that consumers would be transiting from one shopper type to another. It is therefore important to identify the variables linking the groups.

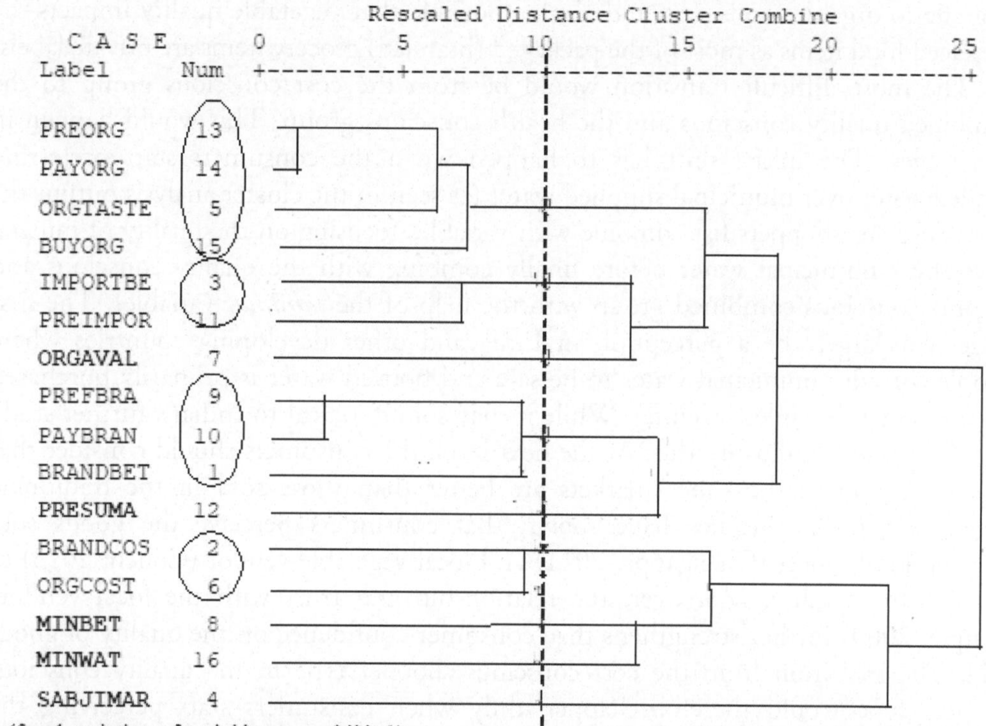

(for description of variables see exhibit 1).
The dotted line denotes the cut off for defining the shopper types. Circled variables indicate the shopper types and the variables in bold indicate the linking variables to combine to the next group.

Figure 1: Cluster Analysis Output: Dendrogram using Average Linkage (Between Groups)

Linking Variables for Transiting between Groups

The status conscious group would move to the heath conscious group only if they are convinced that the organic foods are easily available (from the cluster analysis output it can be seen that this variables joins these shopper types). This seems logical as earlier studies have shown that availability of organic food was a concern.

The transition from quality conscious to the heath and status conscious combined group would happen when the consumers prefer buying food items from super markets as against the traditional food markets (subji mandis). The cluster analysis output shows that preference for purchase of vegetables links the two groups. In India vegetables sold in the super markets are not considered as fresh as the vegetables sold in the traditional vegetable markets. Since most of the packed grocery items are private labels, the vegetable quality could be also impacting the packaged food items. This is supported by Steiner (2010) who states that quality of vegetables sold in supermarkets are not good enough. So, if the quality of vegetables sold in supermarkets is not perceived to be good, it is unlikely that the consumers would upgrade to organic foods. It could also be possible that vegetable quality impacts the packaged food items as most of the packaged (branded) grocery items are private labels.

The most difficult transition would be from the cost conscious group to the combined quality conscious and the health conscious group. This would happen in two stages. The initial shift has to happen when the consumers start preferring bottled water over municipal supplied water (as seen in the cluster analysis output the cost conscious shoppers fist combine with variables focusing on the quality of mineral water over municipal water before finally combing with the quality conscious and organic conscious combined group with the help of the *sabjimar* variable). The first stage may largely be a perception in India and other developing countries where people consider municipal water to be safe and bottled water is primarily purchased for convenience while travelling. While it may sound logical to Indians further study may be required to justify this. At the next level, the consumers should consider that vegetables sold in the super markets are better than those sold in the traditional vegetable vendors. Studies have shown that consumers perceive the goods sold through local grocer (Chengappa, 2011) and local vegetable vendor (Cohen, 2013) to be of better quality. Moreover, the relationship and trust with the local vendors (Gupta, 2009) further strengthens thae consumer confidence on the quality of goods sold. The transition from the cost conscious shopper type to the quality conscious shopper type would therefore happen only when consumers start perceiving the vegetables sold through the super markets are better than the traditional food markets and start considering municipal supplied water to be unsafe.

IMPLICATIONS FOR FOOD RETAILING

A typical transition that retailers should focus on should be "cost conscious group to be upgraded to quality conscious group and finally to the organic conscious group.

To help this transition, food retailers should first ensure that the quality of the vegetables sold is improved. Depending only on the branded and processed food categories to boost their food category sales would be uneconomical as the margins for such brands are low (in India the large companies still have the bargaining power as the brands are not dependent on the retail outlets). Wharton (2009) states that the margins for private labels are on an average 25–30% as compared to national brands where the margins are only between a range of 12–17%. At the second level, organic foods should be prominently displayed. As of now, organic foods are not prominently displayed and consumers have to search for them (Salomi, 2012). Since organic foods counters are not frequented by customers some of them are not maintained properly deteriorating the quality perception of organic foods.

Exhibit 1: Instrument for Data Collection

Rate each of the following questions on a five point Likert type scale ranging from completely agree (5) to completely disagree (1).

1. Branded food is of better quality than unbranded (brandbet).
2. Branded food is more expensive than unbranded (brandcos).
3. Imported food is better than locally grown ones. (importbe).
4. Vegetables brought in Sabji mandis are better than Supermarkets (sabjimar).
5. Food grown organically tastes better than normal food (orgtaste).
6. Organic food is more expensive than normal food. (orgcost).
7. Organic food is available in all stores (orgaval).
8. Bottled Mineral Water is of better quality than city municipal corporation water (minbet).
9. I prefer eating branded over unbranded food whenever possible (prefbra).
10. I prefer paying a higher price for branded packaged food even when cheaper unbranded ones are available (paybran).
11. I prefer buying imported food even if locally grown ones are available (preimpor).
12. I prefer buying vegetable in super markets than in the local sabji mandis (presuma).
13. I prefer organically grown food (preorg).
14. I prefer organic food even if it is more expensive (payorg).
15. I buy organic food in my nearby grocery store (buyorg).
16. I prefer having mineral water from a bottle, even if corporation water is available on tap (minwat)

(Abbreviations in parenthesis are the variable names used in the analysis).

REFERENCES

Acebrón, L.B., Levy Mangin, J-P., Calvo Dopico, D. (2000). A proposal of the buying model for fresh food products: the case of fresh mussels, *Journal of International Food & Agribusiness Marketing*, 11 (3),75–96.

ACNielsen (2006). Indians amongst the top 10 buyers of foods with "health supplements" globally but lack access to organic food products, 20 February, avaliable at: www.acnielsen.co.in/news/20060220.shtml (accessed 12 June 2014),

Ali, Jabir; Sanjeev Kapoor and Janakiraman Moorthy (2010). Buying behaviour of consumers for food products in an emerging economy. *British Food Journal*, 112 (2), 109–124

Chengappa, P.G. (2011). *Food Retail Chain and Super Market Evolution in India.* UAS, Bangalore.

Cohen, Amy J. (2013). Supermarkets in India: Struggle over the organization of Agricultural markets and food supply chain. *Univ of Miami Law Review*, 68(1), 19–68.

Gupta, Kriti Bardhan (2009). Consumer Behaviour for Food Products in India, *International Food & Agribusiness Management Association,19th Annual World Symposium,* Budapest, Hungary, June 20–21, 2009.

Images F&R Research (2007). *India Retail Report 2007,* Images F&R Research, New Delhi, pp. 21.

Kathuria, Lalit Mohan and Paramjeet Gill (2013). Purchase of branded commodity food products: empirical evidence from India. *British Food Journal,* 115(9),1255–1280.

Ling, S.-S., Pysarchik, D.T. and Choo, H.J. (2004). Adopters of new food products in India. *Marketing Intelligence & Planning,* 22 (4), 371–91.

McKinsey & Company (2008). *The Great Indian Bazaar,* McKinsey &Co, Mumbai.

Menon, M. (2009). Organic agriculture and market potential in India. in Willer, H., Kilcher, L. (Eds),*The World of Organic Agriculture – Statistics and Emerging Trends 2009,* IFOAM, Geneva.

Mukherjee, Arpita; Divya Satija, Tanu M. Goyal, Murali K. Mantrala and Shaoming Zou (2012). Are Indian consumers brand conscious? Insights for global retailers. *Asia Pacific Journal of Marketing and Logistics,* 24 (3), 482–499.

Mukherjee, S. (2008). From the ground beneath your feet. *Outlook Money,* April 23.

Rimal, A., Fletcher, S.M., McWatters, K.H., Misra, S.K. and Deodhar, S. (2001). Perception of food safety and changes in food consumption habits: a consumer analysis. *International Journal of Consumer Studies,* 25 (1), 43–52

Salomi, V. (2012). Organic food has few buyers, TOI, Sept, 12.

Saraogi, P. (2006). *Growth of retail in India with pantaloons as a case study,* Nottingham University, Nottingham

Somnath Chakrabarti (2010). Factors influencing organic food purchase in India – expert survey insights. *British Food Journal,* 112 (8), 902–915.

Steiner, Rupert (2010). Oops! Asde Chief has a 'Ratner moment' New Boss admits Supermarket food isn't up to Scratch. *Mail Online,* 19, Aug, 2010.

Wells, L.E., Farley, H. and Armstrong, G.A. (2007). The importance of packaging design for own-label food brands. *International Journal of Retail & Distribution Management,* 35 (9), 677–90.

Wharton (2009). *More Choices in Stores: India's retailers are stocking up on private labels.* K@W, Wharton.

Effect of Green Marketing on the Consumers' Purchase Behavior: A Review

Dr. Malini Majumdar[1]

ABSTRACT: Consumers' purchase behavior plays a pivotal role in shaping the sustainability of the global economy and the environment. The research aims to offer insights into the challenges and opportunities faced by businesses, policymakers, and consumers in the context of sustainable consumption.

The synthesis portion of this study aggregates existing literature on consumers' purchase behavior and green marketing, offering a holistic view of the key factors influencing consumer choices. From psychological aspects to environmental consciousness, this review seeks to identify the multifaceted determinants of green purchasing decisions. Moreover, it highlights the various methodologies employed in prior research, shedding light on the strengths and limitations of these approaches. The review component critically evaluates the effectiveness of green marketing strategies and their influence on consumers. By analyzing case studies across diverse industries, the study examines how various marketing techniques, such as eco-labeling, green product design etc. impact consumer perceptions and behaviors. It also discusses the role of trust and transparency in these strategies and their implications for consumer trust and loyalty.

The study explores the shifting landscape of consumer attitudes and the evolving nature of green marketing. It delves into the challenges faced by businesses in navigating this complex terrain, including issues related to greenwashing, information overload, and consumer skepticism. Moreover, it discusses how advancements in technology, social media, and e-commerce are reshaping the green marketing landscape.

To conclude, the agenda-setting part of this research highlights emerging trends and gaps in the literature. It suggests future research directions, emphasizing the need for a deeper understanding of the interplay between cultural, economic, and social factors in consumers' sustainable choices. It also calls for an exploration of innovative green marketing strategies in an ever-changing global marketplace.

In summary, this study provides valuable insights into consumers' purchase behavior and green marketing, offering a comprehensive overview of existing knowledge while charting a course for future research and practice.

---

[1] Professor, Army Institute of Management.

Keywords: *Green Marketing, Consumer behavior, Consumer choice, Greenwashing, Consumer Skepticism.*

INTRODUCTION

In recent decades, the intersection of consumerism and globalization has generated an unprecedented demand for industrial and consumer goods. Consequently, this surge has exerted abnormal pressure on natural resources and contributed to environmental degradation. Environmentalists have responded with persistent awareness campaigns, elevating environmental consciousness among a segment of consumers. This heightened awareness has cultivated a preference for environmentally friendly processes and products.

Consequently, manufacturers find themselves facing increasing pressure to adopt sustainable practices, designing and producing environmentally friendly and sustainable products, incorporating biodegradable packaging, and embracing other green marketing initiatives. As companies start to align with this environmental ethos, a growing number of consumers become cognizant of and attracted to green products. This shift in consumer awareness and preference ultimately leads to a shift in consumer purchasing behavior.

THEORETICAL FOUNDATIONS OF GREEN MARKETING

Green marketing is operationally defined as "the effort by a company to design, promote, price, and distribute products in a manner that promotes environmental protection" (Polonsky, 2011, p. 1311). A strategic approach is integral to contemporary business sustainability initiatives, notwithstanding the historical emphasis on revenue generation and profit maximization (Akenji, 2014; Maniatis, 2016; Yang *et al.*, 2015).

Organizations that prioritize the preservation of the natural ecological balance throughout their operations exhibit enhanced environmental responsibility while concurrently optimizing financial performance. This dual focus facilitates the reduction of environmental pollution, conservation of natural resources, and overall environmental protection. Thus, such entities gain a distinctive competitive advantage and cultivate new markets, augmenting their corporate image, reputation, and product perception from the consumer standpoint (Chen, 2008).

Consumer awareness of green marketing manifests when individuals place confidence in eco-labels and eco-brands, thereby influencing their purchasing behavior towards green products (Norazah, 2013a, 2013b; Rahbar & Abdul Wahid, 2011) as asserted by Norazah Mohd Suki, Norbayah Mohd Suki, and Nur Shahirah Azman in 2015.

Studies conducted by Dinnie *et al.* (2006), Hartmann and Iba´n˜ez (2006), as well as Norazah (2013a, 2013b), underscore the correlation between consumers' positive awareness of green marketing and the augmentation of environmental knowledge.

MILESTONES AND KEY DEVELOPMENTS IN THE FIELD

In the early stages of green marketing, the literature indicated a perceptible shift in consumer focus towards environmentally friendly products. Initial research primarily concentrated on understanding the change in consumer consumption patterns with regards to green products, resulting in extensive empirical investigations to discern consumer interest in the usage and purchase of such products. During the early 90s, the exploration of green marketing was predominantly from a corporate perspective, revealing that 92% of multinational corporations in Europe modified their products in response to the escalating concerns about environmental pollution (Vandermerwe and Oliff, 1990). Subsequent developments in green marketing research have demonstrated a heightened environmental consciousness among consumers in developed regions, such as the USA and Western Europe (Curlo, 1999). Recent research, spanning the last decade, has indicated a notable consumer awareness and willingness to pay a premium for environmentally friendly products (Lee, 2009; Rahbar and Wahid, 2011; Lee, 2008; D Souza, 2004). However, limited research has explored the impact of green marketing on consumers in emerging economies, such as India (Prakash, 2002).

The burgeoning growth of green marketing and the emergence of "green consumers" are deemed by some as "perhaps the biggest opportunity for enterprise and invention the industrial world has ever seen" (Cairncross, 1992: 177). A green consumer, as defined by Elkington in 1994, is one who consciously avoids products that may cause harm to living organisms, contribute to environmental deterioration during manufacturing or usage, consume a significant amount of non-renewable energy, or involve unethical testing on animals or human subjects.

SHIFTING CONSUMER ATTITUDES

Consumers often express genuine environmental concern, yet this sentiment may not consistently translate into observable purchasing behavior. The correlation between green attitudes, values, and behavior remains somewhat ambiguous, as noted by Essoussi and Linton (2010). Lee (2009) contends that, due to conflicting findings in the literature, additional research is essential to substantiate the connection between environmental attitudes and behaviors. There is a particular need for precise measurement of green behaviors, especially in the context of green buying aspects.

Kalafatis *et al.* (1999) also observe a scarcity of information in existing literature concerning the determinants of the intention to purchase green products. Despite extensive research by various scholars such as Chan and Lau (2000), Cleveland *et al.* (2005), Kim *et al.* (2012), Laroche *et al.* (2002), Lee (2009, 2008), and Straughan and Roberts (1999), a universally accepted and reliable scale for measuring Green Buying Behavior remains elusive. Over the past decade, evidence indicates a noteworthy shift in consumer behavior towards incorporating environmental considerations into lifestyle choices, resulting in changes in consumption habits, such as reduced consumption, resource conservation, and recycling (Barber, 2010). In response, marketing assumes a crucial role and undertakes social responsibility to redirect behavior towards more sustainable consumption practices (Suplico, 2009). The key influencers of consumers' selection of a green product are green features of the product, and environmental awareness related to the particular product (Boztepe, 2012; Thogersen *et al.*, 2012). It is imperative to acknowledge that, although environmentally conscious consumers are generally inclined to purchase sustainable products, their buying behavior is still influenced by traditional factors, including price, brand, and product availability (Jones *et al.*, 2008).

Research by Akehurst *et al.* (2012) underscores a connection between green purchase intentions and the actual purchase of green products, reaffirming the earlier findings of Chan and Yam (1995) and Schuhwerk and Lefkokk-Hagius (1995). These studies suggest that consumers who actively engaged with environmental concerns are likely to choose and purchase green products.

The decision-making process of consumers regarding green purchases is notably influenced by the quality of green products, including factors such as clear product ingredient information, eco-labeling, product appearance, and a general assurance of user friendliness (Tseng & Hung, 2013). Producers strategically position the environmental benefits of green products in consumers' minds to influence their purchasing decisions (Rex & Baumann, 2007, p. 567). Consumers tend to integrate their green knowledge and attitudes with green brand awareness when selecting environmentally friendly products (Matthes *et al.*, 2013; Zhao *et al.*, 2014).

The emergence of new environmental ethics has heightened individuals' awareness and significantly transformed their consumption behavior (Jang *et al.*, 2011). In response, companies have implemented various green initiatives, including the design of green products and services (D'anjelico and Pujari, 2010; Chan *et al.*, 2013), green supply chain management (Wang and Chan, 2013; Tseng *et al.*, 2013a), and innovation practices (Chen *et al.*, 2006; Tseng *et al.*, 2013b). Both profit-oriented and socially responsible firms have embraced the concept of green marketing as a source of competitive advantage, addressing environmental issues in the process (Tan, 2011; Roberts, 1996). These firms actively develop and promote green products to meet the demands of environmentally conscious consumers (Tan, 2011; Kassaye, 2001; Polonsky and Kilboume, 2005). The adoption of environmental or green marketing, as a strategic approach, has become a recent focus in business endeavors (Chen and Chai, 2010; Ottman, 1998). Consumers' pro-environmental concern serves as a significant determinant of their 'green buying' behavior, characterized by the purchase and consumption of products that offer environmental benefits (Mainieri *et al.*, 1997).

ROLE OF CONSUMER AWARENESS AND PERCEPTION INCLUDING FACTORS INFLUENCING CONSUMER PERCEPTION

Consumer awareness and perception play pivotal roles in shaping the dynamics of green marketing. As defined by Polonsky (2011), green marketing encompasses the effort by companies to design, promote, price, and distribute products in a manner that promotes environmental protection. Despite a growing global consciousness regarding environmental issues, consumer attitudes and behaviors remain nuanced. The literature emphasizes the significance of consumer awareness in influencing green purchasing decisions. Additionally, Lee (2009) suggests that the relationship between green attitudes and behaviors is intricate, warranting further investigation to accurately measure and understand the impact of environmental considerations on consumer choices. This interplay of awareness and perception underscores the need for businesses to strategically communicate their environmental efforts, ensuring transparency and fostering consumer trust in green marketing initiatives.

The commitment of consumers to green purchases is still in question, particularly in markets where green products are not sufficiently available (Chan, 1996), and the share of green market activities remains limited (Peattie, 2001; Kalafatis, Pollard, *et al.*, 1999; McCarty & Shrum, 1995). Arbuthnot and Lingg's (1975) studies suggest a positive relationship between environmental concern and green buying behavior. Perceived Consumer Effectiveness (PCE), defined as the belief in one's ability to make a positive impact, plays a crucial role in predicting environmentally conscious behaviors, including green purchases (Ellen *et al.*, 1991; Tan and Lau, 2011). PCE is shaped by knowledge and personal experiences, which promotes pro-environmental behavior (Straughan and Roberts, 1999). Kim and Choi (2005) confirmed PCE as a predictor of green purchase behavior, supported by findings from Tan and Lau (2011). The increase in consumer awareness is expected to elevate environmental concern, leading to greater acceptance of green products (Sharma *et al.*, 2013), aligning with previous research by Grunert and Juhl (1995), Kim and Choi (2003; 2005), and Tilikidou (2007). Notably, PCE is identified as a strong predictor and a moderator between attitude and behavior in pro-environmental contexts (Berger and Corbin, 1992). Seven factors influencing consumer purchase behavior for green products in Central India include environmental awareness and concern, quality and price, availability, PCE, information, environmental attitude, and promotional activity.

ANALYZING GREEN MARKETING COMMUNICATION CHANNELS AND SUCCESSFUL CAMPAIGNS

Analyzing green marketing communication channels and successful campaigns is essential for understanding the dynamics of promoting environmentally sustainable products. Green marketing, aimed at fostering consumer awareness and encouraging environmentally conscious behaviors, employs various communication channels. These channels may include traditional media such as television, print, and radio, as well as contemporary digital platforms like social media, blogs, and eco-friendly websites. Successful green marketing campaigns often exhibit strategic messaging that emphasizes the environmental benefits of products, utilizing compelling visuals and narratives. Case studies of triumphs in green marketing communication reveal the importance of authenticity, transparency, and aligning with consumers' values. The examination of these campaigns allows marketers to discern the most effective channels, messaging strategies, and creative elements, contributing to the development of future environmentally friendly campaigns and enhancing the overall impact of green marketing efforts.

To captivate consumer interest and drive the purchase of green products, it is imperative that green advertising messages are both informative and persuasive, aiming to achieve targeted business outcomes (Belz and Peattie, 2008). Despite the prevalence of terms such as 'eco-friendly' in advertising claims, as noted by Peattie (2001), their effectiveness in influencing green purchasing actions remains largely insignificant. Consequently, businesses are increasingly focusing on identifying and comprehending the factors influencing consumers' purchasing behavior for green products. This understanding is pivotal for crafting compelling and impactful advertisements as part of comprehensive marketing and communication strategies (Chen and Chai, 2010; Tan, 2011).

Green marketing represents a contemporary concern, reflecting how companies engage in activities that promote environmental sustainability, thereby impacting their brand image (Yeng & Yazdanifard, 2015). The emergence of green consumers has compelled industries to prioritize environmental considerations and develop eco-friendly products. Despite this, there remains a lack of universal environmental consciousness among companies, with some engaging in environmentally detrimental marketing practices (Sibarani & Genoveva, 2019). Engaging in green marketing initiatives, however, contributes to the enhancement of a company's brand image, exerting an ultimate influence on consumer purchasing decisions. As consumer awareness regarding environmental issues rises, the adoption of green products has become integral to the lifestyle of environmentally conscious. The trend of companies leveraging green marketing to fortify their brand image is increasingly viewed as a positive and strategic endeavor within the business landscape.

HOW GREEN MARKETING INFLUENCES CONSUMER PURCHASE DECISIONS AND THE ROLE OF TRUST AND CREDIBILITY

Several factors play a pivotal role in motivating green consumers to opt for environmentally friendly products, as evidenced by extensive research conducted over the years (Cherian & Jacob, 2012). These factors encompass heightened awareness of environmental issues, increased accessibility to information on sustainability, corporate green advertising initiatives, a growing concern for the environment, and the rising popularity of green products championed by social and environmental charities. There is an evolving imperative for both marketers and consumers to transition towards green products and services. Despite the initial costs associated with this shift, the long-term benefits are anticipated to be substantial. A wealth of literature explores diverse aspects of green marketing, delving into the intricate relationships between customer attitudes and environmental strategies concerning an organization's marketing practices. Green marketing aims to generate awareness about environmental issues and guide consumers towards adopting a greener lifestyle. Rex and Baumann (2007) suggest that these aspects will drive businesses to develop more environmentally friendly products. Green marketing, being an integral part of marketing, shares key elements with traditional marketing, including price, promotions, products, and place. Furthermore, businesses engaging in green marketing are required to foster robust relationships with suppliers, market intermediaries, and most significantly, consumers (Chan *et al.*, 2012). Corporations are increasingly committing to making their operations more environmentally friendly, prompting heightened awareness among lawmakers, environmental groups, consumers, financial institutions, insurers, and employees, resulting in the formulation of numerous policies and regulations at both national and international levels.

Eco-labeling has proven to be an effective measure bridging the gap between sellers and buyers, providing information on intangible quality measures, including product quality, and presenting recyclability and CSR-related brand prestige (Sammer and Wustenhagen, 2006). Empirical research emphasizes the need to explore how eco-labels directly impact consumers' purchase intentions for environmentally safe products (Sammer and Wustenhagen, 2006). Rashid (2009) identifies that consumer awareness of eco-labels contributes positively to their understanding of green marketing and the subsequent purchase of green products.

Green purchase intention (GPIN) is defined as the intention to buy a service or product that is less or not harmful to society and the environment. Consumers, increasingly conscious of environmental issues, hold environmental beliefs and express a willingness to purchase green products with a minimal impact on the environment (Peattie, 1995). Marketers and manufacturers are compelled to reorganize their manufacturing and business models to align with consumer environmental beliefs (Chen, 2010). Green perceived risk refers to customers' perception that a product may be low-grade or not environmentally friendly. Early in the era of green marketing, some companies falsely claimed non-green products as green to boost sales, eroding consumer trust. Consumers are now reluctant to purchase products due to a lack of trust in sellers, stemming from communication gaps between sellers and buyers (Rizwan *et al.*, 2013). Trust, that encompasses beliefs in honesty, goodwill, and competence, is a crucial factor affecting consumer Green Purchase Trust (GPT). GPT, in turn, is considered a vital determinant of long-term consumer activities, with past literature suggesting a positive impact of GPT on GPIN. Positive experiences with sellers are linked to higher levels of GPIN (van der Heijden *et al.*, 2003).

Perceived risk, associated with negative consumption feelings, has a strong positive correlation with negative emotions, significantly impacting customer trust (Chaudhuri, 1997). It is anticipated that a reduction in perceived risk will enhance the likelihood of product purchase, subsequently elevating consumer purchase intentions (Chang and Chen, 2008). High perceived risk reduces the probability of customer product purchase (Mitchell, 1999), indicating a substantial impact on purchasing behavior.

Green Perceived Value (GPV) encompasses the total benefits, features, and performance of a green product in the consumer's mind. GPV represents the customer's evaluation of the overall benefits derived from a green product, influencing Green Purchase Intention (GPIN) positively. Companies can enhance GPIN by emphasizing the value of their products, with GPV playing a pivotal role both in affecting GPIN and in maintaining long-term customer relationships. Exaggerating the environmental value of products may, however, lead to a loss of customer interest. Existing research establishes a positive relationship between GPV and GPT, with these factors enhancing post-purchase customer assurance (Sweeney *et al.*, 1999).

Consumer studies have delved into various issues related to green consumption, including the ecological consumer, willingness to pay a premium for green products, perceived quality of green products, and attributes motivating green product consumption. Research on corporate green strategies has predominantly focused on their impact on life cycle costs, product differentiation, competitive management, and new market development.

UNDERSTANDING THE DECISION-MAKING PROCESS IN THE CONTEXT OF GREEN PRODUCTS

The Theory of Planned Behaviour (TPB) serves as a widely adopted attitude model for exploring the connections between personal beliefs, social norms, and individual attitudes towards green purchasing (Kalafatis *et al.*, 1999; Kim and Chung, 2011; Ahn *et al.*, 2012). Notably, environmental norms, social conformity, and self-identity emerge as pivotal factors influencing consumers' preferences for green products. Understanding these factors is crucial for comprehending the green buying behavior of

Indian consumers. Pickett-Baker and Ozaki (2008) propose that consumers' pro-environmental values significantly shape their pro-environmental buying behavior. Meanwhile, Rahbar and Wahid (2011) assert that eco-brands and trust in eco-labels play a role in influencing the eco-brand purchase behavior of Malaysian consumers. The awareness and intention to buy eco-brands, in turn, are influenced by a belief in green products and a desire to protect the environment. Companies can enhance consumer awareness about green products and influence purchase behavior through their green marketing initiatives. Ethical consumption not only imparts symbolic meaning to individuals' lifestyles, social values and personal identity, but also influences their green purchase behavior (Niinimaki, 2010). Stets and Biga (2003) further delve into the influence of consumers' identity on green purchase behavior, emphasizing the significance of self-identity and self-concept.

Arpita Khare identifies three pertinent factors in predicting consumers' green buying behavior: group conformance, self-identity, and past buying behavior. Among these, self-identification as "green consumers" emerges as the most influential factor in predicting green buying behavior. In a context where awareness of green marketing, environmentally friendly products, and ecological behavior is limited, consumers tend to associate green buying with self-identity. Firms can strategically employ advertising appeals that highlight "green self-identity" and "peer influence" to promote green products. Emphasizing the advantages of adopting green attitudes, environmentally friendly behavior, and environmental consciousness, such appeals should aim to translate these beliefs from cognitive and conative aspects of attitude to actual behavior. Individual self-image and identification with green initiatives can be leveraged to project a "green self-image," allowing consumers to enhance their societal status by demonstrating commitment to environmental causes. Through advertisements, firms can reinforce the significance of "green consumers" who are dedicated to protecting the environment.

EMERGING TRENDS IN GREEN MARKETING AND INDIAN PERSPECTIVE

The fervent enthusiasm for green marketing that characterized the early 1990s has gradually waned over time (Peattie and Crane, 2005). The second stage of green marketing emerged in the 1990s, marked by a backlash experienced by marketers (Wong *et al.*, 1996). Marketers gradually realized that despite increased consumer concern for the environment and a desire for green products, this sentiment did not necessarily translate into actual purchasing behavior. Among the major impediments, consumer cynicism toward green products, claims, and companies' intentions and practices, stood out as a primary factor contributing to the backlash (Mendleson and Polonsky, 1995; Peattie and Crane, 2005; Wong *et al.*, 1996). From the mid-1990s onward, consumers became progressively more environmentally and socially aware

(Strong, 1996), giving rise to critical consumers who demanded social responsibility from corporations (Gura˘u and Ranchhod, 2005). Against the backdrop of a growing global concern for environmental quality, green marketing has experienced a resurgence. Some researchers argue that green marketing is now "making a comeback", supported by the Global Environmental Survey (GOES), which indicates a gradual intergenerational value shift toward post-materialist priorities, likely leading to increased pro-environmental behavior (Inglehart, 1990).

Although discussions about the green marketing concept began in the 1960s, it was in the late 1980s and early 1990s that the concept began to be formalized and generalized. The American Marketing Association organized the first workshop on the topic in 1974, where green marketing was initially defined as the study of both positive and negative aspects of pollution and depletion of energy sources (Kinnear and Taylor, 1973). According to Polonsky (1994), green marketing encompasses all planned activities aimed at generating and facilitating exchanges to satisfy human needs and desires with the least possible impact on the environment. This definition introduces a more humanistic marketing concept that incorporates ecological and social components and emphasizes the minimization of environmental damage.

Peattie and Charter (2003) provide a comprehensive definition, describing green marketing as a holistic management process responsible for identifying, anticipating, and satisfying customer needs and societal requirements in a profitable and sustainable manner. Soonthonsmai (2007) extends this definition, stating that firms concerned about the environment should develop green products/services to achieve consumer and societal satisfaction.

Many authors argue that green marketing involves a broad spectrum of activities, encompassing R&D, design, manufacturing processes, packaging, and advertising. According to Peattie and Charter (2003), marketers should not only focus on internal production processes, but also consider the impact of production and consumption on the quality of life and the development of a sustainable society. These authors propose expanding the traditional four Ps of marketing to include the four "Ss": customer Satisfaction, product Safety, Social acceptability, and Sustainability of the products.

The emergence of green marketing is a response to the realization that companies are evaluated not only based on product/service performance but also on their social and environmental responsibility. Green marketing is seen as a supportive tool for monitoring, seeking, and fulfilling consumer needs and desires within a context of environmental responsibility.

Given that many authors consider green marketing to influence customer preferences (McDaniel and Rylander, 1993; Pujari and Wright, 1996; Kassaye, 2001), it is crucial to understand the extent of the influence. Despite consumer concern for the environment, marketers have observed that consumers are price-sensitive when it comes to purchasing green products (Mandese, 1991). Additionally, consumers' willingness to pay more for eco-friendly products does not always align with their actual green buying behavior. For instance, individuals who recycle waste may not necessarily want to buy products made from recycled materials (Pickett-Baker & Ozaki, 2008). Pro-environmental concern is conceptualized as a general attitude reflecting the degree to which consumers worry about environmental threats (Alhassan, 2007). Recent studies suggest a high level of concern for environmental problems, indicating a likely increase in green buying behavior (Mainieri *et al.*, 1997). Green Brand Positioning (GBP) is an integral part of brand identity and value creation, occupying a distinctive place in the minds of the target market, valued by customers, unique to a firm, and differentiating the brand from competitors (Aaker & Joachimsthaler, 2000). Effective communication of green brand attributes is crucial for the commercial success of green products (Pickett-Baker & Ozaki, 2008). GBP strategies position brands based on functional, emotional, and green attributes (Mohd Suki, 2016). Green Brand Knowledge (GBK) refers to a green brand node in consumers' memory linked to environmental commitment and concerns (Mohd Suki, 2016). GBK provides information about a product's unique brand attributes, benefits, and environmental contributions, facilitating green product purchases (Mourad & Ahmed, 2012; Sharma & Foropon, 2019; Woo & Kim, 2019; Zhang *et al.*, 2018).

High prices for green products are considered a significant hindrance to green consumption, particularly for young consumers with limited purchasing power (Gleim *et al.*, 2013). While some studies indicate that consumers are willing to pay extra for green products (Ansar, 2013; Erve, 2013; Gotlieb, 2019; Kirmani & Khan, 2018; Mobrezi & Khoshtinat, 2016; Narula & Desore, 2016; Prakash & Pathak, 2017; Shahsavar *et al.*, 2020; Thieme *et al.*, 2015; Wei *et al.*, 2018; Xu & Wu, 2010), others find that eco-friendly consumers may not be influenced by price in their green product purchase intentions (Cronin *et al.*, 2011; Grankvist & Biel, 2001). The perceived high price of green products compared to conventional products, resulting from the low production costs of the latter, poses a challenge to green consumption (Chaudhary & Bisai, 2018; Laroche *et al.*, 2001; Zhang *et al.*, 2018). Despite consumer awareness and willingness to pay more for environmentally friendly options, the actual adoption of green products faces barriers such as lack of awareness, negative perceptions, distrust, high prices, and low availability.

As a strategic approach, green marketing encompasses key elements such as green products, green packaging, green pricing, and green communication (Ottman, 1998). The proliferation of green marketing and the emergence of green consumers are deemed by some as "perhaps the biggest opportunity for enterprise and invention the industrial world has ever seen" (Cairncross, 2003). Richards (2013) explored the impact of green advertising by assessing consumers' connection to the environment and factors influencing trust in advertising and willingness to purchase green products. Similar research conducted by Niazi *et al.* (2012) and Saleem & Abideen (2011) identified a positive relationship between emotional response, attitudinal response, and consumer buying behavior, particularly for products to which consumers were emotionally attached.

Environmental Belief: Environmental belief refers to convictions held by individuals or groups regarding concepts, events, or things. International research indicates that consumers are increasingly concerned about the environment, leading to gradual changes in their behavior (Arbuthnot, 1977; Simon, 1992). Hoyer and MacInnis (2004) emphasize the need to consider consumers' values and beliefs when exploring factors influencing purchase decisions. Ajzen's Theory of Planned Behavior (1991) asserts that environmental beliefs shape attitudes toward behavior, influencing buying intentions (Hoyer & MacInnis, 2004).

Green Packaging: Green packaging involves an approach that considers the full environmental impact of packaging material production and disposal. Sustainable packaging generates less waste and utilizes recyclable materials, emphasizing environmentally friendly practices from product conception to customer product disposal (Prahalad & Hamel, 1994). The ecological consideration of packaging depends on the degree of environmental pollution (Delia, 2010).

Eco-Labeling: Eco-labels are symbols or marks awarded to products that comply with eco-friendly criteria established by governments, associations, or standard certification bodies. Specific product claims, such as "eco-friendly," "recyclable," "biodegradable," and "ozone-friendly," enable marketers to communicate environmental benefits to consumers.

Green Branding: Green brands are those associated with environmental conservation and sustainable business practices. Studies demonstrate that consumers' growing environmental awareness inclines them toward brands perceived as environmentally friendly (Eagly and Kulesa, 1997). Effective communication of green brand attributes is crucial for the commercial success of environmentally sustainable products (Pickett *et al.*, 1995). Green positioning is considered a critical element in the success of green branding strategies (Coddington, 1993).

Green Advertising: Green advertising involves communication that emphasizes the environmentally friendly aspects of a product or organization. The objective is to influence consumer purchase behavior by encouraging the selection of products that do not harm the environment, and by highlighting positive consequences for both the consumer and the environment (Rahbar & Wahid, 2011). Environmental advertisements play a role in shaping consumer values and translating these values into the purchase of green products.

Studies have explored green marketing and production initiatives implemented by Indian companies (Nair and Menon, 2008). Indian companies are adopting green practices to differentiate themselves from competitors (Saxena and Khandelwal, 2012; Agarwal, 2013). However, limited consumer knowledge about green products, organic and recyclable brands, and green production processes poses a challenge. Recent efforts by the government to protect the environment have increased. Studies on Indian consumers' preference for green products indicate interest in green brands, but this interest does not always translate into actual green purchases. Factors such as pro-environmental awareness, concerns, and confidence in the quality of green products play a role in shaping consumer attitudes. However, consumers often lack knowledge about green products, expecting government and companies to lead in adopting green practices. Internal and external factors, including motives, income, environmental concern, and promotional incentives, are identified as significant determinants of green attitudes. Group conformance, social norms, social/peer influence, past green buying behavior, and environmental norms are discussed as influencing factors in green buying behavior, emphasizing the importance of understanding Indian consumers' preferences for green products in the context of cultural values, lifestyle, and social influence.

Effective Sustainable Marketing Campaigns: Strategies and Noteworthy Examples in India (https://www.linkedin.com/pulse/sustainable-marketing-campaign-strategies-india-consumers)

In contemporary marketing, sustainability has emerged as a driving force, encompassing a range of strategies falling under the purview of Environmental, Social, and Governance (ESG) practices. These initiatives not only enhance brand reputation but also contribute to increased sales and heightened customer engagement. Sustainable marketing, often referred to as eco-marketing, transcends traditional product promotion, reflecting a commitment to ethical and eco-friendly practices. Five key strategies delineate successful sustainable marketing campaigns:

1. **Social Media Engagement:** Recognizing consumers' growing interest in eco-friendly products necessitates innovative approaches to connect with them.
2. **Accessible Information:** Companies are urged to integrate quantifiable ESG initiatives and transparent supply chain practices, providing consumers with easily accessible information.
3. **Transparency:** Consumer preferences are increasingly aligned with transparent supply chains that prioritize both the environment and workforce.
4. **Collaboration:** Forming partnerships with environmental organizations amplifies impact and serves as a tangible demonstration of commitment to sustainability.
5. **Seal of Sustainability:** Third-party certifications serve to enhance the visibility of sustainable products, instilling confidence in consumers.

Several Indian brands have exemplified these strategies, notable among them are Schneider Electric's Green Yodha campaign, Tata Group Tea's JaagoRe initiative to combat climate change, Hyundai Motor India Ltd.'s 'Save Water Challenge,' and Nestlé Maggi's '2-minute Safai Ke Naam' campaign. Sustainable marketing is not merely a passing trend; it represents a strategic path to connect, engage, and prosper in a conscious marketplace. Embracing sustainability allows brands to be perceived as beacons of positive change in the eyes of consumers. Seizing this opportunity can empower your brand in the era of eco-conscious consumers, making a meaningful difference in the process.

The significance of green marketing in influencing consumer environmental behavior is underscored by Tan *et al.* The authors emphasize the pivotal role of green communication in fostering customer confidence in a brand's environmental commitment, consequently exerting a positive influence on green purchasing. Consequently, this research endeavor is formulated to augment the understanding of consumers' attentiveness, as perceived from their standpoint, towards companies' green marketing communication, and the subsequent impact on consumers' decisions regarding environmentally conscious purchases.

RECOMMENDATIONS FOR BUSINESSES

1. **Enhanced Transparency in Communication:** Enterprises should accord primacy to transparent communication concerning their environmental initiatives. Articulation of lucid and forthright messages fosters trust among consumers, thereby amplifying the efficacy of green marketing strategies.
2. **Attainment of Recognized Eco-Certifications:** The acquisition of acknowledged eco-certifications serves to validate a corporation's dedication to sustainability. Certifications such as Energy Star, Fair Trade, or organic labels confer upon consumers the assurance that products meet stringent environmental standards.
3. **Perpetual Innovation in Sustainable Practices:** The perpetuation of innovation in sustainable practices affords businesses a distinctive edge. This may encompass endeavors to curtail carbon footprints, embrace renewable energy sources, or institute solutions for eco-friendly packaging.
4. **Implementation of Educational Campaigns:** The initiation of educational campaigns serves to heighten consumer awareness and comprehension of environmental issues. Through the dissemination of information pertaining to the advantages of sustainable practices, businesses contribute to the cultivation of an enlightened and ecologically conscientious consumer base.

RECOMMENDATIONS FOR POLICYMAKERS

1. **Provision of Incentives for Green Practices:** Policymakers are well-positioned to institute incentives, such as tax concessions or subsidies, to incentivize businesses

embracing eco-friendly practices. This initiative not only fosters a wider adoption of sustainable measures but also contributes substantively to the overall mitigation of environmental impact.

2. **Establishment of Robust Regulatory Frameworks:** The formulation and enforcement of unambiguous environmental regulations are imperative to ensure corporate adherence to sustainable practices. Policymakers ought to diligently work towards the creation of a regulatory framework that not only mandates but also incentivizes environmentally responsible business conduct.
3. **Collaboration in Consumer Education Programs:** Policymakers can actively engage in collaborative efforts with businesses and non-governmental organizations to institute consumer education programs. These programs, designed to elucidate the environmental ramifications of consumer choices, empower individuals to make informed and sustainable decisions.
4. **Allocation of Resources for Research and Development:** The allocation of funds towards research and development endeavors in sustainable technologies assumes paramount importance. Policymakers wield a critical role in underwriting initiatives that contribute to the advancement of sustainable production and consumption paradigms.

CONCLUSION

The study suggests that pro-environmental concern is a likely predictor of green buying behaviour. This creates an opportunity for developing green market focusing on more educated consumers—the same proposition which worked in the West. Also, consumers want eco-friendly products from companies which project their image as being "green". The right mix of eco- friendly products and service, sales, marketing, PR and management expertise is needed to target and attract the consumers who may be willing to buy eco- friendly products. Green marketers should identify such segment of consumers and accordingly design and market products at suitable price levels. Since eco-friendly attributes motivate consumers, hence companies should focus on advertising eco-friendly brand labels, in-store displays and pamphlets. Advertisements campaigns may be used to further promote the use of eco-friendly products. Such campaigns can be directed at increasing concerns about environmental issues among consumers and publicize the use of eco-friendly products. Pro-environmental concerns can be raised by advertising that individual buying behaviour can make a difference and can have an impact on the welfare of the environment. It is also important that companies aiming at developing new eco-friendly products should ensure that products perform competitively.

REFERENCES

Aaker, D. A. and Joachimsthaler, E. (2000). The brand relationship spectrum: The key to the brand architecture challenge. *California management review, 42*(4), 8–23.

Ahn, J. M., Koo, D. M. and Chang, H. S. (2012). Different impacts of normative influences on pro-environmental purchasing behavior explained by differences in individual characteristics. *Journal of Global Scholars of Marketing Science, 22*(2), 163–182.

Akehurst, G., Afonso, C. and Gonçalves, H. M. (2012). Re-examining green purchase behaviour and the green consumer profile: new evidences. *Management decision, 50*(5), 972–988.

Akenji, L. (2014). Consumer scapegoatism and limits to green consumerism. *Journal of Cleaner Production, 63*, 13–23.

Arbuthnot, J. and Lingg, S. (1975). A comparison of French and American environmental behaviors, knowledge, and attitudes 1 2. *International Journal of Psychology, 10*(4), 275–281.

Barber, N. A. (2014). Profiling the potential "green" hotel guest: Who are they and what do they want?. *Journal of Hospitality & Tourism Research, 38*(3), 361–387.

Berger, I. E. and Corbin, R.M. (1992). Perceived consumer effectiveness and faith in others as moderators of environmentally responsible behaviors. *Journal of public policy & marketing, 11*(2), 79–89.

Boztepe, A. (2012). Green marketing and its impact on consumer buying behavior. *European Journal of Economic & Political Studies, 5*(1).

Cairncross, F. (1992). *Costing the earth* (Vol. 242). Boston: Harvard Business School Press.

Chan, R. Y. K. and Yam, E. (1995). Green movement in a newly industrializing area: A survey on the attitudes and behaviour of the Hong Kong citizens. *Journal of Community & Applied Social Psychology, 5*(4), 273–284.

Chan, R. Y. and Lau, L. B. (2000). Antecedents of green purchases: a survey in China. *Journal of consumer marketing, 17*(4), 338–357.

Chaudhuri, A. (1997). Consumption emotion and perceived risk: A macro-analytic approach. *Journal of Business Research, 39*(2), 81–92.

Chen, T.B. and Chai, L.T. (2010). Attitude towards the environment and green products: consumers' perspective. *Management science and engineering, 4*(2), 27.

Chen, Y.S. (2008). The driver of green innovation and green image–green core competence. *Journal of business ethics, 81*, 531–543.

Cherian, J. and Jacob, J. (2012). Green marketing: A study of consumers' attitude towards environment friendly products.

Cleveland, M., Kalamas, M. and Laroche, M. (2005). Shades of green: linking environmental locus of control and pro-environmental behaviors. *Journal of consumer marketing, 22*(4), 198–212.

Cronin, J.J., Smith, J.S., Gleim, M.R., Ramirez, E. and Martinez, J.D. (2011). Green marketing strategies: an examination of stakeholders and the opportunities they present. *Journal of the Academy of Marketing Science, 39*, 158–174.

Curlo, E. (1999). Marketing strategy, product safety, and ethical factors in consumer choice. *Journal of Business Ethics*, *21*, 37–48.

D'angelico, R. M., and Pujari, D. (2010). Mainstreaming Green Product Innovation: Why and How Companies Integrate Environmental Sustainability. Journal of Business Ethics, 95(3), 471–486. Deck, C., and Smith, V. (2013). Using Laboratory Experiments in Logistics and Supply Chain Research. Journal of Business Logistics, 34(1), 6–14.

Do Paço, A., Alves, H., Shiel, C. and Filho, W. L. (2014). An analysis of the measurement of the construct "buying behaviour" in green marketing. *Journal of Integrative Environmental Sciences*, *11*(1), 55–69.

D'Souza, C. (2004). Ecolabel programmes: a stakeholder (consumer) perspective. *Corporate Communications: An International Journal*, *9*(3), 179–188.

Eagly, A. H. and Kulesa, P. (1997). Attitudes, attitude structure, and resistance to change. *Environmental ethics and behavior*, *415*, 122–153.

Elkington, J. (1994). Towards the sustainable corporation: Win-win-win business strategies for sustainable development. *California management review*, *36*(2), 90–100.

Ellen, P.S., Wiener, J.L. and Cobb-Walgren, C. (1991). The role of perceived consumer effectiveness in motivating environmentally conscious behaviors. *Journal of public policy & marketing*, *10*(2), 102–117.

Genoveva, G. and Samukti, D. R. (2020). Green Marketing: Strengthen the Brand Image and Increase the Consumers'purchase Decision. *Mix Jurnal Ilmiah Manajemen*, *10*(3), 367.

Gleim, M.R., Smith, J.S., Andrews, D. and Cronin Jr, J.J. (2013). Against the green: A multi-method examination of the barriers to green consumption. *Journal of retailing*, *89*(1), 44–61.

Grunert, S.C. and Juhl, H. J. (1995). Values, environmental attitudes, and buying of organic foods. *Journal of economic psychology*, *16*(1), 39–62.

Hamzaoui Essoussi, L. and Linton, J.D. (2010). New or recycled products: how much are consumers willing to pay? *Journal of Consumer Marketing*, *27*(5), 458–468.

Inglehart, R. (1995). Public support for environmental protection: Objective problems and subjective values in 43 societies. *PS: Political Science & Politics*, *28*(1), 57–72.

Jang, Y.J., Kim, W.G. and Lee, H.Y. (2015). Coffee shop consumers' emotional attachment and loyalty to green stores: The moderating role of green consciousness. *International Journal of Hospitality Management*, *44*, 146–156.

Jones, K. and Leonard, L.N. (2008). Trust in consumer-to-consumer electronic commerce. *Information & management*, *45*(2), 88–95.

Kalafatis, S.P., Pollard, M., East, R. and Tsogas, M.H. (1999). Green marketing and Ajzen's theory of planned behaviour: a cross-market examination. *Journal of consumer marketing*, *16*(5), 441–460.

Kilbourne, W.E. and Polonsky, M.J. (2005). Environmental attitudes and their relation to the dominant social paradigm among university students in New Zealand and Australia. *Australasian marketing journal*, *13*(2), 37–48.

Kim, H., Lee, E.J. and Hur, W.M. (2012). The normative social influence on eco-friendly consumer behavior: The moderating effect of environmental marketing claims. *Clothing and Textiles Research Journal*, *30*(1), 4–18.

Kinnear, T.C. and Taylor, J.R. (1973). The effect of ecological concern on brand perceptions. *Journal of marketing research, 10*(2), 191–197.

Kinnear, T.C., Taylor, J.R. and Ahmed, S.A. (1974). Ecologically concerned consumers: who are they? Ecologically concerned consumers can be identified. *Journal of marketing, 38*(2), 20–24.

Ko, E., Hwang, Y.K. and Kim, E.Y. (2013). Green marketing'functions in building corporate image in the retail setting. *Journal of Business Research, 66*(10), 1709–1715.

Laroche, M., Tomiuk, M.A., Bergeron, J. and Barbaro-Forleo, G. (2002). Cultural differences in environmental knowledge, attitudes, and behaviours of Canadian consumers. *Canadian Journal of Administrative Sciences/Revue Canadienne des Sciences de l'Administration, 19*(3), 267–282.

Lee, A.H., Kang, H.Y., Hsu, C.F. and Hung, H.C. (2009). A green supplier selection model for high-tech industry. *Expert systems with applications, 36*(4), 7917–7927.

Lee, K. (2008). Opportunities for green marketing: young consumers. *Marketing intelligence & planning, 26*(6), 573–586.

Mainieri, T., Barnett, E.G., Valdero, T.R., Unipan, J. B. and Oskamp, S. (1997). Green buying: The influence of environmental concern on consumer behavior. *The Journal of social psychology, 137*(2), 189.

Mandese, J. (1991). New study finds green confusion. Advertising Age, 62(45), 1, 56.

Maniatis, P. (2016). Investigating factors influencing consumer decision-making while choosing green products. *Journal of Cleaner Production, 132*, 215–228.

Mitchell, V. W. (1999). Consumer perceived risk: conceptualisations and models. *European Journal of marketing, 33*(1/2), 163–195.

Mohd Suki, N. (2016). Green product purchase intention: impact of green brands, attitude, and knowledge. *British Food Journal, 118*(12), 2893–2910.

Mourad, M. and Serag Eldin Ahmed, Y. (2012). Perception of green brand in an emerging innovative market. *European Journal of Innovation Management, 15*(4), 514–537.

Nair, S.R. and Menon, C.G. (2008). An environmental marketing system–a proposed model based on Indian experience. *Business Strategy and the Environment, 17*(8), 467–479.

Niinimäki, K. (2010). Eco-clothing, consumer identity and ideology. *Sustainable development, 18*(3), 150–162.

Ottman, J. and Books, N.B. (1998). Green marketing: opportunity for innovation. *The Journal of Sustainable Product Design, 60*(7), 136–667.

Peattie, K. (2015). Sustainability marketing. *Handbook of research on sustainable consumption*, 101–117.

Peattie, K. and Crane, A. (2005) "Green marketing: legend, myth, farce or prophesy?" *Qualitative Market Research: an International Journal,* Vol. 8, No. 4, pp. 357–370.

Peattie, K. and Charter, M. (2003). "Green marketing". In: Baker, M. J. (ed.). The Marketing Book. Burlington: Butterworth-Heinemann, pp. 726–756. 30.

Peattie, K. and Belz, F.M. (2010). Sustainability marketing—An innovative conception of marketing. *Marketing Review St. Gallen, 27*(5), 8–15.

Peattie, K. and Crane, A. (2005). Green marketing: legend, myth, farce or prophesy?. *Qualitative market research: an international journal, 8*(4), 357–370.

Pickett-Baker, J. and Ozaki, R. (2008). Pro-environmental products: Marketing influence on consumer purchase decision. Journal of Consumer Marketing, 25(6), 281–293.

Pickett-Baker, J. and Ozaki, R. (2008). Pro-environmental products: marketing influence on consumer purchase decision. *Journal of consumer marketing, 25*(5), 281–293.

Polonsky, Michael Jay, 2011. "Transformative green marketing: Impediments and opportunities," *Journal of Business Research, Elsevier,* Vol. 64(12), pages 1311–1319.

Prahalad, C.K. and Hamel, G. (1994). Strategy as a field of study: Why search for a new paradigm? *Strategic management journal, 15*(S2), 5–16.

Prakash, A. (2002). Green marketing, public policy and managerial strategies. *Business strategy and the environment, 11*(5), 285–297.

Prakash, G. and Pathak, P. (2017). Intention to buy eco-friendly packaged products among young consumers of India: A study on developing nation. *Journal of cleaner production, 141,* 385–393.

Rahbar, E. and Wahid, N.A. (2011). Investigation of green marketing tools' effect on consumers' purchase behavior. *Business strategy series, 12*(2), 73–83.

Rahbar, E. and Wahid, N.A. (2011). Investigation of green marketing tools' effect on consumers' purchase behavior. *Business strategy series, 12*(2), 73–83.

Rashid, N.R.N.A. (2009). Awareness of eco-label in Malaysia's green marketing initiative. *International journal of business and management, 4*(8), 132–141.

Rex, E. and Baumann, H. (2007). Beyond ecolabels: what green marketing can learn from conventional marketing. *Journal of cleaner production, 15*(6), 567–576.

Rizwan, M., Umair, S.M., Bilal, H.M., Akhtar, M. and Bhatti, M.S. (2014). Determinants of customer intentions for online shopping: A Study from Pakistan. *Journal of Sociological Research, 5*(1), 248–272.

Roberts, J.A. (1996). Green consumers in the 1990s: Profile and implications for advertising. *Journal of business research, 36*(3), 217–231.

Saleem, S. and Abideen, Z. (2011). Effective advertising and its influence on consumer buying behavior. *European Journal of Business and Management, 3*(3), 55–67.

Sammer, K. and Wüstenhagen, R. (2006). The influence of eco-labelling on consumer behaviour–Results of a discrete choice analysis for washing machines. *Business strategy and the environment, 15*(3), 185–199.

Saxena, R.P. and Khandelwal, P.K. (2012). Greening of industries for sustainable growth: An exploratory study on durable, non-durable and services industries. *International Journal of Social Economics, 39*(8), 551–586.

Schuhwerk, M.E. and Lefkokk-Hagius, R. (1995). Green or non-green? Does type of appeal matter when advertising a green product? *Journal of Advertising,* **24**(2), 45–55. https://doi.org/10.1080/00913367.1995.10673475

Sharma, A. and Foropon, C. (2019). Green product attributes and green purchase behavior: A theory of planned behavior perspective with implications for circular economy. *Management Decision, 57*(4), 1018–1042.

Sharma, A. and Kiran, R. (2013). Corporate social responsibility: Driving forces and challenges. *International Journal of Business Research and Development, 2*(1).

Sibarani, L. (2019). The Customer Pressure and Organizational Commitment on Environmental Performance Mediating Proactive Environmental Strategies. *Archives of Business Research (ABR), 7*(7).

Soonthonsmai, V. (2007, June). Environmental or green marketing as global competitive edge: Concept, synthesis, and implication. In *EABR (Business) and ETLC (Teaching) Conference Proceeding, Venice, Italy.*

Stets, J.E. and Biga, C.F. (2003). Bringing identity theory into environmental sociology. *Sociological theory, 21*(4), 398–423.

Straughan, R.D. and Roberts, J.A. (1999). Environmental segmentation alternatives: a look at green consumer behavior in the new millennium. *Journal of consumer marketing, 16*(6), 558–575.

Suki, N.M., Suki, N.M. and Azman, N.S. (2016). Impacts of corporate social responsibility on the links between green marketing awareness and consumer purchase intentions. *Procedia Economics and Finance, 37*, 262–268.

Suplico, L.T. (2009). Impact of Green Marketing on the Students' Purchase Decision. *Journal of International Business Research, 8.*

Sweeney, J.C., Soutar, G.N. and Johnson, L.W. (1999). The role of perceived risk in the quality-value relationship: A study in a retail environment. *Journal of retailing*, 75(1), 77–105.

Tan, Z., Sadiq, B., Bashir, T., Mahmood, H. and Rasool, Y. Investigating the Impact of Green Marketing Components on Purchase Intention: The Mediating Role of Brand Image and Brand Trust. *Sustainability*, 2022;14:5939. doi: 10.3390/su14105939.

Tan, L.P., Johnstone, M.L. and Yang, L. (2016). Barriers to green consumption behaviours: The roles of consumers' green perceptions. *Australasian Marketing Journal, 24*(4), 288–299.

Thøgersen, J., Jørgensen, A.K. and Sandager, S. (2012). Consumer decision making regarding a "green" everyday product. *Psychology & Marketing, 29*(4), 187–197.

Tilikidou, I. (2007). The effects of knowledge and attitudes upon Greeks' pro-environmental purchasing behaviour. *Corporate Social Responsibility and Environmental Management, 14*(3), 121–134.

Tseng, S.C. and Hung, S.W. (2013). A framework identifying the gaps between customers' expectations and their perceptions in green products. *Journal of cleaner production, 59*, 174–184.

Van der Heijden, H., Verhagen, T. and Creemers, M. (2003). Understanding online purchase intentions: contributions from technology and trust perspectives. *European journal of information systems, 12*(1), 41–48.

Vandermerwe, S. and Oliff, M.D. (1990). Customers drive corporations. *Long range planning, 23*(6), 10–16.

Walsh, G., Dinnie, K. and Wiedmann, K.P. (2006). How do corporate reputation and customer satisfaction impact customer defection? A study of private energy customers in Germany. *Journal of Services Marketing, 20*(6), 412–420.

Wong, V., Turner, W. and Stoneman, P. (1996). Marketing strategies and market prospects for environmentally-friendly consumer products 1. *British journal of Management, 7*(3), 263–281.

Wossen Kassaye, W. (2001). Green dilemma. *Marketing Intelligence & Planning, 19*(6), 444–455.

Yang, D., Lu, Y., Zhu, W. and Su, C. (2015). Going green: How different advertising appeals impact green consumption behavior. *Journal of Business Research, 68*(12), 2663–2675.

Yeng, W.F. and Yazdanifard, R. (2015). Opportunities and Challenges in the World of Retailing and the Importance of Adaption to the New Markets. *International Journal of Management, Accounting and Economics, 2*(9), 1110–1121.

Zhao, T. and Cui, R.H. (2014). Research on Green Marketing Strategy in Enterprises Based on Low Carbon (LC) Environment. *Advanced Materials Research, 850*, 1073–1077.

10

Balancing Sustainability and Success: An In-depth Analysis of Home-Based Businesses in India

Dr. Ruchita Burman[1] and Shaiqa Jannat[2]

ABSTRACT: Home-based business (HBB) plays an important role in a country's economic landscape, offering livelihood and opportunities for entrepreneurship and economic growth. This unregulated sector is experiencing exponential growth, yet the comprehensive environmental, social, and economic ramifications of HBBs remain largely uncharted. This paper embarks on a detailed exploration of the sustainability practices employed by HBBs and their multifaceted implications.

It consists of systematic literature review of 30 relevant studies published across the world. Key findings reveal that a substantial portion of these businesses lack awareness and engagement with sustainable practices. Despite the numerous advantages that sustainability can offer to HBBs, entrepreneurs grapple with substantial obstacles, including limited access to finance, societal biases surrounding home-based businesses, and the absence of a supportive infrastructure and regulatory framework.

This paper highlights the potential for implementing sustainable practices by HBB to reduce environmental footprint, foster social security and promote economic resilience. In this pursuit, it identifies research gaps and proposes uncharted research avenues to delve into the emerging facets of HBBs in India. Addressing these research gaps will contribute to a more comprehensive understanding of the sustainability of home-based businesses in India and help shape policies and strategies to enhance their positive impact on the environment, society, and economy.

Keyword: *Home-based Business, Sustainability, Entrepreneurs, Environmental Footprint, Social, Economic.*

INTRODUCTION

In the dynamic landscape of contemporary business-individuals with innovation, initiation, decision-making skills and capital often undertake business activities known as an entrepreneurship. Any business or entrepreneurial venture where the primary office is the owner's home is referred to as home-based business (Cadar &

[1] Assistant Professor, Xavier Business School, St Xavier's, University, Kolkata.

[2] PhD Research Scholar, St Xavier's University, Kolkata.

Badulescu, 2015). The concept of home-based business (HBB) has gained prominence in the recent years. For example, according to 2023 US census, 50% of small businesses in US are home based, which roughly includes 15 million businesses.

The digital transformation of the world tripled with changing work patters, the newly acquired need for flexible work hours and lack of favorable employment opportunities has fueled the growth of home-based entrepreneurial venture (Kautonen *et al.*, 2010). There are growing number of individuals who are opting to begin their entrepreneurial journey from the comfort for their rooms and homes. This is visible by the unparalleled presence of HBB on social media platforms like Instagram, Facebook, and even Twitter and Snapchat where Instagram is considered the main platform for conducting such businesses. This method of home-based business not only offers an individual a better work-life balance, but it also silently contributes to the overall economic development of the country (Alhorr *et al.*, 2017). The aim of this paper is to review the sustainability of such home-based businesses in India, while examining environmental, social and economic implications.

In the recent years, the proliferation of HBB has become a defining characteristic of India's economy. India, as we know, is a diverse populous country- it presents a unique landscape for home-based businesses. With the rich cultural history, Indians have a strong entrepreneurial spirit and have historically engaged in many forms of cottage industries as well as small-scale enterprises. With the advent of internet and the 'Global Village', modern technology has transformed the traditional home-based businesses and enabled them to tap into the larger global market with ease and confidence.

The aim of the study is to dissect the multifaceted dynamics of HBB and the delicate balance of success and sustainability. By delving into the challenges (like lack of financial growth, problems with cash flow, losing passion for the business over time), opportunities and strategies employed by these HBB we seek to unravel the complex web underneath linking responsibility and economic growth. Understanding the dynamics of HBB is crucial for policymakers, researchers and entrepreneurs.

LITERATURE REVIEW

"A person who makes money by starting or running businesses, especially when this involves taking financial risks", is a popular definition of the word entrepreneur by Oxford dictionary. There are many definitions of entrepreneur that explore the many aspects of the phenomenon. For Frank H. Knight (1921), "Entrepreneurship is about taking risks". It was Thomas (2000) who suggested that the research on entrepreneurship should actively include national and international markets to evaluate the conditions and characteristics that foster various entrepreneurial activities in different countries and region. Meuller (2000) also added that it would be reasonable to expect that entrepreneurs reflect the dominant social and cultural beliefs of their nation and that is reflected in their entrepreneurship skills (Thomas & Mueller, 2000). The importance of such an ideology and perception emerges from the fact that research on entrepreneurship should examine both the individual (the entrepreneur) and the society in which they operate (Swanepoel & Strydom 2009).

Home-based business (HBB) is now becoming an increasingly popular method of conducting entrepreneurial activity. Home-based businesses can refer to business that operate from home or at home (Clark and Douglas, 2009–2010). It is defined as the business or entrepreneurship venture that uses family residential property/house for commercial purpose of conducting the business (Dwelly *et al.*, 2005). Anwar and Daniel define HBB as, "a business entity operated by a self-employed person working at home and who is using the internet to carry out a significant proportion of business activities that may include sourcing, selling, providing services and communicating with stakeholders. The business may be operated full or part-time and may utilize building surrounding the home such as studios and garages" (Anwar & Daniel, 2014).

In the recent years there has been an increasing interest by academicians, researchers and policymakers in HBB primarily because of the fact that it is one of the fastest expanding sub-sector of the informal business sector in India. Although the growth and the volume are high, yet this sub-sector is undocumented in nature. There is a lack of official statistics and data, as HBB is not recognized or is given any legal status, as a segment in the SME (Phillipson *et al.*, 2011). It is often viewed as a hobby or a social lifestyle choice and it continues to be invisible and do not receive the awareness and scrutiny that they deserve (Mason, 2010; Mason *et al.*, 2008) HBB are a part of informal enterprise that is often known as the 'invisible workforce'. They are not obligated to possess any license or any legal contract. They are entirely unregulated and unaccounted for, they are also not required to pay taxes, file returns, pay any sort of fee or comply with any regulations. The data about HBB does not appear in any official government statistics or records (Mead and Morrisson, 1996).

Given this sub-sector is free from regulations, those that pursue HBB are seeking to benefit the advantages of reduced government scrutiny and the online environment like reduced cost, better choices and offers, increased socialization or a combination of all. They are offering value at the lowest possible operating cost (Shin, 2014 & Zhang *et al.*, 2014). They include a variety of products like organic beauty products, food production (cloud kitchen/bakery), art and craft, home based boutiques, designing, etc. The nature of these home-based businesses is very heterogeneous which often gives very varied data results and results to a lack of understanding (Anwar & Daniel, 2014).

HBB can play a pivotal role in fostering sustainability by offering individuals to create environmentally conscious enterprises at the comfort of their home. The definition of sustainability presented by Harvard Business School is, "doing business without negatively impacting the environment, community, or society as a whole".

Sustainability in business addresses 3 main categories, namely, its effect on society, its effect on the environment and the economic effect on the business and the community in which it operates. International Institute for Sustainable Development defines sustainability as adoption of such business strategies and methods and activities that fulfills the need of the enterprise and its stakeholders in the present times, while preserving, sustaining the human and natural resources that will be needed in the future. Sustainability plays a very crucial role in long-term success of any business. This idea indicates that any business entity operating a society should contribute to economic growth of the said society through the pursuit of its own financial goals. It should also contribute to social justice through promotion of human resources and be responsible in its contribution towards natural resources preservation, minimizing the carbon footprint of the business and judicious use of the available energy sources (Mamingi, 2011). Society expects sustainability to- "people expect managers to use resources wisely and responsibly; protect the environment; minimize the amount of air, water, energy, minerals, and other materials found in the final goods we consume; recycle and reuse these goods to the extent possible rather than drawing on nature to replenish them; respect nature's calm, tranquility, and beauty; and eliminate toxins that harm people in the workplace and communities" (Marcus & Fremeth, 2009).

For small businesses such as HBB, sustainability is regarded as not important or necessary for extending the life of the business. One of the main reasons being that obtaining such certifications is an expensive and rigorous process. Due to such complexities, sustainability has been a domain of the large corporations and is ignored by small businesses (including HBB). The focus is almost always on large businesses when viewing sustainability for long-term success.

When assessing the sustainability of home-based business, three different aspects can be considered, namely the environmental impact, social impact and the economic impact. Assessing the environmental impact, researchers have been able to uncover that there has been an obvious reduction in commute time and energy consumption associated with working from home, which can lead to lower carbon emission and resource conservation (Hornstein *et al.*, 2015). More importantly, home-based businesses often have smaller physical footprint, thereby reducing the demand for infrastructural development and commercial space (Carfagna *et al.*, 2019). However, it is of utmost importance to examine the possible environmental challenges such as waste management and energy consumption pattern that may arise due to increased consumption and production in residential area (Alhorr *et al.*, 2017).

For environmental sustainability, small businesses can focus on packaging that is hassle-free and convenient without the use of unnecessary plastic elements. HBB can minimize packaging waste by eliminating excessive layers in shipments and using recyclable materials. Environmental friendly packaging can be done by using recycled materials or using packaging materials that can be recycled. There should be a commitment to improve the environment and taking initiatives for the same. HBB can focus on offering organic and green products like organic sourcing and using safer raw materials options.

(Nadim & Luccier, 2010)

Although the sustainability of home-based businesses offers many advantages, there are also a lot of barriers and challenges that entrepreneurs may face. It is essential to recognize such issues like limited access to finance, social stigma associated with home-based business, lack of supportive infrastructure or laws and regulations (Nadim & Luccier, 2010).

In terms of social sustainability, home-based business via the social media offers many lucrative advantages to women. Not only does it support women financially, but to a great extent helps in fulfilling their self-actualization needs. It increases their self-esteem (E.Melissa *et al.* 2015). In India, women face multiple cultural barriers with a wide range of challenges- the most prominent challenge being access to easy and affordable finance options. Conventional entrepreneurship requires a substantial amount of capital (rent money, employee salary, etc). Home-based business solves this issue. It helps women start their business at the home, in their free time with minimal investment. Thus, it helps in creating an equitable society, promote financial independence and create gender equality. It leads to an inclusive economic growth (Bose, 2020).

According to Sicat (2007), there is generally a classification of 2 of types of women who initiates home-based business. The first is the one where women from low or middle-income family are driven to work to generate an income to run the household. They earn to fulfill the basic need of food and shelter for the family. The second type is often defined as the growth entrepreneur; they are the modern, career-oriented, educated women who work to fulfill their self-actualization needs. Many women state that their primary objective to start their entrepreneurial journey is to meet personal and professional goals and go against the gender biasness and stereotypes prevalent in the society (Roffey *et al.*, 1996). Hisrich and Brush conducted one of the first comparative study between women entrepreneurs and minority business owners and they pointed out that the business owners mainly came from middle or upper class of the society and were motivated by their drive for independence (Hisrich & Brush, 1986).

Often, women entrepreneurs seem invisible even though they play an integral part in generating income and well as employment (Sharma, 2018). Globally women entrepreneurs have played an important role in the business development but in India, enterprises by women are still at an early stage with only 7.36% of the enterprises owned by women. Changes in the cultural fabric are needed to increase the number of female entrepreneurs (Garg & Agarwal, 2017).

Economic sustainability is another important factor of home-based business. It helps to create jobs (for the entrepreneurs as well as the few people that they may employ), generation of income and poverty reduction. They help to provide opportunities for micro-entrepreneurs to start an economic venture with minimal capital investment leading to economic participation and economic empowerment of individuals (Kautonen *et al.*, 2010). In addition, home-based business helps in creation of local supply chain, fostering entrepreneurial abilities and skills and promotes additional business associated with it (Anwar & Daniel, 2014).

For any business to have long-term economic success and challenge the ever-increasing competition, it needs to provide a leverage of an improved or innovative product that solves an old problem in a unique way. It often involves taking social responsibility and having deep-rooted edges in the local community as means of long-term sustainability. Sustainability should be treated as competitive advantage (Nadim & Luccier, 2010).

In a market that is becoming more competitive every single day, new paradigm are given importance such as profit is not the only objective of a business, or that profit should be a result of doing the right things. Any business organization, in order to sustain, should have shared interest with the society in which it operates. There is now a limit to economic growth due to the need to preserve natural resources and determining their presence in the future (Barbosa, Castañeda & Ferreira, 2020).

One major aspect of economic sustainability depends on sustainable supply chain, which offers greater opportunity to innovate in the market and help them gain competitive advantage. Appropriate production and distribution is vital for economic growth of such HBB's. They contribute positively towards income generation, employment opportunities and comprehensive growth of the local community and economy in which they operate (Korneeva, Skornichenko & Oruch, 2021).

This review provides a quick encapsulation of the existing literature on HBB. It is a newer phenomenon and it is important to recognize that efforts are to be made towards social, environmental and economic sustainability for the growth and prosperity of any HBB.

CONCLUSION

People have been working at home and from home for time immemorial. However, research has generally failed to draw a clear distinct line between people who are working at home as employees for other businesses and those that are self-employed and run their business from their home. This research paper explored the intricate dynamics of HBB in India. The findings underscore the importance of these enterprises' crucial contributions to employment generation and community development. The study illuminates the challenges faced by HBB like resource/fund scarcity and regulatory hurdles. The comprehensive analysis showcased a symbiotic relationship between success and sustainability visible by the positive impact HBB can have on both environmental and socio-economic aspects. The findings underscore the importance of eco-friendly approaches by HBB that helps in fostering a balance between economic prosperity, social change and environmental stewardship. As HBB continues to evolve, sustainability is not a choice but a strategic decision towards an environmentally conscious and profitable entrepreneurship in India. In essence, this research contributes to the growing body of knowledge on the intersection of entrepreneurship and sustainability. As global landscape evolves, collaborative efforts of policy makers, businesses and society at large can ensure the meaningful contribution of HBB to both economic prosperity and sustainable development in the years to come should be researched.

FUTURE SCOPE

While there is an expanding body of literature on HBB in India, there is a wider future scope that warrants further investigation. The existing literature acknowledges the potential environmental benefits of HBB, such a reduced commuting and physical footprint. However, there is a need for more empirical studies examining the actual environmental practices and impacts of HBB in India. A deeper analysis of energy consumption, waste management, and adoption of eco-friendly practices is needed. While literature also recognizes that HBB can empower women by allowing them to work at their own pace- there is a need for more research that explores the social impact of HBB on women entrepreneurs in India. Research can be done on how HBB owners like assessing the resources, the barriers faced by them and promoting gender equality. While it is acknowledged that HBB contribute to income generation and job creation, there is a need for more in-depth analysis of their economic viability and long-term sustainability. This may include assessing factors such as profitability, expandability, access to finance, and the potential for creating value chains. The existing literature acknowledges also the social stigma associated with home-based businesses. However, further research is needed to explore the specific policy environment and regulatory frameworks in India that impact the sustainability of home-based businesses. This includes examining the effectiveness of existing policies, identifying barriers to growth, and proposing strategies for creating an enabling environment for sustainable home-based businesses.

Addressing future scopes of research will contribute to a more comprehensive understanding of the sustainability of HBB in India and help shape policies and strategies to enhance their positive impact on the environment, society, and economy.

REFERENCES

Anwar, Muhammad Naveed and Daniel, Elizabeth (2014). Online home-based businesses: Systematic literature review and future research agenda.

Alhorr, H.S., Al-Smadi, M.O., Al-Zubi, K.S. and Al-Nassr, M.N. (2017). The Role of Home-Based Businesses in Sustainable Development: An Empirical Study of Women Entrepreneurs in Jordan. *Sustainability,* 9(12), 2229. doi:10.3390/su9122229

Bose, Anjana, Female Entrepreneurship: A Conspectus on Homepreneurs/Mompreneurs (July 15, 2020). Available at SSRN: https://ssrn.com/abstract=3652444 or http://dx.doi.org/10.2139/ssrn.3652444

Carfagna, L.B., Maffei, M.S. and Scorrano, P. (2019). Sustainability and Home-Based Businesses: An Exploratory Study in Italy. Sustainability, 11(9), 2525. doi: 10.3390/su11092525

Dwelly, T., Maguire, K. and Truscott, F. (2005). *Under the Radar: Tracking and Supporting Rural Home Based Businesses.* Report for the Commission for Rural Communities. Live Work Network. Available at: http://www.liveworknet.com/uploads/radar.pdf (accessed 16 May 2013).

Reuschke, D. and Mason, C., "The engagement of home-based businesses in the digital economy," *Futures*, pp. 102-542, 2020.

Garg and Agarwal, *IOSR Journal or Business and Management*, 2017.

Marileide Barbosa, Juan Arturo Castañeda-Ayarza, Denise Helena Lombardo Ferreira, Sustainable Strategic Management (GES): Sustainability in small business.

Hisrich, R.D. and O'Brien, M. (1981). The woman entrepreneur as a reflection of the type of business. In K.H. Vesper (Ed.), Frontiers of entrepreneurial research (pp. 54–67). Boston, MA: Babson College.

Hornstein, T., DeMatteo, D. and Linton, S. (2015). Home-Based Businesses: A Literature Review. *Journal of Research in Marketing and Entrepreneurship*, 17(2), 160-181. doi:10.1108/JRME-02-2015-0016

Hudson, R. (2005). Economic geographies: circuits, flows and spaces, London: Sage.

Journal of Cleaner Production, Volume 258, 2020, 120880, ISSN 0959-6526,

https://doi.org/10.1016/j.jclepro.2020.120880.

Jiao, J., Welch, H. and Moutray, C. (2008/2009). Start-up resources and entrepreneurial discontinuance: The case of nascent entrepreneurs. *Journal of Small Business Strategy*, 19(2), 1–16.

Kautonen, T., Down, S. and Minniti, M. (2010). Ageing and Entrepreneurial Preferences: Global Evidence. Small Business Economics, 34(2), 165-182. doi:10.1007/s11187-008-9156-3.

Knight, Frank H. (1921). Risk, Uncertainty, and Profit. Boston, MA: Hart, Schaffner & Marx; Houghton Mifflin Company.

Korneeva, Elena, Skornichenko, Natalia and Oruch, Tatiana (2021). Small business and its place in promoting sustainable development. E3S Web of Conferences, 250. 06007. 10.1051/e3sconf/202125006007.

Kundu, S.C. and Ray, S. (2018). Impact of Women Empowerment on Entrepreneurship Development in India: An Exploratory Study. *International Journal of Gender and Entrepreneurship*, 10(4), 371-392. doi:10.1108/IJGE-08-2017-0042

Lussier, R.N. and Pfeifer, S. (2000). A comparison of business success versus failure variables between U.S. and Central Eastern Europe Croatian entrepreneurs. *Entrepreneurship Theory and Practice*, 24(4), 59–67.

Mamingi, Nlandu (2011). *Journal of Economics and Sustainable Development* www.iiste.org ISSN 2222-1700 (Paper) ISSN 2222-2855 (Online) Vol.2, No. 11&12, 2011.

Mason, C., Carter, S. and Tagg, S. (2008) *Invisible Businesses: The Characteristics of Home-Based Businesses in the United Kingdom*, WP-o8-01. Glasgow: Strathclyde University.

Mead, D.C. and Morrison, C. (1996). The infor-mal sector elephant, World Development, 24, pp. 1611–1619.

Melissa, Ezmieralda, Hamidati, Anis, Saraswati, Muninggar and Flor, Alexander (2013). Investigating the potentials of social media to support women entrepreneurship in Indonesian urban areas, 2. 92–95. 10.1145/2517899.2517921.

Nadim, A. and Lussier, R.N. "Sustainability as a Small Business Competitive Strategy". *Journal of Small Business Strategy (archive Only)*, Vol. 21, No. 2, May 2010, pp. 79–95, https://libjournals.mtsu.edu/index.php/jsbs/article/view/145.

Wynarczyk, P. and Graham, J., "The impact of connectivity technology on home-based business venturing: The case of women in the North East of England," *Local Economy: The Journal of the Local Economy Policy Unit,* Vol. 28, No. 5, pp. 451–470, 2013.

Roffey, B., Stanger, A., Forsaith, D., McInnes, E., Petrone, F. and Symes, C. (1996). Women in small business: A review of research. Canberra: Australian Government Publishing Service.

Sicat, M. (2007). Impact of improved communication on women's transport needs and empowerment in Bangladesh. In Gender and transport (Transport and communications bulletin for Asia and the Pacific, Vol. 76, pp. 72–88). New York: United Nations Economic and Social.

Sharma, S. (2018). Emerging dimensions of women entrepreneurship: developments & obstructions. Economic Affairs, 63(2), 295372.

Shin, J. (2014). New business model creation through the triple helix of young entrepreneurs, SNSs, and smart devices. *International Journal of Technology Management,* 66(4): 302–318.

Swanepoel, E. and Strydom, J.W. (2009). Analysis of criteria for selecting potential entrepreneurs. Unpublished research. Pretoria: University of South Africa.

Thomas, A.S. and Mueller, S.L. (2000). A Case for Comparative Entrepreneurship: Assessing the Relevance of Culture. *J. Int. Bus Stud Second Quarter,* 31(2), 287–299.

Alkhowaiter, W., "The power of Instagram in building small businesses," in Social Media: The Good, the Bad and the Ugly, *IFIP Conference, Swansea*, 2016, pp. 1–729.

Zhang, H., Lu, Y., Gao, P. and Chen, Z. (2014). Social shopping communities as an emerging business model of youth entrepreneurship: exploring the effects of website characteristics, *International Journal of Technology Management,* 66(4): 319–345.

Impact of Green Packaging and Labeling of Durable Goods on Consumers' Evaluation and Choice: A Study Based in Kolkata Metropolis

Dr. Shivaji Banerjee[1], Sneha Singhania[2] and Subhabrata Mitra[3]

ABSTRACT: Sustainable growth and environmental conservation have emerged as global issues of concern in the recent 21st century. Growing public awareness of the harsh consequences of the depletion of natural resources and consumption of synthetic petrochemicals has generated a group of cautious green consumers who prioritize, prefer and promote products that are cautiously packaged with safe and biodegradable material and have an eco label. This study examines the impact of eco-packaging and eco-labelling of durable goods on consumers' purchase decisions. It shall provide a valuable insight into the preferences and choices of prospective customers which shall enable marketers to boost sales whilst complying to environmental norms. A cross-sectional survey had been employed to collect data from 300 respondents of Kolkata. SPSS was used to analyze the collected data for descriptive study and to test the created hypothesis. The study shall also elucidate the altering trends of packaging and labeling of consumer durables.

***Keywords:** Eco-packaging, Eco-labelling, Green Consumer, Environmental Awareness.*

INTRODUCTION

In an era marked by escalating environmental concerns and a growing awareness of sustainability, the intersection between consumer behavior and eco-friendly practices has become a focal point of scholarly inquiry. Among the myriad avenues through which individuals engage with environmental consciousness, packaging and labeling stand out as pivotal elements influencing consumer perceptions and choices regarding consumer durables. This research endeavors to unravel the intricate dynamics surrounding the impact of green packaging and labeling on consumers' evaluation and decisions concerning product purchase and choice. As industries increasingly pivot toward environmentally responsible practices, understanding how consumers

[1] Senior Assistant Professor in Management, PG and Research Department of Commerce, St. Xavier's College (Autonomous), Kolkata, Visiting Faculty, University of Calcutta and IISWBM.

[2] Former Assistant Professor at St. Xavier's University, Kolkata.

[3] Visiting Faculty, Department of Business Administration, THK Jain College, Kolkata.

respond to and prioritize green packaging and labeling becomes not only academically pertinent but also imperative for businesses striving to align with evolving societal values. This investigation aims to shed light on the nuanced interplay between eco-friendly packaging and consumers' decision-making processes, offering insights that can inform both marketing strategies and sustainable product development. Through a comprehensive exploration of consumer attitudes, preferences, and behaviors based on primary data, this study seeks to contribute valuable knowledge to the ongoing discourse on sustainable consumption, bridging the gap between theoretical understanding and practical implications for businesses and policymakers alike.

SIGNIFICANCE OF THE STUDY

Green packaging and labeling significantly affect a consumers' evaluation and choice in the contemporary global landscape as environmental consciousness has become a pivotal factor in decision-making processes. As consumers increasingly prioritize sustainability, green packaging is viewed by them as the organization's commitment to ecological responsibility and a tangible manifestation of a brand's dedication to reduce its environmental footprint. Consumers, now more than ever, seek products that align with their values and beliefs. Additionally, transparent and informative labeling provides consumers with the necessary information to make eco-conscious choices, fostering trust and loyalty. In essence, the impact of green packaging and labeling extends beyond mere aesthetics, influencing consumers to make ethical and sustainable choices that contribute to a greener and more socially responsible marketplace. This shift in consumer mindset has put adequate pressure on businesses to adopt sustainable packaging practices. As a result, companies are revamping their product strategies to meet the evolving expectations of environmentally conscious consumers. This study shall provide the practitioners with essential details required to execute the theory into profitable practices.

LITERATURE REVIEW

In the wake of escalating environmental concerns and the need for sustainable practices, the realm of packaging has undergone a profound paradigm shift. Green packaging, defined by its commitment to ecological responsibility and resource efficiency, has emerged as a pivotal solution to mitigate the environmental impact of traditional packaging practices.

Eco-packaging or green packaging concepts are designed to help consumers distinguish products that are kinder to the planet than other similar products and promote environmentally conscious consumption. The concept of green packaging is essential for achieving the Sustainable Development Goal (Fonseca*et al.*, 2020). According to Gopinath (2019), customers are concerned about the ingredients when they buy fast-moving edible consumer goods (FMCG). They favor items made with organic, nontoxic ingredients over others. This forces the manufacturers to adapt to their market by being green in all aspects, including marketing and production. One of the competitive tactics that businesses can think about implementing is green packaging (Tuwanku, Rohman and Rofiq, 2018). Green packaging can help businesses optimize their use of materials, resources, and waste to meet their sustainability goals on the economic, social, and environmental fronts (Maziriri, 2018).

Steeniset *al.* (2017) stated customers are receptive to green packaging that is more sustainable. Scott and Vigar-Ellis (2014) revealed that the customers had insufficient understanding of ecologically friendly packaging for organic food, its advantages, and how to distinguish it from conventional packaging. Tomsik and Kutnohorska (2013) proposed that consumers of organic food exhibit distinct attitudes, beliefs, and behaviors towards health care. The majority of customers value their health highly and believe that eating organic food is healthier than eating conventional food. According to Mohamed (2016), green packaging refers to the use of production techniques and materials for goods packaging that have minimal effects on both the environment and energy consumption. Molina-Beach (2016) opined that there are three key characteristics of green packaging: using less packaging that is difficult to break down, choosing packaging that uses less energy, and choosing environmentally beneficial packaging. Recognition of the eco-label positively affects consumers' propensity to purchase green products based on their information. (Rokka and Uusitalo, 2008) revealed that customers now place a higher value on environmental protection, with green packaging being a key factor in their decision-making. The presence of moral reasoning in the selection of product packaging is primarily influenced by the perception of significant environmental impacts and the absence of other significant factors, such as a high price, in the specific purchasing scenario.

Factors like environmental concerns and the absence of other highly involving characteristics play a crucial role in shaping consumer attitudes towards green packaging (Thogersen, 1999) The idea of eco-friendly packaging is relatively new, but it has gained a lot of attention lately. To cut down on resources, increase recycled content, and provide more renewable materials for packaging, global corporations are concentrating on improving packaging.

This literature review aims to provide a comprehensive grasp on the dynamics shaping the green packaging landscape by synthesizing information from a variety of sources. It also aims to offer helpful insights for researchers, industry professionals, and policymakers who are attempting to navigate the complex intersection of packaging practices and environmental sustainability and its impact on the consumer's mind.

RESEARCH GAP

It can be culminated from the available literature that green packaging and labeling is a rapidly evolving concept that impacts the evaluation process and purchase choices of prospective buyers. It also makes consumers more aware and cautious of the deteriorating plight of our natural resources which are limited means supporting our endless wants. Adequate knowledge of the demographic variables of customers who prefer biodegradable packaging and of the various parameters that promote the sales of environment-friendly products is of extreme importance to entrepreneurs in shaping their marketing strategies. However, a thorough analysis of the available secondary data revealed that limited empirical studies have been undertaken to analyze the impact of green packaging and labeling of durable goods on consumers' evaluation and purchase decisions. There is also a dearth of research that analyzes the association between environmental awareness and purchase patterns of durables for urban consumers. This research makes a humble attempt to bridge the gap between the available and desired literature.

RESEARCH OBJECTIVES

- ***Primarily***, to identify the demographic characteristics of consumers who consciously attempt to purchase products with green packages and eco-labels.
- ***Furthermore***, to examine the relationship between environmental awareness and consumers' purchase behaviour.
- ***Lastly***, to summarize the recent eco-friendly trends that are shaping and revamping the industry of durable goods.

THEORETICAL FRAMEWORK

Green Packaging—The New Norm

Green packaging or sustainable packaging is an attempt to employ methods and materials in product packaging that diminishes exploitation of natural resources and energy consumption. It involves a radical shift from plastic and other synthetic substances to biodegradable and recyclable materials that reduce the harmful impacts of packaging on the environment. It is a conscious effort to keep a check on the pollution levels in the environment.

As stated by Mitra and Pandya (2012), sustainable packaging has obtained consistent growth in the last decade due to the budding alarms over environmental hazards, carbon emissions and waste reduction objectives indicated by various countries. There is an accelerated search for bio based packaging material by corporates, government and even eco-conscious consumers as they now have a more holistic view towards packaging efficiency for a safe environment.

Consumers have evolved from the use of leaves, shells, pottery, baskets and hollow logs for product packaging to glass, paper, metallic tins and other hard board containers. The 20th century witnessed the revolutionization of the packaging industry after the introduction of the highly moldable, durable, low cost and lightweight plastic films. The traditional materials used for sealing products were instantly replaced by the widely available plastic sheets. However, plastic was brought under scrutiny when studies indicated the extreme health and environmental hazard created by this synthetic chemical. As per Mishra and Sharma (2010) green packaging seemed to be the solution to the problem of environmental degradation. Hence began the conversion from the traditional plastic dominated packaging industry to environmental friendly, sustainable alternatives of product packaging and handling.

Environmental Performance Certification or Eco Labels

A voluntary method of performance certification, eco labels identify products or services that are environmentally preferable within a specific category. They are attainable, verifiable and measurable and are published for the information and inspection of the prospective consumer segment. It is a deliberate attempt to transparently address the environmental and health impacts of the commodity through its entire product life cycle. Hence as stated by Sahu (2012), eco labels are voluntary market based instruments which are extensively used by corporations to show their environmental responsibility and at the same time to promote sustainable production and consumption.

In India, the intensive demand for eco-friendly products pressurized the government to launch the eco mark scheme in 1991. It is a symbol for ecologically friendly products that comply with the specific quality parameters mentioned as a part of the scheme. An integral part of environmental branding, eco labeling motivates buyers to make aware choices and prefer products and services that are safer for consumption as well as impose no threat on the environment.

Sustainable practices in business operation tamper the cost budget of an organization. It is expensive due to high cost of technology, high licensing cost of eco labels, bureaucratic procedures, premium raw materials and high cost of effective waste disposal management. An insight into the long-term gains motivates entrepreneurs to replace their convention offerings with greener versions that comply with prevailing environmental, social and health regulations of a country.

REVOLUTIONIZING THE INDUSTRY OF CONSUMER DURABLES

In the modern era of globalization, greater awareness, stiffer government regulations, escalated competition and altering trends urge organizations to adopt greener practices in the manufacturing and sale of durable goods. Besides it being a moral obligation for companies to be more environmentally responsible, sustainable practices also smoothen the achievement of the corporate objective of profit maximization. The certain specific measures that have been adopted by companies selling durable goods to make a greener offering are:

- Educating the customers about ***how the packaging material should be disposed of*** or if it can be recycled or reused. For instance shoes like that of Puma come in good quality cardboard boxes that can be reused to reduce the quantity of waste generated.
- Reducing your ecological footprint can be in the form of ***reducing the packaging materials.*** Smaller boxes, bags, and containers not only lowers the shipping cost but also is a more sustainable choice. This can be achieved by using fewer filler materials. For instance, apparels can be tightly folded or bundled so that they fit in smaller boxes.
- ***Recycled packaging*** is a great way to extend the life of previously used materials. Paperboard made by paper pulp is lightweight and can easily be given various forms and is also one of the most common examples of recycled packaging. For instance the global company, Calvin Klein is cent percent committed to using recycled material for packaging.
- ***Plantable packaging*** are materials that can be planted. They have seeds embedded in them that can be planted after they've been used. Apart from being used as fillers or wraps, plantable packaging works great for containing small and lightweight items such as cosmetics or jewelry. For instance, Sow and Grow, a Mumbai-based firm, has plantable packaging composed of paper and seeds that can be planted and grown into various herbs and vegetables.
- ***Paid carry bags*** compel shoppers to be prepared with means to take back their shopped products. This is a conscious attempt made by all the big brands to reduce its generated waste and to encourage reuse. Many companies also have devised the strategy of 'shopping bag for life' wherein additional discounts are given to customers who carry their previously purchased shopping bag.
- In case of specific durables like electronics and furniture, customers are more cautious to check out the eco label to ensure themselves of the controlled impact of the commodity on the environment. Companies go an extra mile to procure such ***eco marks*** in order to sustain in the market.

Hence the industry of durable goods is altering its means of operations in order to maximize its returns in the long run and be aligned with a more ecologically conscious and aware society.

RESEARCH METHODOLOGY

Research Design

The study conducted is descriptive in nature as it provides a detailed understanding of the demographic characteristics of customers who prefer products with bio degradable packages and eco-labels. It also categorizes as an quantitative study as the collection and analysis of data has been quantified to ensure statistically bounded results.

Data Collection

The primary data for the study has been obtained using self-administered, structured questionnaires. It focused upon extracting personal details of the respondents required for detailed demographic analysis. Specific questions were drafted for gauging the level of environmental awareness of the chosen consumers. Response to the parameters that influence product evaluation and purchase behaviour of the prospective customers were obtained on a five-point Likert scale to assess the variation in the frequency of specific purchase habits. Vital details regarding respondents' intentions to purchase products with green packages and eco-labels were also acquired from the questionnaire.

Sampling Design

The urban consumers of Kolkata metropolis constituted the population for this research. Since the study focuses upon biodegradable packaging, eco-labels and green marketing, the rural were eliminated from the population. Environmental awareness, behavioral patterns and the need hierarchy of the rural consumer base is immensely distinct from the urban dwellers. Hence, to avoid complexities the study only focused upon the urban population.

A total sample size of 300 respondents was chosen in order to complete the survey. The sample elements were selected on the basis of the snowball technique because the area of study was vast and the subject of green packaging and eco-labels is comparatively new and in its budding stage in the society. Care was taken to ensure utmost accuracy of data collection by selecting those respondents who *w*ere familiar with the concept of green marketing.

DATA ANALYSIS AND INTERPRETATION

Descriptive Analysis

The above figures summarize the demographic profile of the respondents in relation to their conscious attempt to purchase eco-friendly products. Figure 1 reflects that though the majority of the respondents were male but a greater percentage of female

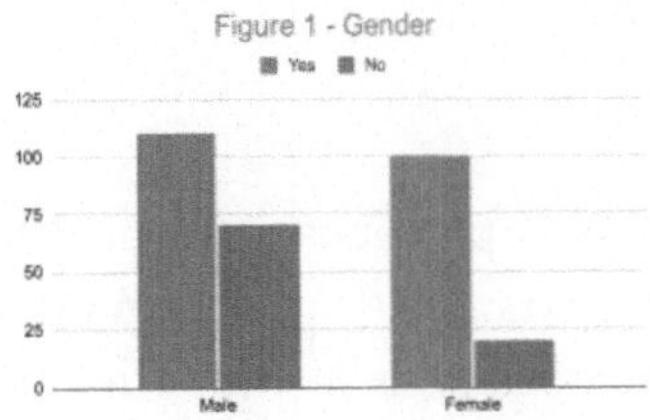

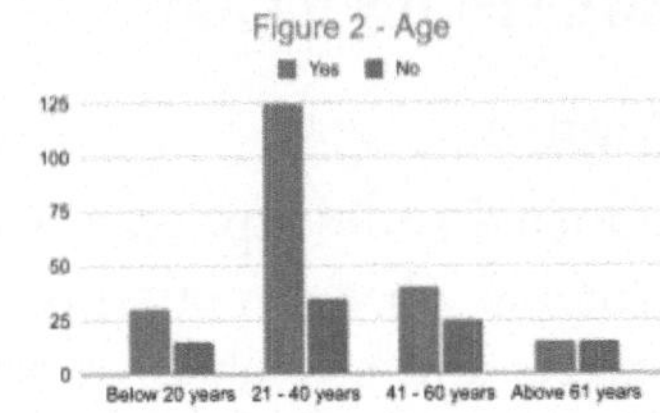

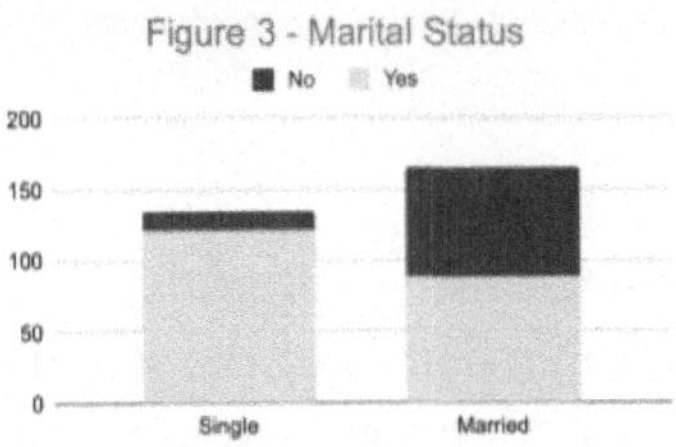

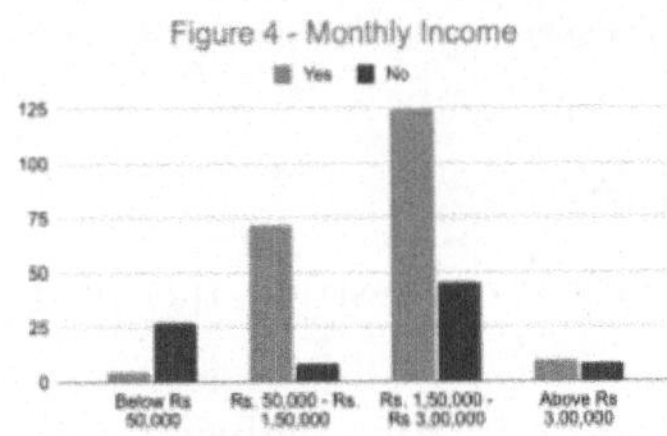

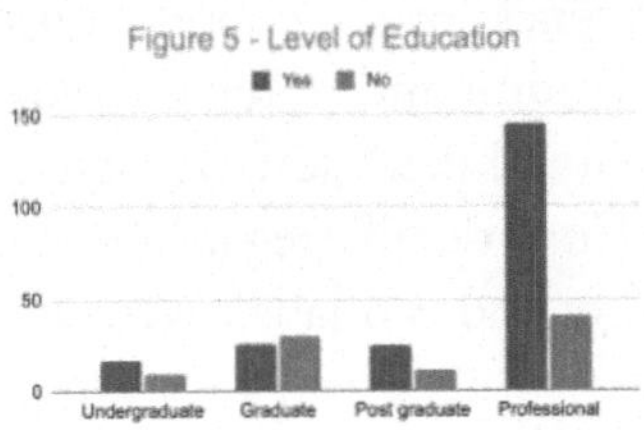

Source: Developed for the study

buyers preferred and purchased green products. In accordance with Figure 2, maximum elements of the chosen sample were in the age group of 21–40 years and that consumers who were above 60 years of age were indifferent toward the environmental impact of their product choices. Figure 3 reveals that though the majority of the respondents were married, a greater percentage of single consumers attempted to make eco-friendly product choices. It can be observed from Figure 4 that maximum respondents earned Rs. 1.5 lacs to Rs. 3 lacs per month and that those consumers who earned less than Rs. 50,000 per month were extremely price sensitive and hence did not willingly purchase greener products that came for a higher cost. Figure 5 highlights that professionals constituted the majority of the sample and that they also mostly preferred to evaluate the environmental impact of their product choices.

Factor Analysis

1. Factor analysis was conducted for the various parameters that indicate the level of environmental awareness of the selected sample. This assisted in reduction of variables and in making the data more composite for hypothesis testing. A KMO Test was used to assess the suitability of the data for Factor Analysis. The chosen significance level was 5% i.e. the value of p should be lesser than 0.05.

Table 1 - KMO and Bartlett's Test

Kaiser-Meyer-Olkin Measure of Sampling Adequacy.		.914
Bartlett's Test of Sphericity	Approx. Chi-Square	5639.621
	Sig.	.001

Source: Developed for the research

Table 2 - Component Score Coefficient Matrix

	Component
	1
Mankind is abusing the environment	0.077
Sustainable Development is the key to growth	0.081
Companies should be bound to comply with environmental laws	0.081
Individual efforts to reduce pollution is vital	0.072
Responsibility of every citizen to protect the environment	0.079
Eco-friendly products should only be promoted	0.082
Green products are beneficial for customers	0.072
Urgent attention is needed to prevent further deterioration	0.075
Extraction Method: Principal Component Analysis.	

Table 1 concludes that the KMO measure is 0.914 which ensures that the variables are suited for factor analysis. Since p value is 0.001 which is lesser than 0.05 it is also significant at 5%. Table 2 summarizes that 1 component was extracted after conducting a factor analysis for the various parameters that judge the level of environmental awareness of the consumers.

2. A factor analysis was also conducted for the purchase habits of consumers. This was done to reduce the volume of data and make it suitable for hypothesis testing. If the KMO measure for the given variables would be more than 0.50 then it would indicate that the chosen variables are suitable for factor analysis.

Table 3 - KMO and Bartlett's Test

Kaiser-Meyer-Olkin Measure of Sampling Adequacy.		.788
Bartlett's Test of Sphericity	Approx. Chi-Square	569.151
	df	45
	Sig.	.001

Source: Developed for the study

Table 4 - Component Matrix

I buy products that have a biodegradable packaging	.776
I prefer packaging in reusable containers	.728
I do not mind paying extra for sustainable packaging	.610
I evaluate sellers on the basis of their product packaging	.730
I believe green packaging improves brand image	.606
I check for eco labels before buying products	.919
I understand the information given in the eco labels	.738
I feel confident in purchasing products with eco labels	.872
I prefer products with eco labels	.801
Eco labels differentiate green products from non-green versions	.923
Extraction Method: Principal Component Analysis.	

Table 3 summarizes that the KMO measure is 0.788 which ascertains that the chosen variables are suitable for factor analysis. One component was extracted using the principal component analysis which can be observed from table 4. The extracted variable summarizes the purchase habits of customers and is an indication of how environmentally inclined a consumer is.

HYPOTHESIS TESTING

H0: There is no relationship between environmental awareness and purchase behaviour of a consumer.

H1: There is a relationship between environmental awareness and purchase behaviour of a consumer.

Table 5: Chi-Square Tests

	Value	df	Asymptotic Significance (2-sided)
Pearson Chi-Square	868.842[a]	153	.001
Likelihood Ratio	713.127	153	.001
N of Valid Cases	300		

Source: Developed for the research

The non parametric test of Pearson Chi Square Test shall be used to solve the above hypothesis. It shall examine whether there is any relationship between environmental awareness and purchase behaviour of consumers related to durable goods. The chosen significance level is 5% i.e. p value of less than 0.05 shal lead to the rejection of the null hypothesis. The adjoining table reveals that the asymptotic significance value is less than 5% and hence the null hypothesis is rejected. This leads to the acceptance of the alternate hypothesis that there is a relationship between environmental awareness and purchase behaviour of consumers.

RESULT AND FINDINGS

The study brought to attention the pressing issue of sustainable development and the need to revamp the production, selling and marketing processes by entrepreneurs required for long term survival and growth of companies. The specific contributions of this paper are:

- The demographic profile of consumers who are more sensitive towards packaging and labeling and opt for environmental-friendly options was highlighted in this research.

- The new trends of sustainable packaging in the industry of durable goods was gathered and summarized as a part of this study. This shall enable practitioners to alter their ways of operation and cater to a larger customer base.
- The formulated hypothesis as a part of the study also revealed that the level of environmental awareness impacts the purchase behaviour of a consumer. Hence indicating the need of making citizens of the country more aware about the plight of their natural resources which shall thereby help them to make wise product choices.

SCOPE OF FUTURE RESEARCH

Eco-friendly packaging and labeling is an emerging area of research that has immense scope in terms of further study. It is a dynamic phenomenon with several of its attributes still in its initial stages of exploration. The study conducted by us can provide valuable data to not only the practitioners but also the scholars. However, it also has several areas of improvement, such as:

1. The findings are based on the analysis of only 300 questionnaires. Future researchers may increase the sample size to increase the accuracy of the research.
2. The sample was collected only from the Kolkata metropolis. In order to gain a more dynamic view, the geographical area of the study should be widened and respondents could be chosen from other countries and states.
3. Several other broader variables such as green branding and green marketing can be included in the study to gain a more comprehensive view and to understand the influence of these attributes upon each other.

IMPLICATIONS OF THE STUDY

The alarming rate at which the natural resources are being exploited and the pollution indexes are soaring up necessitates the need to derive a sustainable approach in fulfilling the demands of the consumer. This study will encourage visionary entrepreneurs to willingly accept the additional costs of eco-friendly products in order to gain an edge in the market and lawfully survive in the long run. Not only does the study highlight the altering notions of the modern consumer but also provides evidence to the claim that the modern, literate customer is concerned about the environment and prefers eco-friendly products. Packaging which contributes to a large percentage of generated waste can be efficiently curbed by adopting the improvised techniques of sustainable packaging as outlined in this study. The impact of environment performance certification has also been detailed for the practitioners indicating the need of acquiring appropriate eco-marks.

CONCLUSION

In conclusion, this academic investigation into "The Impact of Green Packaging and Labeling on Consumers' Evaluation and Choice of durable goods"; has shed light on the multifaceted relationship between environmentally conscious packaging and consumer behavior. The findings underscore the growing significance of sustainable packaging in influencing consumers' perceptions and choices. In recent times there is an evident shift of consumer preferences towards environmentally friendly options. As industries continue to navigate the evolving landscape of consumer awareness and environmental concerns, integrating green packaging strategies presents not only a moral imperative but also a strategic advantage. This research contributes valuable insights to the discourse on sustainable business practices, urging businesses to strive for a more sustainable future. The findings of this study encourage stakeholders across industries to actively engage in eco-conscious practices that resonate positively with consumers and contribute to the global movement toward environmental responsibility.

REFERENCES

Cherian, J. and Jacob, J. (2012). Green marketing: A study of consumers' attitude towards environment friendly products. *Asian Social Science*, 8, 117–126.

Fonseca, L.M.; Domingues, J.P.; Dima, A.M. Mapping the sustainable development goals relationships. *Sustainability* 2020, 12, 3359.

Gopinath, R. (2019 b). Factors Influencing Consumer Decision Behaviour in FMCG. *International Journal of Research in Social Sciences*, 9(7), 249–255.

Maziriri, E.T., Mapuranga, M. and Madinga, N.W. (2018).Self-service banking and financial literacy as prog-nosticators of business performance among rural small and medium-sized enterprises in Zimbabwe. *Southern African Journal of Entrepreneurship and Small Business Management,* 10(1), 1–10.

Mishra, P. and Sharma, P. (2010). 'Green marketing in India: Emerging opportunities and challenges', *Journal of Engineering, Science and Management Education,* Vol. 3, No. 1, pp. 9–14.

Mitra, A. and Pandya, P. (2012). 'Assessing the Environmental Impact', *Modern Packaging & Design,* Vol. 8, No. 2, pp. 30–32.

Mohamed, S.N.S. (2016). The factors of practicing green packaging adoption among the food industry around Melaka. Project Report. Melaka, Malaysia: Universiti Teknikal Malaysia Melaka UTeM.

Molina-Besch, K. (2016). Prioritization guidelines for green food packaging development. British Food Journal, 118, 2512–2533.

Olga Kutnohorska, Pavel Tomsik, "Consumers perception of the health aspects of organic Food" Agric.Econ.czech, 59, 2013 (7): 293–299.

Pirsch, J., Gupta, S. and Grau, S.L. (2007). A framework for understanding corporate social responsibility. *Journal of Business Ethics*, 70,125–140.

Rokka, J. and Uusitalo, L. (2008). Preference for green packaging in consumer product choices – Do consumers care? *International Journal of Consumer Studies*, 32: 516–525.

Sahu, T. (2012). Green marketing: an attitudinal and behavioural analysis of consumers in Pune. *Symbiosis International University*, Pune, 15–20.

Scott, L.; Vigar-Ellis, D. Consumer understanding, perceptions and behaviours with regard to environmentally friendly packaging in a developing nation. *Int. J. Consum. Stud.* 2014, 38, 642–649.

Steenis, N.D., van Herpen, E., van der Lans, I.A., Ligthart, T.N. and van Trijp, H.C.M. (2017). Consumer response to packaging design: The role of packaging materials and graphics in sustainability perceptions and product evaluations. *Journal of Cleaner Production*, 162, 286–298.

Thogersen, J. (1999). The ethical consumer. Moral norms and packaging choice. *Journal of Consumer Psychology*, 439–460.

Tuwanku, A.A., Rohman, F. and Rofiq, A. (2018a). Does green packaging matter as a business strategy? Exploring young consumers' consumption in an emerging market. *Problems and Perspectives in Management*, 16(2), 376–384.

12

Leveraging Sustainability through Green Practices in CSR

Dr. Ratna Sinha[1]

ABSTRACT: Environmental consciousness is no longer a choice for business continuity; rather it is a necessity to ensure the sustainability of the business. The adaptations of green practices, are determined by the mind-set and acceptance to the changes by the workforce. Driven by some of the initiatives such as the agility and resilience built through cultural development, environment of acceptance and training on lateral and creative thinking, have been playing a role in moving in the right direction. The paper examines the dovetailing of environmental management initiatives in business. We frame these sustainable practices under the umbrella of corporate social responsibility (CSR) and discuss the role and relevance environmentally focused CSR plays in professional organization. The research findings suggest that CSR activities be embedded in the organizational environmental strategies for green innovation leading to firm's performance and sustainability.

Keywords: *Green Practices, CSR, Environment, Sustainability, Sustainable Business.*

BACKGROUND

The quest for equitable, inclusive and sustainable growth is a visible need. To build a society, which provides equal access to opportunities, negates disparities is a collective responsibility. Corporate Social Responsibility (CSR) is a strategic issue, which permeates departmental boundaries and influences the way organization does its business and relate with its stakeholders. A.C. Nielsen's 2014 Global Survey on CSR, released on 18th June 2014 shows that 55 percent of global online consumers across 60countries are willing to pay more for such products from those organization practicing the socially responsible environmental norms.

INTRODUCTION

Environmental consciousness is no longer a choice for business continuity; rather it is a necessity to ensure the sustainability of the business. The adaptations of green practices, becomes determining factor led by the mind-set and acceptance to the changes by the workforce. The practise, through some of the initiatives such as the

---

[1] Fellow XLRI in OB, Consultant – HR Advisory.

agility and resilience built through cultural development, environment of acceptance and training on lateral and creative thinking as well as affirmations, reiterations of values, ethical practices that the organization stands for has paved the way. As a concept, green practices through corporate social responsibility (CSR), encourages businesses to think about the environment in which they work in order to improve their reputation and gain the reciprocity of their stakeholders. CSR is ultimately a strategic issue, and not bracketed as a silo function and forms or embedded, in the overall strategy of the company. The quest for equitable, inclusive and sustainable growth is a visible need. To build a society, which provides equal access to opportunities, negates disparities is a collective responsibility. Green practices through, CSR is a strategic issue which permeates departmental boundaries and influences the way organization does its business and relate with its stakeholders. Berman *et al.* (1999) and Kapstein (2001), state that over the past decade firms have come under increasing pressure to pursue socially responsive behaviour from a variety of stakeholder groups including shareholders, employees, investors, consumers and managers.

CSR AND ITS RELATION TO THE ORGANIZATION

CSR refers to strategies that companies implement as part of corporate governance to ensure that their operations are ethical and beneficial to society. In this paper, we have a synopsis of a manufacturing organization, which strives forward in sustainable practices and thereby displaying responsible green behaviour. To maintain confidentiality we name the organization as XYZ Limited. Numerous studies, have affirmed "green behaviour" as an individual behaviour contributes to environmental sustainability. This encourages businesses to develop green innovation. The employees those who are environmentally conscious, add value to the company's image and brand as they work, as face-to-face employees, engaging directly with the customers and community. An organization when it provides volunteering opportunities to its employees, which is a way in XYZ Limited, makes employees even more responsible for their green initiatives and thereby collectively upholding the banner of sustainability. "Green behaviour" includes employees' actions to perform work in an environmentally friendly manner (De Roeck and Farooq); where recycling, resource conservation, participation in environmental initiatives, and the implementation of more environmentally friendly policies are some of the ways, which the organization engages. When a company provides a work environment valuing environmental concerns, the company's innovations always elevate environmental values. This study attempts to bridge this gap by establishing the role of green behaviour as a mediator between CSR and firm performance. The study draws its research and inputs from Social Identity Theory.

SOCIAL IDENTIFICATION THEORY (SIT) AND ORGANIZATION IDENTIFICATION – HOW IT IS RELATED IN CSR

A social identity is the portion of an individual's self- concept derived perceived membership in a relevant social group. Henri Taifel and John Turner originally formulated this in the 1970s and the 1980s. Social Identity Theory (SIT) introduces the concept of a social identity as a way in which to explain intergroup behavior.

In the paper of Tziner *et al.* (2011) mention about social identity theory (Tajfel & Turner, 1986), the perception of a firm as a socially responsible member of society is likely to afford employees an enhanced self-image, pride, the feelings of which impact positively on work attitudes such as job satisfaction (Peterson, 2004). Social identity theory, posits that individuals seek to be part of attractive groups, and upon entry into those groups, describe themselves and others in terms of their group identity (Ashforth and Mael, 1989). Ashforth and Mael, (1989); Dutton *et al.* (1994) state that within SIT, an individual's view of themselves, their 'self- concept', is influenced by their membership of social organization for which the individual works.

Organizational identification has been defined by (Ashforth, Harrison and Corley 2008), as the extent to which a person senses an oneness or being same with the organization. In fact, we can see how an individual addresses in different organizations "ians" after the short abbreviation of the company's name.

Individuals have a strong desire to view their self-definitions in positive terms and seek to enhance their self-esteem through their social identities (Hogg and Abrams, 1990; Tajfel and Turner, 1986).

Sen and Bhattacharya (2001) in their research mention on SIT that organizational identification research draws from SIT suggesting, that people are more likely to identify with an organization when they perceive its identity to be enduring, distinctive and capable of enhancing one's self esteem.

Therefore, we can draw from the above that social identity theory is closely linked with organizational identity and subsequently understanding the theoretical base as a framework and backdrop, employees' participation in individualised green behaviour through CSR initiatives seems a possibility or rather a natural outcome.

RESPONSIBLE CORPORATE CITIZENSHIP

'Responsible Corporate Citizenship' is one of the six strategic pillar objectives of this organization. The company has its plant operating in a locality with nearly 54% population from the SC and ST community. The company is leveraging this scope to plan and implement CSR programs to address various socio-economic issues faced by the people and in turn gain confidence and goodwill from the community. The moral support and confidence of the adjoining community provide comfort and enables improved goodwill, which is important and essential for company's growth plans. Based on various surveys, the understanding of the community requirements is determined. Subsequently the activities and initiatives planned provide support for 6Es i.e., Education, Essential Enablers, Employability, Entrepreneurship, Empowerment and Environment.

The above initiatives are aligned to the Company's Vision, Mission and Values. It is approved monitored and reviewed by the different committees starting from the Board level, to senior leadership apex committee, external members of the council team, as well as the monthly performance committee The objective, to embrace the CSR initiatives is primarily to leverage the sustainable business advantages through community development and betterment. Being at a proximity of underdeveloped society becomes imperative to extend the support and improve the comfort of the adjoining community through objective driven initiatives. The 'Education' and 'Employment' Strategy and Plan is bucketed as 'short term' (3 years) and 'long term' (5 years). Understanding the quality and merit constraints, the organization faces the challenge to groom the prospective youth strength to become eligible for the competition. To do so the company is focusing on improving the quality of education right from the primary level through its Schools Project – working on improving the access, learning and governance in government school for overall improvement in school level education. It further extends to college level – providing scholarships to meritorious students from marginalized communities. Continuing from the Education vertical, Employability initiatives such as Diploma Engineering, BSc. Nursing, General Nursing & Midwifery and Short-term training at its Skill Development Centre with an aim to improve the scope for direct and indirect employment at various levels. Further, focusing on the environmental sustainability, the company through its CSR is promoting plantation in the villages to increase the green cover and carbon sequestration. This principle has given the purpose and context to the short and long-term plan for company's green practices of CSR initiatives.

The CSR initiatives of XYZ Limited, continues to design in ways, which have positive impact on the community and the environment. The programs planned and implemented on participatory mode to ensure sustainability.

The Company has taken few initiatives for preserving our environment. They have planted approximately 50,000 indigenous plants in the surrounding community area. This is an ongoing activity year on year. The community people protect the plantation, as they understand both economic and environmental returns.

The initiatives on livelihood for the people dependent on agriculture and agri-allied are designed in manner that would result in economic development of the people without affecting negatively on the environment. For example – Promoting integrated pond-based livelihood, fish culture using scientific methods, promoting organic farming through use of vermi-compost, promoting System of Rice Intensification (SRI) etc. The technologies are helping in low degradation of soil and other natural resources, hence contributing for sustainable agricultural growth. Further, each house or hamlet in the village has a kitchen garden. The villages are encouraged and supported for 'goatery', 'duckery' and poultry (rearing goats, ducks and Chicken). Self –help groups within the community makes it easier for taking the initiatives forward after the initial hand holding by the company. This is an example of how practices made sustainable, which has helped XYZ Limited to take on newer initiatives, widen their scope, and scale their reach too.

The Company has introduced solar model of drinking water system, which uses solar energy to operate the pump for drawing water and supplying to the marginalized families. The use of solar model is helping in running the drinking water plant without electricity; thus helping to preserve our environment.

The company's performance has affected in a positive way. There is an enhanced year on year performance benefitting all the stakeholders. Within the factory premises too the Green House, solar panels, bio- degradable waste processing. Further, it is ensured through the procurement and marketing team it well cascaded to their vendor partners by laying out norms, are some initiatives which has created a green ambience inside and outside, impacting all stakeholders.

The above narrative gives us a synopsis of how CSR does have a positive impact on employee green behaviour. It also shows an over-all impact, in the organization on the enhanced company performance. The effort ploughed also goes back with even more newer sustained CSR initiatives, which forms a competitive advantage for companies like that of the organization XYZ Limited.

Job Performance

It was Katz and Kahn (1978), who conceptualized on 'job performance' in three ways: (a) joining and staying in the organization b) dependably meeting or exceeding standards of performance prescribed by the organization; and c) innovative and spontaneously going beyond the prescribed role. Another distinction between two types of performance was identified as job-specific task performance and non-job-specific task performance (Campbell, 1990).

Rodrigo and Arenas (2008), describe a committed employee whose personal characteristics based on studies or experience has a concern for social welfare and social justice, therefore is enthusiastic about CSR practices taken up by the organization. This new social role makes one identify with the organization. With this new role gives one a sense of importance and the organizational identity they receive, one performs better than their average performance and enables to perform even better.

Another study where it was dealing with sales staff has shown that participating in CSR initiatives shows enhancement in the performance (Larson *et al.*, 2008).

Korschun *et al.* (2014), state that managers are turning towards CSR as an additional lever to improve job performance. The above depicts that, one who is involved or participates in CSR initiatives especially green practices, would identify himself/herself in a role which would foster identification with the organization enabling one perform better. Keeping the above in mind, we can draw that employees' participation in green practices in CSR positively influences job performance.

Theoretical Implications

The Social Identity Theory and the mediating role of green behaviour, establishes that the study contributes to while expanding on the literature on firm performance and sustainable competitive advantage. Secondly, it depicts the employee's ownership, 'hands on' initiatives by one self or individualization; influence their work and thereby inculcating a visible productive outcome.

Limitations

Further, quantitative collection data collection techniques could be used to understand the relationships between green behaviour, CSR, sustainability of a firm's performance in a more comprehensive way.

Key contribution, Implication

Green practices in CSR is a value – creating activity whose impact on firms goes beyond direct financial benefits. Today's companies ought to invest in green practices through CSR as part of their business strategy to become more competitive. It is increasingly clear that business norms across the world are moving CSR into the mainstream of business practice.

Future Research Perspective

Employees what they perceive to be an environmentally favourable workplace and how they associate with, could be explored in detail. Additionally, since this is a cross-sectional study, future research should consider a longitudinal approach to compare the outcomes.

Data Availability

Available on request from the corresponding author.

REFERENCES

Carroll, A.B. and Hoy, F., "Integrating corporate social policy into strategic management," *Journal of Business Strategy*, vol. 4, no. 3, 1984.

Ashforth, B.E. and Mael, F. (1989), 'Social identity theory and the organization', c, 14, 20 – 39.

Ashforth, Blake E., Spencer H. Harrison, and Kevin G. Corley (2008), "Identification in Organizations: An Examination of Four Fundamental Questions," Journal of Management, 34(3), 325–74.

Roeck, K. De and Farooq, O., "Corporate social responsibility and ethical leadership: investigating their interactive effect on employees' socially responsible behaviors," *Journal of Business Ethics*, Vol. 151, No. 4, pp. 923–939, 2018.

Berman, S.L., Wicks, A.C., Kotha, S. and Jones, T.M. (1999). 'Does Stakeholder Orientation Matter? The Relationship between Stakeholder Management Models and Firm Financial Performance', *Academy of Management Journal,* 42: 488–506.

Chong, M. (2009). Employee Participation in CSR and Corporate Identity: Insights from a Disaster-Response Program in the Asia-Pacific, *Corporate Reputation Review*, Vol. 12, No. 2.

Dutton, J.E., Dukerich, J.M. and Harquail, C.V. (1994). 'Organizational Images and Member Identification', *Administrative Science Quarterly*, 39: 239–63.

Hogg, M.A. and Abrams, D. (1990), "Social Motivation, Self Esteem and Social Identity" in Social identity Theory: Constructive and Critical Advances (Harvester/Wheatsheaf, London).

Katz, D. and Kahn, R.L. (1978). "The Social Psychobgy of Organizations", 2"'Edition, Wiley, New York.

Korschun, D; Bhattacharya, C.B. and Swain, S.C. (2014). Corporate Social Responsibility, Customer Orientation, and the Job Performance of Frontline Employees, *Journal of Marketing*, Vol. 20–37.

Peterson, D.K. (2004). "The relationship between perceptions of corporate citizenship and organizational commitment". Business and Society, 43, 296-319

Peterson, D.K. (2004). "Benefits of participation in corporate volunteer programs: employee's perceptions".

Larson, B.V., Flaherty, K.E., Zablah, A.R., Brown, T.J. and Wiener, J.L. (2008). 'Linking Cause-Related Marketing to Sales Force Responses and Performance.

Sen, S. and C.B. Bhattacharya (2001), '"Does Doing Good Always Lead to Doing Better?" Consumer

Reactions to Corporate Social Responsibility', *Journal of Marketing Research* 38(2), 225–244.

Tziner, A, Oren L, Bar, Y and Kadosh, G (2011), "Corporate Social Responsibility, Organizational Justice and Job Satisfaction: How do They Interrelate, If at All?"

Tajfel, H. and Turner, J.C. (1986) 'The Social Identity Theory of Intergroup Behaviour'. In Austin,

S. and Austin, W.G. (eds) Psychology of Intergroup Relations. Chicago, IL: NelsonHall,

pp. 7–24.

Luu, T.T., "Integrating green strategy and green human resource practices to trigger individual and organizational green performance: the role of environmentally-specific servant leadership," *Journal of Sustainable Tourism*, Vol. 28, No. 8, pp. 1193–1222, 2020.

Su, L. and Swanson, S.R., "Perceived corporate social responsibility's impact on the well-being and supportive green behaviors of hotel employees: The mediating role of the employee-corporate relationship," *Tourism Management*, vol. 72, pp. 437–450, 2019.

13

Playing the Green Game: The Case of BigBasket's Environmental Stewardship

Dr. Shaunak Roy[1]

ABSTRACT: India has evolved as a center of economic growth and entrepreneurial activity, demonstrating resilience and adaptation in the global economy. Amidst urgent environmental issues like climate change and resource depletion, Indian businesses acknowledge the importance of incorporating sustainable practices into their business strategies. This is especially apparent in Bigbasket, the online grocery store backed by Tata Group, which has been leading the way in utilizing technology to improve its sustainability initiatives. The Green Report 2022 by Bigbasket showcases the company's unwavering dedication to environmentally responsible practices, highlighting the harmonious relationship between ecological sustainability and long-term economic feasibility. Bigbasket's ascent from its establishment in 2011 to its position as the dominant force in online grocery delivery is characterized by its embrace of inventive strategies and a diverse selection of products, guaranteeing superior quality and outstanding customer service. The firm's business model combines inventory and hyper-local delivery systems as a strategic solution to the challenges of a digital marketplace and the need to reduce waste and use resources efficiently. Bigbasket's commitment to sustainability is evident in its incorporation of projects such as biomass-powered refrigeration, solar power generation, and rainwater collection into its operations. The present case examines Bigbasket's ecologically conscious tactics, which encompass the minimization of plastic packaging, promotion of organic farming, and implementation of an electric delivery vehicle fleet to mitigate carbon emissions. Bigbasket utilizes automated route planning and delivery technologies to enhance operational efficiency and achieve its environmental goals. This approach minimizes the company's ecological footprint while simultaneously assuring customer happiness and maintaining a competitive position in the market. Bigbasket's eco-friendly activities demonstrate how sustainability can be integrated into fundamental business practices. This is particularly relevant since the e-grocery market in India is expecting substantial growth. Its proactive actions are establishing standards within the industry, promoting a sustainable e-commerce system, and encouraging a future where technology progress and environmental responsibility are closely associated.

[1] Assistant Professor of Management, Department of Commerce & Management Studies (Professor-in-Charge – Management), St. Xavier's College (Autonomous), Kolkata.

Keywords: *Bigbasket, Environmental Stewardship, Online Grocery, Sustainability, Ecommerce, Automation, Resource Efficiency.*

RUDIMENTARY OBSERVATIONS

Over the previous decade, India has gained significant recognition for its vibrant economic environment and broad entrepreneurial spirit (Srikanth *et al.*, 2021). This growth demonstrates its economic might, validating its flexibility and fortitude in the face of adversity worldwide. Through digital and physical infrastructure developments, India continues to undergo a considerable business transformation as the country navigates the intricacies of a fast, globalizing economy.

In light of the pressing global concerns around climate change, the depletion of natural resources, and the widespread need for sustainable practices, comprehending the extensive array of environmentally friendly practices and their prudent integration inside corporate settings is paramount (Ruiz-Pérez *et al.*, 2021). In the given circumstances, Indian enterprises find themselves at a pivotal juncture when they are required to make decisions of significant magnitude with far-reaching implications. These companies are pioneering a novel trajectory due to the impetus provided by technical breakthroughs and a heightened awareness of environmental concerns. One perspective suggests that numerous businesses have implemented environmentally conscious policies and practices due to the urgent imperative for sustainability (Panizzut *et al.*, 2021). It is well-recognized that a strong interconnection exists between long-term economic success and environmental sustainability (Schaltegger & Synnestvedt, 2002). Moreover, it is acknowledged that the advantages derived from this interconnection transcend beyond mere financial profit. These benefits encompass regulatory compliance (Sendawula *et al.*, 2021), establishing stakeholder trust (Wellalage *et al.*, 2022), and enhancing brand reputation (Simão & Lisboa, 2017).

Concurrently, the advent of the digital era has precipitated an unparalleled surge in commercial automation, marked by the proliferation of Artificial Intelligence, Machine Learning, and Data Analytics. Recent research underscores the transformative capacity of automation, showcasing advantages such as heightened efficacy and scalability and fostering an environment conducive to innovation and creativity (Gartner *et al.*, 2022).

CASE OBJECTIVES

The present case investigates the liaison between environmentally sustainable practices and implementing automated business processes regarding TATA Enterprise-backed online grocery retailer Bigbasket, a prominent delivery firm in India, which recently released "The Green Report 2022," a comprehensive account of its steadfast dedication to sustainability. In what ways do technology-enabled procedures facilitate and augment the sustainable operations of the online grocery giant? Are such Indian firms utilizing technology to advance their environmental sustainability initiatives?

AN OVERVIEW OF BIGBASKET

The e-commerce business in India has witnessed momentous growth and the emergence of multiple firms characterized by their dynamic and innovative approaches. However, in online grocery buying, there is a notable standout – Bigbasket. Since its establishment in 2011 by V.S. Sudhakar, Hari Menon, V.S. Ramesh, Vipul Parekh, and Abhinay Choudhari, individuals who had survived the dot-com bubble, Supermarket Grocery Supplies Pvt. Ltd., operating under the trade name Bigbasket, exemplifies the fundamental qualities of entrepreneurial perseverance and flexibility.

Company Overview

Bigbasket, formally registered as Innovative Retail Concepts Private Limited, is recognized as the most extensive online food and grocery shop in India. The widespread scope of its product assortment encompasses over 18,000 products and represents over a thousand distinct brands. Customers are offered diverse products, including fresh produce, essential food items, beverages, personal care products, meats, and similar items.

What distinguishes Bigbasket is its extensive range of products and dedication to maintaining high-quality standards and providing exceptional customer service. Each item is carefully selected, guaranteeing that clients obtain products of superior quality at highly competitive pricing. The company's delivery network covers major cities such as Bengaluru, Hyderabad, Mumbai, Pune, Delhi, and Chennai, guaranteeing prompt and effective doorstep delivery. Bigbasket ensures a smooth buying experience for its users by offering accessible payment alternatives, such as online payments and cash on delivery. Below is a summary of Bigbasket's journey with time (refer to Table 1).

Table 1: Journey of Bigbasket from 2011 to Present

2011	Bigbasket commences operations in Bengaluru with a seed capital of less than USD 1 million.
2012	Raises USD 10 million in Series A funding from Ascent Capital.
2014	Operations expand to other Tier 1 cities.
2015	Commences operations in Tier 2 cities, starting with Mysuru.
2016	Express delivery launched promising deliveries in just an hour.
2017	Milestone of 5 million customers accomplished.

2018	Acquires Raincan (rebranded as bbdaily)
2019	Raises USD 150 million and becomes a Unicorn
2021	Crosses USD 1 billion in annual gross sales; becomes part of Tata Digital and joins the Tata Group.
2022	Enters into Q-Commerce with bbnow.

Source: Company website.

A DIVERSE PRODUCT PORTFOLIO

The assortment of products Bigbasket provides is extensive and customized to meet the needs of various customers. Encompassing a wide range of home necessities, these offerings span from essential items such as fruits and vegetables to more specific products like pet food and hygiene. The company places a strong focus on quality, as indicated by CEO Vipul Parekh's acknowledgment that a substantial amount of the company's revenue is derived from its private-label items. Bigbasket delivers everyday cooking needs, such as ghee (clarified butter), sliced coconut, and fragrant basmati rice. In addition to these things, Bigbasket offers over 40,000 products, including other home goods like bread and laundry detergents, providing clients with a holistic shopping experience. All the products are delivered to the company's doorsteps. The firm's primary objective is to facilitate the convenience of online food shopping to circumvent road congestion and the tedium associated with in-person supermarket visits. To pursue novel avenues, the corporation has additionally initiated three new enterprises, namely bb Daily, bb Instant, and bbnow (refer to Table 2).

Table 2: New Businesses of Bigbasket

Service	*Description*	*Delivery/Availability*
bb Daily	Subscription-based service for milk and fresh groceries.	Order before 10 PM; delivery between 5 AM – 7 AM the next day.
bb Instant	Unmanned vending machine by BigBasket.	Available in corporate offices, tech parks, and apartment buildings in Tier I cities.
bbnow	Rapid grocery delivery service for daily essentials; approx. 3,000–3,500 SKUs on offer	Delivery within 15–30 minutes of placing the order.
bb Express	Approx. 7,500–8,000 SKUs on offer	Delivery within 1 hour

Source: Company website.

Bigbasket effectively utilizes its private label enterprise to optimize consumer value and enhance profit margins. A substantial proportion of the company's total revenue, up to 35%, is derived from its private labels. These labels provide reasonably priced items, particularly within specialized market categories such as organic food and high-end consumer goods. The company's distinctive offering is the idli/dosa batter, which encounters limited competition in the internet marketplace. The commitment to prioritizing value is apparent in the relatively affordable pricing strategies for vital items such as staples and fresh fruit. In addition to serving individual consumers, Bigbasket extends its services to the B2B market. It supplies its private label items to diverse entities, including approximately one thousand Kirana stores, prominent corporations, and organizations in the hospitality, restaurant, and catering (HoReCa) sector.

The firm utilizes a dual business model, encompassing the "inventory model" and the "hyper-local model," as part of its operating strategy. Per the inventory strategy, Bigbasket acquires items from reputable suppliers, such as P&G and HUL, through direct procurement from mills and farmers. The products mentioned above are stored within designated storage facilities, commonly called warehouses, and subsequently distributed to consumers following their orders. To ensure the timely procurement and delivery of perishable items, it is imperative to establish tight connections with local farmers. This collaborative approach allows for order-based procurement and delivery, minimizing the risk of spoilage and ensuring the freshness of the products. In contrast, the hyper-local strategy entails establishing collaborations with more than 2,000 grocery stores around India, enabling expedited deliveries from nearby establishments within one hour. Furthermore, by expanding its presence in the brick-and-mortar retail sector by establishing Fresho locations, Bigbasket is strategically positioned to capitalize on other sources of income, signifying its transformation from a solely internet-based organization to a dominant omnichannel retail force.

A RICH LEGACY

Bigbasket was established in the technologically advanced city of Bangalore in 2011, and a combination of perseverance and foresight characterizes its inception. Bigbasket was established by a group of five entrepreneurs who had experienced the difficulties of the dot-com disaster. The company commenced operations with a substantial capital of USD 10 million from Ascent Capital, a private equity investor.

The company's expansion was additionally accelerated by strategic acquisitions, such as the acquisition of Delyver in 2015 and substantial fundraising rounds, including the one spearheaded by China's Alibaba Group in 2018. By 2019, the company had expanded its operations to encompass 25 cities in India and achieved the notable distinction of being included in the esteemed 'unicorn' club. A summarized representation of the market share of several leading e-grocery apps in India is illustrated below (refer to Figure 1).

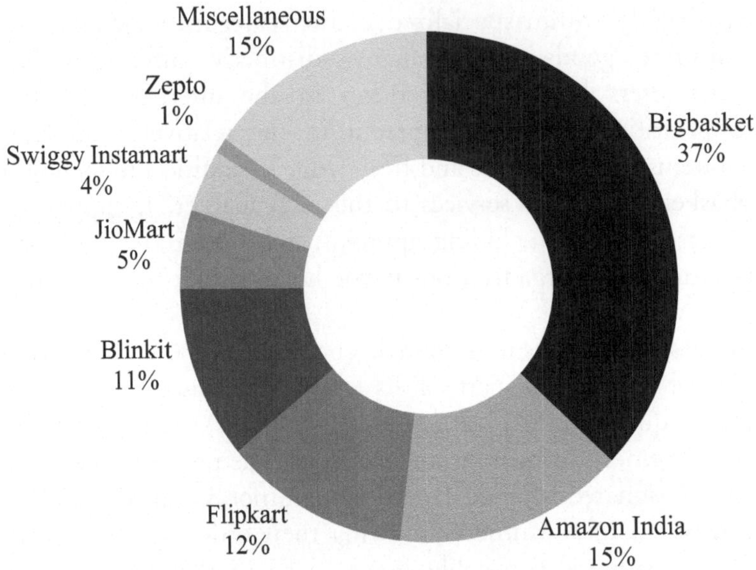

Figure 1: Market Share of Indian e-Grocery Businesses (as of January 2022)
(*Source:* PGA Labs Competitive Intelligence)

Nevertheless, like any entrepreneurial endeavor, Bigbasket encountered its fair share of obstacles during its trajectory. In 2020, the organization experienced a significant data breach that had a detrimental impact on many users. However, the company recovered when the Tata Group obtained a controlling interest in the subsequent year. By 2022, Bigbasket successfully handled a noteworthy 7 million monthly orders. In January 2023, Bigbasket had a significant increase in valuation, reaching an impressive USD 3.2 billion, facilitated by a substantial investment of USD 200 million. The pertinent financial data of Bigbasket from FY2021 to FY2023 is shown below (refer to Figure 2).

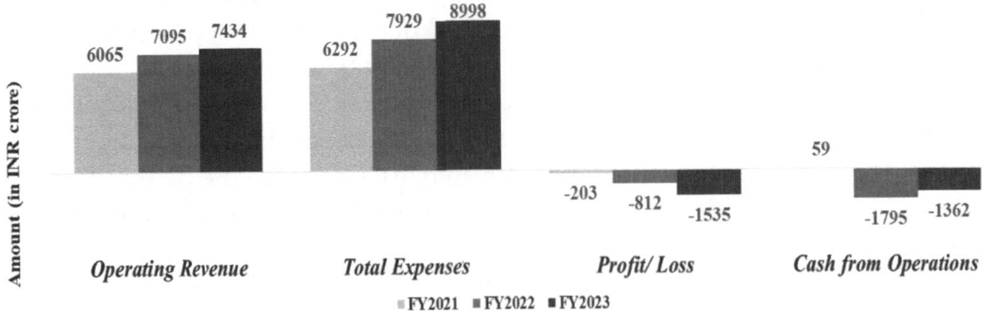

Figure 2: Financials of Bigbasket from FY21 – FY23 (Source: entrackr, 2023)

Bigbasket has secured a cumulative financial amount of USD 1.5 billion through 20 funding rounds. On December 21, 2022, Bigbasket secured a recent round of funding amounting to USD 200 million from its principal stakeholder, Tata Digital. The valuation of Bigbasket was increased to USD 3.2 billion due to the funding round.

In FY2023, BigBasket's B2C division recorded an operational revenue of INR 7,434 crore, indicating a gain of 4.8 percent compared to the preceding year's revenue of INR 7,095 crore. It witnessed a significant rise of 89 percent in its financial losses during the fiscal year 2023, reaching a total of INR 1,535 crore, in contrast to INR 813 crore in FY2022.

The total expenditures in the B2C sector experienced a growth of over 13%, rising from INR 7,929 crore in the fiscal year 2022 to INR 8,998 crore in FY2023. The rise in expenditures primarily stemmed from heightened employee perks, finance charges, and other costs. Innovative Retail substantially increased its allocation towards employee perks during the fiscal year 2023, amounting to INR 916 crore, representing a notable growth of 24 percent compared to the previous fiscal year, where the spending stood at INR 739 crore.

EXPLORING BRICK-AND-MORTAR RETAIL

Bigbasket is strategically focused on maintaining its position as India's leading grocery delivery platform. The proposed strategy entails establishing warehouses in each of the 26 operational cities in India to reduce delivery time to 3 hours.

In November 2021, Bigbasket has just introduced Fresho shops, marking its entry into the offline retail industry with the inauguration of the first store in Bengaluru. This initiative by Bigbasket demonstrates the company's dedication to offering many options for its client base, with a particular focus on fresh food. As per the statements made by Hari Menon, the co-founder and CEO of Bigbasket, the objective is to attain a sales figure of INR 12,000 crore by 2026. This target will be pursued by establishing 800 Fresho outlets across 10 Tier-1 Indian cities.

Bigbasket has consistently reshaped the landscape with its extensive assortment of products, strong historical background, and unwavering dedication to delivering exceptional service. The trajectory from a nascent business to a dominant player in the market is a tribute to the efficacy of foresight, flexibility, and unwavering commitment.

SUSTAINABILITY INITIATIVES OF BIGBASKET: A RETROSPECTIVE

Bigbasket has established a prominent presence in e-commerce grocery retail, primarily recognized for its convenience and extensive product range. Additionally, the company has garnered acclaim for its steadfast dedication to sustainable practices. The brand's dedication was emphasized adequately by the CEO, Hari Menon, ascribing the company's environmentally friendly advancements to the combined endeavor of mindful consumer decisions, constructive input, and mutual regard for the planet. The sustainability accomplishments outlined in Bigbasket's 2022 Green Report have been delved into, emphasizing several collaborative endeavors.

Wet & Dry Waste Management

The fundamental principle underlying Bigbasket's waste reduction strategy is implementing the three-pronged approach: reduction, reuse, and recycling. Using custom-made metal boxes, the firm has effectively reduced the reliance on packaging materials, which frequently contribute to the accumulation of garbage in landfills. The aforementioned robust containers not only guarantee the safe transportation of goods without any harm but also exemplify a circular lifecycle due to their high recyclability. To advance their objectives, surplus food that remains unsold but remains suitable for consumption is sent to charitable kitchens, resulting in a significant reduction in food waste—a matter of great importance within the Indian context. Within the department focused on reusing materials, 42,652 kilograms of waste was prevented by selecting reusable crates instead of single-use cardboard to deliver fruits. In addition, naturally biodegradable cornstarch packaging has been implemented as a substitute for plastics in wrapping fragile agricultural produce. Furthermore, the implementation of repair and refurbishing programs for crates and pallets has been established to facilitate their prolonged usage, hence mitigating the need for new resources.

Electric Delivery Vehicles

Bigbasket has been progressing steadfastly towards sustainability, signifying its influence as a catalyst for environmental transformation. The firm's commitment to sustainability is evident in the utilization of a green fleet consisting of 5,458 electric delivery trucks. This strategic approach has resulted in the successful mitigation of 7,012 tons of carbon dioxide (CO_2) emissions in the year 2022. The steep growth in the firm's electric fleet is noted below (refer to Figure 3).

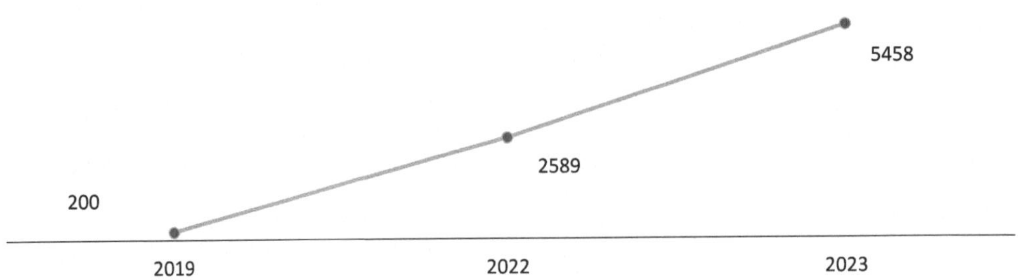

Figure 3: Rise in Electric Delivery Vehicles from 2019 to 2023

Source: Company Data.

This reduction is equivalent to the environmental impact of nearly 3,18,000 trees. The solar initiatives implemented by the company have proven to be highly successful, resulting in significant energy production across 27 warehouses. This level of energy generation is comparable to the positive impact of around 76,000 trees in terms of oxygenation. Notwithstanding, Bigbasket's commitment to sustainability goes beyond just renewable energy. The company actively supports sustainable agriculture by collaborating with 1,782 organic farmers. This support not only advocates for environmentally sustainable agricultural practices but also corresponds with the company's objective of exclusively procuring organic products. Hari Menon expresses this philosophy as a harmonious integration of environmental stewardship, customer satisfaction, and staff well-being, thereby encapsulating the fundamental principles of ethical business practices. The electric vehicles, currently constituting more than 30 percent of the company's delivery fleet, serve as evidence of BigBasket's progressive ideology and also set a standard for the sector. This project is equivalent to the absorption of CO2 by an astounding number of 1,65,000 trees. This achievement is noteworthy, especially when considering that a single tree can absorb just 22 kilograms of CO_2 per year.

Solar Power Generation

Solar power is considered a very sustainable energy, possessing significant potential, particularly in tropical regions such as India. The process of tapping it for our warehouse requirements was initiated in 2016. Bigbasket has achieved notable advancements in solar power generation by effectively utilizing solar energy resources. In the year 2022, a total of 54 million kilowatt-hours of clean energy were generated solely by the 4,512 kilowatt-peak (kWp) solar panels situated on the roofs of 27 warehouses located in 11 different locations, resulting in a reduction of 1,670 metric tons of greenhouse gas emissions. This endeavor not only highlights the utilization of renewable energy but also signifies a progression toward Bigbasket's self-sufficiency in energy usage.

Backing for Organic Farmers

Bigbasket has demonstrated strong advocacy for organic farming due to its recognition of the enduring negative consequences of chemical usage in agriculture. In the year 2022, the company provided support to a total of 1,782 organic farmers, thereby contributing to the development and maintenance of a sustainable food system. These collaborations, enhanced by field geotagging, the exchange of agricultural knowledge, and educational initiatives, align with BigBasket's objective to completely shift to organic produce. Bigbasket invoices are produced using recycled paper, preventing the disposal of 3.1 lakh kilograms of unused paper. Presently, digital invoices are used exclusively for bbnow orders, as the firm intends to implement the same approach for Bigbasket soon.

Biomass-Powered Refrigeration

Bigbasket implemented an innovative initiative by installing GreenCHILL, a biomass-powered cooling system, at their warehouse located in Bengaluru. The energy-efficient modular cooling racks utilize cashew shells and coconut husk as fuel, consuming a mere 8 units per day of power, as opposed to the 90 units consumed by a conventional cooling system. Up to this point, Bigbasket has successfully implemented 9 GreenCHILL units, resulting in an annual reduction of 186 tons of CO_2 emissions. Currently, nine operational units are actively involved in enhancing the sustainability of the supply chain. These units play a significant role in promoting environmentally friendly practices.

Rainwater Harvesting

The implementation of rainwater collection systems in warehouses situated in locations with ample precipitation exemplifies BigBasket's dedication to the preservation of water resources. Implementing this program holds significant importance for a nation such as India, where the issue of water scarcity is increasingly worrisome. Accordingly, 1 lakh liters of rainwater is harvested per season per plant.

Bigbasket has often invoked its stakeholders to pursue green initiatives, conveying that sustainability is an ongoing process of constant enhancement rather than a fixed endpoint. The organization demonstrates a strong commitment to active engagement, continuous improvement, and adaptability, encouraging its community to actively participate in generating ideas that can further its environmental sustainability objectives. Their commitment to sustainability and innovation is evident as it progresses. Their multifaceted strategy has not only improved the sustainability of its operations but has also established a benchmark for the e-commerce business in India.

BIGBASKET: BOTTLENECKS AND POTENTIAL MEASURES ADOPTED

Bigbasket's mission to deliver high-quality, perishable groceries on time presented a significant challenge, especially within the environmental constraints of maintaining a low carbon footprint. The nature of perishable goods demanded not only prompt delivery but also sustainable handling to ensure freshness and minimal waste, aligning with the company's environmental commitment. With the e-grocery sector becoming increasingly competitive, customer satisfaction became paramount, with the added layer of ensuring eco-friendly operations. Delivering fresh produce on time is not just a matter of customer satisfaction but also of reducing food waste, which is a primary environmental concern. Delays or inefficiencies can lead to spoilage, which not only inconveniences customers but also contributes to the more significant issue of food waste, with direct implications on sustainability. Moreover, the logistical challenge of managing short intervals between order and delivery time was amplified through an ecological lens. The need for rapid, manual planning had to be balanced with the imperative to reduce emissions and optimize route efficiency.

Bigbasket has been grappling with the challenge of maintaining an efficient and environmentally conscientious supply chain for fresh food. The perishable nature of their inventory requires a swift farm-to-fork process to avoid spoiling and wastage, which can result in substantial environmental consequences. To address this issue, Bigbasket has significantly invested in a technologically advanced backend system that ensures inventories are constantly being rotated. It maximizes the freshness of the products while minimizing waste, which is a crucial aspect of sustainable practices in the grocery retail industry.

Furthermore, they are confronted with the task of upholding operational efficiency in a business with narrow profit margins. This necessitates monetary investment and a dedication to sustainable practices to guarantee long-term sustainability. Bigbasket, which derives approximately 33 percent of its business from private labels, seeks to improve profitability while potentially managing the environmental impact of these products, including packaging and manufacture.

Bigbasket's effort to address the logistical and environmental obstacles posed by the swift turnover of online grocery purchasing. They are cognizant of their carbon footprint concerning delivery and operations, the consumer exodus, and managing a sizable blue-collar workforce. The use of offline kiosks can be viewed as a measure to decrease emissions by potentially lowering the frequency of home deliveries and the resulting carbon footprint. This is achieved by offering a centralized collection location for customers.

Bigbasket, at present, with the backing of Tata, has been making a deliberate effort to promote environmental sustainability by transforming its packaging methods to minimize significantly the use of plastic. They have been determined to reduce plastic packaging materials by around 60 percent. Vipul Mittal, the National Category Head for Fruits and Vegetables at Bigbasket, opined that they aim to achieve their objective of reducing plastic usage by an additional 30 percent subsequently. Commencing January 2022, Bigbasket's project is progressing towards potentially saving 200 metric tons of paper and 100 metric tons of plastic annually. The company's Environmental, Social, and Governance (ESG) objectives, which have been central to its operations since its founding in 2011, drive these initiatives.

Bigbasket remains at the forefront of the market in providing punctual online grocery delivery while the industry is positioned for significant expansion. According to McKinsey's projections, the online grocery market in India is expected to grow to

USD 10–12 billion by 2025, a substantial increase from USD 2–3 billion in 2020. Bigbasket's dedication to ESG principles, since its conceptualization in 2016, has been strengthening its market position while establishing a more sustainable e-commerce ecosystem (refer to Table 3).

Table 3: Primary Initiatives of Bigbasket towards ESG Goals

Year	*Initiative*	*Performance*	*Goals and Progress*
2016	Launch of Electric Vehicle Program	Bigbasket has integrated 1870 electric two-wheelers and 719 three-wheelers, making up 26.5% of its delivery fleet.	Status as of March 2022
2016	Solar Panel Installation on Shipping Facilities	BigBasket's installation has reached a total solar capacity of 4362 kW.	By the end of 2021, this initiative had cut CO2 emissions by 1,290 tons.
2019	Implementation of Rainwater Harvesting Systems	Nine warehouses are now equipped with rainwater harvesting systems.	Each facility can save up to 1,00,000 liters of water during peak rainfall.
2021	Biomass-Powered Chiller Collaboration	Activation of nine GreenCHILL units.	These units collectively can reduce CO_2 emissions by 186 tons annually.

Source: As reported by the Company.

The firm's dedication to sustainability is evident throughout these challenges, as their strategies prioritize operational and financial objectives while demonstrating awareness of their environmental footprint. This is evident in their approach to acquiring fresh products and the efficiency of their supply chain and delivery methods. Ensuring a harmonious balance between expansion and environmental responsibility shall be the key for Bigbasket to establish a benchmark for the online grocery sector as it grows.

Bigbasket has rapidly amassed a customer base of over 10 million within less than seven years. Upsizing necessitates decision-making abilities that are beyond human intuition. Bigbasket collaborated with Locus as its logistics intelligence partner when it strategically decided to expand its operations nationwide. Locus is a cutting-edge technology company focused on resolving the most complex last-mile issues in worldwide logistics.

By leveraging its technology, Bigbasket overcame its hurdles by generating automated route plans swiftly, ensuring timely deliveries within the promised windows. Locus not only helped them enhance their operational efficiency but also supported their environmental goals. The technology considered real-world constraints like traffic and route restrictions, allowing for the best fleet mix and boosting vehicle space utilization. This optimization not only reduced Bigbasket's freight costs but also their carbon emissions. By improving vehicle loading, Bigbasket not only achieved cost-effectiveness but also lessened the environmental impact by reducing the number of trips and fuel consumption, contributing to a smaller carbon footprint. With the integration of Locus, Bigbasket not only informed customers of accurate ETAs, elevating the customer experience but also proudly maintained an SLA adherence of 99.5 percent, reinforcing its commitment to environmental stewardship.

CONCLUSIVE REMARKS: BIGBASKET'S ROLE IN SHAPING A SUSTAINABLE FUTURE

Bigbasket's primary objective has been to create a sustainable future as it continues developing and progressing. The firm's progression from surmounting obstacles to attaining significant achievements is evidence of the profound impact of resilience and innovation. The Green Report 2022 serves as more than a mere record of previous accomplishments; it represents a commitment to maintain and enhance these environmentally friendly measures. Bigbasket's progress catalyzes other firms, demonstrating the compatibility of sustainability and profitability. Its unwavering commitment to achieving high standards and promoting long-term environmental responsibility is not only facilitating food delivery but also contributing to a more promising future.

Bigbasket's narrative continues to unfold as the prominent e-commerce firm welcomes customers, investors, and other stakeholders to participate in its environmentally conscious journey. It is actively searching for creative solutions and cooperative collaborations that line with its commitment to sustainability as it extends its offerings and reaches. Bigbasket aspires to enhance its strategies and take the lead in creating a more eco-friendly and sustainable e-commerce ecosystem with ongoing support and feedback from its community.

Amidst the increasing environmental challenges, Bigbasket's sustainable activities provide a refreshing solution. Its dedication to ecological sustainability has enhanced the brand's inventive retail techniques. Bigbasket has integrated sustainability into its business model, with a strategic emphasis on lowering its carbon impact. The company's endeavors, ranging from the use of electric vehicles to the establishment of solar-powered warehouses, exemplify a strategic plan for seamlessly incorporating ecological factors into economic operations.

They have strategically integrated technology into its operations to optimize its logistics and supply chain, reducing its environmental footprint. Deploying electric vehicles and solar panels represents only a tiny fraction of the potential advancements in this field. Beneath the surface, the company utilizes data analytics and machine learning to forecast demand and enhance delivery routes, significantly diminishing its carbon footprints. Furthermore, adopting biomass-powered refrigeration and rainwater collection technology demonstrates Bigbasket's comprehensive commitment to sustainability. Bigbasket is seeking to enhance its environmental initiatives to a higher degree, given that it is actively investigating strategies to attain carbon neutrality, such as allocating resources toward renewable energy initiatives and participating in carbon offset programs. The objective is to establish a self-contained system in which waste is minimized and resources are optimally utilized.

In addition to environmental initiatives, Bigbasket acknowledges the significance of community involvement and social accountability. The company's endorsement of organic farmers is a component of a broader dedication to cultivating sustainable livelihoods and advocating for healthy lifestyles. Bigbasket functions as more than simply a retailer; it serves as a platform that facilitates the connection between the local farming community and a broader market. By providing fair prices and a reliable source of revenue, Bigbasket contributes to the socio-economic advancement of the region. The present case exemplifies a commendable paradigm for implementing sustainable business strategies in the era of digitalization. It demonstrates that by prioritizing innovation, community engagement, and environmental stewardship, corporations can effectively make a beneficial impact on the world, thus creating a sustainable and prosperous future.

The present case poses some pressing questions that help assess the rudimentary components of Bigbasket's sustainability framework, examine how eco-friendly practices are incorporated into their business operations, and assess the overall impact on the industry and society. A crucial issue is how Bigbasket has leveraged technological innovations to promote its sustainability goals in the online grocery delivery market. Moreover, to what degree has Bigbasket's environmental initiatives, as outlined in The Green Report 2022, impacted the broader e-commerce sector and regulatory landscape in India? What steps has Bigbasket implemented to safeguard the long-term viability of its product range while simultaneously upholding competitive pricing and quality benchmarks? More importantly, how does Bigbasket's dual business model support implementing sustainable practices in its supply chain and delivery processes?

REFERENCES

Gartner, J., Maresch, D. and Tierney, R. (2022). The key to scaling in the digital era: Simultaneous automation, individualization and interdisciplinarity. *Journal of Small Business Management*. https://doi.org/10.1080/00472778.2022.2073361

Panizzut, N., Rafi-ul-Shan, P.M., Amar, H., Sher, F., Mazhar, M.U. and Klemeš, J.J. (2021). Exploring relationship between environmentalism and consumerism in a market economy society: A structured systematic literature review. *Cleaner Engineering and Technology*, *2*, 100047. https://doi.org/10.1016/J.CLET.2021.100047

Ruiz-Pérez, F., Lleo, A. and Ormazabal, M. (2021). Employee sustainable behaviors and their relationship with Corporate Sustainability: A Delphi study. *Journal of Cleaner Production, 329*, 129742. https://doi.org/10.1016/J.JCLEPRO.2021.129742

Schaltegger, S. and Synnestvedt, T. (2002). The link between 'green' and economic success: environmental management as the crucial trigger between environmental and economic performance. *Journal of Environmental Management, 65*(4), 339–346. https://doi.org/10.1006/JEMA.2002.0555

Sendawula, K., Turyakira, P., Ikiror, C. M. and Bagire, V. (2021). Regulatory compliance and environmental sustainability practices of manufacturing entrepreneurial ventures in Uganda. *Asia Pacific Journal of Innovation and Entrepreneurship, 15*(1), 62–74. https://doi.org/10.1108/APJIE-08-2020-0122

Simão, L. and Lisboa, A. (2017). Green Marketing and Green Brand – The Toyota Case. *Procedia Manufacturing, 12*, 183–194. https://doi.org/10.1016/J.PROMFG.2017.08.023

Srikanth, M., Kumar, G. N. and Reddy, W. R. (2021). Entrepreneurship, Innovation, and Economic Development: An Indian Experience. *Https://Doi.Org/10.1177/0970846 4211042100, 47*(3), 279–292. https://doi.org/10.1177/09708464211042100

Wellalage, N.H., Kumar, V., Hunjra, A. I. and Al-Faryan, M.A.S. (2022). Environmental performance and firm financing during COVID-19 outbreaks: Evidence from SMEs. *Finance Research Letters, 47*, 102568. https://doi.org/10.1016/J.FRL.2021.102568

14

Green Human Resource Management in Indian Organizations

Dr. Monalika Dey[1]

ABSTRACT: Green Human Resource Management, often known as Green HRM, is an emerging field of study that takes into account all facets and practices of Human Resource Management that are geared toward achieving environmental sustainability. Methods of Green Human Resource Management comprise of all strategies, processes, and protocols for making use of an organization's resources in a way that is sustainable not only for the organization but also for the surrounding natural environment. Green practices are currently being implemented, and Human Resource Strategies are being established to encourage environmental management initiatives as a direct result of the focus that top management places on sustainability and the dedication that they have shown toward it. Companies in the modern day are required to give equal consideration to the social and environmental issues, in addition to consider ways to reduce their ecological footprints. In the past, the primary emphasis placed on the success of a corporation was the enhancement of its economic value. In today's world, however, economic and financial elements are not the only things that are essential for success in the corporate world; social and environmental aspects are also of equal importance. The study also emphasises the impact Green Human Resource Management has had and the competitive advantage these companies have obtained as a result of the activities taken by these organisations as a product of these efforts. This study is carried out at an opportune time because there has been a significant increase in the level of environmental pollution and waste generated by factories. As a direct consequence of this, there has been a rise in the number of the implementation of policies by both the public and private sector organizations with the goal of minimizing the rapid depletion of non-renewable resources and the negative societal consequences that result from this. The current necessity of Green Human Resource Management in the Indian context is addressed by this research. To establish GHRM knowledge, the paper uses a systematic review with a descriptive research method to explore the application of GHRM and its impact in Indian context. This research follows the field's development from the initial GHRM investigations in the literature. This methodological approach takes the form of a multi-case study in which literature reviews are studied in the context of Green HRM practices in both the global and

[1] Assistant Professor in Management in HR & OB, Faculty of Commerce and Management, St. Xavier's University, Kolkata.

the Indian backgrounds. Also reviews of case study and observational studies of the Organizations which have incorporated Green HRM practices have been thoroughly studied and inferences are drawn from their implementations as well as their outcome. The primary objective of this study is to determine whether or not Green HRM practices have a significant impact on the long-term viability of a firm as well as the number of employees who remain with that organization. The findings of this research study recommend that some of these practices be implemented in Indian organizations at the present time.

Keywords: *Green Human Resource Management, Green Human Resource Practices, Human Resource Strategies.*

INTRODUCTION

Green Human Resource Management (Green HRM) is a relatively new research subject that encompasses all aspects and practices of human resource management that aim to achieve environmental sustainability. Green human resource management (GHRM) has evolved as an academic concept concerning corporate sustainability and sustainable development. The purpose of GHRM is to analyze and interpret on specific GHRM practices that are linked to basic human resource management functions. A broader definition describes GHRM as "phenomena relevant to understanding relationships between organizational activities that impact the natural environment and the design, evolution, implementation and influence of HRM systems."

In a world of declining natural capital, the "green way" of doing business may be the next competitive edge. Green innovation is becoming more popular among companies. Lee (2009) defines green management as firms' environmental management initiatives. Businesses must balance economic growth and environmental protection to preserve the environment for future generations (Daily and Huang, 2001). Green HRM in India is an initiative for environmental protection and is becoming more important in a company's operations because the HR department is so important.

Organizations adopt innovative methods to maximize resource use and minimize time, resulting in cost-effectiveness. Today ignoring green raises operating costs and damages the company's reputation. Green management saves money and inspires environmentally conscientious companies. Researchers can work on process improvements for environmental sustainability even if most corporations have focused on product innovation. Green human resource management (GHRM) is a poorly researched topic, and while some Indian organizations have adopted green management, the notion is still young. This essay explains why Indian Central Public Sector Enterprises (CPSEs) require GHRM practices. GHRM promotes carpooling, job-sharing, teleconferencing and video interviews, recycling, telecommuting, online training, and energy-efficient office buildings. GHRM identifies innovative ways to integrate "people" to green organisations, an ancient idea. As GHRM ensures, any new change must be implemented, enforced, and authorised by "people," making green initiatives difficult to start.

Green Human Resource Management (Green HRM or GHRM) is a novel concept that is gaining traction around the world. Green HRM, according to Anjana Nath, is defined as environmentally friendly HR strategies that result in improved efficiencies, lower costs, and higher levels of employee engagement. Green HRM initiatives assist businesses in finding cost-cutting alternatives without sacrificing top personnel. The strategic focus on Green HRM encourages sustainable corporate practises. As a result, GHRM methods can be used to create a new organizational culture.

Typical Green HRM activities include video recruiting and, the utilization of online and video interviewing to meet travel requirements. Electronic filing, car-sharing, job-sharing, teleconferencing, and virtual interviews, recycling, telecommuting, online training, energy-efficient office spaces, are some other environmentally friendly GHRM initiatives. These GHRM practices result in greater efficiencies, lower costs, and better employee engagement and retention, which in turn help organisations reduce employee carbon footprints.

Potential model for Green Human Resource Management Model

Here is a potential model for Green Human Resource Management (GHRM) for Corporate Sustainability:

1. *Green Recruitment and Selection*: The organization should incorporate environmental sustainability considerations into its recruitment and selection processes, such as by seeking out candidates with relevant environmental expertise or experience. The organization should attract and retain employees who share its commitment to sustainability by incorporating sustainability criteria into recruitment and performance management processes.
2. *Environmental Training and Education*: The organization should provide environmental training and education for all employees to raise awareness of sustainability issues and equip them with the knowledge and skills needed to implement sustainable practices in their work.
3. *Sustainable Performance Management*: The organization should integrate environmental sustainability into its performance management system, such as by setting environmental performance targets for employees and including sustainability considerations in performance evaluations. Employees should be held accountable for their role in achieving the organization's sustainability goals through performance management systems that include sustainability metrics and rewards for sustainable behavior.

4. *Environmental Policy and Strategy Development*: The organization should develop an environmental policy and strategy that outlines its commitment to sustainability and defines the specific actions it will take to reduce its environmental impact. This policy should be communicated to all employees and integrated into the organization's overall business strategy.
5. *Leadership and commitment*: The organization's leadership team should demonstrate a commitment to environmental sustainability by setting clear goals and policies, and by leading by example through their own actions.
6. *Employee Engagement and Empowerment*: The organization should involve employees in sustainability initiatives and provide opportunities for them to take ownership of sustainability efforts within the organization. This can include employee suggestion programs, green teams, or employee volunteer programs. Employees should be actively engaged in the organization's sustainability efforts through communication, training, and involvement in decision-making. This can include programs such as green teams, sustainability training, and employee suggestion schemes.
7. *Continuous Improvement*: The organization should continuously monitor and evaluate its GHRM practices and policies, and make improvements where necessary to ensure they align with sustainability goals and meet the needs of employees. The organization should continuously monitor and improve its GHRM practices and policies through regular audits, performance evaluations, and employee feedback.
8. *Collaboration and Partnership*: The organization should communicate its GHRM practices and policies to stakeholders and report on its sustainability performance to increase transparency and accountability. The organization should foster partnerships and collaborations with other organizations and stakeholders to share knowledge, resources, and best practices related to GHRM and sustainability.

This concept is adaptable and should be connected with the organization's sustainability plan. All employees must actively participate and evaluate its efficacy. This model could be a starting point. This model can be customised to fit the organization's needs, but it can give a foundation for incorporating sustainability into human resource management. To fit the organization's needs, the legal and regulatory framework, resource availability, and industry features must be considered.

Global Practices of Green HRM

Incorporating environmentally-friendly ideals generated from the firm's vision and goal into the recruitment and selection of prospective workers; prioritising the appropriateness of prospective employees' environmentally friendly personalities with an eco-friendly company. Organizing orientation events to instill environmentally conscious principles and culture, as well as building an environmentally conscious work culture. Routine training activities relating to environmentally friendly competency are being organised. Employee development is being carried out globally and through the employee exchange programme in order for employees to have the same view of global Green Business. Providing as many opportunities as possible for all employees, both individually and in groups, to actively participate in shaping environmentally responsible behaviour in the organisation. Having a defined organisational system in place to engage staff at all levels in eco-office activities in office buildings. Having benchmarks for measuring environmentally friendly behaviour using key performance indicators (KPI). Including criteria for evaluating environmentally friendly behaviour in integrated performance assessments. Creating regulations and rules to reward employees that exhibit environmentally responsible conduct. The rewards were presented either intrinsically or extrinsically. Maintaining a close eye to employee health and safety through the Corporate Safety Committee, whose purpose was to ensure the implementation of OSH standards that complied with national and international regulations, ultimately ensuring the safety of not just employees but also customers and other stakeholders.

GHRM Practices in Indian Context

Green HRM in India supports sustainable workplace practises, encourages employees to reduce their carbon footprint, and provides incentives for public transit and carpooling. Indian businesses adopt green HRM practises include promoting sustainable workplace practises, offering environmentally friendly benefits like flexible working hours, telecommuting, and green commute allowances, and encouraging employees to take public transit or carpool. Public transportation and carpool incentives are other green HRM practises. Green human resource management in India includes encouraging employees to reduce their carbon footprint, providing incentives for public transportation or carpooling, providing green benefits like flexible working hours, telecommuting, and green commuting allowances, providing green training and education, and implementing green policies like energy-saving and waste reduction. Companies can also implement energy-saving, waste-reduction, and employee-training programmes.

Significance of GHRM

Business buzzword "Green HRM" is growing in importance. As global awareness of environmental sustainability and sustainable development has grown, this word has become a popular research issue. Green HRM now encompasses environmental, social, and economic well-being. Sustainability plans are rapidly expanding within thousands of businesses today as a response to the dangers and disasters that has resulted from climate change, and continuously threatens to bring, into our world. The private sector is critical to the fight against negative impacts from climate change. A top-down approach is required for firms to flourish and progress in their overall sustainability efforts, along with the backing of the Top Management, including Human Resources.

Objective of GHRM Study

- *OBJ 1*: To enquire about the perception of Green HRM among employees in select Indian Companies.
- *OBJ 2*: To analyze the initiatives taken by Indian Companies toward GHRM environment.

LITERATURE REVIEW

Green Human Resource Management (Green HRM) is a new academic field that covers all HRM methods that promote environmental sustainability. GHRM is an academic idea for business sustainability and sustainable development. In their 2022 research study, Sharma, Sakhuja, and Nijjer focused on data mining unstructured data. It repeats important terms from the corpus and assigns scores to each term. This research uncovers and predicts GHRM trends and core areas. Semi-automated literature reviews are used to interpret the newest trends in the relevant field of research. This study analyses 317 Scopus-published GHRM articles from 2008 to 2021. Text, latent semantic analysis (LSA), and network analysis are used to examine Green Human Resource Management research trends and link qualitative and quantitative literature. The research uses KNIME and VOSviewer. This study ran an SLR on the GHRM Scopus database to solve these constraints. Keyword network analysis shows that Green HRM literature has contributed to Grounded Theory, Ability Motivation Opportunity (AMO) Theory, and Resource-Based View (RBV). Additionally, many works use keywords to study GHRM in the workplace. The data shows that India can do more in this field, and the keywords above could be a good start. Keywords show hospitals, hotels, universities, and airlines that have implemented GHRM. Semantic similarity between keywords helps future scholars identify current trends. This study will help GHRM researchers find keywords, relevant subjects, and new research fields using natural language processing. K-mean clustering revealed five GHRM research themes. Future academics can use those tendencies to solve environmental issues, green the environment, and urge businesses to use GHRM.

Muisyo, Qin, *et al.*, 2022, illustrate how Green Innovation Culture (GIC) affects GHRM and Green Competitive Advantage (GCA). Consumers' environmental concerns are greening businesses. Green innovation is crucial for most manufacturers. Green human resource researchers have neglected this research area, which could boost green management scholarship. Research has two main goals. Determine how GHRM and Green Innovation Culture (GIC) affect Green Competitive Advantage (GCA). Second, how Green Innovation Culture (GIC) affects GHRM practices and Green Competitive Advantage (GCA) in Zhejiang, China. These studies surveyed 324 Chinese factory workers. The writers collected data from all company levels. Two direct and one interactive model equations were created by the authors. The authors tested their models and hypotheses using AMOS 24 and SEM. The findings showed that GHRM practices, which include recruiting and selection, training and development, reward and remuneration (green incentive), and employee engagement and leadership (green opportunity), significantly improved the GCA of the organizations. GIC-encouraged enterprises' GCA encompasses Green Product Innovation (GPDI) and Green Process Innovation (GPI) (GPRI). The analysis also shows that businesses who combine GHRM with Green Innovation Culture (GIC) obtain higher GIC than those that do not.

Amjad, Abbas, Rehman *et al.*, 2021, examine and interpret GHRM practices related to essential human resource management functions in textile industry. The study focused on "organisational sustainability" basic principles (OS). This study examines how GHRM practices including training and development, performance appraisal, and reward and pay affect organizational sustainability through environmental and employee performance. 165 Pakistani textile industry managers were surveyed to acquire primary data. Based on strategic choice theory and the attribution model, secondary data from current literature suggests that green human resource management (GHRM) practices are crucial to environmental management and organizational sustainability. Performance appraisal, training and development, and reward and compensation all affect organizational sustainability, according to the study. This study also examines how the environment and employee performance mediate the relationship between GHRM practices and organizational sustainability. The study supports mediation. The GHRM is new to developing countries, so additional research is needed to identify sustainability challenges and evaluate its implications on Pakistan's textile and manufacturing industries.

Stakeholders have pushed companies to go green in recent years. Sustainable HRM practices are growing in importance. Although there are few research on green HRM, most are in developing nations, scholars are intrigued. Mousa, Othman (2020) studies Palestinian healthcare organizations' green HRM practices and their long-term performance. This research examines how Palestinian healthcare organizations implement green human resource management and how it affects long-term performance. The combined study method included 14 semi-structured interviews with West Bank hospital CEOs, operational managers, and HR managers. 69 managers who implemented green HRM were surveyed. PLS-SEM analyzed data. Green HRM was mildly adopted, averaging 2.42 on a 5-point scale. 3.42 for sustainability. Green HRM enhanced sustainability, according to the path coefficients test. "Green hiring" and "green training and involvement" were most crucial. Environmental sustainability had the highest path coefficient (0.478), while social performance had the lowest (0.372). This report discusses creating country green HRM. Green HRM improves employee behavior and performance. Legislators were taught how to promote and implement green HRM for long-term success. Sustainable organizations use Green HRM. Green HRM policy must be integrated into recruiting and selection, training and development, performance and pay management, and employee participation in green HR activities to execute them, communicate them to employees, motivate them to follow green projects, and reward them. Employee participation improved Management Review Checking and Corrective Action, the study found.

Social, environmental, and ethical goals are increasingly important to companies. Organizations are defining new goals that include financial profit, human, communal, and environmentally responsible performance and development. SHRM promotes "green" companies. Chams, Blandón (2019) explores the antecedents and consequences of SHRM and highlights the hurdles to sustainable deployment at the company level and globally, based on conceptual and empirical publications. This extensive literature analysis examines how Sustainable Human Resource Management (SHRM) can create a sustainable workplace and achieve SDGs. This multi-stage review examines SHRM and SDG predictors. 1995–2017 SHRM literature was examined. First search a database, then a reference. Future research may test four hypotheses. Sustainable management research gaps are identified and suggested. New sustainable strategies and ecological approaches by the organization's human capital achieve sustainable development goals (SDGs). This article discusses Sustainable Human Resource Management (SHRM), sustainable performance, and HR practices that support sustainable development goals (SDGs). It examines SHRM's personal, organizational, and cross-national causes and effects. Competitiveness, legitimacy, and eco-responsibility drive organizational reform (Bansal and Roth, 2000). This paradigm changes to "green" management with social and economic goals (Harris and Tregidga, 2012).

Intellectuals and businesspeople have joined the green movement in recent decades. Green purchasing (Zhang *et al.*, 2018), green management (Mustapha *et al.*, 2018), green HR management (Przychodzen *et al.*, 2018) (Renwick *et al.*, 2013; Zaid, 2018), green supply chain management (Kazancoglu *et al.*, 2018), green finance (Ng, 2018), green innovation (Li, 2018), and green IT (Zaid, 2018). (Przychodzen *et al.*, 2018). Yong, Yusliza, *et al.*, 2019, pioneered the study of green intellectual capital and green human resource management. Green relationship and human capital influenced green human resource management. HRM is crucial to this green agenda, according to Renwick *et al.* (2013). To determine if green HRM practices improve firm sustainability. A quantitative postal survey was used to obtain data from 112 of Malaysia's major industrial businesses. Partial Least Squares Regression Analysis analyzed the association. Green structural capital and green HRM were unrelated. No worldwide evidence-based framework evaluation has been found in ISI Web of Knowledge or Scopus.

Pinzone, Guerci, *et al.* (2016) investigated how "Green" Human Resource Management (GHRM) practices encourage employees to go the "extra mile" to protect the environment. The study takes an innovative approach to Environmental Management (EM) by transforming the company with strong employee support. This allows us to explore the mediation function of collective commitment to transformation—specifically to Environmental Management (EM)—in relation to the interaction between "Green" HRM practices and common voluntary environmental behaviors. This study was part of England's National Health Service (NHS) transformation to improve hospital environmental performance. This study employed primary and secondary data. We found that "Green" HRM strategies encourage collectively voluntary environmental behavior. Employees' EM assistance also mitigates this relationship. By conceptualizing three separate "Green" HRM practices, our findings highlight their relative importance and their different consequences on collective environmental behavior. This study offers EM scholars and managers evidence-based advice for using "Green" HRM to improve staff environmental attitudes and actions.

Jabbour & Jabbour (2016) emphasize on the greater gap between HRM and supply chain management, even if researchers in both fields are growing the roles of Green Supply Chain Management (GSCM) and Green Human Resource Management (GHRM) in creating more sustainable firms. Although "Green Human Resource Management" (GHRM) and "Green Supply Chain Management" (GSCM) are popular disciplines in "Green Operations Management" (OM) and "Human Resource Management" (HRM), respectively, these two current subjects have been slow to merge. The supply chain management (SCM)-HRM integration gap is larger. This paper proposes a synergistic and integrative framework for the GHRM-GSCM relationship and an integrated research agenda. Conceptual research. This conceptual study aims to unite GHRM and GSCM, two emerging organizational sustainability challenges. Integrating concepts/theories is essential for linking domains that rarely interact (Sarkis, 2012, Boudreau *et al.*, 2003, Daily and Huang, 2001). Although "Green Human Resource Management" (GHRM) and "Green Supply Chain Management" (GSCM) are popular disciplines in "Green Operations Management" (OM) and "Human Resource Management" (HRM), respectively, these two current subjects have been slow to merge. This is because supply chain management (SCM) and HRM integration is weaker. This essay discusses how the GHRM-GSCM merger affects academics, managers, and practitioners in organizational sustainability and really sustainable supply chains.

Mehta and Chugan (2015) examine how GRHM is changing to create a sustainable workplace. Customers, government authorities, and management experts are all concerned about environmental sustainability. The HRM function involves participating in stakeholder struggles and environmental issues. This report describes green HRM and the firms' HRM practices. This article explains "Green Human Resource Management," including organizations' strategies, benefits, policies, and practices. This report analyses current green human resource management trends in enterprises. It also shows how HRM contributes to "green" business cultures. Green HRM concepts are growing in the HR business, sometimes supplementing sustainability-based programmes. New processes, rules, products, and tools actually improve compliance and efficiency. The study shows how HRM policies and practices can promote environmental sustainability.

O'Donohue, W., Torugsa, N. (2015) examines the relationship between proactive environmental management and corporate success. Environmental policies save firms money, generate new revenue, and avert trouble. GHRM's implications on small enterprises are examined in this article. Few studies have examined the relationship between proactive environmental management and company performance, especially in small enterprises. Green Human Resource Management (GHRM) practises affect this relationship. This research examines HRM's impact on environmental management and financial performance in 158 small Australian machinery and equipment manufacturers. Green HRM's additional value as a facilitator of strategic sustainable development should reassure small enterprises that rising societal and government expectations for environmental sustainability won't cost them too much. Green HRM moderates the relationship between green innovation managerial and financial performance, so a high concentration of Green HRM increases the financial benefits of proactive sustainable development. Green firms think turning green is cheaper than polluting. Going green boosts a company's image and revenue.

Jam, M. and Jamal, W.N. (2020) examined how environmentally friendly human resource management (HRM) practices affect educational institutions in South Punjab, Pakistan, and their organizational lifespan and staff retention rates. Green human resource management includes all strategies, methods, and procedures that use organizational resources to sustain organizations and the environment. This research in South Punjab, Pakistan, examines whether educational institutions use green HRM. South Punjab educational institutes provide statistics for the purpose. Schools, colleges, and universities are included. The responders are the H.R. manager, school principals, and data from 150 randomly selected south Punjab schools. Green human resource management practices improve South Punjab educational institutions' sustainability and employee retention, according to the findings. Green management approaches appear to promote educational institution sustainability. Few educational institutions employ eco-friendly management practices and their sustainability benefits. Some universities partially use these methods due to resource restrictions. South Punjab is booming, and fresh and globally established practices are not commonly accepted. Lack of awareness and resources prohibit these activities from being integrated into the workplace. These difficulties can be remedied by spreading green practices and ensuring resources. Green policies improve staff retention more than sustainability. Green management education can change governance. Government green incentives should boost education and industry. The survey indicated that green initiatives in south Punjab schools improve sustainability and employee retention. Time, financing, and data shortages hampered study. This study was limited to South Punjab, hence its results may not apply to other Pakistani provinces.

Green HRM is the latest business term. Arora, M. (2020) examines top management's commitment to sustainability, green practises, and human resource methods to promote environmental management programmes. A corporation's success historically depended on economic value marketing. Modern firms must reduce ecological footprints and balance economic, social, and environmental factors to be competitive and benefit shareholders. This article discusses Indian companies' practices. The article also emphasizes Green HR's impact on organizations' competitiveness. This study is timely since factory pollution and waste have increased, prompting public and private sector initiatives to slow non-renewable resource depletion and severe social impacts. This study's methodology describes the theory's logical development. This study employs qualitative approaches. Secondary data helped this research article achieve its goals. This study employed secondary data. Green HRM prevents environmental and global crises. Thus, future generations must preserve and develop the human habitat. Incorporating green HRM into management philosophy, HR policies and practices, employee training, and environmental standards in these and other companies may transform the sector. It will teach workers and community members resource efficiency and promote eco-friendly products. HRM goes green. This article discusses GHRM's financial and environmental improvements. This form of GHRM practice evaluation may promote employee health by improving the workplace and satisfying an increasingly environmentally conscious workforce. GHRM improves employee well-being and business profitability. Green HR lowers environmental waste and enhances HR resources, equipment, and processes, saving money.

SAMPLING DATA AND METHODOLOGY

1. ***Sample Selection***: The sample units for the study are collected from selected HR employees working in companies across India.
2. ***Sample Size***: The sample size of 34 has been selected for this research study.

3. ***Data Collection***: The data collection is done from primary and secondary sources.
   (a) *Primary Data*: Primary data is collected through structured questionnaire by conducting surveys among HR employees of different companies.
   (b) *Secondary Data*: Secondary data is collected from research paper, journals, thesis and journalistic websites.
4. ***Sampling Technique***: Convenience Sampling method is used for the collection of data from the employees of different companies.
5. ***Type of Research***: This is a descriptive research. The use of GHRM and its influence in the Indian setting are the topics that are investigated in this work through the use of a descriptive research approach and a systematic review. This descriptive research traces the evolution of the field back to the first GHRM investigations that were published in the relevant literature. This methodological approach is presented in the form of a multi-case study, in which literature studies are investigated within the framework of Green HRM practises in both the global and the Indian backdrops. The research involves surveys to collect data from the respondents with an objective to know the respondents' opinion about the current state of affairs.

FINDINGS

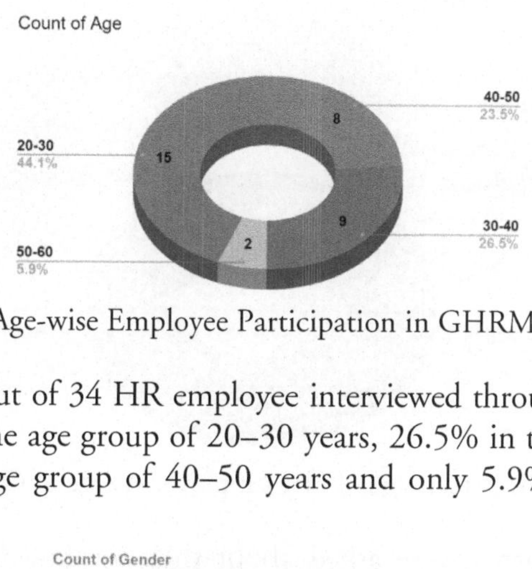

Dia.1: Age-wise Employee Participation in GHRM Survey

Here we see that out of 34 HR employee interviewed through online survey 44% of them were within the age group of 20–30 years, 26.5% in the age group of 30-40 years, 23.5% in the age group of 40–50 years and only 5.9% in the age group of above 50 years.

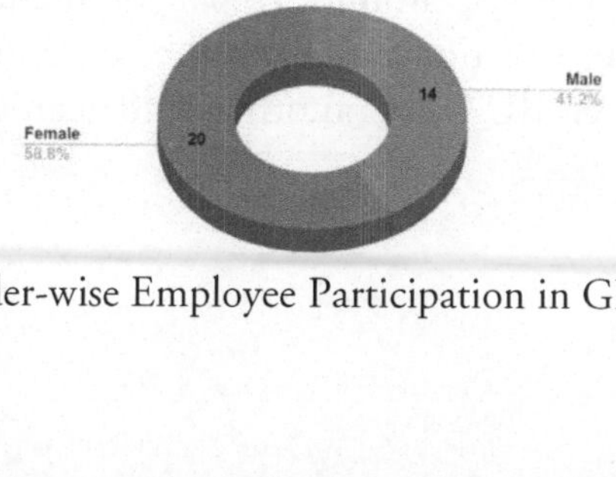

Dia. 2: Gender-wise Employee Participation in GHRM Survey

Here in the survey 58.8% of the employees surveyed were Female participants and 41.2% were Male candidates.

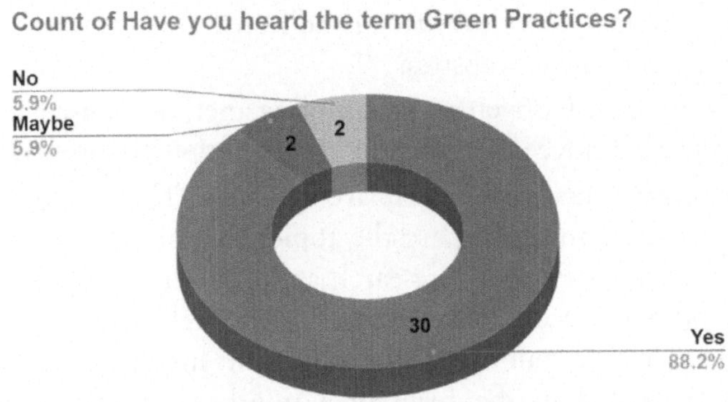

Dia. 3: Percentage of People Aware of Green Practices

When the participants were asked about their knowledge about Green Practices in Corporates, majority of them, around 88.2% of them were aware of the term Green in their Corporate working environment. Among the rest interviewed, 5.9% of them have never heard the term Green Practices, and another 5.9% were not sure if they heard the words Green Practices.

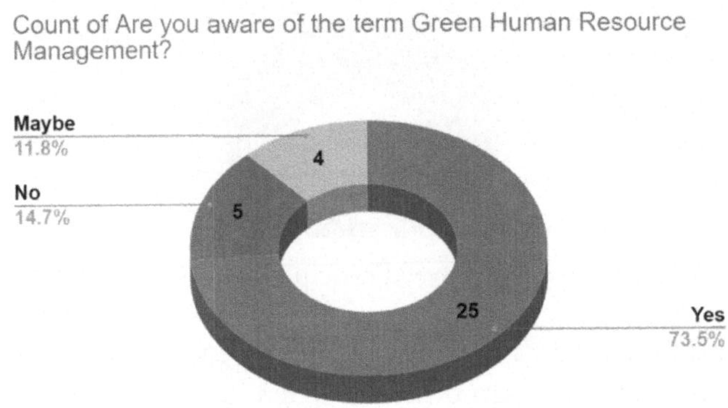

Dia. 4: Percentage of HR Employee Aware of GHRM

When the participants were asked about their awareness about Green Human Resource Management (GHRM), around 73.5% of them were aware of the term GHRM in their Corporate functions. Among the rest interviewed, 14.7% of them have never heard the term GHRM, and another 11.8% among them were not certain about GHRM practices.

Table 1: Green Recruitment & Selection Practices

Green Recruitment & Selection	*% Positive Response*
Sustainability Awareness in Recruitment	41.20%
Online Submission	67.60%
Telephonic/Video Interview	76.50%
Candidate's Green Awareness	14.70%
Job Description with Environmental Awareness	14.70%
No Green Recruitment & Selection Activities	5.90%

The participants were asked if their Companies use any of the mentioned Green Recruitment & Selection practices. Among the given options the most commonly used practices were Telephonic/Video Interview, which got 76.5% of the positive responses, 67.6% were already doing Online Submission of job applications, 41.2% had asked about sustainability awareness during Recruitment process. When interviewed about Candidates' Green Awareness during interview 14.70% showed positive awareness. When HR employees were interviewed 14.70% responded that Job Description were inclusive of environmental Awareness. 5.90% of the respondents confirmed there were no Green Recruitment & Selection activities practiced in their organization.

Table 2: Green Training & Development

Green Training & Development	*% Positive Response*
Environmental Awareness at Induction	33.30%
Green Training Need Analysis	24.20%
Green Training for Environmental Awareness	42.40%
Availability of Online Training Materials	51.50%
Training on Environmental Practices	33.30%
No Green Training & Development	21.20%

The participants were asked if their Companies use any of the mentioned Green Training & Development activities. Among the given options the most commonly used practices were Availability of Online Training Materials, which got 51.5% of the positive responses, 42.4% were acquainted with Training for increasing environmental awareness. 33.3% suggested that candidates are made aware of green sustainability at the time of Induction, and other 33.3% of them said that training on best Environmental Practices takes place in their organizations. 24.2% of the participants agreed to Green Training Need Analysis Awareness and 21.2% of the interviewed personnel said that there are No Green Training & Development practices in their organizations.

Table 3: Green Performance Appraisal Management

Green Personal Appraisal Management	*% Positive Response*
Support for Employee Green Performance	32.40%
Team Awards for Sustainability	29.40%
Recognition for Good Environmental Practices	32.40%
Rewards for Sustainability Suggestions	29.40%
Rewards for Green Skills Acquisition	17.60%
No Green Performance Appraisal System	38.20%

The participants were asked if their Companies use any of the mentioned Green Personal Appraisal Management practices. Among the given options the most commonly used practices were Recognition for Good Environmental Practices, which got 32.4% of the positive responses, and another 32.4% said there was Support for Employees' Green Performance. 29.4% of the employees said there were Team Awards for Sustainability efforts and another 29.4% respondents agreed that their company Rewards for Sustainability Suggestions. 17% of the respondents confirmed rewards for Green Skill Acquisition. But majority of 38.2% of the interviewed candidates said there were no Green Performance Appraisal Management system in their organizations.

Table 4: Green Employee Participation and Empowerment

Green Employee Participation & Empowerment	*% Positive Response*
Company Encourages Environmental Responsibility	52.90%
Employees Help Improve Sustainability Challenges	29.40%
Workshops to Help Employees Go Green	44.10%
Employees' Share Company's Green Management Vision	20.60%
Teamwork Helps Management in Sustainability Efforts	23.50%
No Green Employee Participation & Empowerment	26.50%

The participants were asked if their Companies use any of the mentioned Green Employee Participation and Empowerment activities. Among the given options the most commonly used practices were Encouragement towards Environmental Responsibility, which got 52.9% of the positive responses, 44.1% were acquainted with Workshops to help Employees Go Green in their work environment. 29.4%

suggested that Employees are actively involved to Help Improve Sustainability Challenges in the company. 23.5% said that Teamwork Helps Management in Sustainability Efforts, and 20.6% of the Employees Share Company's Green Management Efforts. 26.5% of the interviewees said that there are No Green Employee Participation & Empowerment activities in their organizations.

Table 5: Green Organizational Culture

Green Organizational Culture	*% Positive Response*
Company Vision States Environmental Sustainability	18.20%
Top Management Supports Employees for Sustainability	21.20%
Company Allocates Budget for Green Initiatives	12.10%
Company Actively Supports Green Initiatives	27.30%
No Green Organizational Culture	21.20%

When the participants were asked about their awareness about Green Organizational Culture in their Company, around 27.3% of them said Their Company Actively Supports Green Initiatives, 21.2% said that Top Management Supports Employees for Sustainability efforts, 18.2% said Company Vision Clearly states Environmental Sustainability, and 12.10% said that Company Allocates budget for Green Initiatives. 21.20% of the employees interviewed said that there is no clearly stated Green Organizational Culture present in their Company.

Table 6: Green Exit Policy

Green Exit Policy	*% Positive Response*
Online Exit Interview Policy	68.80%
Enquiry About Green Practices During Exit	25.00%
To Measure Positive Effects of Sustainability	25.00%
Negative Impact Enquiry due to any Green Practice	18.80%
If Green Practices Reason For Resignation	9.40%
No Green Exit Policy	3.10%

The participants were asked if their Companies use any of the mentioned Green Exit Policy. Among the given options the most commonly used practices were Online Exit Interview Policy, which got 68.8% of the positive responses, 25% suggested that Employees were enquired about Green Practices During Exit and another 25% responded Exit Policy enquired Positive Effects of Sustainability of employees. 18.8% said their company enquires about Negative Impact of any Green

Practices during Exit Interview. 9.4% positively responded that company enquires if Green Practices are Reason for Resignation. 3.1% said that there Company has no Green Exit Policy.

Table 7: Online Practices to reduce Paperwork

Online Practices to Reduce Paperwork	*% Positive Response*
Online Leave Application	91.20%
Online Budget Approval	58.80%
Online Storage for Files	64.70%
Duplex Printing Rule	38.20%
Digital Forms for Appraisal Management	55.90%
Use Digital Modes of Communication	2.90%

The participants were asked if their Companies use of Online Practices to reduce Paperwork. The mentioned Green Exit Policy. Most commonly used practices were Online Leave Application, 91.2%, followed by Online Storage for Files at 64.7%. Online Budget Approval scored 58.8% of the positive responses, and 55.9% agreed that they use Digital Forms for Appraisal Management. 38.2% of the respondents said that their company follows Duplex Printing Rule and only 2-9% said that their Company has no Online Practices to Reduce Paper work.

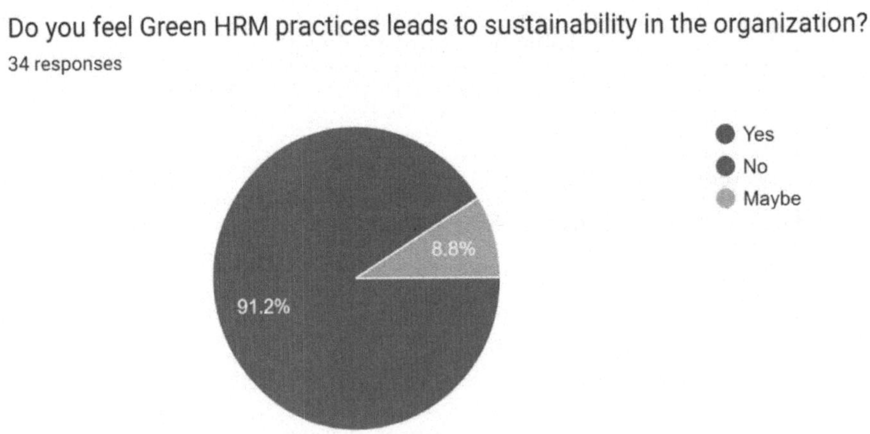

Chart 8: GHRM Sustainability

When asked if the interviewees feel that Green HRM will lead to overall sustainability in the Organization, a majority of them, 91.2% responded positively, and only 8.8% of them were not sure of its effects.

CONCLUSION

This study gives a preliminary outlook on the strategic implementation of Green HRM in Indian Context. The fundamental goal of Green HRM is to educate employees on the challenges of environmental management, such as what actions are required, how they work, and how they benefit the environment. The practice of GHRM stimulates employees and instils a sense of pride in them for participating in the green initiative. The objective is to harmonize corporate goal and societal aims without sacrificing corporate objectives.

REFERENCES

Jam, M., and Jamal, W.N., Impact of Green Human Resources Management Practices on Organizational Sustainability and employee Retention: An Empirical Study Related to Educational Institutions. (2020). iRASD *Journal of Management*, Vol. 2, No. 1, 2020, pp. 34–48. https://doi.org/10.52131/joe.2020.0201.0014

Sharma, C., Sakhuja, S. and Nijjer, S. Recent trends of green human resource management: Text mining and network analysis. *Environ Sci Pollut Res* (2022). https://doi.org/10.1007/s11356-022-21471-9 Recent trends of green human resource management: Text mining and network analysis | SpringerLink

Muisyo, P.K., Qin, S., Ho, T.H. and Julius, M.M. (2022), "The effect of green HRM practices on green competitive advantage of manufacturing firms", *Journal of Manufacturing Technology Management*, Vol. 33 No. 1, pp. 22–40. https://doi.org/10.1108/JMTM-10-2020-0388

Amjad, F., Abbas, W., Zia-UR-Rehman, M. *et al.* Effect of green human resource management practices on organizational sustainability: The mediating role of environmental and employee performance. *Environ Sci Pollut Res* **28**, 28191–28206 (2021). https://doi.org/10.1007/s11356-020-11307-9 Effect of green human resource management practices on organizational sustainability: the mediating role of environmental and employee performance | SpringerLink

Sharifa K. Mousa, Mohammed Othman, The impact of green human resource management practices on sustainable performance in healthcare organisations: A conceptual framework, *Journal of Cleaner Production*, Volume 243, 2020, 118595, ISSN 0959-6526, https://doi.org/10.1016/j.jclepro.2019.118595. (https://www.sciencedirect.com/science/article/pii/S0959652619334651)

Nour Chams, Josep García-Blandón, On the importance of sustainable human resource management for the adoption of sustainable development goals, Resources, *Conservation and Recycling*, Volume 141, 2019, Pages 109–122, ISSN 0921-3449, https://doi.org/10.1016/j.resconrec.2018.10.006.(https://www.sciencedirect.com/science/article/pii/S0921344918303719)

Jing Yi Yong, M.-Y. Yusliza, T. Ramayah, Olawole Fawehinmi, Nexus between green intellectual capital and green human resource management, *Journal of Cleaner Production*, Volume 215, 2019, Pages 364–374, ISSN 0959-6526, https://doi.org/10.1016/

j.jclepro.2018.12.306. (https://www.sciencedirect.com/science/article/pii/S09596526183 4037X)

Marta Pinzone, Marco Guerci, Emanuele Lettieri, Tom Redman, Progressing in the change journey towards sustainability in healthcare: the role of 'Green' HRM, *Journal of Cleaner Production*, Volume 122, 2016, Pages 201–211, ISSN 0959-6526, https://doi.org/10.1016/j.jclepro.2016.02.031. (https://www.sciencedirect.com/science/article/pii/S0959652616001761)

Charbel José Chiappetta Jabbour, Ana Beatriz Lopes de Sousa Jabbour, Green Human Resource Management and Green Supply Chain Management: linking two emerging agendas, *Journal of Cleaner Production*, Volume 112, Part 3, 2016, Pages 1824–1833, ISSN 0959-6526, https://doi.org/10.1016/j.jclepro.2015.01.052. (https://www.sciencedirect.com/science/article/pii/S0959652615000566)

Mehta, Kathak and Mehta, Kathak and Chugan, Pawan Kumar, Green HRM in Pursuit of Environmentally Sustainable Business (June 1, 2015). *Universal Journal of Industrial and Business Management*, Vol. 3, No. 3, pp. 74–81, June, 2015, ISSN: 2332-3310 (Print), ISSN: 2332-3329 (Online), Horizon Research Publishing Corporation, Alhambra, USA., Available at SSRN: https://ssrn.com/abstract=2627211 Green HRM in Pursuit of Environmentally Sustainable Business by Kathak Mehta, Pawan K. Chugan:: SSRN

O'Donohue, W. and Torugsa, N. (2015). The Moderating effect of 'Green' HRM on the association between proactive environmental management and financial performance in small firms, August, 2015, 239–261. https://doi.org/10.1080/09585192.2015.1063078

Arora, M., Green HRM in India: An Initiative for Environmental Protection. – Palarch's *Journal of Archaelogy of Egypt/Egyptology*, 17(10). ISSN 1567-214x.

Deconstructing AMO framework: a systematic review | Marin-Garcia | Intangible Capital.

Top 100 companies in India for CSR and Sustainability in 2021 – The CSR JournalTop of Form Bottom of Form.

Green Practices and Business Augmentation: Reality or an Illusion

Kausik Chakraborty[1] and Dr. Manodip Ray Chaudhuri[2]

ABSTRACT: It is true to say that the world is becoming complex and multifaceted day by day with rising tensions of deglobalization and ongoing wars. Survival and Profit making remains as one of the major concerns for various business houses across the nation and for that organizations are focusing on various techno-structural changes within the organization for better health.

On the other hand, with the rising level of pollution, nurturing a green environment and crafting a green business is the call of the hour. Environmental consciousness now strikes us almost every day in the current times. Resource limitation concerns and environmental concerns did raise a question on the very concept of sustainable use of assets and pollution (Wang and Song, 2014) Opinions were that developments pertaining to the economy and pollution reduction could not go hand in hand. Striking a proper balance between constant high consumption of resources in order to develop the economy and at the same time also thinking about eco-friendly environmental concerns is a challenge (Chan *et al.*, 2012). The excessive consumption and usage of the non-renewable resources with an aim of speedy economic developments did adversely affect the environment and raised huge concerns (Atlin and Gibson, 2017).

Now amidst all these there have been numerous investigations where there were serious concerns raised for factors altering green innovation practices with respect to environmental regulations, ethics, legal system and the supply chain. Moreover, there has been extensive pressure from various government bodies, society and customers at large to practice such initiatives religiously.

In the opinion of (Chen, 2008b; Chang, 2011) it is the manufacturing sector across the globe that is the highest waste producing sector. The very concept of Green Innovation can be further bifurcated into green products, green marketing, green processes, and green management that are focused and oriented towards eco-friendly initiatives and work practices like recycling, controlling the pollution emission levels at large (Seman *et al.*, 2019).

[1] Ph.D. Scholar in Management, Xavier Business School, St Xavier's University, Kolkata.

[2] Professor of Management in HR & OB and Former Dean, DRC-PhD Convener in Management, Xavier Business School, St. Xavier's University, Kolkata.

The chapter paper will focus on the importance of the same in current business context. With respect to the same green initiatives of few organizations like Reliance and Flipkart will be discussed in this chapter as to how these companies are balancing both development on one hand and environmental conscious initiatives on the other hand. Also, how such initiatives are contributing towards overall business development which can be used for further study.

Keywords: *Pollution, Resources, Green Washing, Green Business, Sustainability.*

INTRODUCTION

In today's world the word "Sustainability" has become an essence of major business operations. In order to operate by the principles of sustainability; "Green Practices" which emphasizes on adopting principles and processes helps in realizing the goal of sustainability. However lately it has been realized and felt that implementation of green practices in reality is a challenging affair, reasons could be like mobilizing the capital, resources, information flow etc. (G20 Green Finance Synthesis Report, 2016). Now with the advancement of businesses across the world and rise in competition for survival, the extent of natural resources usage has been increased by many folds which in a way does create an adverse effect on the environment. So it is the need of the hour that we use such natural resources in an optimum way so that productions are environment friendly and for that adoption of green business practices by the business houses are necessary.

With increase in population and developments in the field of technology, the usage of various kinds of resources are at an all-time high which does create an adverse effect on the environment. As a result of which both the employees, organization and government jointly have to take certain initiatives which helps in addressing the rising concern. Some of the initiatives by the government are the Green Hydrogen Mission, GOBARdhan (Galvanising Organic Bio-Agro Resources Dhan Scheme), the Green Credit programme, MISHTI, Amrit Dharohar, and more. Also notably few major business houses in India did take great initiatives and actions with respect to Sustainability and Green Initiatives which the paper deals with in depth.

LITERATURE REVIEW

Studies conducted by Ahmad, M. (2016) stated that productivity does gets enhanced with the effective usage of resources, an aim of good will creation in the market with proper planned investment opportunities all directed towards green business practices which will enhance the objectives of sustainable development.

Gupta, R. (2011) in his study stated that the awareness level amongst the Indian customers is not that much aware about the eco-friendly products and its benefits.

Moreover, the Indian customers were very less aware about the initiatives taken by companies as such for the cause.

Smith, E.E. and Perks, S. (2010) in their study suggested that the General Management Team and HRM Team in an organization must actively take initiatives for promoting various initiatives that promote green causes.

Agarwal, K., Sutra Dhār, S.P. and Agarwal, R. (2020) in their study found that the majority of the respondents in their study are moderately aware of the concept of Sustainability and Green Initiatives. The major factors upon which they worked were eco-friendly packaging initiatives, respondent's awareness about the various symbols and certifications which declares a product as green, the benefit of the same with respect to health perspectives, consumable and eco-friendly electricity concern, initiatives on plantation of trees, green initiatives by government. So post their study it was revealed that the majority of the respondents were moderately aware about the products which are eco-friendly and also moderately aware about the brands which offered such products.

RESEARCH GAPS

Post conducting a brief literature Review, the gaps identified were:

1. Very less study has been found which focused on organizations "Green Initiatives" practices with respect to Sustainability and what exactly they were doing to educate the mass population about "Green Products".
2. It has been found that the majority of the population in general only have moderate knowledge about the concept of Sustainability, Green Initiatives and Green Products.

RESEARCH OBJECTIVES

1. To study the degree and extent of the various Green Initiatives Practices with respect to Sustainability practiced by major organizations.
2. To study the degree and extent of initiatives taken by the organizations to aware the mass populations regarding Green Initiatives and Sustainability.

RESEARCH METHODOLOGY

This Qualitative study is based on secondary data. The secondary data were obtained from various journals, statements, newsletters and social media platforms.

Case Study Analysis

A Case Study from Flipkart

In India, the e-Commerce industry is actually very young and with lots of potential to grow as compared with other industries present. Flipkart happens to be one of the early players in this segment who plays a key role in influencing the population to adapt to online shopping. At present it is the No. 1 E-Commerce platform for India. The founders who initially started the organization with selling books online with country wide shipping; now the very same organization deals with probably everything which a human could think of purchasing in their online portal or platform.

But with the growing business and expansion they also work extensively on various Sustainability Initiatives which is actually one of their values in order to be a responsible value chain.

Some of the major initiatives taken by the organization happens to be in the area of:

- **Sustainable Packaging**: Here the organization made humongous initiatives to replace the bubble wrap papers used for packaging with honeycomb wrapping papers and shredders. Thus, eliminating the plastic made bubble wrap papers which was actually increasing the carbon footprint and also a concern for environmental issues.
- **Electrification of Last Mile Fleets:** It was notable to see that for the last mile operations from Delivery Hubs to Customers while delivering happiness as they say for products. They transformed the majority of their vehicles from diesel owned to electricity charged two-wheelers. The very same helped the organization to attain their objectives of Sustainability with immense ROI in terms of fuel cost and vehicle maintenance. So this very same initiative served both the purposes of Cost Saving and also a responsibility towards Green Concern through methods of reducing carbon emission.
- **Renewable Energy**: In Haringhata, West Bengal, Flipkart established their biggest warehouse which is also the biggest in entire Asia. The site boasts of on major ground breaking initiatives taken in the field of Sustainability and Green Initiatives such as 2.75 MW Solar rooftop PV plant installation, Energy efficient equipment's which are sensor enabled, 100% re-usage of wastewater and treatment, installed water efficient fixtures which gave a 25% goodness on water consumption at the facility, re-using the rain water via harvesting the same in a pond of 8000 cubic meter.

In order to sensitize the mass population, Flipkart has started using labeling of their products which they call as "Green Label" where >15% of the total cost of materials, products and equipment are eco labeled.

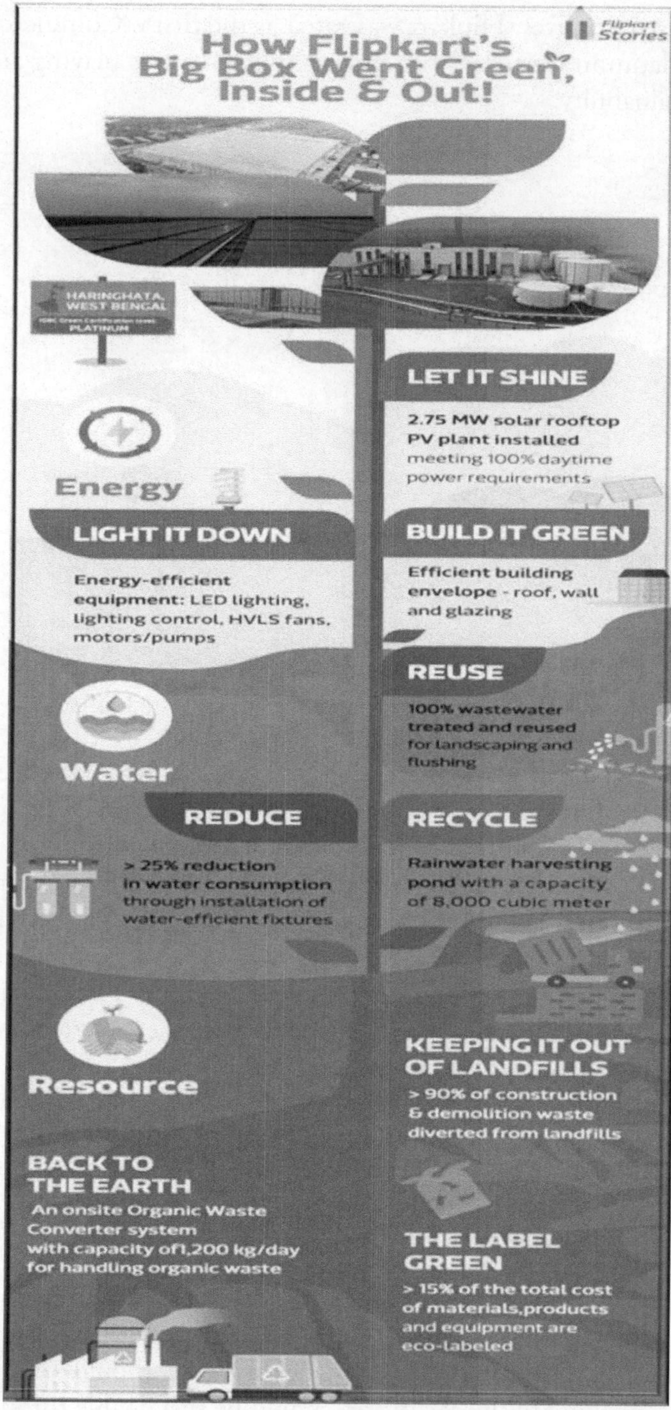

Source: https://stories.flipkart.com/flipkart-sustainable-green-building-haringhata/

With all these initiatives, Flipkart was rated as the first e-Commerce organization to have been "Platinum Certified" warehouse by IGBC thus playing an active role in the field of Sustainability.

Source: https://stories.flipkart.com/repair-refurbish-reuse-reduce-solar-power-jeeves

The initiatives taken at Haringhata Site; West Bengal have also been reciprocated at other major hubs across India. Such as Solar Panels for electrification, water reuse, using EV vehicles inside the side for transportation and movement, Plantation initiatives. In fact, in order to increase the awareness, there are competitions held within the site amongst the employees to come up with the best projects which addresses the sustainability concern.

So with the above initiatives taken by Flipkart for all its Fulfillment Centers (FC) and Mother Hubs (MH) it gets pretty evident with the practices Flipkart follows with respect to Sustainability and Green Practices.

In order to promote and create awareness about their activities they mention all these initiatives over their social media handles like LinkedIn, Facebook, Instagram and also through Newspaper publications.

A Case Study from Reliance

At Reliance, Sustainability is viewed as a responsibility of the organization towards environment and society. As a part of their principle, they have included "Product Life Sustainability" which means that the organization should produce goods and services which contribute to the safety and should be sustainable throughout their life cycle. Also, the aspect of "Environment" is one of their core principles where they strive towards respecting, protecting and making serious efforts to restore the environment at large through their services.

As per their annual report of 2022, the organization has about 233 subsidiaries and they try to engage through all their subsidiaries to contribute in terms of sustainability principle. Through means of suppliers, distributors and local communities, government and other entities in the value chain.

With respect to its continuous strive towards a Sustainable environment, the organization took some remarkable steps in attaining the same. Some of them are mentioned below:

- **R|ElanTM – Fusion Technologies:** The organization leveraged on the technical front and developed fusion technologies solutions which are created through eco-friendly and sustainable rout like moisture management (R|ElanTM Kooltex), thermal insulation (R|ElanTM AirTherm), all- weather comfort (R|ElanTM AllClima) and all of the same are created from waste PET bottles (R|ElanTM GreenGold). So through the same we could see how the organization worked upon the major issues to provide eco-friendly and sustainable solutions. Thus bringing forward the novel commitment of the organization to introduce innovative technologies that promote sustainability.
- **RelWoodTM as a Replacement to Wood:** This product offering from Reliance happens to be the substitute product of wood which is again sustainable and eco-friendly. It is known that India has a forest cover area of 21% whereas the demand for wood is 31%. Also, our country India happens to be the largest importer of wood for the rest of the world.

  So with such ground breaking initiative by the organization to bring a 100 % substitute product of wood is really commendable. As the very same initiative is directly having effect on sustaining the natural forest cover, recyclable in nature and also it does not release hazardous fumes and gasses with much better quality and resistance than wood. It is said that the products are long lasting and thermoforming friendly which could be the selling point proposition material for those customers who are eco-friendly and sustainability cautious.
- **Fabric Recycling (PET-Polyethylene terephthalate):** Reliance as an organization is deeply concerned with the increasing post usage consumer products which become wastes. As the very same is highly hazardous for our environment.

Addressing this environmental burden caused due to discarded wastes in the environment, the organization with the help of technology is attempting to segregate the PET from the fabric blends and eventually convert the same to re-usable fabric fibers through cost-effective technologies for producing new fabrics and garments. Also, to improve the valorization process the recovered PET fibers are used as reinforcement fillers in concrete composites for improving the strength of the compression. This is how the organization is striving towards sustainable production and helping in reducing climatic impact.

Reliance in order to promote the principles of a circular economy which are Reduce, Reuse and Recycle have intensively worked on the various waste management initiatives. Some of those initiatives are Recron® Green GoldTM Polyester Staple Fibre (rPSF), Green Polyolefin (gPO) and Waste to Road (W2R). Further to promote the principles of circular economy the various hazardous wastes are recycled as an alternative fuel and raw materials for the cement industry.

By 2035, the target for the organization is to be Net Carbon Zero. For the same the organization has reported an increase of 115% renewable energy consumption in FY 2022–23 as compared with the previous financial year of 2021–22. The company also aimed for setting a 20 GW solar energy generation capacity by 2025 which will be fulfilling the energy requirement. The organization has made significant effort to use bio-energy for bridging the demand and they have replaced 5.3% of energy consumption at their Dahej and Hazira, India sites with green power and green steam with a focus on making CO_2 a recyclable resource through means of technology by harnessing photosynthesis biological pathways which will play a pivotal role.

Some of the Pictorial Representation of Sustainability Practices at Reliance

Note: Images taken from Business Responsibility and Sustainability Report of 2021–22 and 2022–23.

CONCLUSION

Sustainability should always be a social goal for people and business organizations to co-exist. Keeping that in mind the three principles of sustainability which are environmental, economic and social have to be kept in mind especially for all the organizations operating. As through sustainability the major environmental concerns are addressed at large. According to UNESCO, "Sustainability" is a long-term goal whereas "Sustainable Development" refers to the various processes and ways to achieve the same.

Likewise in the above two major cases, one from Flipkart which is currently the best e-Commerce player in the market in terms of Supply Chain and the another is Reliance Industries which is again the best in its segment that how these two organizations in lieu with their objectives are working on the sustainability policies with their various initiatives which are noble in nature and can be replicated by other business organization as well. So that together the principle and goal of Sustainability could be achieved.

All though we have seen that in today's scenario manufacturing industries are the biggest waste producing sectors, so here comes the concept of "Circular Economy" which can play a major differentiator in achieving the sustainability goal for those organizations which are in the manufacturing sector, as practiced by Reliance.

Another major concern area is that in India other than the big organizations, the majority of the MSME enterprises don't practice religiously 100% on the principles of Sustainability. So, it becomes very imperative that such enterprises which comprise the major chunk should think about the same by looking into the ways which other giants in the industry are practicing to bring about a change in the ecosystem.

So Green Practices and Business Augmentation is actually a reality for the major houses but for the MSME enterprises which operate in sub-rural, rural or suburban areas needs support from the government and big organizations on the ways as to how with the help of technology and innovation they are able to bring the changes. Lastly a mass awareness by the enterprises for the end consumers as to how they as an organization is contributing towards the sustainable environment doing their part and how the end consumers can learn, be aware and contribute from their end towards the cause. As at the end its a joint collaboration where collectively both the business houses, enterprises and people at large need to come together for a Sustainable Development.

BIBLIOGRAPHY

https://www.thehindubusinessline.com/companies/reliance-industries-aims-for-100gw-green-energy-ambani-unveils-ambitious-plans-for-energy-transition/article67244727.ece#:~:text=Reliance%20Industries%20intensifies%20green%20energy,charting%20a%20transformative%20energy%20transition.

https://www.fibre2fashion.com/services/promotion/enhanced-sustainability/reliance.asp

https://www.reliancepower.co.in/environmental-initiatives

https://www.ril.com/OurBusinesses/New-Energy.aspx

https://www.livemint.com/companies/news/ril-ready-to-double-its-green-energy-investment-to-1-5-trillion-11691432801242.html

https://www.livemint.com/opinion/online-views/reliances-big-green-bet-reflects-a-strategic-shift-11624550790875.html

https://indiacsr.in/esg-at-the-core-how-reliance-industries-takes-bold-steps-towards-sustainable-progress/

https://www.frontiersin.org/articles/10.3389/fpsyg.2020.553625/full

https://www.researchgate.net/publication/344224437_Impact_of_Green_Practices_on_the_Financial_Performance_A_Study_of_Indian_Automobile_Companies

https://iaeme.com/MasterAdmin/Journal_uploads/IJM/VOLUME_11_ISSUE_8/IJM_11_08_175.pdf

Ahmad, M. Green Business Practices: Balancing Environment and Economic Desires. International Journal of Multidisciplinary Research and Development, 3(5), 2016.

Gupta, R. An Empirical Study of Impact of Green Retailing on Customers Buying Behaviour. Numero, 2(4), 2011.

Smith, E.E. and Perks, S. A Perceptual Study of the Impact of Green Practice Implementation on the Business Functions. *Southern African Business Review*, 14(3), 2010.

Agarwal, K., Sutra Dhār, S.P. and Agarwal, R. (2020). Green Business Practices: A Study on Retailers, *International Journal of Management (IJM),* Volume 11, Issue 8, August 2020, pp. 1988–1997, Article ID: IJM_11_08_175

https://thecsruniverse.com/articles/flipkart-progresses-on-sustainability-commitments-diverts-approximately-3000-tonnes-from-landfills-in-a-year#:~:text=With%20a%20proactive%20stance%20towards,with%20its%20broader%20sustainability%20vision.

https://stories.flipkart.com/flipkart-sustainable-green-building-haringhata/

https://stories.flipkart.com/category/sustainability

Green Finance: Prerequisite Towards Sustainability

Dr. Gautami Chattopadhyay[1]

ABSTRACT: Green finance is a new word in the financial world that encompasses innovative ways of farming. Green Finance is an important tool for maintaining green growth and ensuring environmental and economic development. It plays a crucial role by promoting green financial products and attracting investment in green business and technology. Given the huge financing needs in our nation's renewable energy projects, it has caught the international attention. Banks have found that reputed investors are reluctant to lend to projects if some of them do not receive green certification. The concept of green banking is also beneficial to the environment. Ongoing climate change has enabled India to create its own green growth.

Green finance contains the responsibility of creating a new and sustainable platform. While fintech strives to streamline financial services and streamline processes, green fintech in India is also focusing on reducing emissions and supporting biodiversity. Essentially, green finance refers to environmentally sustainable and socially responsible financial investments. This type of financing is considered an effective tool for mitigating climate change and promoting sustainable development. It has gained popularity in India in recent years as the Indian government has implemented various measures to promote green investment. Green finance shoulders the responsibility of creating a new and sustainable platform. While fintech strives to streamline financial services and streamline processes, green fintech in India is also focusing on reducing emissions and supporting biodiversity. This current generation is committed to using technology to promote environmental sustainability and create a healthy world.

Keywords: *Green Finance, Green Growth, Sustainability, Renewable Resource, Green Banking, Climate Change.*

INTRODUCTION

Green finance is a wide area where the financial investment keeps flowing towards any project which connects to sustainable development, environmental products, and policies to boost the growth of a better economy. India is in a mission to reduce its emissions intensity by 30-35 per cent as per reports within 2030 and assemble 40 per cent of its population to depend on renewable energy sources in order to achieve its Nationally Determined Contribution (NDC) goals [2]. This mission will only be possible when the external funds are obtainable to finance this green transition.

[1] Assistant Professor, University Alliance, ICA Edu Skills Pvt. Ltd.

Green finance serves as an essential tool to protect green growth for environmental and economic sustainability. It has an enormous role to offer by promoting green financial products and engaging the opportunities for investing in green industries and technology. Considering the huge financial requirement of our nation renewable projects are receiving global importance. It has been observed by bankers that reputed investors are not keen on extending their loans on projects if a portion of it is not certified as green. Further, financial institutions are now promoting green products and services for offering these to consumers [1]. Banks are also following green practices to develop sustainability without harming the environment. This paper tries to explain the concept by scrutinizing the key words and countries framework.

Role of Green Finance

Finance works as a pivotal tool in each phase of business cycle whether it is at micro level, or large scale. Green finance is considered innovative and as the term goes with a broad range of funding for projects, environment-oriented technologies, industries or businesses. Green finance is an elemental agent of low carbon green growth while it binds the financial industry, environmental progress and economic growth which are essential for country like India to sustain. People are aware of the ecological imbalance caused due to over emission of carbon in the atmosphere resulting in the occurrence of global warming [13–14]. This has pushed the governments around the globe to think about it seriously for the sake of generations to come. Here emerges the thought of green funding or green investment or green technologies and other green initiatives [5] which gets collaged into one term- Green Finance. The Reserve Bank of India has incorporated the renewable energy sector as the priority sector. Thus, it turned out that, banks must concentrate a certain portion of their overall lending book towards the priority sector, which will support in bringing the credit flow in this sector. Banks and non-banking finance companies have been the main source of funding for renewable energy. However, banks have limited need for a major role as providers of long-term debt for renewable energy projects because of reasons that goes by the risk of an asset-liability mismatch. The long-term funds available with insurance and pension funds in India are not properly projected to meet the debt requirement of the renewable energy sector due to regulatory restrictions. Likewise, the existing traditional financing sources are not enough to manage any sort of capacity addition, and looking at the enormous financial requirement of the renewable energy sector, it is essentially required to identify alternate sources to supplement or fulfill as well as broaden the options of renewable sector funding.

Green Banking system was introduced to remain competent in the area and it is the one which adopts certain policies of sustainable green practices for everyone like the employees, products and services and facilities. Green banking [3] always carries the idea to protect environment by making people aware about the initiatives which the bank takes so as to keep the environment safe and green. Banks perform green practices generally by installing electronic devices which are environmentally safe, which reduces carbon footprint [8]. Any green bank can be differentiated from a normal bank by going through the dissimilarities. Green banks give more priority to those factors which are concerned with the environment. Their prime objective is to generate fair environmental and social business practice. These banks keep a check on each and every factor before lending any loans, company will only get a loan if the venture undertaken by that company is environmental friendly [7].

Following are the Characteristics of Green Banking:

(a) Payments of any kind of bills are done using online mode.
(b) Online banking is preferred rather than using branch banking.
(c) Opening of the accounts are done with the help of online banking system.
(d) Green banking products include: 'ATMs', 'Mobile Banking', 'Online Banking', 'Green Credit Cards', 'Green Savings Accounts', 'Green Mortgages', 'Green Loans', 'Green Credit Cards', etc.

Any consumer can conserve paper by selecting the products and services of green banking system and it will be helpful for protecting the environment. Green banking is a combination of technology and operational improvements, therefore, the best possible green banking initiative would be the one where customers as well as the banks becomes equally involved and the best example is online banking [11].

Recently some of the measures taken in the area of Green Banking are: [4]

- State bank of India launched Green Pin facility in Mumbai in February 2016 which would save the customer's time for visiting the branches and help the bank in saving the costs on courier and stationary services
- Axis Bank, made furniture from the recycled materials and started using water from rain water harvesting and water treatment plants. This group also started Remote Management Service Program to monitor the energy usage in the offices and develop the green data centers. Under its "Root For Planet" program it has been awarded the certificate by Limca Book of Records for accomplishing a national record of planting 24 varieties of 1,27,199 saplings in a day across 24 centers involving 7000 volunteers in 687 branches.

After this comes green bonds [12] which are the debt instruments that raises money to fund clean energy projects. The introduction of Green Bonds may resolve the issue of funding, which results in delay of these 'green' projects, in the evolving renewable energy sector. Companies that raise money through these bonds were to invest it only in areas that are environment-friendly such as renewable energy, waste management, clean transportation or sustainable land use. Even though solar power is increasingly competitive compared with power from conventional sources and offers attractive long-term cash flows with zero fuel risk, barriers are still noticed within the financial system. India's banks, for example, face regulatory exposure limits curbing the amount that they can lend to specific sectors. Hence, funding for clean energy gets merged with the power sector as whole due to which these limits are already gets covered. This calls for leading to proposals to set a separate exposure limit for renewables only. With the issue of Green Bonds by Indian corporate, there has been a positive effect on account of investor diversification, which may reflect in increased capital inflow from global investors who would invest in green ventures and access to finance at various stages of the project lifecycle. It also enhances issuer's goodwill as it helps showcasing their commitment towards sustainable development. At the same time, there is limitation of Green Bonds because the risk of project performance stays with the issuer rather than the investor and investors are at times hesitant to buy bonds with lesser ratings. Indian Renewable Energy Development Agency (IRDA) in the year 2014 issued a tax free Green Bond for Rs. 1,000 each. [10] These bonds were issued with 10 year, 15 year and 20 year terms carrying interest rates at 8.16%, 8.55% and 8.55% p.a. respectively, CARE and Brick Works gave it AAA rating. Yes Bank has tied up with KPMG India to provide assurance services for specified term in accordance with the green bond principles. Yes Bank issued a 10 year Green Infrastructure bond in 2015 raising an amount of Rs. 1,000 crores, this amount raised would be diverted towards the financing of the Green Infrastructure projects such as solar power, biomass, wind power and small hydel power projects.

Since the economic recession and global financial crisis, green growth has been drawing worldwide attention as one of the new economic accelerator, which can achieve both environmental protection and economic sustainability. Specifically, green finance is one of "targeted financing" and futuristic in approach since it focuses on green economic activities and financing for the IT industry. This combination of necessity and chance provides correct moment to identify necessary steps for sustainable finance. Environment sustainability being a matter of concern at global sphere has increased the scope for investment in green projects utilizing renewable energy resources [14]. Therefore, many banks and financial institutions would look forward at these kinds of growing sectors. The reasons for going green are many, and the main among them are: due to the increasing energy consumption and energy prices, growing consumer interest in environmentally-friendly goods and services, higher expectations by the public on enterprises' environmental responsibilities and emerging strict regulatory and compliance requirements [6]. Banking sector is one of the major sources of financing investment for commercial projects which is important for economic growth, thereby can plays a vital role in highlighting environmentally sustainable and socially responsible investment.

CONCLUSION

Looking ahead a decade we can predict about complete change in economy where green growth has its major role. Green growth is becoming a lucrative option for countries around the world to achieve environmental protection, reducing poverty and economic advancement [9]. Green banking is emerging with operational instruments to promote renewable energy sectors. For India a huge opening is available which needs to be explored and looked forward. Financial institutions and government have to take regulatory steps to create awareness to the society. Arranging proper trainings and awareness programs in the coming years will help to structure a complete democratization of green finance in India to take place, so that individual investors, corporations, banks and all financial institutions and intermediaries will have their financial tools at their disposal to shift the economy towards sustainability. Though there are risks associated, the shift to green is clear, consistent and cannot be prevented.

REFERENCES

Chadichal Shilpa and Dr Misra Sheelan (2013). "Exploring Web Based Servqual Dimensions In Green Banking Services Impact on Developing e-CRM". *Asia Pacific Journal of Management and Entrepreneurship*, 1(3), 285–312.

Nishikant, Jha and Shraddha, Bhome (2013). "A Study of Green banking trends in India". *Abhinav International Monthly Refereed Journal of Research in Management & Technology*, 2, 127–132.

Kandavel, D. (2013). "Green Banking Initiatives of Commercial banks in India", *SIT Journal of Management*, Volume 3, No. 2, 213–225.

Nagarjuna, Loluru (2015). "Green Financial Management Practices in Public and Private Sector banks—A case study of SBI and ICICI bank", *International Multidisciplinary E-Journal,* Volume 4, No. 8, 295–306.

Heim, G. and Zenklusen, O. (2005). "Sustainable Finance: Strategy Options for Development Financing Institution" Eco: Fact, Stampfenbachstrass, Zurich.

Sibabrata, Nanda and Suresh, Bihari (2012). "Profitability in banks of India: An Impact Study of implementation of Green banking." *International Journal of Green Economics,* 6(3), 217–225.

Sharma, Neetu; Chaudhary, Richa and Purohit, Harsh (2015). "A Comparative study on Green Banking InitiativesTaken by Select Public and Private Sector banks in Mumbai", *IOSR Journal of Business and Management*, 32–37.

Sharifi, Omid and Hossein, Bentolhoda Karbalaie (2015). "Green Banking and Environment Sustainability By Commercial banks in India", *International Journal of Science Technology & Management,* Volume No. 4, No. 11, 294–304.

Javedkar, Prakash and Lavasa, Ashok (2014). "India's Progress in Combating Climate Change, Briefing Paper for UNFCCC COP 20 Lima, Peru", *Issue Paper by Ministry of Environment, Forests and Climate Change,* December.

Agarwal, Richa G. (2015). "Concept Paper on Issuance of Green Bonds ", *Concept Paper by SEBI*, December.

Raghupati, M. and Sujhatha, S. (2015). "Green Banking Initiatives of Commercial Banks in India", *International Research Journal of Business and Management*, Volume 8, No. 2, 74–81.

Kala, Vinod and Garg, Vivek (2014). "Issue paper on Green Bonds in India", *Issue Paper by PACE*, December.

Rambalak, Yadav and Govind, Pathak (2014). "Environmental Sustainability through green banking: A Study on Private and Public sector banks in India", *International Journal of Sustainable Development*, 6(8), 37–47.

Singh, Yadwinder (2015). "Environment Management Through Green Banking: A study of Commercial Banks in India", *International Journal of Interdisciplinary and Multidisciplinary Studies*, Volume 2, No. 4, 17–26.

Websites

www.sbi.co.in

www.axisbank.com

www.yesbank.in

www.business-standard.com

www.climatepolicyinitiative.org.

www.oecd.org/greengrowth

'Sustainable is Attainable'— Tata Power's Transition to Green Energy

Sumit Ray[1]

BRIEF HISTORY OF THE ELECTRICITY SECTOR IN INDIA

The Tata Power Company Limited is India's largest integrated power company with an installed electricity generation capacity of 14,384 MW. The company was incorporated as Tata Hydroelectric Power Supply Company in 1916 but finally on 18th September 1919 it was formally formed into The Tata Power Company Limited.

Electricity which is now almost synonymous to oxygen, is a resource whose commercialization set-off the wheels of a new revolution and changed the entire world. Though Shri. Jamsetji Nusserwanji Tata wanted to bring this innovative energy source to our country in 1875, it wasn't until much later that it could become a reality. The first hydroelectric power plant in India at Darjeeling was established in 1897 with the help of the Maharaja of Burdwan, Sir Bijoy Chand Mahatab Bahadur and the British Government. This plant supplied power to the district of Darjeeling.

Hydroelectric Power Plant in Darjeeling, Circa 1897
Source: Tata Power History Archives.

[1] Chief Operating Officer, Allindia Technologies Limited.

The first thermal power plant of The Calcutta Electric Supply Corporation Limited was commissioned at Emambagh Lane near Princep Ghat in 1899 heralding the beginning of thermal power generation in India.

In 1910 the British India Government passed the first Electricity Act for India. Post-independence in 1947 both the Government of India through its public sector undertakings and the private sector have worked towards making India the third largest producer of electricity in the world as on date. During the fiscal year (FY) 2022–23, the total electricity generation in the country was 1,844 TWh, of which 1,618 TWh was generated by utilities.

The gross electricity consumption per capita in FY2023 was 1,327 kWh. In FY2015, electric energy consumption in agriculture was recorded as being the highest (17.89%) worldwide. The per capita electricity consumption is low compared to most other countries despite India having a low electricity tariff.

The Indian national electric grid has an installed capacity of 416.0 GW as of 31 March 2023. Renewable energy plants, which also include large hydroelectric power plants, constitute 43% of the total installed capacity.

The total installed utility power generation capacity as on 31 March 2023 by type is shown in the table below.

Breakdown of Installed Generation Capacity as on 31/03/2023		
Source	**Installed Capacity (MW)**	**% of Share in Total**
Fossil Fuels	***2,37,269***	***57.7%***
Coal	2,05,235	49.3%
Lignite	6,620	1.6%
Gas	24,824	6.0%
Diesel	***589***	***0.1%***
Non-Fossil Fuels	***1,78,790***	***43.0%***
Hydro	46,850	11.3%
Wind	42,633	10.2%
Solar	66,780	16.1%
Bio Mass	10,248	2.5%
Waste to Energy	554	0.1%
Small Hydro	4,944	1.2%
Nuclear	6,780	1.6%
TOTAL	***4,16,059***	***100.0%***

Source: "Power Sector at a Glance | Government of India | Ministry of Power". powermin.gov.in

Introduction to Tata Power

Tata Power's journey over a century has been a fascinating saga of pioneering initiatives, responsible business practices that have a minimal impact on the environment. Today, Tata Power in one of India's largest integrated power company with a significant international presence. The Company has an installed generation capacity of 14110MW in India and a presence in all the segments of power sector, viz Fuel & Logistics, Generation (thermal, hydro, solar and wind), Transmission, Distribution and Trading. It has successful public- private partnerships in Generation, Transmission and Distribution in India namely "Tata Power Delhi Distribution Limited" with Delhi Government for distribution in North Delhi, 'Powerlinks Transmission Ltd.' with Power Grid Corporation of India Ltd. for evacuation of Power from Tala Hydro plant in Bhutan to Delhi and 'Maithon Power Ltd.' with Damodar Valley Corporation for a 1050 MW Mega Power Project at Jharkhand. It is one of the largest renewable energy players in India and has developed the country's first 4000 MW Ultra Mega Power Project at Mundra (Gujarat) based on super-critical technology.

TATA POWER AT A GLANCE		
	DELIVERING GROWTH AT SCALE	
1	Installed/ Managed Energy Capacity	14,384 MW
2	Customers Served	12.5 million
3	Renewable Energy Portfolio (operational and under implementation)	7800 MW
4	Manufacturing Capacity of Solar Cells & Modules (present & upcoming)	5100 MW
5	Large Utility-Scale Solar EPC Oder Book	4000 MW +
6	Public EV charging Points	4370+
	LEADING THE WAY IN SUSTAINABILITY	
7	Clean & Green Energy Portfolio	38%
8	S&P Global CSA (Percentile)	85
9	Lives Touched with CSR Initiatives	3.7 Million +
10	Students Reached by Club enerji Programme	62,210
11	Youth Certified and Trained for Jobs	12,000+
12	Years of Conserving the Mahseer Fish	50+

Source: Tata Power Website www.tatapower.com

Its international presence includes strategic investments in Indonesia through 30% stake in the leading coal company PT Kaltim Prima Coal (KPC) in Singapore through Trust Energy Resources to securitize coal supply and the shipping of coal for its thermal power generation operations and in Bhutan through a hydro project in partnership with The Royal Government of Bhutan. With its track record of technology leadership, project execution excellence, world class safety processes, customer care and driving green initiatives, Tata Power is poised for a multi-fold growth and committed to 'lighting up lives' for generations to come.

Tata Power's Foray into Renewable Energy

As one of India's largest renewable energy players, Tata Power is positioned at the top to deliver to the changing landscape of India's renewable energy focus. Through its subsidiaries, Tata Power Renewable Energy Limited (TPREL), Tata Power Solar Systems Limited (TPSSL) and Walwhan Renewable Energy Limited (WREL), the company is a front- runner across the renewable spectrum.

The Company aims to energise consumer lifestyles by providing sustainable power. It hopes to inspire efficient use of energy and endeavours to educate the benefits of implementing energy conservation practices. It aims to set higher benchmarks in the implementation of cutting-edge eco-friendly technologies and processes of energy management.

With sustainable development at the heart of its operations, Tata Power leads the way in the generation of clean and green energy contributing to the reduction of carbon emissions. With a 30% clean energy portfolio, Tata Power commits to being Carbon 'Net Zero' before 2045. To achieve this vision, Tata Power focuses on an entire gamut of alternate clean sources of power, enabling customers and stakeholders with sustainable and smart energy solutions.

As Tata Power strives to lead the reform process for sustainable green power, it is also committed to safeguarding the environment for future generations. The founder, Shri Jamshetji Tata, vowed to provide the country and its people with cheap, clean, and abundant power. Tata Power continues to make good on that promise and takes pride in lighting up lives sustainably!

Harnessing Hydro Power

The Company has an installed hydro capacity of 1762 MW. Tata Power has a JV with the Royal Government of Bhutan, under which it has commissioned the 126 MW Dagachhu Hydro Project with Druk Green Power Company. Tata Power, through its subsidiary Tata Power International Pte Ltd, has signed an agreement with Clean Energy AS (Clean Energy) and IFC InfraVentures (IFC) for developing hydro projects of an aggregate capacity of 400 MW in Georgia. The company has synchronised of 187 MW Shuakhevi Hydro Project in Georgia. The company has commissioned two units of 60 MW each of its 120 MW Itezhi Tezhi hydro Power Project in Zambia, in which Tata Power has a 50 percent stake.

Foray into Solar Power

With over 4.5 GW of renewable energy under construction, Tata Power has a strong portfolio of 2995 MW of solar generation capacity. Further accolades are:

- Won LOA to set up a 150 MW solar project in Solapur, Maharashtra through competitive bidding followed by an e-reverse auction.
- Commissioned a 120 MW landmark solar project in Mesanka, Gujarat.
- Commissioned a 300 MW Project in Dholera, using India's largest single-axis tracker system generating 774 MU's annually.
- Executed India's first floating solar project for NTPC in Kayamkulam, Kerala.

The power generated by these solar panels is expected to take the lighting load of the entire building. TP Renewable Microgrid Limited (TPRMG) plans to set up the world's largest number of decentralised solar microgrids that will position India as the global leader in clean, decentralised, affordable and reliable power supply.

Solar Farms

Harnessing Wind Energy

Tata Power has an installed capacity of 932 MW and plants spread across five states of Maharashtra, Gujarat, Tamil Nadu, Karnataka, Andhra Pradesh, Jharkhand, Madhya Pradesh and Rajasthan the leading states in promoting wind power generation in India.

Wind Farms

Waste Heat Recovery/BFG

Tata Power has set up various plants at Haldia and in Jamshedpur (Power 6) based on the blast furnace and coke oven gases which are waste gases from steel making process which help in reducing greenhouse gas emission significantly. It's looking at other similar projects with Tata Steel. Tata Power through its Joint Venture company Industrial Energy Limited (IEL), has successfully commissioned 2 units of 67.5 MW each of the 202.5 MW IEL, Kalinganagar—Orissa project. The company's installed generating capacity from waste gas generation stands at 443 MW.

New and Service-Led Businesses

The Company is looking to scale-up its service businesses, i.e. EV Charging, Home Automation, Distribution services, Thermal O&M services, Solar Rooftop and Solar EPC and is also evaluating opportunities in emerging business areas such as microgrids, rooftop solar, energy efficiency solutions and EV charging stations. It has collaborated with Tata Motors Limited to roll-out EV charging infrastructure and aims to expand its presence further in high EV adoption cities in India. The Company has also launched its rooftop services program in more than 90 cities.

The Company is also working on developing a robust software platform for customers of Tata Power's extensive EV charging infrastructure, includes over 59,000+ home chargers, 4800 public and semi-public charging points, and 430+ bus-charging points, spans across 420+ cities. The company plans to set up 25,000 charging points in the next five years, further supporting the growth of the EV ecosystem in the country.

TP Renewable Microgrid (TPRMG) is set to roll out 10,000 microgrids to provide innovative solutions for the under- served communities and expand the global microgrid footprint. The Company marked first anniversary by commissioning its 100th Solar Microgrid Project in Ratnapur, Uttar Pradesh. The company also partnered with Airtel Payments Bank to enhance customer convenience while also inaugurating its first 5kW Bio-gas generating plant in Bihar.

Taking Strides in Businesses of Interest—Going Green

Rooftop Solar

Tata Power Solar Systems Limited, TPSSL has been India's top solar rooftop EPC player since the past six years.

Compelling economics, especially for the commercial and industrial segment, favourable government policies, and increased environmental awareness have been the key growth drivers. It serves customers across residential, commercial and industrial segments and institutions. The approach to rooftop solar can be broadly classified into two categories – own and operate solar rooftop assets under PPA and build rooftop projects for other customers under EPC contract. Our total portfolio is about 421 MW (as on 31st March 2020), of which 28 MW is under PPA.

Solar Water Pumps

India is seeing a sharp increase in energy consumption, which is being driven by both economic expansion and rapid population expansion. India has set a target of becoming net zero by 2070 in order to grow sustainably. However, this will require India to reduce its net carbon emissions by 1 billion tonnes by the year 2030, which is a challenging goal to achieve.

One of the many industries experiencing growth is agriculture which is predicted to increase to US$ 24 billion by 2025. As per First Advance Estimates for FY 2022-23 (Kharif only), total food grain production in the country is estimated at 149.92 million tonnes.

India is also one of the major players in the agriculture sector worldwide and it is the primary source of livelihood for about 58% of India's population. Thus, farmers also become an integral part of the sector.

However, the World Bank predicts that India will see unusual and unprecedented spells of hot weather, more frequently and covering much larger areas. It also predicts that we can expect drier years to be drier, and wet years wetter.

This increases the dependence on groundwater, and therefore, on groundwater pumps. Out of the total electricity consumed in the country, 20% of the electricity is used for agriculture practices, mostly in irrigation. For farmers who rely on grid-connected pumps, especially during the summer months, this can be an exercise in frustration: power cuts during the day, when watering is needed, and power supply at night, when watering can't be done.

Farmers have taken 12 million electricity connections and 9 million diesel pump sets to pump up groundwater for irrigation.

Farmers turn to diesel-powered pumps, only to find that not only do these pumps inflate their costs, but are also prone to breakdowns. These inflate costs further and often lead to costly delays which ultimately affect crop yield. Moreover, diesel-powered pumps are also notorious for their outsized output of smoke and particulate matter. In essence, it's a solution that doesn't work well and creates another host of problems.

Solar Pumps wipe the slate clean. Once installed, a solar pump runs like clockwork, matching its output to when it is needed most: the sunny summer months. No more stress when the power goes out, no more trips to buy diesel (and no more expensive diesel costs!), and no more unexpected and messy breakdowns either. Moreover, solar pumps are a dream to maintain.

The biggest fillip to Solar Pump adoption comes from the PM-KUSUM (Pradhan Mantri Kisan Urja Suraksha evam Utthaan Mahabhiyan) Scheme which aims at creating energy security for Indian farmers while also contributing to the share of installed capacity from non-fossil-fuel sources. Under this scheme, individual farmers will be supported to install standalone solar agriculture pumps of up to 7.5 HP capacity in off-grid areas.

The aim is to install 20 Lakh pumps by March 2026. Under this scheme, the farmer bears just 40% of the total cost, and within that 40%, up to 30% can be availed through bank finance.

As always, the devil lies in the details, and this is where the GoI needed strong industry partners for implementation. Tata Power, India's No.1 Solar EPC company for the last 8 years was an obvious choice of partner. Tata Power has installed over 85000 pumps across India, under the PM KUSUM scheme. For context, by replacing just 1 million diesel pumps with solar ones, we can expect to mitigate the usage of 9.4 billion litres of diesel, which translates into direct savings for farmers. It also helps us save 25.3 million tonnes of CO_2.

The solar modules have a warranty of 25 years with over 0.1% warranty claim over 2 decades. The solar pumps also come with safety features such as reverse polarity, low voltage and lightening arrestor, and dry runs that ensure the consumer's protection. Moreover, Tata Power also provides assistance in the paperwork and best-fit maximising for the customer's optimum benefit, providing a comprehensive installation experience to simplify the transition from conventional diesel-powered pumps to solar pumps.

Companies like Tata Power are making decentralized renewable energy technologies easily accessible, thereby enabling the smallest communities of the country to partake in the country's sustainable action. Reducing energy usage from fossil fuel sources and moving towards renewables, will not only reduce carbon footprints in the agriculture sector but also enhance the livelihoods of key stakeholders such as the farming community of the country.

With strong industry partners like these, India's ambitious net zero targets, emissions targets, and green energy targets are being rendered achievable. As our installed capacity for renewable power grows, Indian businesses will be able to make a seamless switch to green power, giving Indian products an equal platform in a global marketplace – particularly where regulations such as Carbon Border Adjustment Mechanism (CBAM) are concerned.

Moreover, India will achieve what developed, western countries have been unable to so far: create more jobs, more industry, and more wealth, while reducing emissions, improving air quality, and being kinder to the planet.

Renewable Microgrids

India is home to over six lakh villages and over 70% of the country's population resides here. However, every minute, 25–30 people migrate to Indian cities in search of better livelihoods and lifestyles.

With India's rapid economic growth, the local village economies must also be strengthened through reliable electrification to partake in this development. The government in its commitment to electrification has successfully electrified all villages in India.

However, there are several rural pockets where topographical challenges have made setting up conventional transmission and distribution infrastructure and their maintenance difficult.

Tata Power: India's largest integrated power company that has been operating across the electricity value chain for 107 years, catering to 12 million+ people across urban India through its various distribution companies in states like Mumbai, Odisha, Delhi and Rajasthan—recognizes the need for bringing electricity to rural pockets where conventional supply is intermittent.

Rural electrification plays a significant role in promoting economic growth and energy independence in rural India. So why must rural pockets stay behind when the rest of the country is moving forward? To empower rural India and enable sustainable development, Tata Power has reached states like Uttar Pradesh and Bihar, to provide a reliable power supply that will help bridge the gap between modern India and 'Bharat'. To enable this transformation, Tata Power has come up with a unique proposition – So what if conventional electricity can't come to them? They can make their own!

Enter: Solar Microgrids. Integrated networks or 'grids' of power capture, store and distribute clean electricity to an entire rural community. These Microgrids consist of a network of small-scale solar panels and battery storage systems that can provide clean and reliable electricity to power rural businesses, homes, and other community infrastructure. Components can be brought to the site and assembled to create a grid that needs no input other than the sun to provide electricity.

Solar Microgrid

Solar Microgrids can be a game-changer for small businesses in remote villages that face unreliable electricity supply. Businesses can reduce their dependence on expensive and unreliable diesel generators, which are commonly used in rural areas. Resulting in significant cost savings over time. They can also provide a stable and uninterrupted power supply, which is critical for businesses that require electricity to operate. This can lead to increased productivity and profitability, as well as improved product quality and consistency.

Tata Power Renewable Microgrid (TPRMG), a wholly owned subsidiary of Tata Power, was launched in October 2019, for setting up Renewable Microgrids to supply clean, affordable, reliable & quality power supply to rural India. So far, around 200 Microgrids are commissioned in the states of Uttar Pradesh and Bihar. A pilot Microgrid programme is also underway in Odisha. The goal is to roll out 10,000 Microgrids in the near future.

The beautiful village of Indrapur makes for an interesting story of how Microgrids are transforming rural lives through easy electrification. Set amid the Sundarbans, it is only accessible via a 90-minute ferry ride. The village used to pack all their activities into the limited sunlight hours, as they had no electricity, and connecting them to the grid was an extremely expensive (and technically challenging) undertaking. TPRMG's 110 kW grid matches the average sunlight that the village gets (one bright day followed by one cloudy day) by design: a two-day autonomy mechanism in which the battery bank was altered to discharge a 25–30% per day irrespective of a sunny or cloudy day.

Aside from the positive impact on businesses, and the general health of the population, electrification has had another pleasant side effect: an increase in literacy rates. Children are now able to use dependable, high-quality light in their homes to do their homework and studies, resulting in better student outcomes, and more children staying in school. Moreover, the community now enjoys other benefits of light: a bustling night market.

TPRMG is bringing electricity to not just the villages and rural entrepreneurs but to the remotest of towns and tribes across the country as well. The story of TPRMG's implementation of 100+ Solar Microgrids in Chattisgarh reads like an adventure tale. The tribal communities here are located centrally in the dense forests of Chhattisgarh, with absolutely no access to power. TPRMG was able to successfully implement the project in the village and also trained and educated the local communities in its maintenance, creating employment and acceptance of the project.

While the other villages enjoy nights with bright lights, the Hanle Observatory at Ladakh communes with the dark. Indian Institute of Astrophysics (IIAP), Bangalore wanted TPRMG to build a 35 kWp solar plant at the IIAP's Hanle Observatory to power India's highest telescope. The project entailed various challenges such as being located high in the Himalayas where materials to Hanle could only be transported via mules and yaks. Ladakh also faces unpredictable and extreme weather conditions throughout the year which does not suit standard solutions, so TPRMG designed a solution that was specific to their use case.

Today, the solar Microgrid not only provides uninterrupted power to the Hanle Observatory but also helps them realise significant cost savings. Of course, they don't have to spend anything on the transportation of fuel, which traditional sources of power would have necessitated, even if the fuel were transported by the most untraditional means.

Moreover, the solar grid at Hanle is quiet. It produces no unsightly pollution, nor does it demand anything other than timely maintenance, and sunlight. It doesn't disturb the dark skies Hanle needs to do its important work of unravelling the mystery of the stars. There's something poetic about Hanle being powered by the energy of a star itself.

That then, is the promise of solar Microgrids. Light where we need it. Quiet where we need it. Power wherever we need it. Energy that comes from the same source that powers life on this planet. What could be cleaner, more dependable than that?

As Tata Power puts it so succinctly, #DependableAsTheSun.

EV Charging Infrastructure—Towards Greener Mobility

Tata Power intend to provide our state-of-the-art and customised EV charging solutions to form the infrastructure backbone for a growing EV ecosystem and provide customers access to this energy efficient option with ease. Tata Power is a strong supporter of the government's National Electric Mobility Mission. Being part of the Tata Group enables us to derive synergies from other group companies, particularly Tata Motors' planned roll-out of electric cars. The Company has collaboration with MG Motors and Jaguar India. Starting from our first EV charging station set up in Mumbai, Tata Power's extensive EV charging infrastructure, includes over 40,000 home chargers, 4000+ public and semi-public charging points, and 250 bus-charging points, spans 350 cities with a presence in 550 cities. The company plans to set up 25,000 charging points in the next five years, further supporting the growth of the EV ecosystem in the country.

EZ Home Automation Solutions

Tata Power EZ HOME is an IoT solution which allows you to operate, schedule, monitor appliances like lighting, fans, ACs, washing machines, geysers, TVs, refrigerators, etc. with your phone and with voice control via Google Assistant or Alexa.

You can now operate home appliances more efficiently, with the convenience of managing them through your smartphones. These smart switches/devices will be integrated with your home appliances like lighting, fans, AC, curtains, geyser etc. for remote monitoring, control and operation through a smart phone or smart voice device.

This IoT solution from Tata Power enables you to have Safe, Easy & Efficient control from anywhere!

POWERING A GREENER WORLD—PIONEERING INITIATIVES TOWARD SUSTAINABILITY

As India's largest integrated power company, Tata Power is conscious of their role as sustainability stewards and embraces the challenges of climate change. They strive to lead the path towards growth with responsibility. Their commitment to this sustainable future has been categorical and consistent. Their sustainability initiatives comprise investments in clean coal technologies; several well-planned projects that generate power from wind, solar, and geothermal energies that are renewable sources; an unflinching commitment towards biodiversity conservation; streamlining water use; and planting thousands of trees in the vicinity of their power plants to reduce carbon footprint. They are continuously working towards innovating and implementing eco-friendly technologies, and undertaking various projects under the Clean Development Mechanism, including wind power projects and various small-scale energy efficiency projects.

Environment

Over the next five years, Tata Power plans to increase its generation capacity exponentially. Tata Power has executed a number of measures in order to reduce emissions. Tata Power's power plant emissions are well within the norms laid down by the National Ambient Air Quality Standards (NAAQS). Sourcing clean coal is another significant way of reducing emissions and increasing efficiency. Tata Power has been consciously exploring clean coal sources, including imports, for its thermal power plants. Committed to complying with all regulations pertaining to the preservation and enrichment of the environment, Tata Power uses world- class innovative and environment-friendly technologies.

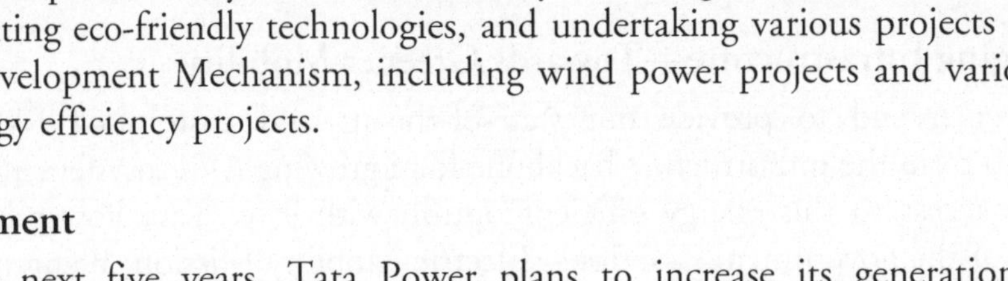

The Company is committed to the cause of ensuring a greener and sustainable planet. In line with this it has launched two new properties under the aegis of Greenolution in 2015. 'Act for Mahseer', is a sustainable programme focused at conservation of the Mahseer, an endangered species of fish. It is a call to action public campaign aimed at spreading awareness about the mighty Mahseer to help preserve this valuable fish species in a big way at national level.

The Company also embarks on several initiatives to spread awareness about saving power, conserving energy and combating climate change issues. One such initiative is the Tata Power Club Enerji (previously known as Tata Power Energy Club) that educates the masses about how to use energy efficiently and curb energy wastage, along with conserving resources and civic & moral values. The Club reaches out to school children through various interactive mediums and sensitizes them on the need to conserve energy, resources and civic & moral values. The Club started in 2007 with 12 schools in Mumbai and has today become a nationwide movement reaching about 500 schools and covering ten cities—Mumbai, Pune, Bengaluru, Kolkata, Delhi, Ahmedabad, Jamshedpur, Lonavla and Belgaum. Over the last several years, it has reached out to number of schools in India and has sensitised over 29 million citizens who in turn have helped save more than 33 million units of electricity till date. This saving is equivalent to saving 25,000 tonnes of CO_2. Club Enerji program is now more than 10 years old.

In FY15, Tata Power Club Enerji launched an online module of the Club Enerji programme. The module is hosted on the Club Enerji website.

The objective of this initiative is to reach out to a larger audience and impact a larger group of IT skilled children with a vision to transform by adopting a holistic and robust approach towards conservation.

The module aims to not only urge the wider audience to conserve energy, resources, and their civic and moral values, but also give them a detailed understanding of the ways in which depletion of resources is occurring, and its various repercussions.

In 2017, Club Enerji won Bronze award Club Enerji Disaster Management module under the category Multimedia CD-Rom Based Presentation at ABCI awards, Mumbai. In the year 2014, Tata Power Club Enerji has been declared as a 'promising practice' in Tata Group Companies in TATA Deep Dive Collaborative Benchmarking (DDCB) Study on "Advertising, Branding & Corporate Communication (ABCC)" by TQMS.

Club Enerji's Resource Conservation module won in the Digital Communication Category at the Association of Business Communicators of India (ABCI) Awards in 2014. Club Enerji had been shortlisted as BEST PRAX for presentation at International forum in Auckland in December 2012.

It has also been bestowed with the Eco Advocate Award by Asia Pacific Enterprise Leadership Awards (APELA) at Singapore. It was recognized at the "2012 International Business Awards" with Gold Stevie Award for being the best Marketing Campaign of the Year 2012 – Energy category. It has also been awarded Gold at the ABCI awards in the category Best Communication material and Bronze for its Resource Conservation Module.

COMMUNITY RELATIONS

The Company is committed to being sensitive about resource conservation, environment protection and enrichment, and the development of local communities. The Company has continued its focus on Corporate Social Responsibility activities to make a difference to the communities in its area of operations. Over the last thirty years, Tata Power has continued to participate in an eco-restoration and eco-development programme in the Western Ghats, which is one of the most sensitive ecosystems in the world. Through this period, over seven million saplings of 60 tree species have been planted. Even today, over 600,000 trees are being planted regularly as a re-forestation measure. A number of training programmes are carried out for developing self-employment opportunities among the rural population.

The Company also carries out regular medical check-ups, provides medicines at its health centres, and carries out a number of health awareness programmes such as eye check-ups and blood donation camps at several locations.

TATA POWER SKILL DEVELOPMENT INSTITUTE (TPSDI)

The Tata Power Skill Development Institute (TPSDI) was established by Tata Power Company Limited to bridge the skill gap in the Energy Sector and equip individuals with employable skills. Founded in 2015 during Tata Power's Centenary Year Celebrations, TPSDI has successfully trained over 200,000 people to date (Sept 2023).

TPSDI's vision is be the Best-in-Class Technical Training Institute for Contemporary and Future industrial Skills to empower people in a sustainable manner. To achieve this vision, TPSDI has established six Training Hubs and four Training Spokes across the country, utilizing Tata Power's joint ventures and subsidiaries' resources.

These training "centres" are staffed with capable and experienced faculty who are backed by Tata Power's deep and extensive expertise in the traditional power sector, safety, and green energy skills.

Apart from these centres, TPSDI conducted training at numerous locations across the country (more than 43) and internationally, in Bhutan, Ethiopia, and Liberia.

The modular training and certification programs offered by TPSDI equip trainees with a wide range of Power Sector skills, covering Renewable, Green, and Traditional Energy sources, Power Generation, Transmission, and Distribution. TPSDI offers training in Green Energy, Safety Health & Environment, Transmission & Distribution, Power Systems, and Soft Skills, utilizing a unique training approach designed for delivering skills with speed, scale, and standards. TPSDI's courses and approach heavily emphasize "hands-on" training on skills. All TPSDI centres are equipped with life-sized industrial equipment, instruments, and models on which trainees can practice and hone their skills.

CONCLUSION

The story of Tata Power truly outlines what a leader in the industry has to undertake to make paradigm shifts in the business keeping in mind the future of the world we live in. Their commitment toward the environment and sustainability is testified by their conscious shift from conventional to new technologies and their determination to educate everyone that 'sustainable is attainable' if we all put our heart and minds to it together for the better future of this world.

BIBLIOGRAPHY

https://tatapower100.tatapower.com/heritage/power-generation-over-the-years.aspx

"BP Statistical Review of World Energy 2021 (page 63)" (PDF).

Growth of Electricity Sector in India from 1947–2023" (PDF).

Growth of Electricity Sector in India from 1947–2020" (PDF). Central Electricity Authority. October 2020.

Power Sector at a Glance ALL INDIA | Government of India | Ministry of Power". powermin.gov.in.

Tata Power Corporate Profile 2023.

Tata Power Website www.tatapower.com

Tata Power Annual Report 2022–23.

World Bank Environment Report https://www.worldbank.org/en/topic/environment

Tata Power Blog Articles https://www.tatapower.com/blog

Tata Power Media Releases https://www.tatapower.com/media/media-releases.aspx?utm_medium=301&utm_source=direct&utm_campaign=/media/media-releases.aspx

Tata Power Featured Stories https://www.tatapower.com/media/featured-stories.aspx

Learning Organization and Green Practices

Dr. Rita Basu[1]

ABSTRACT: Theses day's people are very health conscious. They are highly observant about the effect of environmental pollution in their life and naturally concerned about the industrial pollution also. Therefore environmental management happen to be the part of the every organization's objectives. But at the same time there is a need to overcome any financial constraints of the firm and to promote growth through industrialization. So, it becomes organizations' responsibility to plan sustainable development that facilitates not only the protection of the environment but also the growth of the organization. Greenness ensures that organization reduces the amount of waste and pollution, discharged into environment and it ensures better use of resources. The success of this strategy can be activated by the intervention of competent human resources of the organization through organizational development. This organizational development should be the part of green human resource development (GHRD). Now the required competency development of the organizations' members for green organizational development depends on acquisition of information, absorption of it, modify it (if necessary), and transferring it into knowledge within the organization. This process demands the generation of need within the organization to improve knowledge capacity, such that it can accommodate external demand and utilize external knowledge for greenness. This can be done through organizational learning, which implies innovation and it is always related to change. But, for the implementation of change, to support change, it is necessary to develop an appropriate organizational culture, where the common beliefs, values, attitudes and standard of behaviour of the members of the organization are nurtured and modified properly through the process of learning to develop synergy for green practices by transforming the organization into learning organization. Therefore, Green organizational development not only depends on the competency of the organizations' members but also the existence of this supportive culture ie, learning organization culture which facilitate in adopting pro-environmental behaviour for sustainable development.

Keywords: *Greenness, Sustainable Development, Green Human Resource Development, Organizational Development, Organizational Learning, Learning Organization.*

---

[1] Professor and Head of the Department, Department of Applied Psychology, University of Calcutta.

INTRODUCTION

Now a days people are very health conscious. These consciousnesses develop the attitude of the individual to remain active about health related issues (Becker, *et al.*, 1977; Gould, 1990; Jayanti and Burns, 1998). Naturally a person regularly update their information and level of knowledge in relation to their health and tries to chalk out the plan for maintain and improve the health by preventing the causes of ailments and by reducing the severity of it. *As a part of this activity, they are highly observant about the effect of environmental pollution in their life and naturally concerned about the air pollution caused by industry also.*

AIR POLLUTION AND INDUSTRIALIZATION

Air pollution is the contamination of the indoor or outdoor environment by any chemical, physical or biological agent that negatively modifies the natural characteristics of the atmosphere. Household combustion devices, motor vehicles, industrial facilities and forest fires are common sources of air pollution. Pollutants of major public health concern include particulate matter, carbon monoxide, ozone, nitrogen dioxide and sulphur dioxide. Outdoor and indoor air pollution cause respiratory and other diseases and are important sources of morbidity and mortality (WHO).

National Programme on Climate Change & Human Health, National Centre for Disease Control (NPCCHH, 2022) reported about the recent study done by Indian Council for Medical Research (ICMR), showed the following findings:

1. 1.7 million Deaths (18% of the total deaths) in India (2019) were attributable to air pollution a) Chronic Obstructive Pulmonary Disease (32.5%), b) Ischemic heart disease (29.2%), c) Stroke (16.2%) and d) Lower respiratory infections (11.2%).
2. 11.5% of the total DALYs (Disability-Adjusted Life Year) in India (2019) attributable to air pollution are – a) 39.5% from lung diseases – COPD (22.7%), Lower respiratory infections (15.5%), Lung cancer (1.3%); b) Other DALYs – Ischaemic heart disease (24.9%), Stroke (13.7%), Diabetes (5.5%), Neonatal disorders (14.5%), Cataract (1.5%).

According to the findings major sources of air pollution in the country are:

1. Ambient (outdoor) air pollutions from both anthropogenic and natural—Industrial emissions (through fossil fuel burning/process and fugitive emission), vehicular exhaust, re-suspension of road dust, construction and demolition activities, refuge burning (garbage, horticulture wastes, crop residues etc.), use of solid fuels for cooking and burning of firecrackers etc.

2. Household (indoor) air pollutions caused by burning biomass such as—wood, coal, dung, kerosene in chulhas or fireplaces for cooking and heating purposes. Others such as: by burning mosquito coils, incense sticks, cigarettes, bidis, use of sprays, solvents and fumes from chemicals used in building interiors etc.
3. ***Sick Building Syndrome (SBS):*** Building occupants experience acute health and comfort effects which appear to be linked to time spent in a building, but no specific illness or cause can be identified is called Sick Building Syndrome (SBS).

The complaints may be localized in a particular room or zone, or may be widespread throughout the building. The major sources are inadequate ventilation, chemical and biological contaminants (molds and fungi) from indoor sources or outdoor sources, dust, smoke, fumes, fabric fibres, bright or flickering lights and problems with cleaning and layout.

Central Pollution Control Board, Government of India enacted: The Water (Prevention and Control of Pollution) Procedure for Transaction of Business) Rules, 1975, The Air (Prevention and Control of Pollution) Act, 1981 (as amended to date), The Environmental Protection Act, 1986 (as amended to date), The Public Liability Insurance Act, 1991, The Biological Diversity Act, 2002, The National Green Tribunal Act, 2010 (Pollution Control Acts, Rules & Notifications Issued There under, 2021). But at the same time there is a need for exhaustive inspection and vigilance whether all these laws and rules are followed by the industry or not as well as it is also the social responsibility of the organizations those produce pollution in daily activities to mitigate waste and emissions. *Therefore environmental management happen to be the part of the every organization's objectives. But at the same time there is a need to overcome any financial constraints of the firm and to promote growth through industrialization.*

As opined by Khan and Tarique (2015), introduction of liberalization measures in 1991 simplified the entry of private and foreign investment & technology in industrial sector in India. Due to this India was able to develop a strong and diversified industrial structure, which put our country in the league of emerging economies. However, rapid industrialization carried with it the seeds of environmental damage. Further they said that pollution of natural environment not only affects people but also have adverse impact on economic growth in the long run. Behrer *et al.* (2023) in their research under World Bank on Development Economics found that air pollution has a variety of negative impacts on workers and economic sectors that manifest at the macro level in the form of reductions in economic growth. The most obvious mechanisms through which air pollution affects year-to-year changes in GDP are that pollution reduces worker productivity on the job, increases worker absenteeism due to illness, and directly harms agricultural productivity. Data from the Reserve Bank of India suggests that the effect is non-trivial— the median annual increase in the level of particulate pollution reduces year-to-year changes in gross domestic product by 0.56 percentage points. *So, it becomes organizations' responsibility to plan sustainable development that facilitates not only the protection of the environment but also the growth of the organization.*

SUSTAINABLE DEVELOPMENT AND GREEN MANAGEMENT

Sustainable Development

To address the challenges of climate change, extreme poverty, scarce resources, cultural conflicts, political instability, human migration-based disruption, and globalization, a universal set of goals, targets, and indicators, namely Sustainable Development Goals (SDGs), was Introduced by the United Nations. Referring the remark made by Halisçelik & Soytas (2019), that the social development, economic growth, and environmental protection being the three mutually reinforcing pillars continuously interacting with different stakeholders develop the complex nature of sustainable development, Iqbal and Ahmad (2020), commented that this proposed initiatives are applicable for all type of business units without any exemption. According to them in sustainable development, organizations view nature as an integral part of their corporate businesses and create a win-win solution for planet, society, and organization itself. Also, to be in competitive advantage resources are the leading objects for the development of dynamic competencies in the rapidly changing environments. So, there is a need to develop a sense of balance for high resource consumption for economic development and to face constant challenge that forces organizations to run-through eco-friendly professional manners. It has a close association with the concept of corporate social responsibility. *Greenness ensures that organization reduces the amount of waste and pollution, discharged into environment and it ensures better use of resources.*

The Green Management

The Green management is the responsibility of the whole organization. According to the goals and strategies of the business, management tries to develop or adopt suitable innovative approach to get environmental support for sustainable development. Green management is defined as the process inside a company that uses innovation to accomplish sustainability, waste reduction, social responsibility, and competitive advantage via continuous learning and improvement(Matheus *et al.*, 2023). So, there is big responsibility of an organization to align the organizational goals and practices with the goals and practices for implementation of green organization. From the study of Khare *et al.* (2023), Stakeholders' demand, organisation resources, expertise, managing environmental uncertainty, and product uniqueness affect green management and Small Scale Industry's (SSI) sustainability performance in India. According to them, green management boosts SSI's sustainability. *The success of this strategy can be activated by the intervention of competent human resources of the organization through green organizational development as a part of green human resource management.*

GREEN HUMAN RESOURCE MANAGEMENT

It could be realized that environmental disruptions are often a result of certain human activities. Restraining of such disruptions can be done by investigating and changing the underlying human behaviour. The success of this strategy demands for green human resource management. As the employees are coming from the different parts of the society, naturally they are aware of the significance and need of greenness in their workplace and are concerned for green human resource management. Our personal and professional lifestyle is affected due to many consequences. The reasons for green HRM are:

1. To protect the environmental aspects to make the work ethical and build the internal and external environment of workplace safe & healthy
2. To train and encourage the employees to perform their activities in an environment friendly way.
3. To advance organization environmental performance by HR functions like training, employee empowerment, and Environmental Management System (EMS), rewards etc.
4. To motivate employees, for involving employees in corporate environmental management initiatives and efforts.
5. To develop green environmental culture.

Through literature survey Masood (2018), conglomerated, that Green HRM is concerned in the development, execution and on-going maintenance of a system, which aims to make employees of an organization to be with greenness. It is the transformation of employees into green employees so that they can significantly contribute to the environmental goals for realization of environmental sustainability. He added that Green human resource management (GHRM) process includes the environmental responsibility in the tasks and duties of human resources, so that they are motivated to collaborately implement the innovative environmental programs for their organization. Therefore it is obvious that besides the development of awareness, planning and implementing reduction of use of such product which can directly or indirectly responsible for generation of pollution in the organization, the functions of GHRM are also involve the green human resource policies such as planning, recruiting, selecting, maintaining and developing the employees and the organization as a whole. Green human resource management boost up the value of the employees and the organization for Green Human Resource Development. As a branch of green human resource management philosophy, green human resource development (GHRD) are continuously explores the need of the development of the mindset of the human resource towards greenness of the environment for the benefit of the general health of the people as well as for sustainable development. The study of Mishra (2017) suggests that, there is high scope for Indian manufacturing sector to improvise GHRM practices. The employees have accepted the value and need for greening, interested to clarify their role in greening of organization, ready to explore new and innovative measures, show interest in incorporating employee involvement and representatives from organizations liked the idea of having" green teams". According to his findings, top-management support, facilitate and desire environment friendly practices in the Indian organization because the country has a power-distance culture, where employees look for their seniors' consent and preference in initiating any new behaviour. Leader's environmental descriptive norms, leadership style and demonstration of pro-environmental behaviours play an important part in the greening of organizations. Greening of the organization also demands a supportive environment-friendly culture, which in turn demands new leadership competencies, behaviours and mindsets. The other key concern was that though the need for mutual learning and integration of greening practices across departments had been felt by all the representatives, there was no provision reported for the same.

According to conventionally, practising Organizational Development (OD) involves strategic planning, leadership development, team building, learning and development, cultural change and implementation of strategy. OD must involve systematic change effort for improvement of the organization's system and at the same time capacity building of the system for future development through spontaneous responses and involvement of the members of the organization (Cummings and Worley, 2008). *This organizational development should be the part of green human resource development (GHRD).*

GREEN ORGANIZATIONAL DEVELOPMENT

By "Green OD" Yeganeh and Glavas(2008) referred that organization focuses change of core practices for the sustainability of the societal good and preservation of natural environment as well as adding value to the organization in terms of reputation, stock prices and viability. They told that, in the field of OD, sustainability describes lasting change. While Green OD is about sustainable change, sustainability alone is not Green OD. Effective Green OD requires trust, learning, empowerment, buy-in, and relational capacity.

Now the required competency development of the organizations' members for green organizational development depends on acquisition of information, absorption of it, modify it (if necessary), and transferring it into knowledge within the organization.

This process demands the generation of need within the organization to improve knowledge capacity, such that it can accommodate external demand and utilize external knowledge for greenness. This can be done through organizational learning, which implies innovation and it is always related to change.

ORGANIZATIONAL LEARNING AND GREENNESS

The practice of organizational learning involves: the identification of the present level of knowledge within organization; As per the environmental requirement acquire new knowledge; the diffusion of the existing and new knowledge; the integration and modification of the knowledge and the use of the knowledge for changing the behaviour of the members of the organization.

Huber (1991) said that it is a complex process for potential development of new knowledge for the betterment of organizational behaviour. According to Miller (1996) organizational learning is the acquisition of knowledge from individuals and groups, to influence others in an organization. Similarly Desai (2010) also said that it is the process of acquiring information, absorbing that information, modifying it if necessary, and transferring that knowledge within an organization. Therefore it can be said that organizational learning is basically concern for social relations among individuals of an organization. It is the institutionalization of knowledge gained by any member of the organization. As per Crossan and White (2011), this learning change the cognitive structures as well as the behaviours of the members of the organization, to enlarge the capability of the organization to comply with its surroundings. So, it could be said that positive attitude for organizational learning could give direction to the organization towards sustainable development for competitive advantage.

Iqbal, and Ahmad (2020) studying on Small and medium-sized enterprises (SMEs) in South Asian Association of Regional Cooperation (SAARC) found that there is a significant impact of organizational learning on sustainable performance. This study views organizational learning as a source of sustained competitive advantage for sustainable developmental goals. Zhang *et al.* (2018) conducting survey on 300 organizations in China identified that the organizational learning and environmental proactivity played moderating role in dynamic capability development for green innovation.

Surveying on manufacturing enterprises Obeng *et al.* (2022)), established that the relationship between GHRM practices and organizational competitiveness of manufacturing enterprises, was positively moderated by the organizational learning potentials of the firms. They have realized that the accomplishment of superior competitiveness and sustainable development is based on the capability of the firm to engage in GHRM or in specific term GHRD practices and also exerting attitude towards organizational learning, than to adopt only in GHRD.

But the organization that learn for organizational learning demand an appropriate organizational environment. This organizational environment depends on systematic development of a different organizational culture called Learning Organization. The organizational learning is a procedure or practice, whereas the Learning Organization is at the same time the state and the root of that process which generates, stimulates and directs members of the organization to learn for organizational learning.

For the implementation of change, to support change, it is necessary to develop an appropriate organizational culture, where the common beliefs, values, attitudes and standard of behaviour of the members of the organization are nurtured and modified properly through the process of learning to develop synergy for green practices by transforming the organization into learning organization.

THE LEARNING ORGANIZATION AND GREENNESS

Senege (1990) focused on the role of individual and of organization to define learning organization. According to him, 'where people continuously expand their capacity to create the results they truly desire, where new and expansive patterns of thinking are nurtured, where collective aspiration is set free, and where people are continually learning how to learn together'.

Learning organization model by Senege (1990) proposed

Senege suggested learning organization is founded on five disciplines:

1. **Personal Mastery**: Essential to the process is building self-awareness and understanding personal strength and weakness.
2. **Mental Models**: Allows individual to unearth the assumption and generalization that influence their understanding of the world and shape how action is taken.
3. **Building Shared Vision**: The vision is created collectively to realize the vision that fosters genuine commitment.
4. **Team Learning**: Individual share and transmit own thoughts and learning for the betterment and maintaining balance of knowledge for all the members of the team.
5. **System Thinking**: A business organization is a complex system with many subsystems and applying systems thinking means viewing each function as part of the larger system rather than as a collection of isolated tasks.

The conceptual framework for the present proposition is significantly relevant with the concept of the most popular model proposed by Senege (1990). From this model it was found that learning organization is a one of the intervention of Organizational Development where organizational culture is going to be modified and it would obey the principal of individual differences in terms of innovation, commitment and learning behaviour styles etc. and phenomena also vary under changes of circumstances with major climate of the organization and variation of work team and leadership.

The Culture of the Learning Organization and Greenness

The ability of the organization to acquire new knowledge from the surroundings, depends to a great extend on the prevailing attitude among the employees, especially the managers as a transformational leader in relation to the organization and the surroundings. Building-up of the learning organization, depends on the formerly developed and established organizational culture. For development of green organization it is realized that the following cultural components of the learning organization are the best means:

- A key characteristics of the culture of the learning organization, is the continuous examination and experimentation of the truth. Obviously the members of the learning organization inclined to enquire constantly, to collect and analysis the data for greenness and investigate the basic requirement for the green environment through the organizational learning. As a result the process of green organizational development is also enhanced.
- The learning organization is open to its internal and external environment. Such openness makes it possible to get the information from everywhere easily and spontaneously so organization remain updated about any kind of change or any kind of development related to greenness.
- Trust, beliefs and respects for internal and external members, even for boundary members are the characteristics of the learning organization. This mindset encourages the members of the organization to spontaneously sharing of their knowledge, opinion and learning for the creation and development of green organization and everyone also reciprocate this by positive acceptance.
- The members of the learning organization are getting opportunities, encouragement and feel free to test the hypotheses or assumptions whatever they have in their mind for betterment of green organization. This kind of organization culture helps to nurture the innovative ideas for greenness, within the organization fearlessly and happily.
- The members of the learning organization are highly focused and oriented towards the real questions and problems. They accept reality and fact. Their decision-making is based on real facts and data, never influenced or guided by any intention and or interests of any authority or influential person. This exactly helps learning organization to properly build green organizational environment rapidly and smoothly.
- Members of the learning organization believe in synergy for the organizational development. As a consequence they respect team relationship and like to get the

credit as a member of a team than as an individual. Their synchronized energy amplifies the capability of the organizational learning for greenness.

- Learning organization is customer centric and one of the major goals of learning organization is to move beyond the customer satisfaction by providing superior value for consumers. The basic reason of learning is to enable an enterprise to value for green organization for its internal and external customers.
- The learning organizational culture should be like the one where the employees and manager are not afraid of any risk of doing any task or apply any innovative ideas, because they believe that, if there is no acceptance of any risk in the organization, then there are no innovations, no changes and consequently, there is no learning. So to implement greenness in organization, members accept any kind of risky behaviour.
- The members of the learning organization believe that even they can learn from mistakes. The tolerance of mistake helps in new learning and helps to proceed forward for implementation of innovative idea. The culture of the learning organization is characterized by the attitude that the mistakes are in fact, the opportunity to learn something new, that the mistakes are unavoidable and that the admittance of mistakes is not a reflection of weakness but is a strong support for learning.

Green organizational development not only depends on the competency of the organizations' members, implementation of new technologies or huge capital investment but also the existence of this supportive culture i.e., learning organization culture which facilitate in adopting pro-environmental behaviour for sustainable development. Therefore the advancement of learning organization is the best avenue for the green practices.

REFERENCES

Becker, M.H., Maiman, L.A., Kirscht, J.P., Haefner, D.P. and Drachman, R.H. (1977). The health belief model and prediction of dietary compliance: A field experiment. *Journal of Health Social Behavior*, 18:348–366.

Behrer, A. Patrick Rishabh and Choudhary. Dhruv Sharma. Air Pollution Reduces Economic Activity Evidence from India. *World Bank Group. Development Economics Development Research Group* June 2023 http://www.worldbank.org/prwp Policy Research Working Paper 10515.

Cummings, Thomas G. and Worley (2008). Christopher G. Organization Development & Change, *South-Western Cengage Learning*, USA, 9th ed.

Crossan, M., Maurer, C. and White, R. (2011). Reflections on the 2009 AMR decade award: Do we have a theory of organizational learning? *Academy of Management Review*, 36, 446–460.

Desai, D.A. (2010). Co-creating learning: Insights from complexity theory. *The Learning Organization*, 17(5), 388–403. https://doi.org/10.1108/09696471011059796

Gould, S.J. (1988). Consumer attitudes toward health and health care: A differential perspective. *Journal of Consumer Affairs*, 22:96–118.

Huber, G. (1991). Organizational learning: The contributing processes and the literatures. *Organization Science*, 2, 88–115.

Iqbal, Qaisar and Ahmad, Noor Hazlina (2020). Sustainable development: The colors of sustainable leadership in learning organization. wileyonlinelibrary.com/journal/sd © 2020, *ERP Environment and John Wiley & Sons Ltd.* (Aug, 2020) DOI: 10.1002/sd.2135

Jayanti, R.K. and Burns, A. C. (1998). The antecedents of preventive health care behaviour: An empirical study. *Academy of Marketing Science*, 26(1), 9-15

Khare, Vikas Kumar, Raghuwansi, Sandeep, Vashista, Anil and Verma, Priyanka (2023). The Importance of Green Management and its Implication in Creating Sustainability Performance on the Small-Scale Industries in India. *Journal of Law and Sustainable Development* 11(5):e699. DOI:10.55908/sdgs.v11i5.699. August 2023

Maria Khan1 and Md. Tarique (2015). Industrial Pollution in Indian Industries: A Post Reform Scenario. *Journal of Energy Research and Environmental Technology* (JERET). Print ISSN: 2394-1561; Online ISSN: 2394-157X; Volume 2, Number 2; January-March, 2015; pp. 182–187.

Masood, Rana Zehra (2018). Green Hrm: A Need for 21st Century. *Journal of Emerging Technologies and Innovative Research* (JETIR). www.jetir.org. June 2018, Volume 5, Issue 6. ISSN-2349-5162.

Matheus, Juliano, André Takeci Iamamoto, Bidin, P. and Silva. (2023). *The Dynamic Capabilities of Cleantechs and Eco-Innovation in the Use of Green Fiscal Public Policies.* 11(1), e0248–e0248. https://doi.org/10.37497/sdgs.v11i1.248

Miller, D. (1996). A preliminary typology of organizational learning: Synthesizing the literature. *Journal of Management*, 22(3), 485–505. https://doi.org/10.1177/01492063 960220030

Mishra, Pavitra (2017). Green human resource management, A framework for sustainable organizational development in an emerging economy. *International Journal of Organizational Analysis.* Vol. 25 No. 5, 2017 pp. 762–788. © Emerald Publishing Limited, 1934-8835.

Obeng, Patrick, Dogbe. Courage Simon Kofi and Boahen. Patience Ama Nyantakyiwaa (2022). Nexus between GHRM and organizational competitiveness: role of green innovation and organizational learning of MNEs. *Bussiness and Society Review*, 2023;1–29. wileyonlinelibrary.com/journal/basr.

Senge, Peter M. (1990). *The Fifth Discipline*, Doubleday, New York.

Yeganeh, Bauback and Glavas, Ante (2008). Green Organization Development. OD PRACTITIONER Vol. 40, No. 2 2008.

Zhang, Yali, Sun. Jun, Yang. Zhaojun and Li, Shurong (2018). Organizational Learning and Green Innovation: Does Environmental Proactivity Matter? Sustainability 2018, 10, 3737; doi: 10.3390/su 10103737. www.mdpi.com/journal/sustainability

Notice

Health Advisory on Air Pollution, National Programme on Climate Change & Human Health National centre for Disease Control (NPCCHH), Directorate General of Health Services, Mohawk, September 2022. https://www.who.int/health-topics/air-pollution#tab=tab_1 dt 15/11/2023 Definition of Air Pollution.

Pollution Control Acts, Rules and Notifications Issued Thereunder (2021). Central Pollution Control Board (Ministry of Environment, Forest & Climate Change, Government of India) Parivesh Bhawan, East Arjun Nagar, Delhi – 110032 Website: http://www.cpcb.nic.in April, 2021.

Green Hospitals: A Perspective on Future of Sustainable Healthcare in India

Dr. Ipsita Patranabis[1], Dr. Supti Mandal[2] and Dr. Soma Bose Biswas[1]

ABSTRACT: Post COVID the Indian healthcare sector is sensitised to the fact that both government and private initiatives are needed to bridge the gap between demand and supply. The healthcare industry is varied and vast. It comprises of hospitals, medical devices and equipment, health insurance, telemedicine and medical tourism. Among these the hospital industry accounts for approximately eighty percent of the total healthcare market (Jain, 2022). Studies suggest that, hospitals are considered as energy-intensive buildings because throughout the year there is a need of different forms of energy to maintain the complex medical equipment and uphold a pristine environment in the hospital. Reports cite that in India, the rate of generation of hospital waste is estimated to be approximately 2 kg/day/bed in India which witnessed an upsurge during COVID 19 during 2020 and 2021 generating tons of biomedical wastes (Chand et al., 2021). With reference to energy usage and waste management programs in Indian hospitals, this article aims to explore the strategic initiatives undertaken by the hospitals to address the emerging issues so that the future can be secured from threatening fatal diseases or diseases secured from any unforeseen disaster. Some important programs initiated by hospitals is towards implementing Common Bio Medical Wastes Treatment Facility (CBMWTF), installation of solar lights, water harvesting and treatment plants, usage of natural lighting, eco-awareness training and awards, farming of organic vegetables and fruits, treating ground-water, recycling waste-water and aiming towards a digitally-enabled paperless organization. The present study will critically evaluate the concept and development of green hospitals and the challenges and issues towards building a sustainable healthcare system in India.

***Keywords:** Green Hospital, Sustainable Healthcare, Energy Efficiency, CBMWTF.*

SUSTAINABILITY: MEANING AND SIGNIFICANCE

Our world is changing, evolving, and growing older. Mother Nature has provided fundamental support for life on Earth, which is equitable and plentiful for all

[1]Associate Professor, Department of Management Science, Techno International, New Town, Kolkata.

[2] Professor and HOD, Post Graduate Institute of Hospital Administration Peerless.

living species on Earth. However, human greed is ruining the habitat and hence, efforts for saving the planet is the need of the hour. This can only save and sustain human life on earth. The four pillars of sustainability are human, social, economic and environmental. Environmental sustainability is the topmost priority followed by human who in turn will ensure social and economic sustainability and growth. Herein, the government commitments and initiative has to be supported by professionals, corporate houses and other stakeholders for an eco-friendly and a green future.

HEALTHCARE ECOSYSTEM IN INDIA: PRESENT AND FUTURE

The healthcare ecosystem in India majorly includes infrastructure, medical equipments, health insurance, telemedicine, and medical tourism. In terms of revenue and employment, the Indian healthcare sector has become one of the top-ranking sectors. The sector is expected to grow exponentially and create lakhs of jobs (Lal, 2023). But data reveals, India has around 5 hospital beds per 10,000 people, according to the World Health Organization reports. With a continually increasing population, India needs large number of hospitals to effectively meet the healthcare demands of its citizens (Srinivasan, 2023). The recent pandemic has thrown enormous challenges in areas of mobilising beds, organizing required medical devices and uninterrupted medical attention for non-COVID patients. In the midst of all challenges, India has responded well during the times of crisis and also fulfilled all globally laid down medical protocols. Nevertheless, the experts identified the gaps to ensure future sustainable healthcare. Further to this, the Human Development Report (2020), features India in an disturbing position in terms of availability of beds, which also clearly indicates the need of expansion in the healthcare sector. India which has around 18 per cent of the total world population and hence, has to immediately plan and prepare for strengthening its future healthcare system. Technological advancement in medical sciences has revolutionized treatment but along with this the hospitals of tomorrow has to envision and practice environment-friendly strategies because human life and nature are intertwined and preserving the environment is crucial for the enhancement of life.

GREEN HOSPITALS: THE CONCEPT & FRAMEWORK

Leadership in Energy and Environmental Design (LEED), established by the United States Green Building Council, had been launched as a pilot in 1998 and was formally offered as a rating system in 2000. The Confederation of Indian Industry (CII) formed the Indian Green Building Council (IGBC), in the year 2001. The vision of the council is, “To enable a sustainable built environment for all and facilitate India to be one of the global leaders in the sustainable built environment by 2025”. IGBC is attempting to indigenize LEED according to the environmental conditions prevalent in India. IGBC defines ‘green buildings as buildings which use less water, optimize energy efficiency, conserve natural resources, generate less waste and provide healthier spaces for occupants, as compared to conventional buildings'. The rating framework of IGBC is based on the five elements of nature namely, Earth, Water, Fire, Air and Ether because Indian philosophy and ancient medical science has firmly stated that these five elements strongly affect the physical, emotional, intellectual and social well-being of each and every existing individual (IGBC Green New Buildings Rating System Version 3.0, 2014).The objective of the IGBC Health and Well Being rating is to 'facilitate the buildings to incorporate people centric measures for enhancing the health & well-being'. The IGBC framework will facilitate hospitals and other institutions to remain aware about factors like quality of indoor air, water quality, hygiene, food and lifestyle. This will enable to consciously practice healthy lifestyle and the measuring criteria will have a check on the sickness rate, spread of diseases and associated health impacts. These good practices will lessen health issues and vulnerability for other contagious and also non-contagious diseases (IGBC Health and Well-being). According to the IGBC, 'a green hospital building can be defined as one which enhances well being of patients by optimising natural resources through an efficient and environment friendly manner'. Past research suggests that the components of a green hospital include energy savings, greener source for creating energy, waste management, lighting, air quality and saving water.

GREEN HOSPITALS: A DIRE NECESSITY

As per the Bio-medical waste management (BMWM) rules 2016, "Bio-medical waste means any waste, which is generated during the diagnosis, treatment or immunization of human beings or animals or research activities pertaining thereto or in the production or testing of biological or in health camps". The BMWM 2016 has also strictly mentioned that the wastes which may cause serious damage to the surrounding environment or can infect a healthy person has to be taken into cognizance and managed suitably. According to World Health Organization (WHO) the biomedical wastes constitute 15 per cent of the total healthcare waste but if not managed properly can be extremely hazardous and of immense threat to human life. The remaining 85% of the waste constitute general and other wastes which also need attention according to Solid Waste Management Rules, 2016, Construction & Demolition Waste Management Rules, 2016, E-Waste (Management) Rules, 2016, Batteries (Management & Handling) Rules, 2001, and Rules/guidelines under Atomic Energy Act, 1962 as applicable. Hence, to protect health and environment, green initiatives are a directive for all the stakeholders including policy-makers, hospital management, doctors, nurses, staff, patients and friends and family of patients.

Strategic Initiatives Towards Creating Green Hospitals in India

Green hospitals or energy efficient hospitals are aimed to optimise and save energy and support the environment through proactive measures of waste management. The objective is to ensure physical and mental well-being of the patients. As consultants say that a big corporate private hospitals spend 600 rupees per day per bed on electricity wherein air conditioning system contributes around 50–60 percent of the electricity bill in hospitals. So hospitals are initiating intelligent building management system to save on the electricity cost wherein the air conditioning will be able to sense the people density in a particular room and function accordingly. Mechanically adjusted lighting system are also installed which can function depending on the required lighting levels. The infrastructure is built in green buildings in such a way that they can make maximum use of natural light by having large windows and open sky lights. Saving water is another strategic initiative of green buildings by installing intelligent pumping system, sensor based urinals and also conserving water for future use. But a keen observation of the hospital industry reveals a disparity in the facilities available in the urban and rural India. Among the various challenges that the rural India has to combat, cost of healthcare, is the most vital issue which frequently makes treatment unreachable for them not even for critical diseases but also for the non-critical ones. Accumulation of fund and managing financial burden for diagnosis and treatment of life-threatening diseases is a concern for rural India and this can pose a serious threat towards public health in India. The following sections discuss in-depth the problems and probable measures for the enhancement of eco-friendly and people-friendly medical facilities in India.

CHALLENGES AND ISSUES IN THE HEALTHCARE SECTOR IN INDIA

The population of India, comprising both rural and urban, 2018–2021 is presented in the following Table 1.

Table 1: Rural and Urban Population in India (2018–2021)

Year	*Rural (in millions)*	*Urban (in millions)*
2018	903.13	465.87
2019	906.33	476.79
2020	908.68	487.7
2021	909.38	498.18

Source: India; Macrotrends; World Bank; United Nations; 2018 to 2021. https://www.statista.com/statistics/621507/rural-and-urban-population-india

The above table depicts clearly the year-on-year growth of the rural and urban population in India (Rathore, 2023). Adding to this, the age distribution data indicates, as on the year 2022, 6.9 per cent of the Indian population is above 65 years of age (Neill, 2024). These figures clearly indicate the significance of healthcare facilities in a country like India.

However, according to statistical records, an estimated sixty-nine thousand hospitals, both public and private, were recorded in India in 2019. Out of these, approximately forty three thousand hospitals belong to the private sector and nearly twenty five thousand are public hospitals (Minhas, 2023). The major share of private hospital facilities are being accessed by the urban population whereas around 72 per cent rural population can avail only 33 per cent of the hospitals. The major reasons for this are accessibility during emergency, affordability, distance from the villages and many more. Thus the rural population is compelled to use some minimal medical facilities which they feel is within their capability to pay. Smaller hospitals are mostly family owned. These hospitals have a dearth of adequate infrastructure, modern medical amenities, and insufficient medical support staff. Incidents of violence are far more common in smaller hospitals due to loss of lives resulting from deficient medical attention. Thus these institutions are too far from the standards of 'GOING GREEN'. Not only the smaller private hospitals or the rural healthcare centres and hospitals but the conditions are even worse for government run units. They lack hygiene, infrastructure, medical equipments and also other basic amenities. The article wants to draw attention of the healthcare industry, medical practitioners and future researchers to the fact that the concept of GREEN HOSPITALS is applicable to large multinational private hospitals because they have the financial capability and technical competence to compete according to the global rating standards. Also simultaneously they have the potential to provide high-end treatment to patients at a premium cost. But healthcare should have be inclusive and equitable. Presently there is a gap between green corporate hospitals and smaller or government hospitals who have not even achieved the bare minimum standards of the green concept.

CONCLUSION AND WAY FORWARD

The future of the healthcare industry in India has to become further strong and robust. If India is young today with 50 per cent population below the age of twenty-five years then it is important to realise that in the next thirty-five years India will become old as well. So this is the right time to build. Government, corporate houses, medical professionals have to initiate a green movement at all levels or else would result in a broken healthcare system. Only quantity in terms of number of hospitals concentrated in cities will not be sufficient for a healthy ecosystem. Every big hospital which intends to enter the competition of the healthcare industry should also have a pre-condition to facilitate the medical infrastructure of at least one or two hospitals in the rural India. The authors believe that this way equilibrium in the medical facilities can be slowly established contributing to the sustainable green culture for both rural and urban India. On one hand as energy efficient green buildings and green environment is encouraged for the overall patient well-being also on the other hand accessibility to affordable treatment is an important factor towards a sustainable healthy future. Energy efficient green building can save on financial resources which can be utilised for development of hospitals in rural India. The authors plan to propose a simple process flow model for achieving sustainable healthcare facilities through optimization of resources and green initiatives (Figure 1).

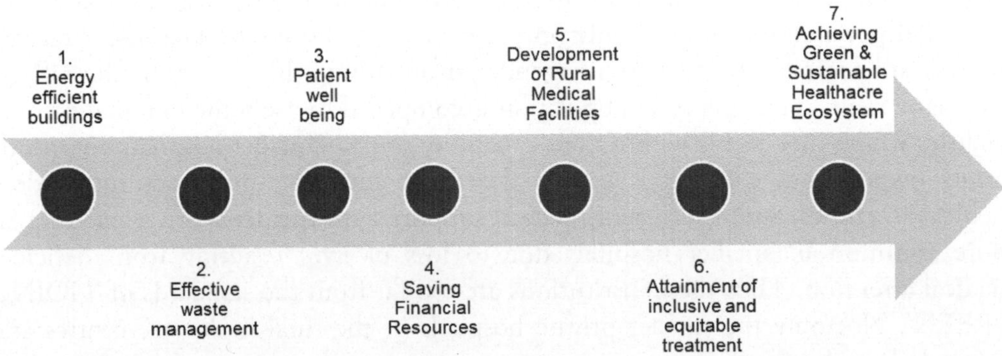

Figure 1: Process Flow Model for Achieving Sustainable Healthcare

(Authors' perspective)

The aim of the model is to depict the fact that sustainable healthcare system is the future of India and it is at the core of all the stakeholders' interest. This can only be achieved through a appropriate balance in energy savings, efficient waste management and proper utilisation of the financial resources in the development of rural healthcare facilities.

REFERENCES

Chand, S., Shastry, C.S., Hiremath, S., Joel, J.J., Krishnabhat, C.H. and Mateti, U.V., Updates on biomedical waste management during COVID-19: The Indian scenario. *Clin. Epidemiol. Global Health,* 2021;11:100715. doi: 10.1016/j.cegh.2021.100715

Jain, K. (2022, January 19). *The boom in India's healthcare firms isn't showing signs of slowing.* Retrieved December 28, 2023, from https://economictimes.indiatimes.com: https://economictimes.indiatimes.com/industry/healthcare/biotech/healthcare/the-boom-in-indias-healthcare-firms-isnt-showing-signs-of-slowing/articleshow/88966321.cms?from=r

Lal, T. (2023, August 24). *Indian hospital industry garnering investors' attention.* Retrieved December 20, 2023, from tpci.in: https://www.tpci.in/indiabusinesstrade/blogs/indian-hospital-industry-garnering-investors-attention

Minhas, A. (2023, July 12). *Estimated number of public and private hospitals across India in 2019.* Retrieved December 26, 2023, from https://www.statista.com/: https://www.statista.com/statistics/1128425/india-number-of-public-and-private-hospitals-estimated

Neill, A.O. (2024, Januray 5). *India: Age distribution from 2012 to 2022.* Retrieved January 23, 2024, from https://www.statista.com: https://www.statista.com/statistics/271315/age-distribution-in-india

Rathore, M. (2023, July 10). *Rural and urban population in India from 2018 to 2021.* Retrieved December 28, 2023, from https://www.statista.com/: https://www.statista.com/statistics/621507/rural-and-urban-population-india

Srinivasan, A. (2023, July 20). *ETHealthworld.com.* Retrieved November 23, 2023, from Health Infrastructure, Capacity Building & Investments: The focal points to improve Healthcare in India: https://health.economictimes.indiatimes.com/news/industry/health-infrastructure-capacity-building-investments-the-focal-points-to-improve-healthcare-in-india/101970232

(2014). *IGBC Green New Buildings Rating System Version 3.0.* Hyderabad: Indian Green Building Council.

(2016). *Guidelines for Management of Healthcare Waste as per Biomedical Waste Management Rules.* Central Pollution Control Board Ministry of Environment, Forest & Climate Change.

A Study on Green HRM Post-Pandemic: An Emerging Trend in the New Era

Sananda Halder[1] and Dr. Saikat Chakrabarti[2]

ABSTRACT: The journey of HRM is indeed adventurous; it has faced a lot of ups-and-downs. Challenges faced by the managers dealing with human resources are multi-dimensional which may even vary from one era to the other. In this present era of modernization & globalization we are blessed with thehighly automatized technology, production, business activities and also with the increase in the human standards of living. The other side of the coin shows a different picture of ecological imbalanceand threats to human being because of the said development. Green HRM has been initiated to protect environment from the ill effect, if anything, of technological advancement.The practices of Green environment may help the managers to take part inthe new era of sustainable business development. Green HRM can be referred to as using every employee interface to promote and develop sustainable environment friendly practices. Also it aims at increasing employee awareness and commitments towards environment friendly HR practices. Green HRM initiatives should involve lower costs and better employee engagement, retention and reduction of employee carbon foot prints. Also it focuses on implementing virtual recruitment and on-boarding process, online training and energy efficient office spaces etc. After the pandemic crisis we have observed shift in the business houses from traditional approaches to taking sustainable HR practices which will explore green economic facts of business.This chapter will focus on the implementation of Green HRM initiatives in the organizational aspects, also aiming at cost saving and sustainable growth of business in the new era. It will also emphasize on the chronology and development of Green HRM initiatives of business organization.

Keywords: *Environment Friendly, Green HRM, Sustainable, New Era.*

INTRODUCTION

In recent days the degradation of natural environment due to human exploitation has bought the need of sustainable practices within the different level of

[1] Assistant Professor, Department of Business Administration, Institute of Engineering & Management, UEM-Kolkata.

[2] Associate Professor, Department of Business Administration, Institute of Engineering & Management, UEM-Kolkata.

organization. This emphasizes on the necessity of re-developing the organizational goals, strategies & process. The need of converting incommodious technologies with eco-friendly practices have been observed to create eco-friendly, viable & rational organizational structure. Human resource management plays a vital role in shaping the organizational culture and create sustainability. HRM functions are the key drivers within the organization in developing environmental sustainability by aligning the organizational strategy, values, ideology and agenda with the process of creating eco-focus and developing sustainable organizational environment. The HRM strategy should motivate and inspire the employee's ambition to create diversity and growth. GHRM refer as the process of creating sustainable practices and increase employee awareness towards the environment. GHRM does not only limit within creating environmental sustainability but also focuses on development of green workplace by adapting 4R's (Re-use, re-cycle, reduce, re-placement). Green HRM does not only emphasize on shaping the organization but also emphasized on green recruitment, green learning & development, green appraisal, green rewards & recognition. After the very recent effect of pandemic in the society it has made us think again on the concept of going green in the workplace and developing sustainable, eco-friendly work premises by not only shifting to online process also saving cost and reusing resources through the concept. This pandemic has showed huge economic crisis all over the globe which has created bulk termination of employees, crunch in the resources, shortage of financial funds as well. Now the time has come to reshape the businesses again by providing green cost beneficial solutions to it.

The objective of this research is to identify the determinants which will help to implement GHRM policies within the organizational work process. It will also focus on creating a structure which will show the determinants and its association with different levels of HRM process in an organization which can built Green Human Resource development in work place.

LITERATURE REVIEW

The HR strategy should reflects organization values & culture, sustainable return to investors, analyzing social trends and government regulatory, and also focus on the public policy agendas. That's why there is a need for the integration of environment managed into HRM named as Green HRM (Patil, *et al.*, 2015).

In the era of modernization our day to day activities on the environment has triggered the need to go green in all the aspects of an organization. With the growing need in corporate's to adopt environment friendly and sustainable development the HRM functions have become one of the major contributor in bringing sustainability in the organization by adapting Green HRM (Mehta, *et al.*, 2015).

Green HRM has become the necessity in the current century as Green HRM refers to using every employee interface to promote sustainable practices which help to increase employee awareness and commitments towards sustainability in the organizational level (Hussain, 2018).

The concept of sustainable development can be referred as ensuring a better quality of life for everyone without exhausting the present resources completely. The excessive stress on environment has influenced the organizations as well as researchers to take initiatives in transforming their operations into green management practices (Dwivedi, *et al.*, 2021).

Green HRM not only focuses on environment sustainability, it also helps in cost cutting by spreading awareness of protection within employees and employers of the organization. These activities help not only in cost saving but also increase in sales, reducing expenses, providing knowledge to the employees, pool recruitment, reducing labor turnover and absenteeism (Gupta, 2021).

Adoption of Green HRM practices within the organization has many advantages which benefit both organization & employee as well. By adopting Green practices it is possible to become ecological, economical & practical at the same moment (Perzadh, *et al.*, 2018).

Nowadays it has become necessary for organizations to work for environment sustainability as business environmental factors like legal, social and ethical are creating pressure on the organizations and also making it necessary for corporate to create transactions towards environmental management (Mohammed, 2021).

In organization a leader who promotes and motivates his employees to focus on Green HRM Practices for creating organizational commitment to sustainable development goals and performance is the one who is leading the organization through green transformation leadership (Iftikhan, 2021).

Green HRM also helps to minimize the expenditure and maximize the profit of an organization by adapting 3R's such as reduce, recycle and reuse. It helps to reduction of waste, recycling of products and reuse of materials which leads into enhancement of return on investment (Durai, *et al.*, 2020).

The Covid-19 pandemic has created both positive & negative impact on the practices made by organizations towards Green HRM Practices. As through work from home concept they are reducing carbon foot prints, in the same place due to global recession it has become difficult to invest on Green HRM Practice (Madhu, 2022).

In India, the implementation of Green HRM is still a fantasy. Through CSR programs awareness on the usage of Green HRM & environment friendly HR practices has been made. HRM has the opportunities to create impact on the green movement (Bhalla,*et al.*, 2016).

OBJECTIVE OF THE STUDY

- To identify the different literatures on green HRM to find out a link between green organizational culture and organizational environmental sustainability.

- To identify the different factors under the green organizational culture which can affect the organizational and environmental sustainability.

THEORETICAL FRAMEWORK

Green Recruitment

Recruitment being the most important function of HRM and Green Recruitment process is changing the dynamics in this process. It can be referred as a process with reduced negative impact on the environment to create sustainable environmental organizational culture (Begum, *et al.*, 2023). Green recruitment is providing the organizations with the scope to be unique in the recruiting process. Time has come for all employers to implement the best green practices to show their commitment towards sustainable environment and also to spread eco-friendly messages with its recruitment process (Gupta, *et al.*, 2013). Green recruitment is having a significant sustainable company performance. By understanding the process companies can develop more effective strategies which will help them to create sustainable goals (Ruma, 2023). Using Green HRM in the organization, it will help to seek candidates and communicate to them about using of less paper and more electronic platforms. In the Green HRM process green selection, recruitment, onboarding process and adoption of those processes creates a vital role in the organization (Tsymbaliuk, *et al.*, 2022).

Green Learning and Development

Effective utilization of human resources is a crucial part in any organization. Therefore, Training & Development of employees in any organization helps to create competencies and sustainability. Today's organizations have understood that only economic activities are not enough in the fast changing world where without environmental and people development organization won't be able to succeed (Jamal, 2021). Every organization wants to improve its own capabilities and achievements need to focus on its employees learning & development (Piwowar, *et al.*, 2021). Green training will help the employees to understand and implement green creativity in the organization (Gunjan, *et al.*, 2020). Green L&D is a vital part of GHRM and it focuses on taking proactive decisions towards green initiative and building employees green activities such as waste reduction, energy savings etc (Rawashdesh, 2018). The outcomes of green L&D are green awareness, green skills development, green competency creation which will effect on positive pro-environmental behavior. This employee pro-environmental behavior will also build a relationship between Green L&D and environmental sustainability (Olaiya, *et al.*, 2022).

Green Appraisal

Green auditing and information systems are commanding for environmental sustainability by setting up green performance management system (Renwick, 2013). In this process organization can only create sustainable HRM practices when green appraisal process is directly linked to green goals, task and green job allotments (Mandip, 2013). Green performance management helps to build green performance indicator within employees. It also focuses on setting green goals & responsibilities with departments and integrating green criteria during employee appraisal (Mashala, 2018). It is also an initiative towards green environmental practices. It is also having a positive impact on employee performance (Ardiza, *et al.*, 2021).

Green Employee Engagement

Green Employee relation can be built by involving employee participation in organizational green initiatives results in better green management practices. It builds a positive culture within employees in achieving environmental management initiatives (Mashala, 2018). Research showed, green employee relation practices include introducingand involving employees in green practices, consultation in resolving environmental issues and also in green whistle blowing (Renwick, 2013). Green employee relation has a significant impact on employee engagements, vigor of the employees, dedication of the employees, and absorption of the employees (Singh, *et al.*, 2020). Creation of green work climate in organization by creating an environment friendly workplace positively influences green employee behavior (Huo, *et al.*, 2022). Nowadays top talents are attracted by those organizations that all are having high environmental values and employees are taking those sustainable values into their personal life (Welmilla, *et al.*, 2020).

Green Rewards and Recognition

Rewards and compensation should be taken as a key element for reinforcing employees green work engagements towards creation of environmental sustainability (Mehta, *et al.*, 2015). Providing incentives and rewarding employees for their eco-friendly initiatives and also acquiring green skills should be introduced in organization for employee's rewards & compensation system (Mashala, 2018). Green rewards & recognition in an organization can be both financial & non-financials system which will contribute to organization's green environmental goals (Rael, 2018). Green rewards, recognition and compensation affect the employee performance. Recognition for green environmental performance, bonuses on competence can be added as dimensions of green rewards (Ardiza, *et al.*, 2021).

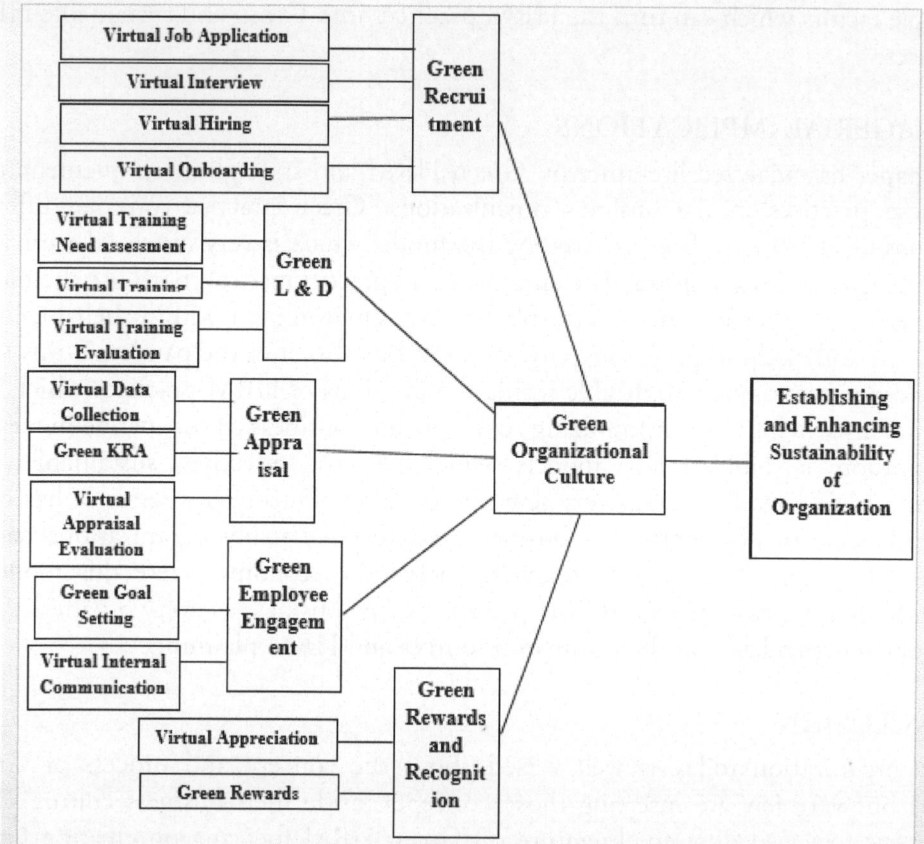

Source: Authors' own creation.

Model Re-presenting Green HRM Practices with HRM Structure Inside Organization

Based on empirical studies, the review has revealed that Green HRM practices in the divisions of learning and development, recruitment, pay and rewards are essential factors which can penetrate sustainable environment practices inside the business (Pham, *et al.*, 2019). Green HRM determines the growing capability within the divisions of HRM and drops out the environment desecration and inserting HRM tools and events significant in lowing cost and creating competency by recycle and reusing business resources to create ecologically sustainable style (Trivedi, 2015).

In this model the researchers have tried to show five major divisions of HRM practices of today's modern day organization and the determinants which are part of the divisions and can turn the HRM practices into Green and sustainable HRM. This article has shown the factors which can make the divisions of HRM in an organization into Green HRM practices. In every division this model has shown multiple factors which can turn the HRM practices into Green and sustainable HRM practices.

MANAGERIAL IMPLICATIONS

This paper has analyzed literature on Green HRM and strategically implementation of those practices in the business organizations. Green practices on the different divisions of HRM have been showed by the model which is very much relevant with today's organizational culture. The employer and practitioner can both use the model and create cost effective and sustainable business environment within their business. It will not only help in protecting environment but also after the pandemic this kind of concept is very much applicable inside the divisions of HRM practices which will be immense helpful in minimizing cost of the business. Post pandemic every organization is looking for models which is cost effective, sustainable and organizational friendly having very few maintenance. During pandemic it has been observed, due to degradation of business and revenue many organizations has to choose demission of employees which impacted the economy. Here this model is trying to create a cost effective HRM process for the business as every organization is very much dependable on their human resources and HRM planning.

CONCLUSION

Every organization today is well versed about the concept and process of Green HRM but very few are inserting those concepts inside their business culture. This paper has reviewed different literature on Green HRM focusing on creating Green HRM inside the organization to establish and enhance the sustainability in organization and also offered a model based on that. Green HRM is the future ahead in creating sustainable business environment. It does not only focus on environment sustainability but also it can be used for cost effective HRM practices as well. Both the employee and the employer can use this model to create a multi dimensional Green organizational culture. The effective utilization of this model can help the organization to minimize the cost for example, using virtual process during recruitment, and training of the employees, during appraisal, employee engagement, rewarding and encouraging the employees. This model clearly unveils the multi dimensional HRM practices in an organization. It can also be used to build Green Organizational Culture which can influence in the establishment and enhancement of sustainability in organization.

REFERENCES

Ardiza, A., Nawangsari, F. and Sutawijaya, P. (2021). Green Rewards, Recognition, and Compensation: Impact on Employee Performance in a Sustainable Context.

Begum, S., Kavitha, R. and Premkumar, R. (2023). Green Recruitment: Transforming HRM Dynamics for Sustainable Organizational Culture.

Bhalla, A. and Mehta, S. (2016). The fantasy of Green HRM implementation in India and the role of CSR programs in creating awareness.

Durai, V. and Nalini, R. (2020). Minimizing expenditure and maximizing profit through the 3R's in Green HRM.

Dwivedi, A. and Gaidhani, A. (2021). Sustainable development initiatives through Green HRM practices.

Gunjan, A. and Rajib, D. (2020). Green Training: Fostering Green Creativity among Employees.

Gupta, R. (2021). Green HRM: Balancing environment sustainability and cost-cutting in organizations.

Huo, J., Azhar, S., Rehun, N. and Mojed, M. (2022). Creating a Green Work Climate: Influence on Employee Behavior and Engagement.

Hussain, F. (2018). Green HRM and its role in promoting sustainable practices and employee awareness.

Iftikhan, M. (2021). Leadership role in promoting Green HRM Practices for organizational commitment to sustainable development goals.

Jamal, A. (2021). Employee Training & Development: A Crucial Element for Sustainable Organizations in a Changing World.

Madhu, K. (2022). Positive and negative impacts of the Covid-19 pandemic on Green HRM Practices in organizations.

Mehta, A. and Chugan, P.K. (2015). Green HRM: A major contributor to sustainability in organizations.

Mohammed, S. (2021). Necessity for organizations to work towards environment sustainability and the role of Green HRM.

Olaiya, O. and Olaosebikan, O. (2022). Green L&D Outcomes: Building Green Awareness, Skills, and Competencies for Pro-Environmental Behavior.

Patil, S. and Das, R. (2015). Integration of environment management into HRM: The concept of Green HRM.

Perzadh, N., Mufti, I. and Nazir, A. (2018). Advantages of adopting Green HRM practices for both organizations and employees.

Piwowar, A. and Sules, D. (2021). Focusing on Learning & Development for Organizational Capabilities and Achievement in a Green Context.

Rael, A. (2018). Green Rewards & Recognition: Financial and Non-Financial Systems Contributing to Organizational Environmental Goals.

Rawashdesh, A.M. (2018). Green Learning & Development: Proactive Decisions and Employee Green Activities.

Renwick, D.W.S. (2013). Involving Employees in Green Practices and its Impact on Employee Engagement.

Ruma, N. (2023). Significance of Green Recruitment in Enhancing Sustainable Company Performance.

Singh, A. and Pandey, N. (2020). Green Employee Relations: Impact on Employee Engagement, Vigor, Dedication, and Absorption.

Tsymbaliuk, I., Vasylyk, Y. and Stoliaruk, I. (2022). The Role of Green HRM in Candidate Seeking and Communication through Eco-Friendly Platforms.

Welmilla, I. and Ranasinghe, P. (2020). Attracting Top Talents: The Role of High Environmental Values and Sustainable Practices in Organizations.

Influence of Green Packaging on Consumers' Purchase Decision: An Exploratory Analysis

Dr. Soumik Gangopadhyay[1] and Doyel Mukherjee Prodhan[2]

INTRODUCTION

Packaging design is not only a functional and aesthetic element of a product, but also a powerful communication tool that can influence consumer behavior and preferences. Termed as the fifth P in the marketing mix, it holds significance in both safeguarding products and promoting sales. Consequently, it constitutes an essential component in the distribution of goods. Post consumption of the product, packaging loses some of its functional importance and improper disposal of used packaging causes significant environmental pollution. Packaging has an adverse impact on the environment from three facets—through resource consumption, creation of waste leading to solid, liquid, and gas pollution, and the dissemination of bacteria and pests. This is where sustainable packaging becomes crucial as it addresses the adverse environmental impact caused by traditional packaging. Decent growth of green packaging in international market, but marginal growths in Indian market indicate the necessity of exploring the influence of green packaging among the consumers. Current study is an attempt to explore the same among Indian consumers in adherence with 'Theory of Planned Behaviour'. 200 respondents belonging to z generation have been interviewed with the help of a structured close ended questionnaire to understand their viewpoint on sustainable packaging to purchase a FMCG product. Statistically analysed primary data reveals that 'responsible consumption' oriented mindset is not a guarantee to 'sustainable purchase'.

LITERATURE REVIEW

In the 21st century, there has been a surge in global awareness towards green consumption. This trend is prompting marketers to adopt a more environment friendly approach and expand their portfolio of green products to meet the demands of the evolving consumer preferences. Increase in green consumerism and with corporate environmentalism fast catching up the world over; corporates have started making use of green marketing strategies and techniques (Sanjoy *et al.* 2018).

[1] Professor, Institute of Engineering & Management (IEM-UEM), Kolkata, India.
[2] Research Associate, Globsyn Business School, Kolkata, India.

Increasing awareness on the various environmental problems has prompted a shift in the way consumers go about their life. There has been a change in consumer attitudes towards a greener lifestyle (Tiwari *et al.*, 2014). This was followed by the effect of brand awareness, brand associations, brand loyalty including the impact of attitude towards green cosmetics and brand equity on the willingness to purchase green cosmetics among young consumers (Hayat *et al.,* 2022). Bhattarcharya *et al.*, (2011) observed that maintaining ecological balance is a significant challenge with which the corporate world is confronted today. Sarkar *et al.*, (2012) showcased that in the modern era of globalization, it has become a challenge to keep the customers as well as consumers in fold and even keep our natural environment safe and that is the biggest need of the hour. Consumers are also aware of the environmental issues like; global warming and the impact of environmental pollution. Svkrishna *et al.*, (2013) studies cracking the code of customer purchase behaviour is a challenge for market researchers as myriad of factors interfere. Marketers are puzzled as competitors position a new product category in the market to create demand. Indian consumers perceive the composition of cosmetics as a blend of healthy chemical extract. Jonsaan *et al.*, (2014) noted a discernible surge in the demand for green innovations over the past decade, attributed to heightened consumer awareness of the environmental challenges that the world is facing.

In response to this, the global discourse on environmental sustainability in recent years, has seen a paradigm shift, prompting industries across different sectors to re-evaluate their existing operations and embrace eco-friendly alternatives. One such significant initiative in this endeavor is the increasing importance of sustainable packaging. According to Phillip Kotler, packaging can be traditionally defined as all the activities involved in the design and production of containers for a product for its protection, storage, distribution and sale. Additionally, in this modern age of self-service, a package can also be seen as the unspoken sales person, serving a crucial function in marketing communication (Stewart, 1995).

Due to the growing environmental concerns and the evolving awareness regarding the significant environmental harm caused by products and their conventional packaging materials, sustainable packaging is now evolving into a powerful tool for reducing environmental impact (Svanes *et al.*, 2010). As a result, the emphasis on sustainable packaging is increasing significantly for both brands and consumers, more so than ever. “Eco-friendly packaging” is not just a trendy term; and incorporating environmentally conscious packaging is no longer a choice but a mandatory requirement for the organizations.

However, in practical terms, there has been a noticeable shift in recent decades, moving away from reusable packaging towards the prevalence of single-use packaging, driven by the popularity of smaller portion packs. Glass bottles for milk, fruit juices etc. were all replaced by single use packaging thereby posing a challenge to the fundamental idea of sustainable packaging (Coelho *et al.*, 2020). Additionally, Dey *et al.* (2021) is of the opinion that due to the swift depletion of green spaces, prolonged time needed for designing packaging materials, and the subsequent increase in packaging expenses, single use packaging (SUP) quickly gained widespread popularity. But the negative consequences arising from the use of single-use packaging, leading to waste generation, water, land, and marine contamination, surpass the advantages associated with its easy availability, cost reduction, or durability (Chen *et al.*, 2021). Hence, embracing sustainable packaging emerges as the sole rational choice, considering the imperative need to address environmental concerns and mitigate the adverse impacts of conventional packaging on ecosystems.

According to Siracusa & Rosa (2018), packaging that is recyclable or biodegradable, particularly those made from biopolymers, not only mitigates the harmful impacts of single-use plastics but also extends the shelf life of the products thereby contributing to a reduction in both food and packaging waste. Furthermore, adopting eco-friendly or sustainable packaging aligns with the preferences of environmentally conscious consumers, leading to increased sales for organizations. This choice not only resonates with the purchasing intentions of green consumers but also enhances the overall brand image of the company (Xin *et al.*, 2019). However, the corporates grapple with a dilemma as poor packaging is often associated with inferior product quality in the eyes of consumers. Thus, when employing sustainable packaging, it becomes crucial to uphold the image and perception of luxury associated with the product. Therefore, the packaging must not only be environment friendly but also appealing enough to effectively enhance product promotion (Georgakoudis *et al.*, 2018). Granato *et al.* (2022) is also of the opinion that while adopting sustainable packaging can result in sustainable logistics and enhance consumers' perception of higher product quality and organic attributes, it may also lower the perceived aesthetic quality.

In the midst of this ongoing dilemma, environmentally conscious millennials are urging brands to be more socially and environmentally conscious than before. However, the adoption of recyclable or renewable alternatives is contributing to an increase in packaging costs (Tran *et al.*, 2019). Thus from the consumer standpoint, sustainable packaging can be described as packaging that either implicitly or explicitly conveys the eco-friendliness of both the product and its packaging. However, the concept of sustainable packaging is not effectively communicated to consumers, leading to challenges in identifying packaging that is environmentally friendly or green (Boz *et al.*, 2020).

Studies indicate that products with eco-friendly packaging, offering convenience in both use and disposal, have a positive impact on the purchasing intentions of consumers who favour sustainable products. However, these consumers are unwilling to pay an additional premium for green packaging and expect manufacturers to bear the cost (James and Kurian, 2021). In contrast, Kashif and Rani (2021) asserted that consumer attitudes positively influence the intention to purchase green packaging. According to their findings, consumers not only express a readiness to buy products with environmentally friendly packaging but are also willing to pay a premium for the advantages associated with eco-friendly packaging. Another research carried out by Martinho *et al.* (2015) found that a significant portion of environmentally conscious consumers favours recyclable packaging over visually striking and attention-grabbing packaging. They place greater importance on the functionality of the packaging than its design. Rita Antunes Guerra (2019) also suggested that stronger the connection between the consumer and the environment, the greater the likelihood that environmentally friendly packaging products are pertinent and influence customer decisions

Therefore, despite consumers' positive attitudes toward green packaging, there is a reluctance to pay a premium for eco-friendly alternatives, emphasizing the need for manufacturers to absorb the additional costs. While some studies suggest a willingness to pay more for environmentally friendly packaging, consumer preferences vary. Ultimately, the connection between consumers and the environment plays a crucial role in influencing their choices, highlighting the importance of sustainable packaging in shaping consumer decisions. Therefore association between Behavioural Belief, Normative Belief, Intention of use of green packaging has to be explored.

METHODS

Present study is based on both secondary as well as primary data. Secondary sources were from books, magazines, brochures and web sites. Primary data was collected by a well-structured questionnaire prepared by approaching people in a face to face interview.

The entire study was carried out in two stages.

Stage I: A survey was undertaken to collect the primary data. We have approached 100 respondents spanning ages from below 18 years to above 50 yearshaving disparity in profession, with the help of a structured questionnaire at Kolkata and Howrah area. Responses have been collected on a 5- point scale anchoring from Strongly disagree to Strongly agree. Strongly disagree, Disagree, Neutral, Agree and Strongly agree have been coded as 1, 2, 3, 4, 5 respectively.

Stage II: Extensive analysis was done in this stage based on the primary data collected from the field survey and suggestions were made to the management for implementing strategies for improvement. Data clean, preparation, Tabulations of data collected through questionnaire, graphs, correlational analysis and heat map created using Python IDE.

Constructs of the study are Behavioural Belief which has been measured from three perspectives i.e. Tensile strength (BB1), Durability (BB2) and Selective product usage

(BB3); Normative Belief which has been measured from three perspectives i.e. contribution to environmental greening (NB1), Attractiveness (NB2) and Cost effectiveness (NB3); Control belief which has been measured by Reusability (CB1), Understanding information (CB2) and Accessibility (CB3). Intention of use of green packaging has been measured by Subjective preference (I1), Intention to pay extra (I2) and Intention to recommend (I3). Adoption behavioural intention has been measured by B1.

Data Analysis & Interpretation

33% of respondents belong to above 100000 monthly family income group. 18% of the respondents belong to the group below 25000. 15% belong to the group 85001–100000. 12% belong to the group 25001–45000. 13% belongs to the group 45001–65000. The smallest group of9% is shared by the respondents belonging to 65001–85000. 38% respondents are dependents. 8% have business, 10% are professionals and 7% belong from service background. 37% respondents have other occupations. 60% respondents are Graduates while 23% are High school pass outs. 17% have completed their post-graduation. 71% of the respondents belong to the age group of 18–26 years. 21% respondents were of the age group 27–34 years. The percentage is identical, standing at 3%, for both the age groups of 35–42 and those aged above 50 years. 2% belong to the age group 43–50 yrs.

Table 1: Description of Response Collected

Statement	*Strongly Agree (%)*	*Agree (%)*	*May be (%)*	*Disagree (%)*	*Strongly Disagree (%)*
Traditional packages have more tensile strength as compared to eco-friendly packages (BB1)	14	44	33	5	4
Traditional packages are more durable. (BB2)	12	48	27	11	2
Traditional packages are typically usable for selective products (BB3)	12	38	38	11	1
My purchase of products with green packaging will be a potential contribution toenvironmental greening (NB1)	23	53	17	5	2
Traditional packaging is more attractive than green packaging	8	37	35	16	4

Statement	*Strongly Agree (%)*	*Agree (%)*	*May be (%)*	*Disagree (%)*	*Strongly Disagree (%)*
(NB2)					
Traditional packages are cost effective than green packages (NB3)	16	41	27	14	2
Traditional packages are reusable, rather than green friendly (CB1)	5	41	27	22	5
I understand information regarding to contents, instructions and benefits of green packaging (CB2)	13	55	26	6	0
Green packages are easily accessible during product purchase (CB3)	12	56	24	7	1
I will prefer to buy a product having green packaging (I1)	9	32	45	14	0
I am willing to pay extra to avail a product with green packaging (I2)	11	47	30	12	0
I will use products with green friendly packaging if recommended by friends and family (I3)	21	56	21	2	0
Adoption of product of green packaging is the future (B1)	21	56	21	2	0

Table 2: Quantitative Description of Data

	BB1	*BB2*	*BB3*	*SN*	*NB2*	*NB3*	*CB1*	*CB2*	*CB3*	*I1*	*I2*	*I3*	*B1*
count	100	100	100	100	100	100	100	100	100	100	100	100	100
unique	5	5	5	5	5	5	5	4	5	4	4	4	5
top	4.0	4.0	3.0	4.0	4.0	4.0	4.0	4.0	4.0	3.0	4.0	4.0	4.0
freq	44	48	38	53	37	41	41	55	56	45	47	56	39

Next, a similarity analysis has been done on the responses based on Likert scale level. Spearman correlation has been applied on each pair or ordinal variable of the survey.

Although the heat map does not reveal dependency or similarity of high strength, it reveals strong positive correlation between I3 & B1. Peer recommendation has strong positive impact on adoption of product with green packaging and that is the future of adopting products with green packaging.

Table 3: Similarity Analysis

	BB1	BB2	BB3	NB1	NB2	NB3	CB1	CB2	CB3	I1	I2	I3	B1
BB1	1.00	0.38	0.05	0.14	0.05	-0.01	0.14	0.17	0.07	0.17	0.15	0.22	0.09
BB2	0.38	1.00	0.03	0.08	0.12	0.10	0.19	0.16	0.20	0.03	0.19	0.14	0.17
BB3	0.05	0.03	1.00	0.23	0.08	-0.03	0.01	0.03	0.00	0.11	0.26	0.23	0.25
NB1	0.14	0.08	0.23	1.00	-0.11	0.12	0.07	0.31	0.16	-0.10	0.07	0.20	0.02
NB2	0.05	0.12	0.08	-0.11	1.00	0.10	0.07	-0.07	-0.07	-0.01	0.07	-0.07	-0.06
NB3	-0.01	0.10	-0.03	0.12	0.10	1.00	0.05	0.15	0.04	-0.13	-0.00	-0.13	-0.11
CB1	0.14	0.19	0.01	0.07	0.07	0.05	1.00	0.13	0.14	0.04	-0.11	0.00	-0.12
CB2	0.17	0.16	0.03	0.31	-0.07	0.15	0.13	1.00	0.35	0.00	-0.09	0.10	0.04
CB3	0.07	0.20	0.00	0.16	-0.07	0.04	0.14	0.35	1.00	-0.10	-0.09	0.09	0.09
I1	0.17	0.03	0.11	-0.10	-0.01	-0.13	0.04	0.00	-0.10	1.00	0.12	0.13	0.24
I2	0.15	0.19	0.26	0.07	0.07	-0.00	-0.11	-0.09	-0.09	0.12	1.00	0.45	0.38
I3	0.22	0.14	0.23	0.20	-0.07	-0.13	0.00	0.10	0.09	0.13	0.45	1.00	0.58
B1	0.09	0.17	0.25	0.02	-0.06	-0.11	-0.12	0.04	0.09	0.24	0.38	0.58	1.00

CONCLUSION

It was observed that customers are concerned with environmental issues, and their purchase decisions about green-packaged products are dependent on different variables, including their environmental concern regarding the packaging's design; the typology, biodegradability, and recyclability of packaging materials; and the origin of the products, among others. Nevertheless, it was observed that the willingness to acquire green-packaged products of a significant number of customers is also dependent on price. In addition to contribute significant ecological benefits, consumers also regard price as a crucial factor influencing their purchasing decisions. While examining consumer behaviour towards functions of sustainable package, the findings showed positive evaluation from both non-experienced and experienced participants relating to functions of protecting product quality, promoting product and providing convenience of ecological packaging. The reliability of information on packaging was determined as an aspect impacting customer behaviour in terms of promoting and providing convenience to the consumer. Theory of planned behavior was also discussed to understand the consumer behavior and intentions. The study signals that respondents are interested to pay more for a product using green packaging if tensile strength is acceptable and strongly recommended by peers. The willingness to pay has a significant relationship with consumer buying behavior.

Interesting to observe that customers are stressing on the social trend of using product that uses green package. Hence, it can be inferred that the choice to purchase eco-friendly products, including those with green packaging, is significantly influenced by factors such as environmental concerns, societal norms, and consumers' willingness to pay for sustainable and environmentally conscious options.

REFERENCES

Abdullah, N.A., Nuruddin, H.H. and Abdullah B.A. (2020). Determinants of among young the halal cosmetics adoption consumers in the klang valley. *Journal of Islam and the Contemporary world,* 13(2), 55 83.

Adrita, U.W. (2020). Consumers Actual Purchase behavior towards Green Products: A study on Bangladesh. *Int. J. Bus. Innov. Res,* 1(1)

Amberg, N. and Fogarassy, C. (2019). Green Consumer Behavior in the Cosmetics Market. Resources, 8(3)

Auliandri, A.T., Rohman, F.A. and Rofiq, A. (2018). Does green packaging matter as a business strategy? Exploring young consumers' consumption in an emerging market. *Problems and Perspectives in Management,* 16(2), 376–384. doi:10.21511/ppm.16(2).2018. 34.

Boz, Z., Virpi, K. and Claire, K.S. (2020). Consumer considerations for the implementation of sustainable packaging: A review. Sustainability, 12(6), 2192.

Chen, Yuan, *et al.* (2021). Single-use plastics: Production, usage, disposal, and adverse impacts. *Science of the total environment* 752, e141772.

Chitra, K. (2007). In search of the green consumer; A perception study, *Journal of service research,* 7(1), 173–191.

Chitra, K. and Roost A. (2007). A Perceptual study abr *Services Research Journal of services,* 7(1), 173–191.

Chakrabarti, S., Gangopadhyay, S., Lahiri, I., Sur, S., Chattopadhyay, S. and Sharma, R.R. (2023). Perspectives in Sustainable Management Practices, ROUTLEDGE, London, 1–7. https://doi.org/10.4324/978103264048-1.

Coelho, Patricia Megale, *et al.* (2020). Sustainability of reusable packaging–Current situation and trends. Resources, *Conservation & Recycling,* X(6), 100037.

Dey A. *et al.* (2021). Challenges and possible solutions to mitigate the problems of single-use plastics used for packaging food items: A review. *Journal of Food Science and Technology* 58(9), 3251–3269.

DHL trend research (2019). Rethinking Packaging: A DHL perspective on the future of packaging in the logistics industry. https://www.dhl.com/content/dam/dhl/global/core/documents/pdf/glo-core rethinkingpackaging-trend-report.pdf.

Flores, P.J. and Jansson, J. (2022). Determinants of consumer green innovation adoption across domains, A systematic review of marketing journals and suggestions for a research agenda. *International Journal of Consumer Studies*, 46(5), 1761–178.

Georgakoudis, E.D., Tipi, S.N. and Bamford, G.C. (2018). Packaging redesign–benefits for the environment and the community. *International Journal of Sustainable Engineering* 11(5), 307–320.

Granato, Giulia, Arnout R.H. Fischer and Hans C.M. van Trijp. (2022). The price of sustainability: How consumers trade-off conventional packaging benefits against sustainability. Journal of Cleaner Production 365, 132739.

Hao, Y., Liu, H., Chen, H., Sha, Y., Ji, H. and Fan, J. (2019). What affect consumers' willingness to pay for green packaging? Evidence from China. Resources, Conservation & Recycling, 141, 21–29.

Herbes, C., Beuthner, C. and Ramme, I. (2020), "How green is your packaging a comparative international study of cues consumers use to recognize environmentally friendly packaging", International Journal of Consumer Studies, Vol. 44, No. 3.

Jafarzadeh, S., Jafari, S.M., Salehabadi, A., Nafchi, A.M., Kumar, U.U. and Khalil, H.A. (2020). Biodegradable green packaging with antimicrobial functions based on the bioactive compounds from tropical plants and their by-products. Trends in Food Science & Technology, 100, 262–277.

James, Felix and Aju, Kurian (2021). Sustainable Packaging: A Study on Consumer Perception on Sustainable Packaging Options in E-Commerce Industry." *Nveo-Natural Volatiles & Essential Oils Journal*, 10547–10559.

Jain, S.K. and Kaur, G. (2004). Green Marketing: An Attitudinal and Behavioural Analysis of Indian Consumers. Global Business Review, 5(2), 187–205. https://doi.org/10.1177/097215090400500203.

Kashif M. and Rani T. (2021). Customers' Attitude towards green packaging: A case of sapphire, Pakistan. *Journal of Marketing Strategies*, 3(1), 1–28.

Kaur, B., Gangawar, V.P. and Dash, G. (2022). Green marketing strategies, environmental attitude, and green buying intention, A multi-group analysis in an emerging economy context. Sustainability, 14(10), 6107.

Ker, Wong, Yap Kar Sen, and Salini Devi Rajendran. "A study on the benefits of eco-friendly packaging on sustainable supply chain management in fast moving consumer goods industry." E3S Web of Conferences. Vol. 136. EDP Sciences, 2019.

Kesari, B., Atulkar, S., Pandey, S. (2021). Consumer Purchasing Behaviour towards Eco-Environment Residential Photovoltaic Solar Lighting Systems, Global business review, 22(1), 236–254.

Khare, A. (2019). Antecedents to green buying behaviour: a study on consumers in an emerging economy. Marketing Intelligence& Planning, 33(3), 309–329. doi:10.1108/MIP-05-2014-0083.

Khan, S., Salim, A. (2021). Saudi females buying behavior of green cosmetics, A pertinent motivational aspect. Journal of Marketing Communications, 27(6), 594–606.

Kotler, Philip. (1991). Principles of Marketing. Englewood Cliffs, N.J.: Prentice Hall.

Kumar, A., Bam. L. (2023). Eco-labels trigger green Product Purchase intention among emerging Journal of Indian Buriness, 15(3), 1755–4195.

Kumar, S.D., Sharma, R. (2015). A study of Consumers' perception and attitude. towards green Products, International Journal of Advanced Research in Management, and social, 8, 285–00 297.

Laheri, K.V. (2015). Consumer behaviour towards purchase of green products with specific product category. Indian journal of management science, 5(1), 66–73.

Limbu, Y.B., Pham, L., Nguyen, TTT. (2022). Predictors green cosmetics Purchase intentions among of young female consumers in Vietnam. Sustainability, Vol. 19, Issue 14

Luthra, C., Deshwal, P. (2022). Determinants of green purchase behaviour–A literature review on specific product categories. Academy of Marketing Studies Journal, 26(1), 116–120.

Martinho, Graça, *et al.* (2015). Factors affecting consumers' choices concerning sustainable packaging during product purchase and recycling. Resources, Conservation and Recycling 103, 58–68.

Mishra, J. (2017). Have Green, Pay More An Empirical Investigation of Consumer's Attitude Towards Green Packaging in an Emerging Economy. In Essays on Sustainability and Management, 125–150.

Nandi, P. (n.d.). (2023). Green packaging market size, share, growth: Report, 2030. Green Packaging Market Size, Share, Growth | Report, 2030. https://www.marketresearchfuture.com/reports/green-packaging-market-2995.

Nekmahmud, M. and Fekete-Farkas, M. (2020). Why Not Green Marketing? Determinates of Consumers' Intention to Green Purchase Decision in a New Developing Nation. Sustainability, 12. doi:7880

Nguyen, A. T., Parker, L., Brennan, L. and Lockrey, S. (2020). A consumer definition of eco-friendly packaging. Journal of Cleaner Production, 252.

Satapathy, S., Sangle, S., Unnikrishnan. S. (2018). Determinants of technology – bared Product adoption by Consumers, World Review of science, Technology and Sustain- able Development, 14(1), 85–99.

Sharma S, (2022). How ethical are my millennials 1 A qualitative study, journal of information. communication and Ethics valли 20 Society 20(4), 531– 545.

Singh, G. and Pandey, N. (2018). The determinants of green packaging that influence buyers' willingness to pay a price premium. *Australasian Marketing Journal*, 26(3), 221–230.

Siracusa, Valentina and Marco D. Rosa (2018). "Sustainable packaging." Sustainable food systems from agriculture to industry. Academic Press, 2018. 275–307.

Souri, M. E., Sajjadian, F., Sheikh, R. and Sana, S.S. (2018). Grey SERVQUAL method to measure consumers' attitudes towards green products—A case study of Iranian consumers of LED bulbs. *J. Clean. Prod*, 177, 187–196.

Stewart, Bill. Packaging as an effective marketing tool. CRC Press, 1995.

Sumi, R.S. and Kabir, G. (2018). Factors affecting the buying intention of organic tea consumers of Bangladesh. *J. Open Innov. Technol.* Mark, 4.

Svanes, E. *et al.* (2010). Sustainable packaging design: a holistic methodology for packaging design. *Packaging Technology and Science: An International Journal,* 23(3), 161–175.

Taufique, K.R. and Vaithianathan, S. (2018). A fresh look at understanding Green consumer behavior among young urban Indian consumers through the lens of Theory of Planned Behavior. *Journal of cleaner production*, 183, 46–55.

Technavio, https://www.technavio.com (2021, September). *Market research reports – industry analysis size & trends.* https://www.technavio.com/report/green-packaging-market-industry-analysis.

Testa, F., Pretner, G., Iovino, R., Bianchi, G., Tessitore, S. and Iraldo, F. (2021). Drivers to green consumption: a systematic review, *Environment, Development and Sustainability: A Multidisciplinary Approach to the Theory and Practice of Sustainable Development*, 23(4), pages 4826–4880.

Witek, L. and Kuzniar, W. (2020). Green Purchase Behavior: The Effectiveness of Socio-demographic Variables for Explaining Green Purchases in Emerging Market. Sustainability, 13(1).

Wandosell, G., Meroño, M.P., Alcayde, A. and Baños, R. (2021). Green Packaging from Consumer and Business Perspectives. *Sustainability*, 13(3), 1356.

Yadav, R., Giri, A. and Chatterjee, S. (2022). Understanding the users' motivation and barriers in adopting healthcare apps: A mixed-method approach using behavioral reasoning theory, Technological Forecasting and Social Change, BM Sharma, GK Bharat, S. Tayal, L. Nizzetto, The legal framework to manage chemical pollution in India and the lesson from the Persistent Organic Pollutants. 490, 733–747.

https://corporate.mcdonalds.com/corpmcd/ourstories/article/renewable_packaging.html

ANNEXURE

Questionnaire

Gender

(a) Male (b) Female

Age

(a) Below 18 (d) 35– 42
(b) 18–26 (e) 43–50
(c) 27–34 (f) Above 50

Education

(a) Undergraduate (c) Post Graduate
(b) Graduate (d) P.hD.

Occupation

(a) Dependent (c) Service (e) Others
(b) Business (d) Professional

Monthly Family Income (in INR)

(a) Below 25000 (d) 65001–85000
(b) 25001–45000 (e) 850001–100000
(c) 45001–65000 (f) Above 100000

1. Traditional packages have more tensile strength as compared to eco-friendly packages.
   (a) Strongly disagree (b) Disagree (c) Neutral
   (d) Agree (e) Strongly agree

2. Traditional packages are more durable.
   (a) Strongly disagree (b) Disagree (c) Neutral
   (d) Agree (e) Strongly agree

3. Traditional packages are typically usable for selective products.
   (a) Strongly disagree (b) Disagree (c) Neutral
   (d) Agree (e) Strongly agree

4. My purchase of products with green packaging will be a potential contribution to environmental greening.

(a) Strongly disagree (b) Disagree (c) Neutral
(d) Agree (e) Strongly agree

5. Traditional packaging is more attractive than green packaging.
(a) Strongly disagree (b) Disagree (c) Neutral
(d) Agree (e) Strongly agree

6. Traditional packages are cost effective than green packages.
(a) Strongly disagree (b) disagree (c) Neutral
(d) Agree (e) Strongly agree

7. Traditional packages are reusable, rather than green friendly packages.
(a) Strongly disagree (b) Disagree (c) Neutral
(d) Agree (e) Strongly agree

8. I understand information regarding contents, instructions and benefits of green packaging.
(a) Strongly disagree (b) Disagree (c) Neutral
(d) Agree (e) Strongly agree

9. Green packages are easily accessible during product purchase.
(a) Strongly disagree (b) disagree
(c) Neutral (d) Agree
(e) Strongly agree

10. I will prefer to buy a product having green packaging.
(a) Strongly disagree (b) disagree (c) Neutral
(d) Agree (e) Strongly agree

11. I am willing to pay extra to avail a product with green packaging.
(a) Strongly disagree (b) disagree (c) Neutral
(d) Agree (e) Strongly agree

12. I will recommend friends and family to purchase products with green friendly packaging.
(a) Strongly disagree (b) disagree (c) Neutral
(d) Agree (e) Strongly agree

13. Every civilized individual should only prefer product having green package.
(a) Strongly disagree (b) disagree (c) Neutral
(d) Agree (e) Strongly agree

A Study on Stakeholders' Influence on Green Practices by Firms

Dr. Soma Sur[1] and Arundhati Das Chatterjee[2]

ABSTRACT: Stakeholder pressures and its influence on green practices by organizations continue to be an important topic for sustainability. Often there are sample size constraints which limits researchers to conclude the main motivations behind green practices by firms and the type of stakeholders' influence behind the same. The first part of this study includes a literature review on stakeholders' pressure on firms relating to green practices. Taking 19 empirical studies the authors explored the relationship between stakeholders' pressure and green practices by firms using a meta-analysis in the second part of the study. The results confirm that despite heterogeneity and publication bias the study has been robust. The moderated effect of economic factors on stakeholders' pressure on green practices shows that in developed countries, stakeholders' influence plays a key role. The last part of the study involves a conceptual framework relating to the motivations behind green practices by the firm. The paper provides a clear insight into the relationship of stakeholders' influence on green practices by firm through meta-analysis. Conducting meta-analysis in this case assures the positive relationship between stakeholders' pressure and green practices. The proposed framework can be taken up for further studies in future.

INTRODUCTION

For thousands of years, business existed only at the fringes of society. Society thought little of people in business, and people in business expected little of society. Profit was their only reward because power, social status, and even social acceptability were closed to them. In this context, the idea that making a profit was the only goal of business might have some sense (Solomon *et al.,* 1983)

In pursuant of this economic benefit business units over time have been exploiting wealth from nature. The call for consideration of environment coupled with social issues led business houses to rethink their stance on ecosystem for a better long-term survival. Since the value of a business world echoes the societal value, in recent times a need has been felt to expand the objective of business beyond just economic profit.

[1] Professor Xavier Business School, St. Xavier's University Kolkata.

[2] Research Scholar (Management), St. Xavier's University Kolkata.

A plethora of stakeholders contributed in this (Henriques & Sadorsky, 1996). Sustainability may be explained as "the development that meet the needs of the present without compromising the ability of future generations to meet their own needs" (Brundtland Commission, 1987). A company's sustainable practices are usually analysed against environmental, social and governance metrics. Enterprises that strive to meet this triple bottom line are connoted as green business. However, there are different factors that has driven firms to take up green practices. Beginning with a highlight on green marketing (GM) practices by the firms this article reviews the stakeholders' pressure in motivating a firm to adopt green practices (GP) through a meta-analysis. In the process it then develops a conceptual model of firm's motivations behind GP.

GREEN MARKETING AND GREEN PRACTICES

Green Marketing activities or Green Practices are widely used firm's responses to environmental concerns (Rodriguez LS, 2016). Green Practices focusses on integrating environmental theories into dimensions of marketing mix (Pujari *et al.*, 2003). Thus, according to (Polonsky, 1994) Green Marketing includes "all activities designed to generate and facilitate any exchanges intended to satisfy human needs and wants such that the satisfaction of these needs and wants occurs with minimal detrimental impact on the natural environment." These activities that are part of Green Marketing are thus GP by firms (Jansson *et al.*, 2010). The formal definition of green marketing was given by American Marketing Association in Austin, way back in 1975. The concept of "Ecological Marketing" where companies sought to find remedies for environmental issues, was initiated with it. This phase persisted for some time and gradually the focal point for the companies shifted in adopting clean technology, green product innovation and finally moving towards sustainability which gained prominence in early 2000s. Advent of an environmental concern overtime is viewed as a very big opportunity in recent past for inventions in this regard (Cairncross, 1992). Through green business, companies have started to give attention to environmental issues.

There are many activities which is termed as GP like green supply chain management (GSCM) which is mainly implementation of environmental thoughts into supply chain activities of a firm (Sheyadi & Al Sheyadi, 2022), green packaging, green purchasing and green manufacturing (Shaharudin *et al.*, 2018). Green manufacturing products include hardware and software innovations (Song & Yu, 2018) or green innovations (GI) which is a part of corporate environmental practices (Lin C.Y *et al.*, 2008). This is again part of green product innovation and green process invention (H. Wang *et al.*, 2021) and in works of (Tang M *et al.*, 2018).

LITERATURE REVIEW

In recent times there is a surge in green products requirements. As customers are a vital force to reckon with in this regard most of the research studies concerning green marketing centres round consumers' behavioural attitude or intention or awareness towards environmental products (Jain & Kaur, 2004); (Agrawal *et al.,* 2023). There has been a consistent dearth of exploring the perspective of manufacturers, their motivations, stakeholders' pressure (SHP) and finally the outcome of their green practices in business. A review literature on the motivations of firms in adopting green practices may start with the stakeholder's theory with stakeholders being the initial influencers in this study. Stakeholders according to (Freeman & R.E, 1984) are organizations or individuals that contribute resources in the long run activities of business. If a firm wants to maximise its value, then it cannot ignore the interest of associated stakeholders (Jo e*t al.,* 2015). Mentions in this regard can be made of (Buysse & Verbeke, 2003) and in the writings by (Henriques & Sadorsky, 1999) and in article by (Sharma & H. Vredenburg, 1998) studies.

Henriques and Sadorsky, 1999 were the first of its kind study in this regard. They used empirical data to establish a relationship between firm's environmental practices and stakeholders' influence. The results show a positive relationship between plans regarding and pressure imposed by customers and shareholders. However, the same study indicated a negative relationship when the pressure exerted is by the lobby group. Pressure exerted by stakeholders, higher degree of interaction among member firms (Scott 1983) motivates a firm to go for green practice.

(Zhang H *et al.,* 2020) studied the association between SHP and green innovation with the aid of structural equation model or SEM. He considers government pressure and customers' pressure on a firm to establish a relationship through an empirical study based on Chinese firms.

(Awan *et al.,* 2017) studied the association between stakeholders' pressure and green supply chain practices. The study is on manufacturing firms in Pakistan and empirical testing is done using SEM. The study has got a huge potential in the field of environment management practices (EMP) of manufacturing firm.GP is a part of EMP (Mohd Rizaimy Shaharudin *et al.,* 2018) that aims to minimise environmental negative effects (Eltayeb *et al.,* 2011) and also by (Ramayah *et al.,* 2011). A similar study on stakeholder's influence on EMP was carried out by (Latip *et al.,* 2022) using SEM on food manufacturing firm of Malaysia which are a part of SME that highlights that though there are intentions by the firms to adopt EMP it has not as yet been realised to a full scale in Malaysia owing to several obstacles. In this regard the role of the managers has been mentioned. Infact if SME owner-manager increase their investment then many a times the hurdles of achieving EMP can be dealt with. A firm's managers play an important role in these activities and their perceptions play a crucial role (Donaldson & Preston, 1995) also many of them want to reduce inherited environmental risk (Klassen & Whybark, 1999).

Stakeholders can be primary, that is those involved in transactions or can be secondary, that is those who are not involved directly in transaction (Klievink *et al.*, 2012). In the context of green practices by the firm primary stakeholders are shareholders, suppliers, employees and customers. On the other hand, local government, environmentalists and society are secondary stakeholders. Freeman, 1984 classified stakeholders into 10 classes, (Lee JW *et al.*, 2018) focussed on internal and external stakeholders and (L. Wang *et al.*, 2020) categorises pressure exerted by both internal and external stakeholders into internal pressure, market pressure, coercive pressure and social pressure. Internal stakeholders are concerned with how the environmental issues may impact their jobs (Fineman and Clarke, 1996) and the external stakeholders are often environmentally more conscious (Etzion, 2007). Previous studies stress on the fact that SHP on GP can be analysed best if the pressure exerted by different group of stakeholders can be classified. In this regard the theoretical framework of a study (Lin & Sheu, 2012) based on institutional theory can be mentioned which states that firms within a societal set up are not confined as per a dyadic relationship and this aspect leads firms imitating the behaviour of their peer group of firms known as isomorphism. This means that firms often exhibit same behaviour under same context. The relationship study between SHP and GP can be explored from two theories—a stakeholders' aspect that highlights on how a firm's various stakeholder influences their implementation of GP and an -institution based understanding, that highlights a firm's reaction to institutional pressures like NGO, governmental pressure (Lixiang Wang *et al.*, 2020).

Ru-jen Lina, Chwen Sheu, 2012 mentions three major types of pressure catagorized on the basis of (Dimaggio & Powell, 1983). They are coercive, normative and mimetic pressure. Coercive pressure arises when a firm's regulatory SHP occurs. It is usually exerted by other organizations with interest on a firm's legal matter. Placed in these circumstances it is seen a firm is implements GP more often in order to reduce political, economic costs (Xie, 2017). Normative pressure arises from NGOs and social groups. It often occurs between members of the same firm level environment. It can yield reputational advantage for a firm. Mimetic pressure arises when firms imitate other firms' behaviour when placed under uncertainty (Ning *et al.*, 2022), Ru-jen Lina, Chwen Sheu, 2012). competitors working in same field may exert pressure initiating reconfiguration of policies (Durand & Georgallis, 2018), also stated as mimetic pressure (DiMaggio and Powell,1983) media, labour unions often exerts pressure (Hoffman & A.J, 2000) and may influence firms for adopting GP (Gunningham *et al.*, 2004). Again, there may arise supplier pressure that will influence environmental certification by firms (Ong *et al.*, 2019)

META-ANALYSIS

This study opts a limited meta-analytic approach while performing statistical analysis on previous empirical studies related to SHP and GP. Meta Analysis is a subset of systematic reviews. It is a process which is a systematic combination of relevant qualitative and quantitative data from many previous articles to come up with a conclusion with higher statistical strength. The end result is statistically sounder than the result of a single study, as there are more subjects, more variation among subjects, or accumulated effects and results (Himmelfarb health science library). For this study, Meta Essential software (Eramus Research Institute of Management) is used. This open-source software has been inspired by (Borenstein M *et al.*, 2009)

Research Design

On the basis of the literature reviews with a special focus on stakeholders' and institutional theories followed by DiMaggio and Powell, 1983, this study proposes the following framework for meta-analysis.

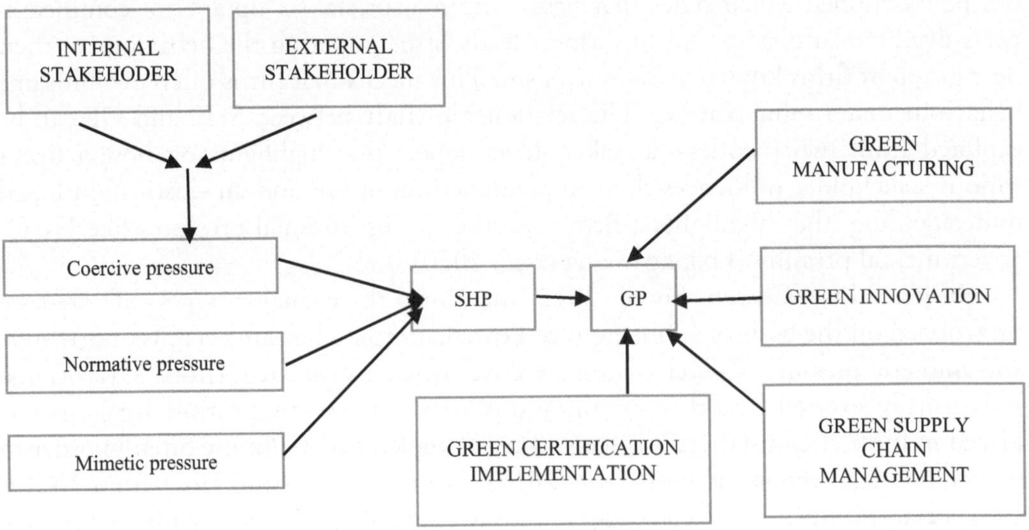

This study defines GP as the dependent variable and the SHP as the independent variable upon it.GP encompasses green manufacturing, green innovation, green supply chain management and green certification implementation.

Data Collection

The initial step of the analysis is to collect articles related to the study of SHP on GP. For the purpose web search is conducted. Initially a total of 26 articles were selected based upon the keywords. It was also checked whether the selected articles have used correlation analysis and whether correlation matrix was provided in it. On the basis of the second criteria 7 articles were eliminated. Finally, a total of 19 articles were found valid here. The results are summarized in the following Table 1.

Table 1

Keywords	*Publications*	*Articles*
	1. Elsevier	6
Stakeholder's pressure,	2. Semantic Scholar	3
Green practice,	3. Jstor	1
Green manufacturing,	4. Frontiers	1
Green innovation,	5. MDPI	1
Green supply chain,	6. Research Gate	2
Green certification	7. Emerald	1
	8. Wiley	1
	9. EBSCO	1
	10. Medwin	1
	11. Log-forum	1

Table 2 below provides a complete summary of all the sample articles collected for the purpose of meta-analysis with the author's name, sample size, correlation coefficient and the location of the study specification.

Table 2

Author	*Participants*	*N*	*r*	*Countries*	*HDI*	*Eco status*
Awan U *et al.*, 2017	Exporter	272	0.462	Pakistan	0.544	Dg
Awan U *et al.*, 2017a	Exporter	272	0.522	Pakistan		Dg
Lin R, Sheu C,2012	Managers	112	0.508	Taiwan & US	0.921	D
Yu *et al.*, 2014	Employees	167	0.303	UK	0.929	D
Yu *et al.*, 2014 a	Employees	167	0.447	UK		D
Ning S, Jie X, Li X 2021	companies	222	0.185	China	0.768	D
Ning S, Jie X, Li X 2021 a	companies	222	0.012	China		D
Wang H, Khan M,*et al.*, 2021	Employees	515	0.777	Pakistan		Dg
Wang H, Khan M,*et al* 2021a	Employees	515	0.544	Pakistan		Dg
Wang H, Khan M,*et al.*, 2021b	Employees	515	0.563	Pakistan		Dg
Sanjay Kumar Singh *et al.*, 2021	Managers	248	0.68	Abu Dhabi	0.911	D

Author	*Participants*	*N*	*r*	*Countries*	*HDI*	*Eco status*
Latip M, Sharkawi *et al.*, 2022	Managers	367	0.511	Malaysia	0.803	D
Latip M, Sharkawi *et al.*, 2022a	Managers	367	0.735	Malaysia		D
Latip M, Sharkawi *et al.*, 2022b	Managers	367	0.597	Malaysia		D
Zuraidah Raja Mohd Rasi *et al.*, 2014	Managers	248	0.097	Malaysia		D
Zuraidah Raja Mohd Rasi *et al.*, 2014a	Managers	248	0.004	Malaysia		D
Zuraidah Raja Mohd Rasi *et al.*, 2014b	Managers	248	0.57	Malaysia		D
Zuraidah Raja Mohd Rasi *et al.*, 2014c	Managers	248	0.328	Malaysia		D
Zhang H, *et al.*, 2020	Managers	282	0.574	China		D
Zhang H, *et al.*, 2020 a	Managers	282	0.707	China		D
Hossain *et al.*, 2022	Managers	140	0.21	Bangladesh	0.661	Dg
Hossain *et al.*, 2022a	Managers	140	0.135	Bangladesh		Dg
Huang *et al.*, 2009	Managers	235	0.33	Taiwan	0.926	D
Huang *et al.*, 2009a	Managers	235	0.54	Taiwan		D
Huang *et al.*, 2009b	Managers	235	0.37	Taiwan		D
Baah *et al.*, 2021	Managers	210	0.509	Ghana	0.632	Dg
Baah *et al.*, 2021a	Managers	210	0.54	Ghana		Dg
Kitsis A M & Chen I J, 2021	Managers	206	0.19	US		D
Li *et al.*, 2020	Managers	544	0.74	China		D
Li *et al.*, 2020a	Managers	544	0.47	China		D
Li *et al.*, 2020b	Managers	544	0.45	China		D
Li *et al.*, 2020c	Managers	544	0.45	China		D
Li *et al.*, 2020d	Managers	544	0.22	China		D
BERRONE P *et al.*, 2013	Managers	20	0.05	US	0.921	D
BERRONE P *et al.*, 2013a	Managers	20	0.04	US		D
El-Kassar & Singh, 2019	Managers	215	0.374	MENA	0.734	Dg
El-Kassar & Singh, 2019a	Managers	215	0.396	MENA		Dg
Sheyadi & Al Sheyadi, 2022	Managers	138	0.283	Oman	0.816	D
Sheyadi & Al Sheyadi, 2022a	Managers	138	0.399	Oman		D
Sheyadi & Al Sheyadi, 2022b	Managers	138	0.178	Oman		D
Sheyadi & Al Sheyadi, 2022c	Managers	138	0.304	Oman		D
Hajikhani M *et al.*, 2012	Managers	200	0.578	Malaysia		D
Hashmi & Akram, 2021	Managers	277	0.361	Pakistan		Dg

Empirical Results

The meta-analysis has been done findings on heterogeneity, publication bias and moderating effect and subgroup analysis has been done. The following sections shows the findings and the results.

Heterogeneity

For the purpose of the analysis, correlation coefficient between the two variables are collected from the correlation matrix of past studies. Then heterogeneity test on the meta-analysis is done to determine whether there exists heterogeneity among the combined studies. This study uses Cochran's Q and Higgin's I^2 value to run the

Table 3

Meta Analysis Model	
Model	Random Effects Model
Confidence Level	95%
Presentation	
Sort By	Entry Number
Order	Ascending
Combined Effect Size	
Correlation	0.43
Confidence Level LL	0.37
Confidence Level UL	0.49
Prediction Interval LL	-0.06
Prediction Interval UL	0.75
Z Value	11.74
One tailed P value	0.00
Two tailed P value	0.00
Number of incld. Subjects	11714
Number of incld. Studies	43
Heterogeneity	
Q	769.61
PQ	0.00
I^2	94.54%
$T^2(Z)$	0.06
T(Z)	0.25

heterogeneity test. If the existing study outcome is homogeneous, then there is a probability that in future it will have the similar result when applied to new subjects. But if the studies show heterogeneity, then unless the reason for heterogeneity is well understood the effect shown by new subjects will be hard to comprehend (von Hippel, 2015). A forest plot is a graphical display used in meta-analysis for the purpose of studying heterogeneity. It is represented by lines in a box which symbolises point estimate like effect size e.g odd ratio, risk ratio etc (Dettori *et al.*, 2021). Forest plot of the study reveals high heterogeneity. As per (Hunter & Schmidt, 2000) there will be heterogeneity in this kind of combined study and hence random effect model should be used (Lixiang Wang *et al.*, **2020**). The results are shown in Table 3 below reveals P_Q as less than .01 which rejects the null hypothesis of homogeneity. Null hypothesis of homogeneity is rejected by the Q value under the main effect ($p < 0.01$), while the I^2 is greater than 94% in this paper.

Publication Bias

The study next checks for publication bias which means that the failure to incorporate studies owing to strength of the study finding (Nair, 2019) which simply points to the fact that only studies which are statistically significant positive are often published. It is a common practice to not publish results with negative outcome which are considered as failed results. However, studies with small sample size, no difference between groups and many other reasons may contribute in negative results (Joober *et al.*, 2012). Failsafe-N is used for testing publication bias which was first described by (Rosenthal R, 1979). It is a test of combined significance where the failsafe number indicates the number of studies missing that which averages a z-value of zero which is aggregated for making the combined effect size statistically insignificant (Eramus research institute of management online) Here Rosenthal Fail-Safe N (Nfs) shows that the coefficient Nfs is more than 5K + 10 (K = the size of the sample). This indicates although the publication bias exists it is a robust study (Rosenthal, R, 1979). *Table 4* shows the result

Table 4

Failsafe Tests	
Rosenthal	
Overall Z score	50.82
Failsafe-N	41000
Ad-hoc rule	FALSE

Moderator Effect and Subgroup Analysis

This article analyses the moderated effects of economic factors on the SHP on GP. For the purpose the countries based on which the studies had been conducted are grouped into developed countries (D) and developing countries (Dg) using HDI as an indicator. Countries with HDI of less than 0.8 is considered as Dg and above are considered as D (as per UNDP criteria). Limitation of the study in this regard has been taking the HDI value of Taiwan which is not included under UNDP but is incorporated from the list HDI of administrative divisions of Greater China. On the other hand, HDI for MENA countries is taken based on an average of 18 countries which falls within the group. The analysis results point to the fact that SHP in D play a vital role in GP. The results are summarised in *Table 5.*

Table 5

Economic Development Level	*N*	*95% Confidence Interval*		*Q test*	I^2	*Z*
		Lower Level	*Upper Level*			
Developed Countries	31	0.33	0.49	568.41	94.72%	9.14
Developing Countries	12	0.35	0.58	180.79	93.92%	7.65

CONCLUSION

This paper highlights stakeholder pressure on green practices by firms through meta-analysis in order to get a general conclusion and provide fruitful inputs for future research on the topic. One of the keys finding of the study is about categorising different pressure groups and to find the kind of pressure exerted by them. Literature review has also shown that stakeholder pressure helps to enhance the implementation of green practices through green innovation in production design and green supply chain. Since the articles included under meta-analysis have different context it can be concluded that stakeholder pressure on firms is contingent. The study is heterogeneous signifying the scope of further analysis. However meta-analysis done here is not exhaustive since only few papers were included in the process and this is one of the main limitations of this study.

REFERENCES

Agrawal, M., Kalia, P., Nema, P., Zia, A., Kaur, K. and John, H. B. (2023). Evaluating the influence of government initiatives and social platforms on green practices of Gen Z: The mediating role of environmental awareness and consciousness. *Cleaner and Responsible Consumption, 8.* https://doi.org/10.1016/j.clrc.2023.100109

Awan, U., Kraslawski, A. and Huiskonen, J. (2017). Understanding the Relationship between Stakeholder Pressure and Sustainability Performance in Manufacturing Firms in

Pakistan. *Procedia Manufacturing, 11*, 768–777. https://doi.org/10.1016/j.promfg.2017.07.178

Baah, C., Opoku-Agyeman, D., Acquah, I.S.K., Agyabeng-Mensah, Y., Afum, E., Faibil, D. and Abdoulaye, F.A.M. (2021). Examining the correlations between stakeholder pressures, green production practices, firm reputation, environmental and financial performance: Evidence from manufacturing SMEs. *Sustainable Production and Consumption, 27*, 100–114. https://doi.org/10.1016/j.spc.2020.10.015

Berrone P., Fosfuri A., Gelabert L and Luis R. Gomez. (2013). Necessity As The Mother Of "Green" Inventions: Institutional Pressures And Environmental Innovations. *Strategic Management Journal, 34*(8), 891–901.

Borenstein M, Hedges L.V, Higgins J.P.T and Rothstein H. (2009). *Introduction to Meta-Analysis* (1st ed.). John Wiley & Sons, Ltd.

Buysse, K. and Verbeke, A. (2003). Proactive environmental strategies: A stakeholder management perspective. *Strategic Management Journal, 24*(5), 453–470. https://doi.org/10.1002/smj.299

Cairncross, F. (1992). Costing the Earth: The Challenge for Governments, the Opportunities for Business. *Boston: Harvard Business School Press, 14.*

Dettori, J.R., Norvell, D.C. and Chapman, J.R. (2021). Seeing the Forest by Looking at the Trees: How to Interpret a Meta-Analysis Forest Plot. *Global Spine Journal, 11*(4), 614–616. https://doi.org/10.1177/21925682211003889

Dimaggio, P.J. and Powell, W.W. (1983). The Iron Cage Revisited: Institutional Isomorphism and Collective Rationality in Organizational Fields. In *Source: American Sociological Review* (Vol. 48, Issue 2).

Donaldson, T. and Preston, L. E. (1995). The Stakeholder Theory of the Corporation: Concepts, Evidence, and Implications. In *Source: The Academy of Management Review* (Vol. 20, Issue 1). https://www.jstor.org/stable/258887

Durand, R. and Georgallis, P. (Panikos). (2018). Differential Firm Commitment to Industries Supported by Social Movement Organizations. *Organization Science, 29*(1), 154–171. https://doi.org/10.1287/orsc.2017.1170

El-Kassar, A.-N. and Singh, S.K. (2019). Green innovation and organizational performance: The influence of big data and the moderating role of management commitment and HR practices. *Technological Forecasting and Social Change, 144*, 483–498. https://doi.org/10.1016/j.techfore.2017.12.016

Eltayeb, T.K., Zailani, S. and Ramayah, T. (2011). Green supply chain initiatives among certified companies in Malaysia and environmental sustainability: Investigating the outcomes. *Resources, Conservation and Recycling, 55*(5), 495–506. https://doi.org/10.1016/j.resconrec.2010.09.003

Etzion, D. (2007). Research on Organizations and the Natural Environment, 1992-Present: A Review. *Journal of Management, 33*(4), 637–664. https://doi.org/10.1177/0149206307302553

Freeman and RE. (1984). Strategic Management: A Stakeholder Approach. *Prentice Hall: Bergen, NJ, USA.*

Gunningham, N., Kagan, R.A. and Thornton, D. (2004). Social License and Environmental Protection: Why Businesses Go Beyond Compliance. *Law and Social Inquiry*, *29*(2), 307–342. https://doi.org/10.1086/423681

Hajikhani M, Wahiza binti abdul wahat N and Bin IDRIS, K. (2012). Considering on Green Supply Chain Management Drivers, as a Strategic Organizational Development Approach, Malaysian perspective. *Australian Journal of Basic and Applied Sciences*, *6*(8), 146–165.

Hashmi, S.D. and Akram, S. (2021). Impact of Green Supply Chain Management on Financial and Environmental Performance: Mediating Role of Operational Performance and the Moderating Role of External Pressures. *Logforum*, *17*(3), 359–371. https://doi.org/10.17270/J.LOG.2021.602

Henriques, I. and Sadorsky, P. (1996). The determinants of an environmentally responsive firm: An empirical approach. *Journal of Environmental Economics and Management*, *30*(3), 381–395. https://doi.org/10.1006/jeem.1996.0026

Henriques, I. and Sadorsky, P. (1999). The Relationship between Environmental Commitment and Managerial Perceptions of Stakeholder Importance. In *Source: The Academy of Management Journal* (Vol. 42, Issue 1). https://www.jstor.org/stable/256876

Hoffman and A.J. (2000). Competitive environmental strategy: A guide to the changing business landscape. *Washington, DC: Island Press.*

Hossain, M.I., Ong, T. S., Teh, B. H., Said, R.M. and Siow, M.L. (2022). Nexus of Stakeholder Integration, Green Investment, Green Technology Adoption and Environmental Sustainability Practices: Evidence from Bangladesh Textile SMEs. *Pertanika Journal of Social Sciences and Humanities*, *30*(1). https://doi.org/10.47836/pjssh.30.1.14

Huang, Y.-C., Ding, H.-B. and Kao, M.-R. (2009). Salient stakeholder voices: Family business and green innovation adoption. *Journal of Management & Organization*, *15*(3), 309–326. https://doi.org/10.1017/S1833367200002649

Hunter, J.E. and Schmidt, F. L. (2000). Fixed Effects vs. Random Effects Meta- Analysis Models: Implications for Cumulative Research Knowledge. *International Journal of Selection and Assessment*, *8*(4), 275–292. https://doi.org/10.1111/1468-2389.00156

Jain, S.K. and Kaur, G. (2004). Green Marketing: An Attitudinal and Behavioural Analysis of Indian Consumers. *Global Business Review*, *5*(2), 187–205. https://doi.org/10.1177/097215090400500203

Jansson, J., Marell, A. and Nordlund, A. (2010). Green consumer behavior: determinants of curtailment and eco- innovation adoption. *Journal of Consumer Marketing*, *27*(4), 358–370. https://doi.org/10.1108/07363761011052396

Joober, R., Schmitz, N., Annable, L. and Boksa, P. (2012). Publication bias: What are the challenges and can they be overcome? *Journal of Psychiatry & Neuroscience*, *37*(3), 149–152. https://doi.org/10.1503/jpn.120065

Kitsis, A.M. and Chen, I.J. (2021). Do stakeholder pressures influence green supply chain Practices?Exploring the mediating role of top management commitment. *Journal of Cleaner Production*.

Klassen, R.D. and Whybark, D.C. (1999). The Impact of Environmental Technologies on Manufacturing Performance. *Academy of Management Journal, 42*(6), 599–615. https://doi.org/10.2307/256982

Klievink, B., Janssen, M. and Tan, Y.H. (2012). A stakeholder analysis of business-to-government information sharing: The governance of a public-private platform. *International Journal of Electronic Government Research, 8*(4), 54–64. https://doi.org/10.4018/jegr.2012100104

Latip, M., Sharkawi, I., Mohamed, Z. and Kasron, N. (2022). The Impact of External Stakeholders' Pressures on the Intention to Adopt Environmental Management Practices and the Moderating Effects of Firm Size. *Journal of Small Business Strategy, 32*(3). https://doi.org/10.53703/001c.35342

Lee, J.W, Kim M.Y. and Kim E.Y. (2018). Antecedents of Adopting Corporate Environmental Responsibility and Green Practices. *Journal of Business Ethics, 148*, 397–409.

Li, G., Lim, M.K. and Wang, Z. (2020). Stakeholders, green manufacturing, and practice performance: empirical evidence from Chinese fashion businesses. *Annals of Operations Research, 290*(1–2), 961–982. https://doi.org/10.1007/s10479-019-03157-7

Lin C.Y, Ho and Y.H. (2008). 60 An Empirical Study on Logistics Service Providers' Intention to Adopt Green Innovations. *J. Technol. Manag. Innov., 3*, 17–26.

Lin, R. and Sheu, C. (2012). Why Do Firms Adopt/Implement Green Practices?–An Institutional Theory Perspective. *Procedia – Social and Behavioral Sciences, 57*, 533–540. https://doi.org/10.1016/j.sbspro.2012.09.1221

Nair, A. (2019). Publication bias – Importance of studies with negative results! *Indian Journal of Anaesthesia, 63*(6), 505. https://doi.org/10.4103/ija.IJA_142_19

Ning, S., Jie, X. and Li, X. (2022). Institutional pressures and corporate green innovation; empirical evidence from chinese manufacturing enterprises. *Polish Journal of Environmental Studies, 31*(1), 231–243. https://doi.org/10.15244/pjoes/139926

Ong, Lee, Teh and Magsi (2019). Environmental Innovation, Environmental Performance and Financial Performance: Evidence from Malaysian Environmental Proactive Firms. *Sustainability, 11*(12), 3494. https://doi.org/10.3390/su11123494

Polonsky, M.J. (1994). An Introduction To Green Marketing. *Electronic Green Journal, 1*(2). https://doi.org/10.5070/G31210177

Pujari, D., Wright, G. and Peattie, K. (2003). Green and competitive influences on environmental new product development performance. *Journal of Business Research, 56*(8), 657–671. https://doi.org/10.1016/S0148-2963(01)00310-1

Ramayah, T., Samat, N. and Lo, M. (2011). Market orientation, service quality and organizational performance in service organizations in Malaysia. *Asia-Pacific Journal of Business Administration, 3*(1), 8–27. https://doi.org/10.1108/17574321111116379

Rodriguez, L S. (2016). Green marketing and a broader stakeholder orientation. *Academy of Marketing Studies Journal, 20*(3).

Rosenthal R. (1979). The file drawer problem and tolerance for null results. *Psychol. Bull., 86*, 638–641.

Shaharudin, M.R., Akbar, J., Zainal, N.N., Hassam, S.F., Zainoddin, A.I., Fadli, M. and Nizam, M. (2018). Factors That Influence Green Practices Adoption Amongst Logistics Services Providers. In *Int. J Sup. Chain. Mgt* (Vol. 7, Issue 6). http://excelingtech.co.uk/

Sharma, S. and H. Vredenburg. (1998). Proactive corporate environmental strategy and the development of competitively valuable organizational capabilities. *Strategic Management Journal, 19.*

Sheyadi, A. and Al Sheyadi, A. K. (2022). *Open Access Journal of Waste Management & Xenobiotics Committed to Create Value for Researchers Stakeholder Environmental Concerns and Adoption of Green SCM Practices: Role of Stakeholder Characteristics J Waste Manage Xenobio Stakeholder Environmental Concerns and Adoption of Green SCM Practices: Role of Stakeholder Characteristics.* https://doi.org/10.23880/oajwx-16000177

Solomon, Robert C and Hanson. (1983). Above the Bottom Line: An introduction to Business Ethics. *New York: Harcourt Brace Jovanovich.*

Song, W. and Yu, H. (2018). Green Innovation Strategy and Green Innovation: The Roles of Green Creativity and Green Organizational Identity. *Corporate Social Responsibility and Environmental Management, 25*(2), 135–150. https://doi.org/10.1002/csr.1445

Tang M, Walsh G, Lerner D, Fitza, MA, Li and Q. (2018). Green innovation, managerial concern and firm performance: an empirical study. *Bus, Strat. Environ, 27*(1), 39–51.

von Hippel, P.T. (2015). The heterogeneity statistic I2 can be biased in small meta-analyses. *BMC Medical Research Methodology, 15*(1), 35. https://doi.org/10.1186/s12874-015-0024-z

Wang, H., Khan, M. A. S., Anwar, F., Shahzad, F., Adu, D. and Murad, M. (2021). Green Innovation Practices and Its Impacts on Environmental and Organizational Performance. *Frontiers in Psychology, 11.* https://doi.org/10.3389/fpsyg.2020.553625

Wang, L., Li, W. and Qi, L. (2020). Stakeholder pressures and corporate environmental strategies: A meta-analysis. *Sustainability (Switzerland), 12*(3). https://doi.org/10.3390/su12031172

Yu, W., Ramanathan, R. and Nath, P. (2014). The impacts of marketing and operations capabilities on financial performance in the UK retail sector: A resource-based perspective. *Industrial Marketing Management, 43*(1), 25–31. https://doi.org/10.1016/j.indmarman.2013.07.014

Zhang H, He J, Shi X, Hong Q, Bao j and Xue S. (2020). Technology characteristics, stakeholder pressure, social influence and green innovation. *Sustainability, 12.*

Zuraidah Raja Mohd Rasi, R., Abdekhodaee, A. and Nagarajah, R. (2014). Stakeholders' involvements in the implementation of proactive environmental practices. *Management of Environmental Quality: An International Journal, 25*(2), 132–149. https://doi.org/10.1108/MEQ-11-2011-0054

Linkage between Sustainable Development Goals 7 & 13 – Challenges & Way Forward

Anirban Datta[1] and Sushmita Choudhury[2]

ABSTRACT: On 25 September 2015, 193 members of the United Nations General Assembly adopted the 2030 Agenda for Sustainable Development, which comprises a set of 17 sustainable development goals (SDG) with 169 specific targets. Out of the 17, Goal 7 is for ensuring access to clean and affordable energy, which is crucial for the development of all pillars of the society, viz. agriculture, business, communications, education, healthcare and transportation. Generation and consumption of energy is one of most dominant contributor to climate change, accounting for around 60% of total global greenhouse gas emissions, thus having a direct linkage with Goal 13, which focuses on climate action. Warranting universal access to affordable energy (electricity) by 2030 needs propagation of clean energy sources such as solar, wind, biomass, micro-hydro and geo-thermal, which, perpetually, requires expansion of infrastructure and upgradation of technology to supply clean energy in affordable and sustainable way, with least carbon foot-print, across the globe, for which, holistic energy transition policies for regional, national and local levels are essential. The underlying challenges are many, as the energy transition policies cannot be same for all corners of the globe, that is, it would be different for developed and developing countries, as well as for different geographical regions. This poses a critical challenge towards achievement of 'Net Zero', particularly for those countries, such as India, where per capita energy consumption is much lower (and yet to reach the point of saturation) than USA, European Union, Australia or China, and whose primary & predominant source of generation of electricity is though the route of combustion of fossil fuels, and that needs gradual phasing down, not sudden phasing out, as that would lead to acute energy shortage, because of gross disproportionate between energy consumption versus number of consumers. Therefore, the formulation of effective and sustainable energy transition policy must be country specific to strike a balance between SDG 7 and 13.

Keywords: *SDG, Energy, Climate Action, Policy, Sustainability, Net-zero.*

---

[1] Founder & CEO – PIMECAS Engineering Solutions; Honorary Secretary, West Bengal State Centre, The Institution of Engineers (India); MIE, C Eng, PE.

[2] DGM – Human Resources, Pinnacle Infotech.

INTRODUCTION

The 2030 Agenda for Sustainable Development, which comprises 17 sustainable development goals (SDG) with 169 specific targets, promotes national/country-specific target-setting and adaptation of the SDGs into national policies, strategies, and developmental process, in the structure of National Development Plans (NDPs), number of which are rapidly increasing in last 20 years. These NDPs form the crucial part of the way forward of different countries to mitigate the various challenges and complexities of socio-economic, infrastructural, industrial and environmental processes at the national and global levels as well as to align with different international agreements (e.g., the Paris Agreement) and global agendas, setting path for the policy direction, development priorities, and implementation strategies for a country, and is often zeroed down through a national consensus process. NDPs are required to be aligned with the global goals in different forms and degrees, which vary from nation to nation, based on varying national priorities across the globe. One significant leaning observed is the adoption or alignment of the SDGs to formalise existing approaches and narratives of national interests. The countries which attempt to integrate the SDGs explicitly into national development plans, they need to define the linkages between goals and indicators, as well as the role of the NDP in mainstreaming the SDGs (Katramiz and Okitasari, 2021).

BACKGROUND

Figure 1: Sustainable Development Goals (SDGs)

(*Source:* https://www.un.org/sustainabledevelopment/blog/2015/12/sustainable-development-goals-kick-off-with-start-of-new-year)

Gap in Research and Approach towards Synergies in SDG 7 & 13 and Suggestive Pathway

Apart from the co-benefits of climate action (SDG 13) on ambient air quality and health, and their synergies with a low-carbon (clean) and affordable energy transition (SDG 7), there is a general lack of data and indicators to assess the synergies between the SDG goals, target and indicators at local, national, and international levels as well as across different sectors, including co-benefits of adaptation of decarbonisation and resilience measures and issues concerning protection of biodiversity. Furthermore, research gaps are also persistent on the interlinkages between climate action and the energy transition, including the implications for a 'just transition'. Increase in the level of collaborative research would not only bridge the knowledge gaps but also lead to capacity building. Similarly, decarbonisation of energy generation, transmission, distribution, usage and universal energy access would also bring co-benefits and trade-offs, in the forms of reduction of emissions, conservation of resources and increase in revenue, largely driven by the energy efficiency measures for household appliances, which can lower costs by 20%, having significant economic value, with air quality improvements frequently being of the same or even greater order of magnitude than mitigation expenditures. Energy transition pledged under the Paris Agreement, with 1.5°C temperature reduction target, can significantly reduce global air pollution and avert between 70000–90000 premature deaths (globally) per annum in 2030 depending on the strictness of air pollution control measures, or by as much as 175000–345000 per annum in 2030 under a more ambitious 2°C compliant pathway. In addition to decarbonisation, another important step towards meeting the 1.5°C goal is reforming global energy consumption patterns. This, of course, must transpire in line with the existing frameworks, as millions of people all across the world still do not have adequate access to affordable, reliable, sustainable, and modern sources of energy. A study projected a 40% reduction in global final energy demand by 2050, based on existing evident trends in low energy demand, despite growths in population, and economic activity and progress. Decisions about pathways to meet energy demand can have an impact on the welfare and wellbeing of people, the resilience and effectiveness of physical and social infrastructures, and the health of the natural environment, and must therefore be made in a way that is sustainable. Demand-side measures like selection of technology, consumption pattern, behaviour, lifestyles and associated socio-technical outlook are increasingly receiving attention all across the world. Overall, these have the potential to reduce emissions by 40%–80% in different user sectors, while contributing significant co-benefits (about 80%) through improvements in wellbeing by delivering across the boundaries of SDGs. One such approach that has received considerable attention is the implementation of energy conservation and efficiency measures. Globally, increases in energy efficiency across many sectors have prevented more than 200 Mt of energy-related GHG emissions in 2019 alone. This also bring co-benefits linked to various SDGs, including health, wellbeing, and productivity, employment & income generation, better energy security, and reduced rate of depletion of resources.

One of the key strategy for this can be upgradation of old buildings in cities to be more energy-efficient to reduce GHG emissions. This can have the potential to create 2 million jobs per annum till 2050 in OECD cities alone (OECD: Organisation for Economic Co-operation and Development; a unique forum where the governments of 37 democracies with market-based economies collaborate to develop policy standards to promote sustainable economic growth and can compare experiences, seek answers to common challenges, identify good practices, and develop high standards for economic policy, together with its sister agencies, the International Energy Agency (IEA) and the Nuclear Energy Agency (NEA)). In non-OECD cities, the same level of investments may generate between 2–16 million net new jobs per annum within the same time frame. In addition to this, improved working conditions and decline in rate of sickness make employees 1–16% more productive in energy-efficient buildings, aligning to the SDGs 3 & 8.

Apart from the buildings, energy efficiency measures in transport sector wherein transition towards battery powered electric vehicles lead to reduction of emission from combustion of fossil fuels, and synergies can be made between improved physical activity, reduced injuries and health risks, improved air quality, and reduced heat exposures. More impetus on the use of electric vehicles has the potential to create 24 million jobs by 2030. For example, studies have indicated that for Ahmedabad city of India alone, high uptake of low-carbon vehicles in the can reduce 74% of NOx and 83% of PM2.5 from the passenger transport sector compared to business-as-usual in 2035.

Thus, by pledging to eradication of emission through improvements in energy efficiency, cities not only add the global effort to combat and mitigate climate change, but may also gain locally by getting several associated advantages.

Main Challenges Pointed Out by Stakeholders

In various discussions (across-the-table and online) involving multiple stakeholders, following challenges in the pathway synergy between SDG 7 & 13 have been pointed out.

- Access to clean, affordable, reliable and sustainable energy is not gaining adequate momentum due to extensive and continued dependence on emitting and unsustainable fossil fuel resources, mostly due to reliance on traditional practices and infrastructures, and a general lack of awareness of new and existing renewable energy technologies that can support clean and safe energy access to all.
- Transition to affordable and clean energy is not adequately supported by economic incentives. Moreover, lack of synergised policies does not focus on the urgent

need to make the transformation to a low carbon society where emissions are halved by 2030 and net zero emissions by 2050 (however, net zero target set by India is 2070).

- Multi-stakeholder interactions and partnerships were perceived as a key to drive the implementation of SDG 7 and related targets, with full consideration of communities and affected populations at national and local level, to guarantee that no one is left behind.
- Technological transfer between developed and developing countries is grossly disproportional, undermining the dynamic learning process needed to adapt propagate low-carbon technologies in developing economies. Moreover, high-risk in green investment projects is a pronounced barrier in developing new technology solutions in many countries.

In subsequent sections, more focus is given on the way forward.

Sectoral Analysis

Universal access to affordable and clean energy, simultaneously reducing air pollution and mitigating climate change, can be achieved, with an appropriate mix of renewable energy, generation of energy in conventional route (with gradually phasing down) in a more improvised manner, introduction of efficient supply and conversion technologies, modification of energy consumption pattern and efficiency & conservation in end-use.

Larger portion of CO_2 emissions come from direct fossil-fuel use in the transport and industry sectors, while energy supply sector emissions (mostly from the power sector) are limited by a rapid approach to net zero CO_2 emissions until mid-century.

Four central options for reducing fossil-fuel emissions are:

1. Lowering energy demand,
2. Electrification of energy services
3. Decarbonisation of the power sector
4. Decarbonising non-electric fuel use in energy end-use sectors.

The energy system connects energy supply with energy demand through final energy carriers, including electricity and liquid, solid or gaseous fuels, tailored to their end-uses. To map energy-system transformations in mitigation pathways, four macro-level decarbonisation indicators associated with final energy are useful:

- Limit on the increase of final energy demand
- Decrease in the carbon concentration of electricity
- Rise in the share of final energy provided by electricity
- Decrease in the carbon concentration of final energy other than electricity.

Measures for reduction in demand of energy are key to reduce CO_2 emissions from end-use sectors for low-carbon pathways. The reductions in upstream energy can be several times larger than the initial end-use demand reduction. There are inter-dependencies among the supply and demand (end-use) sectors which necessitate the importance of a wide, systematic approach, driven by demand & use in energy services for mobility, residential & commercial activities (buildings), and manufacturing.

Industry

Industrial sector is the largest end-use consumer, both with respect to final energy demand and Green House Gas (GHG) emissions, with direct CO_2 emissions currently account for about 25% of total energy-related and process CO_2 emissions, and increased at an average annual rate of 3.4% between 2000 and 2014, significantly faster than total CO_2 emissions. In addition to emissions from the combustion of fossil fuels, usage of fossil fuels in the petrochemical industry and smelting of metals, as well as non-fossil fuel process emissions (e.g., from cement manufacturing) account for a small amount (about 5%) to the industrial sector's CO_2 emissions. Industries producing metallurgical and chemical materials are energy and emissions intensive in particular, viz.:

- Steel
- Non-ferrous metals
- Chemicals
- Non-metallic minerals
- Pulp and paper

These industries accounted for around 66% of final energy demand and 72% of direct industrial emissions in 2014.

Buildings

In 2014, the buildings sector accounted for 31% of total global energy usage, 54% of final electricity demand, and 8% of energy-related CO_2 emissions (excluding indirect emissions due to usage of electricity). When the generation of electricity at upstream is considered, buildings were responsible for 23% of global energy-related CO_2 emissions, with one third from direct fossil fuel consumption. Historically, growth in consumption of energy has been driven mainly by population and economic growth, with more access to electricity, and higher use of electrical appliances and space cooling resulting from elevating standards of living, particularly in developing countries and/or third world countries. These trends will continue in the future, and in 2050, energy consumption in this sector is projected to increase by 20% and 50% compared to 2010 in the Integrated Assessment Models (IAM) of 1.5°C-overshoot and 2°C-consistent pathways, respectively. However, sectoral studies project something different trends, indicating that the energy consumption in 2050 would come down compared to 2010 in Energy Technology Perspectives 2017-Beyond 2°C Scenario (ETP-B2DS), and the reduction rate of CO_2 emissions is higher than in IAM pathways.

Transport

Transportation sector accounted for 28% of global final energy demand and 23% of global CO_2 emissions related to energy in 2014, with annual rate of increase in emissions by 2.5% between 2010 and 2015, and in the last 50 years, this sector has observed faster rise in emissions than any other sector. It may be noted that this sector is the least diversified energy end-use sector, consuming 65% of global oil final energy demand, with 92% of transport final energy demand consisting of oil & its derivatives (ETP 2017), posing severe challenges for unfathomable decarbonization.

The projections of IAMs are more pessimistic than IEA-ETP scenarios, though both of them clearly project deep slash in energy consumption and CO_2 emissions by 2050. 1.5°C-overshoot pathways from IAMs project a reduction of 15% in energy consumption between 2015 and 2050, while ETP-B2DS predicts a reduction of 30%. Furthermore, IAM pathways are generally more pessimistic in the projections of CO_2 emissions and carbon intensity reductions. In IPCC's 2013 physical science report (AR5), similar comparisons between IAMs and sectoral studies were performed, those matched closely with each other, with identification of two important changes:

- Rapid growth in sales of electric vehicle in passenger cars segment.
- Increased attention towards structural changes in this sector.

The former one contributes to reduction of direct CO_2 emissions and the latter to reduction of energy consumption.

MITIGATION AND WAY FORWARD

Industry

Industrial sector's mitigation strategies can be categorized in terms of the following five pathways:

(i) Reduction of demand
(ii) Improvement in energy efficiency
(iii) Increase in electrification of energy demand
(iv) Reduction in the carbon content of non-electric fuels
(v) Introduction of innovative processes and application of carbon capturing systems.

Figure 2: Sustainable Development Goals (SDGs)

(*Source:* https://wedocs.unep.org/bitstream/handle/20.500.11822/22742/7_Affordable%20and%20clean%20energy%20for%20all_FINAL.pdf; https://wedocs.unep.org/bitstream/handle/20.500.11822/22748/13_Climate%20ActionFINAL.pdf)

As projected in IEA ETP, the relative contribution of different measures for reduction of CO_2 emission in B2DS scenario compared with their reference scenario in 2050 are as presented in Table 1.

Table 1

Energy efficiency	42%
Innovative process and CCS	37%
Switching to low-carbon fuels and feed stocks	13%
Material efficiency	8%

Reduction in the use of industrial materials, while delivering similar services, or improving the quality of products could help to reduce energy demand and overall system-level CO_2 emissions. Strategies include using materials more intensively, extending product lifetimes, increasing recycling, and increasing inter-industry material synergies, such as substitution with clinker in cement production (Allwood *et al.*, 2013; IEA, 2017a). Related to material efficiency, use of fossil-fuel feedstocks could shift to lower-carbon feedstocks, such as from oil to natural gas and biomass, and end-uses could shift to more sustainable materials, such as biomass-based materials, reducing the demand for energy intensive materials (IEA, 2017a).

Reaping energy efficiency potentials hinges critically on advanced management practices, such as energy management systems, in industrial facilities as well as targeted policies to accelerate adoption of the best available technology. Although release of excess energy, usually as waste heat, is inevitable, recovering and reusing this waste heat through technically and economically viable conditions benefits the overall energy system. Moreover, demand-side management strategies could modulate the level of industrial activity in line with the availability of resources in the power system. This could imply a shift away from peak demand and as power supply decarbonizes, this demand-shaping potential could shift some load to times with high portions of low-carbon electricity generation (IEA, 2017a). In the industry sector, energy demand increases more than 40% between 2010 and 2050 in baseline scenarios. However, in the 1.5°C-overshoot and 2°C-consistent pathways from IAMs, the increase is only 30% and 5%, respectively. These energy-demand reductions encompass both efficiency improvements in production and reductions in material (resource) demand, as most IAMs do not differentiate these two factors.

CO_2 emissions from industry are to increase by 30% in 2050 compared to 2010 in baseline scenarios. By contrast, these emissions are reduced by 80% and 50% relative to 2010 levels in 1.5°C-overshoot and 2°C-consistent pathways from IAMs, respectively. By middle of the century, CO_2 emissions per unit of electricity are projected to decrease to near zero in both approaches of pathways. A fast-tracked electrification of the industrial sector thus would be powerful mitigation option. In the IAM pathways, the share of electricity increases up to 30% by 2050 in 1.5°C-overshoot pathways from 20% in 2010. Some industrial fuel uses are substantially more difficult to be replaced with electricity than others, and electrification would also have other effects on the process, including impacts on plant design, cost and available process integration options (IEA, 2017a).

In 1.5°C-overshoot pathways, the carbon intensity of non-electric fuels consumed by industry decreases to 16 gCO_2 per MJ by 2050, compared to 25 gCO_2 per MJ in 2°C-consistent pathways. Considerable carbon intensity reductions are already projected to be achieved by 2030, largely via a rapid phase-out of coal. Biomass is becoming gradually more important energy carrier in the industrial sector in deep-decarbonization pathways, but primarily in the long (in 2050, biomass is projected to account for only 10% of final energy consumption even in 1.5°C-overshoot pathways). In addition, hydrogen plays a crucial role as a substitute for fossil based non-electric energy demands in some pathways.

Without gross propagation of low-carbon industrial processes, the 1.5°C-overshoot target is difficult to attain. Bringing such technologies and processes to commercial deployment requires significant investment on R&D, technology upgradation & skill development. Some examples of innovative low-carbon process routes include: new steelmaking processes such as upgraded smelt reduction and upgraded direct reduced iron, ironmaking from poor quality of iron ore as well as from scrap, inert anodes for aluminium smelting, and full oxy-fuelling kilns for clinker production in cement manufacturing (IEA, 2017a).

Carbon capture and storage (CCS) plays a major role in decarbonizing the industry sector in the context of 1.5°C and 2°C pathways, especially in industries with higher process emissions, such as cement, iron and steel industries.

In 1.5°C-overshoot pathways, CCS in industry is projected to reach 3 $GtCO_2$ per year by 2050, although with strong variations across pathways. Given the projected long-lead times and need for technological innovation, early scale-up of industry-sector CCS is essential to achieving the stringent temperature target. Development and demonstration of such projects has been slow, however. Currently, only two large-scale industrial CCS projects outside of oil and gas processing are in operation (Global CCS Institute, 2016). The estimated current cost of CO_2 avoided (in 2015 US $) ranges from $20–27 per ton of CO_2 for gas processing and bioethanol production, $60–138 per ton of CO_2 for fossil fuel-fired power generation, and up to $104–188 per ton of CO_2 for cement production (Irlam, 2017).

Buildings

In building sector, mitigation options are reductions in energy consumption and CO_2 emissions, through the route of decrease in energy demand and aggressive electrification in the buildings sector. Share of electricity in 2050 would be 60% in 1.5°C-overshoot pathways, compared with 50% in 2°C-consistent pathways; this would contribute to the reduction of direct CO_2 emissions by replacing carbon-intensive fuels, like oil and coal. Moreover, when combined with a rapid decarbonization of the power system, it would also support further reduction of indirect CO_2 emissions from electricity.

Sectoral bottom-up models generally estimate lower electrification potentials for the buildings sector in comparison to global IAMs. Besides CO_2 emissions, rising demand for air conditioning system in buildings across the Globe may also lead to increased emissions of GHGs in form of HFCs in this sector over next few decades. Although HFCs are currently a relatively small proportion of annual GHG emissions, their use in the air conditioning sector is expected to rise rapidly over the next few decades if sustainable alternatives are not adopted. However, their projected future impact can be significantly mitigated through better operation, servicing and maintenance of equipment and transition of cooling gases.

IEA-ETP (IEA, 2017a) analysed the relative merits and demerits of various technology measures toward the reduction of energy consumption and CO_2 emissions in the buildings sector. The largest energy savings potential is in heating and cooling systems, principally due to improvements in building envelope and introduction of high efficiency equipment. In the ETP-B2DS, energy demand for space heating and cooling is 33% lower in 2050 than in the reference scenario, accounting for 54% of total reductions from the reference scenario. Energy savings from transition to high-performance as well as energy-efficient lighting, appliances, and water heating equipment account for another 24% reduction from the total demand. The long-term, strategic shift away from fossil-fuel use in buildings, alongside the rapid uptake of energy efficient, integrated and renewable energy technologies (with clean power generation), leads to a drastic reduction of CO_2 emissions. In ETP-B2DS, the direct CO_2 emissions are 79% lower than the reference scenario in 2050, and the remaining emissions originate mainly from the continued use of natural gas.

The buildings sector is characterized by very long-living infrastructure, and immediate steps are utmost important to avoid lock-in of inefficient carbon and energy-intensive buildings, through the routes of advanced renovation technologies. This is required for both to new buildings in developing countries where substantial new construction is expected in the near future and to retrofits of existing buildings in developed countries. This embodies both a significant risk and opportunity for mitigation. Apart from the effect of building envelope measures, adoption of energy-efficient technologies such as heat pumps and, more recently, light-emitting diodes (LED) are also important for the reduction of energy consumption and CO_2

emissions. Choices, behaviour and building operation of habitats and/or consumers can also significantly affect energy consumption pattern and play the role of a guiding factor in conservation of energy and resources, thereby leading to reduction in CO_2 emissions.

Transport

Substantial reductions in emissions in the transport sector are projected to be achieved by several means, such as technology-focused measures like energy efficiency and fuel-switching. Structural/social changes that avoid or shift transport activity are also important. While the former solutions (technologies) always tend to figure into deep decarbonisation pathways in a major way, this is not always the case with the latter, especially in IAM pathways. Comparing different types of global transport models, Yeh *et al.* (2016) find that sectoral (intensive) studies generally envision greater mitigation potential from structural changes in transport activity and modal choice. Though, even there, it is primarily the switching of passengers and freight from less to more efficient travel modes, more specifically, shifting from private mode to public mode of transport (e.g., from cars, trucks and airplanes to buses and trains) that is the main strategy; other actions, such as increasing vehicle load factors (occupancy rates) and outright reductions in travel demand (e.g., as a result of integrated transport, land-use pattern and urban planning), are significantly much less. Whether these dynamics accurately reflect the actual mitigation potential of structural changes in transport activity and modal choice is an area of investigation. According to the recent IEA-ETP scenarios, the share of avoid (reduction of mobility demand) and shift (shifting to more efficient modes) measures in the reduction of CO_2 emissions from the reference to B2DS scenarios in 2050 amounts to 20% (IEA, 2017a).

The potential and strategies to reduce energy consumption and CO_2 emissions differ significantly among different modes of transportation. In ETP-B2DS, the shares of energy consumption and CO_2 emissions in 2050 for each mode are rather different (Table 2), indicating the challenge of decarbonizing heavy-duty vehicles (HDV, trucks), aviation, and shipping. The reduction of CO_2 emissions in the entire transport sector from the reference scenario to ETP-B2DS is 60% in 2050, with varying contributions per mode (Table 2). Since there is no prescribed readymade capsule to achieve this deep decarbonisation target, every possible measure would be required for this stringent emissions outcome.

Table 2: Transport Sector Indicators by Mode in 2050 (IEA, 2017a)
Share of energy consumption, biofuel consumption, CO_2 emissions, and reduction of energy consumption and CO_2 emissions from 2014
(CO_2 emissions are well-to-wheel emissions, including the emission during the fuel production)
LDV: light duty vehicle, HDV: heavy duty vehicle

	Share of Each Mode (%)			*Reduction from 2014 (%)*	
	Energy	*Biofuel*	*CO_2*	*Energy*	*CO_2*
LDV	36	17	30	51	81
HDV	33	35	36	8	56
Rail	6	–	–1	–136	107
Aviation	12	28	14	14	56
Shipping	17	21	21	26	29

The contribution of various measures for the CO_2 emission reduction from the reference scenario to the IEA-B2DS in 2050 can be seen in Table 3.

Table 3

Efficiency improvement	29%
Biofuels	36%
Electrification	15%
Avoid/shift	20%

It is noted that the share of electrification increases compared with previous studies, due to the recent growth of electric vehicle sales worldwide. Another new trend is the allocation of biofuels to each mode of transport.

In road transport, incremental vehicle improvements (including engines) are significant, especially in the short to medium term. Hybrid electric vehicles are also contributory to empower the transition from IC engine vehicles to EVs, especially plug-in hybrid EVs. Electrification is a powerful step to decarbonize short-distance plying vehicles (passenger cars and two and three wheelers) and the rail sector. In road freight transport (trucks), systemic improvements (e.g., in supply chains, logistics, and routing) would be effective measures in tandem with efficiency improvement of vehicles. Shipping and aviation are more challenging to decarbonize, while their demand growth is projected to be higher than other transport modes, and both need to follow highly go-getting efficiency improvements and use of low-carbon fuels. In the near and medium term, this would be advanced biofuels while in the long term it could be hydrogen as direct use for shipping or an intermediate product for synthetic fuels for both modes (IEA, 2017a).

A study (in US) by Forbes reveals that if an EV runs 30,000 miles in a year, then break-even would be reached in 1 year, but this would only be about 0.4% of vehicles. If the same is driven up to 10,000 miles in a year it would take 5 years before reaching break-even with the CO_2 emitted by an IC engine vehicle. That would be about one-third of vehicles. Another one-third of EV running only 5,000 miles in a year will take 24 years to break-even with an ICE vehicle's CO_2 output. This clearly denotes that fewer the miles driven, the longer it takes to reach the break-even CO_2, and for about one-third of vehicles, they will never be driven enough to justify for investment for the purposes of reducing carbon emissions. This is somewhat true for other countries as well; rather because of the fact that US citizens drive much further every year than other nationalities, it makes the US much more suitable for vehicle electrification, compared to other countries.

The share of low-carbon fuels in the total transport fuel mix increases to 10% and 16% by 2030 and to 40% and 58% by 2050 in 1.5°C-overshoot pathways from IAMs and the IEA-B2DS pathway, respectively. The IEA-B2DS scenario is on the more ambitious side, especially in the share of electricity. Hence, there is wide variation among scenarios, including the IAM pathways, regarding changes in the transport fuel mix over the first half of the century.

These differences can be explained by more thrust on efficiency improvements and avoid/shift decreasing energy consumption, and increased share of biofuels and electricity accelerating the speed of decarbonization in ETP scenarios. Although biofuel consumption and sales of EV have increased significantly in recent years, the growth rates projected in these pathways would be exceptional and far higher than reached so far.

The 1.5°C pathways require an acceleration of the mitigation solutions already featured in 2°C-consistent pathways (e.g., more efficient vehicle technologies operating on lower-carbon fuels), as well as those having received lesser attention in most global transport decarbonization pathways up to now (e.g., mode-shifting and travel demand management). Current-generation, global pathways generally do not include these newer transport sector developments, whereby technological solutions are related to shifts in commuter's behavioural pattern.

Key Messages and Recommendations in a Global Perspective

Sustainable access to clean energy and the targets supported by the Sustainable Development Goal (SDG) 7 of the 2030 Agenda can only be achieved through strong investment on energy transition and the mobilization of financial planning. Governments, private sector and other stakeholders need to create the ecosystem for enabling the production, distribution and raising awareness for percolation of clean energy sources backed up by the strategic recommendations provided by multi-stakeholder consultations.

An efficient and timely energy transition must be supported by adequate policy incentives for development of renewable energy sources including wind, solar, sustainable conventional and non-conventional hydro and geothermal power generation, as in the long run, the environmental benefits of switching to renewable energy would likely far outweigh the short-term investments of installing the technologies and infrastructure.

Governments must look into energy efficiency and conservation regulations including provision of incentives for investments in energy efficient processes and products. Special emphasis must be given on reduction of system losses in electric power transmission and distribution. Furthermore, governments must furnish distinct information through policies about the effects of non-rational use of energy for the environment, economy, and society, with improved electricity demand side management.

In the longer term, a shift towards renewable energy and greater energy efficiency would slow the depletion of many types of natural resource and would generally support environmental targets. However, shifting to large-scale use of bioenergy or hydropower could add stress on terrestrial and inland freshwater ecosystems with strong negative effects if not governed well. For example, minerals will be required and without efficient recycling, targets seeking to protect natural resources, conserve ecosystems and biodiversity will be constrained. Ocean-based energy production, like offshore wind farms, can compete spatially with marine and coastal habitats and protected areas.

Recycling materials before they may go to a landfill can help to reduce GHG emissions by reducing the need for virgin materials. Manufacturing products from recycled materials requires less energy, typically, than making products from virgin raw materials.

Government and policy makers across the world must emphasize on reduction of routine hydrocarbon gas flaring in oil & gas sector, as well as focus on technology and regulation on capture and use of methane from landfills, and effective waste-to-energy combustion.

There is a need to build a more dynamic and sustainable model of technology, innovation, data collaboration, and capacity building: this should be addressed both between developing and developed countries, and in multilateral partnerships. Co-innovation is the key to give impetus to technological collaboration, sharing, and development.

Smooth and streamlined administrative and permitting process for green investments is urgent to catch up with the ambitious investment pathways needed to meet climate neutrality by 2050. Finance and investment for sustainable, reliable, affordable and clean energy are essential catalysts to meet SDG 7.

Conflict in the Pathway of Synergies between SDG 7 and 13

Studies of Stockholm Environment Institute vide their SEI report February 2023 (Dzebo & Shawoo, 2023) have noted that countries' commitments under the Paris Agreement, especially commitments to reduce emissions, have the potential to undermine or inhibit progress toward a range of development goals. For example, there would be potential negative implications of climate mitigation for land use and energy access. Climate change mitigation actions can also sometimes undermine achievement of SDGs by exacerbating social vulnerability, inequity and uneven power relations, particularly if the root causes of vulnerability are not accounted for. However, World Health Organization (WHO) has focused on the critical nexus between climate change, health and air pollution. Air pollution is a major and increasing threat to human health; according to WHO, exposure to fine particulate matter from indoor and outdoor air pollution results in approximately 7 million premature deaths per year. The issues of climate change and air pollution are closely linked because many major sources of air pollution are also major sources of GHGs. If the progression in climate change is not halted, there may be new, more frequent, and more severe climate-related illnesses, adding to the already high burden of health care providers, and adding significantly to future health care costs. Even if transitioning to a low-carbon and low-pollution energy and transport future appears costly, some estimates suggest that those costs may well be much lower than future health care costs in a warming world. Thus, policies and measures seek to address climate change, air pollution, health, safety, and other concerns in a synergistic manner.

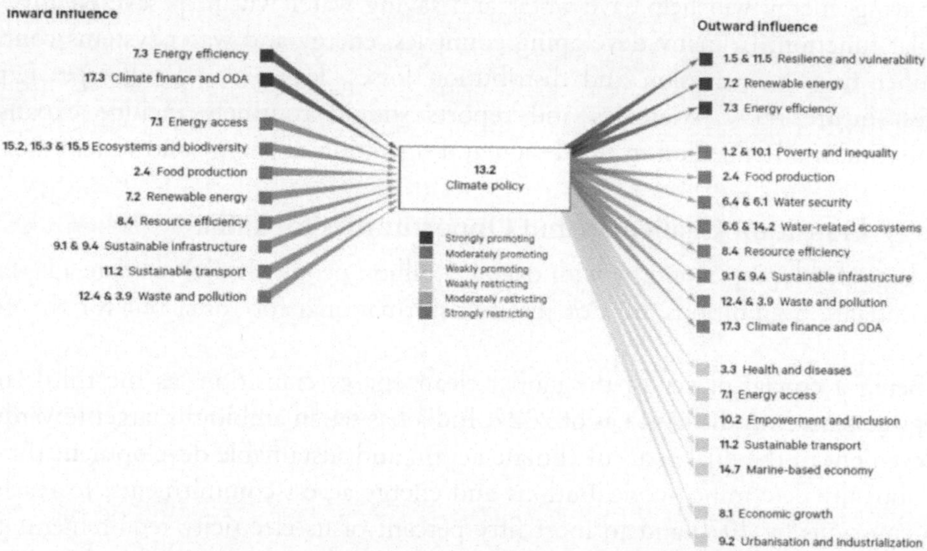

Figure 3: Outward Influence of Target 13.2 (climate policy)

(*Source:* SEI report February 2023, Adis Dzebo, Zoha Shawoo, Stockholm Environment Institute)

For example, water and energy are highly interlinked. Water is needed for generation of energy production in hydro-electric route as well as for water-based cooling systems in thermal power plants. On the other hand, energy is needed to operate all pumps in drinking, industrial, and agricultural water supply and distribution systems, and wastewater collection and treatment. Desalination of sea-water using renewable sources of energy is increasingly important in water-scarce regions. Conventional and integrated energy and water systems need to be planned and operated in an integrated manner to realize synergies and co-benefits, and to curb growing emissions of greenhouse gases. Following steps can be very much pertinent on this area:

- Surfaces of reservoirs can be used in part for floating PV solar farms; this has already gained momentum worldwide.
- Gravity-fed water supply systems can be used to co-generate electricity from small turbines.
- Seaside cities in the tropics can install water-based air-cooling systems to lower their operational energy costs and emissions
- Wastewater treatment systems can capture heat and biogas for reduction of emissions as well as for power generation, which may be of particular importance and commercially feasible in large-scale facilities.
- Water conservation, efficiency, and demand management are also crucial for attaining synergies in SDGs and climate protection.

Saving energy will help save water and saving water will help save energy, in a circular function. In many developing countries, energy and water systems continue to suffer from transmission and distribution losses, leakage, and pilferage. Experts suggest future NDC strategies and reports should routinely include expansion, repairs, and modernization in the design and operation of energy and water systems.

Energy Transition Challenges and Opportunities for India

As a large developing economy with over 1.3 billion people, India's climate adaptation and mitigation ambitions are not just transformational for India but for the entire planet.

Being a crucial player in the global clean energy transition, as the third-largest energy consumer in the world as of 2022, India has set an ambitious target towards the achievement of the dual goals of climate action and sustainable development through its nationally determined contributions and energy access commitments, to reach net zero emissions by 2070 and to meet fifty percent of its electricity requirements from renewable energy sources by 2030, and committed to 3 targets, which are to be achieved by the year 2030:

1. By 2030, 40% of India's cumulative electric power installed capacity will come from non-fossil fuel-based energy sources.
2. India will reduce the emission intensity of its gross domestic product (GDP) by 33–35% (vis-à-vis 2005 levels).
3. India will create an additional carbon sink of 2.5–3 billion tonnes of CO_2 equivalent (through additional forest and tree cover).

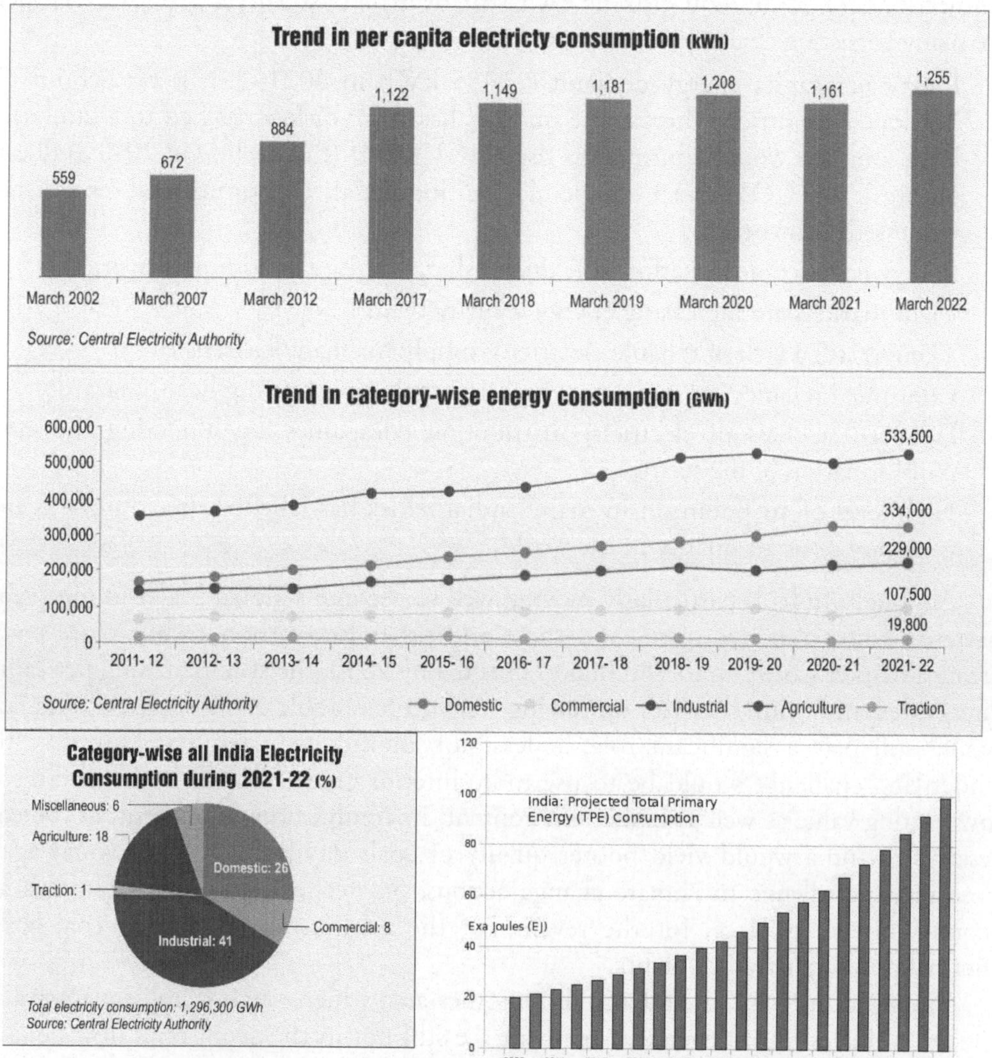

Figure 4: Trend of Energy Consumption in India

(*Source:* https://powerline.net.in/2023/04/04/key-statistics-electricity-consumption-per-capita-and-category-wise/and https://ef4india.wordpress.com/2012/01/04/estimating-the-energy-requirement-in-2030/)

With a stunning scale of transformation, having its economic growth among the highest in the world over the past two decades, and adding up to infrastructure development, with construction of new buildings, factories and transportation networks, it has also become the third highest annual CO_2 emitting nation, due to the rapid growth in fossil energy consumption, as coal and oil have so far served as fuel for India's industrial growth and modernisation, inclusive of adding new electricity connections for 50 million citizens each year over the last 10 years. However, there are many persisting challenges underneath:

- India's per capita energy demand (~1255 kWh in 2021–22), is far behind the developed countries, wherein the number has more-or-less reached to a saturation level, and this would continue to rise (FIGURE 4) (the decline in 2021 is due to outbreak of COVID-19 pandemic, as industrial & commercial established witnessed a downturn).
- Energy has become less affordable due to sharp increase in commodity prices.
- Tight markets are increasing energy security risks.
- There is still a lack of reliable electricity supply for many citizens.
- Continued reliance on traditional fuels for cooking is causing health hazards.
- Financial sickness of electricity distribution companies are hindering the rapid transformation of the sector.
- High level of air pollution in many Indian cities has labelled the country as one with very poor air quality in the world.

Although, India is particularly moving well to become a global leader in renewable batteries and green hydrogen, and these and other low-carbon technologies could create a market worth up to $80 billion in India by 2030, the still increasing per capita energy demand cannot be met up relying only on renewable energy sources, and coal would still play a significant role, at least for another two decades. However, the underlying challenge would be to use more inferior grade of coal, both in terms of low heating value as well as higher ash content, in combustion equipment, as the coal reserves in India would yield poorer quality of coals day by day. This would again pose severe challenge to climate change actions. So, technological advancements are required to be in place, for the revamp of the combustion system in coal based thermal power generating plants.

Propagation to EV in India is also another area which needs a holistic approach. Electric vehicles in passenger car segment are still not in the economies of scale, and the preceding discussions revealed the longer break-even period for the EV, which more challenging for a country like India with dense population and less road surface area compared to developed nations.

Even though India's energy goals are predominantly defined at the national level, its energy transition would have different perspectives in different states, as some of the states face greater challenges to formulate, adopt and implement the national level clean & affordable energy access commitments than others. In addition to this, technical challenges with integration of renewables in the grid, changes in consumer behaviour, electricity generation ownership patterns, and institutional arrangements pose questions on consumer tariff design and utility revenue models. Regulators and policymakers will need to find the right balance between stability and flexibility in this era of decreasing costs of renewable energy generation systems and improved performance of new technologies.

CONCLUSIONS

From the elaborations, it is evident that the strategy for energy transition, provision of affordable energy and climate change mitigation actions needs a synergized and holistic approach, and so are the implementation sustainable development goals along with their targets & indicators. The policies, strategies and implementation would vary from country to country, between regions, and even between different zones within a country. Thus, localization of SDGs and their targets & indicators are crucial for the maximum benefit to the stakeholders.

REFERENCES

International Energy Agency (IEA) (2017). *World Energy Outlook 2017.*

United Nations. Department of Economic and Social Affairs (2023). *Synergy Solutions for a World in Crisis: Tackling Climate and SDG Action Together – REPORT ON STRENGTHENING THE EVIDENCE BASE,* First Edition 2023.

Stockholm Environment Institute (SEI) (2023). *Sustainable Development Goal interactions through a climate lens: a global analysis.* SEI report February 2023: Adis Dzebo, Zoha Shawoo.

The World Bank (2022). *Tracking SDG7: The Energy Progress Report 2022.* A joint report of the World Bank, the International Energy Agency, the International Renewable Energy Agency, the United Nations, and the World Health Organization.

The World Bank (2022). *Tracking SDG7: The Energy Progress Report 2019.* A joint report of the World Bank, the International Energy Agency, the International Renewable Energy Agency, the United Nations, and the World Health Organization.

United Nations. Department of Economic and Social Affairs (2021). *Stakeholders Thematic E-Consultation for the United Nations High-Level Dialogue on Energy Summary Report,* May 2021.

United Nations (2021). *Harnessing Climate and SDGs Synergies – Raising Ambition in the Era of Paris+5 and Pandemic Recovery: Synthesis Report of Climate and SDGs,* Synergies Learning Series, December 2020 – February 2021.

United Nations. Department of Economic and Social Affairs (2021). *Leveraging Energy Action for Advancing the Sustainable Development Goals: Policy Briefs in Support of The High-Level Political Forum.*

Stockholm Environment Institute (SEI) (2019). *SDGs and the environment in the EU: A systems view to improve coherence,* Report commissioned by the European Environment Agency 2019: Nina Weitza, Henrik Carlsena, Kristian Skånberga, Adis Dzeboa, Vincent Viaudb.

Intergovernmental Panel on Climate Change (IPCC) (2018). *Global Warming of 1.5°C. An IPCC Special Report on the impacts of global warming of 1.5°C above pre-industrial levels and related global greenhouse gas emission pathways, in the context of strengthening the global response to the threat of climate change, sustainable development, and efforts to eradicate poverty.* Masson-Delmotte, V., P. Zhai, H.-O. Pörtner, D. Roberts, J. Skea, P.R. Shukla, A. Pirani, W. Moufouma-Okia, C. Péan, R. Pidcock, S. Connors, J.B.R. Matthews, Y. Chen, X. Zhou, M.I. Gomis, E. Lonnoy, T. Maycock, M. Tignor, and T. Waterfield (eds.).

United Nations. Department of Economic and Social Affairs (2022). *SDG Good Practices: A compilation of success stories and lessons learned in SDG implementation.* Second Edition.

United Nations University. Institute for the Advanced Study of Sustainability (2021). Policy Brief No. 25, 2021. *Accelerating 2030 Agenda Integration: Aligning National Development Plans with the Sustainable Development Goals.* Tarek Katramiz and Mahesti Okitasari.

https://www.forbes.com/sites/neilwinton/2023/06/29/high-mileage-evs-win-co2-race-but-low-use-favors-hybridsreport/?sh=48b543082a6b

https://www.iea.org/commentaries/india-s-clean-energy-transition-is-rapidly-underway-benefiting-the-entire-world

https://www.teriin.org/article/indias-energy-transition-challenge-decision-making-time-rapid-change

https://www.businesstoday.in/magazine/industry/story/despite-challenges-indias-plans-for-energy-sector-are-ambitious-it-needs-proper-execution-369010-2023-02-05

https://www.imf.org/en/Publications/fandd/issues/2022/12/bumps-in-the-energy-transition-yergin

https://www.thehindubusinessline.com/news/challenges-that-come-with-energy-transition/article65556854.ece

https://www.bu.edu/gdp/2022/10/11/critical-challenges-in-realizing-the-energy-transition-an-overview-of-indian-states/

https://timesofindia.indiatimes.com/blogs/voices/indias-energy-transition-challenges-and-opportunities-for-a-sustainable-future/

Building Sustainable Green Businesses for Bharat

Dr. Ruma Basu Gomes[1] and Kanishk Gomes[2]

ABSTRACT: In the rapidly evolving contemporary Indian business landscape, decision-making extends beyond the traditional objective of profit maximisation to embrace the critical influence of corporate actions on social and environmental spheres. In order to do so, it is imperative to integrate sustainability throughout the chain of business processes. For our country, this is much simpler said than done since our distinct cultural and economic context presents complex challenges. Our unique set of risks and opportunities makes us a fertile ground for innovating new business strategies for the green transition. Our use of "Bharat" underscores a commitment to formulating industry-agnostic strategies that are attuned to the nuances of our national context. These strategies must be crafted to bridge the rural-urban divide, harness the full potential of available natural and human resources, and positively contribute to uplifting the underserved populations. As we aim to evidence, a commitment to social advancement complements the ultimate objective of business expansion. This chapter seeks to delve into forging a sustainable trajectory for domestic enterprises to follow to enhance their responsibility towards nature, the community, and their own stakeholders. By deconstructing the supply chain, we are able to identify points where an organisation can bolster their resilience. Through evidence-based research, we provide measures that can be undertaken by companies and whose effects can be amplified at scale. The objective of this chapter is not only to improve the ESG (Environment, Social, and Governance) ratings of organisations but also to effectuate real positive social change while reducing overall operational costs. The shift towards a green economy enables us to respond to market demands and increase long-term organisational sustainability while ensuring that our actions do not overburden our resource pool.

Keywords: *Bharat, Business Strategy, Climate Crisis, Green Innovation, Localisation, Social Impact, Sustainability.*

INTRODUCTION

The climate polycrisis we are presently undergoing, marked by global warming, is a multifaceted problem with varied causes and repercussions across sectors, communities, nations, and industries. The health and economic prosperity of current

[1] Consultant – HR and Behavioural Sciences.

[2] Student and Author, Social Sciences.

and future generations are at stake, making it imperative to find solutions for a cleaner, more sustainable future. Climate change presents a complex, threefold challenge with far-reaching consequences (Torkington, 2023). First and foremost, the escalating pollution levels constitute a significant risk to both the environment and public health. Secondly, it accelerates biodiversity loss and exacerbates land degradation, issues that are especially critical in agricultural economies such as India, where a substantial segment of the population relies on farming for their livelihood. Finally, the growing difficulty in managing waste efficiently represents a pressing concern in the face of climate change. This demands an urgent response from key stakeholders, including national authorities, local governments, affected communities, and those vulnerable to the vagaries of climatic disasters. This list would, however, be incomplete without acknowledging the role businesses have to play in the deliberation to resist the most adverse impacts of unsustainable resource use. In the face of an escalating climate crisis and increasing levels of pollution, it is imperative for contemporary businesses to embrace sustainable practices. The growing influence of the private sector in national economies globally, coupled with the expanding network of multinational corporations, underscores the reality that the journey towards sustainability cannot be undertaken by governments alone. As the global population burgeons and economic activities intensify, the strain on our planet's finite resources becomes more pronounced. This situation compellingly highlights the necessity of integrating sustainability into every facet of development and economic sectors, transforming it from an optional approach to an indispensable element in our collective response to environmental challenges.

Amidst the escalating urgency of environmental concerns, businesses globally are beginning to acknowledge the adverse impacts that climate change can have on their profitability. This evolving awareness is catalysing a shift in corporate strategies, steering them towards sustainability as a pivotal approach. Recognising that their long-term success is inextricably linked to their capacity for environmentally responsible operations, businesses are increasingly adopting innovative means to address and minimise their negative externalities. The past decade has seen a heightened focus among top executives and eco-entrepreneurs on the rise of climate-related natural disasters, drawing significant attention to the need for sustainable practices in business operations. At the international level, there is a discernible movement towards sustainability, albeit progressing at a modest pace. This gradual global shift is primarily observed in the Global North, including the Nordic countries, Western Europe, North America, and affluent East Asian nations. However, the scenario is somewhat different, closer to home in India. Here, market leaders are becoming increasingly aware of trends and adapting their business models to meet India's ambitious sustainability goals. Yet, the trajectory of sustainability in India is influenced by a myriad of additional factors. The Indian landscape, distinct from advanced industrial economies, faces unique challenges, including limited resources that constrain public spending on green initiatives and the prominence of micro, small, and medium enterprises. Moreover, the social context in India, marked by its vast cultural diversity, plays a significant role in shaping its approach to sustainability. With a linguistic diversity that quadruples that of the entire European continent, it becomes clear that solutions in India cannot be standardised but must instead be tailored to reflect the diverse needs and contexts of its people. Consequently, the transition to a green economy in India necessitates a localised approach, one that integrates sustainable processes in a manner that best suits specific regional and cultural contexts. This approach underscores the importance of customising sustainability initiatives to effectively address the unique environmental, economic, and social challenges faced by different areas within the country.

ROOTING OURSELVES IN BHARAT

Nearly two-thirds of the Indian population, as per the Census of India (2011) data, live in "Bharat" – our rural areas. This is extremely distinct from the countries where the green transition has been successful. Data from 2005 to 2023 shows that consistently, the top 100 most sustainable companies have been disproportionately present in the Global North- Europe, and North America (Scott, 2023). In the rankings' latest iteration, there is only one company from Africa (Investec) and sixteen from Asia. These sixteen companies are nearly evenly distributed among Japan, China, South Korea, and Singapore. Notably, none of the companies are from India, and none of the countries represented above remotely resembles India's unique demographic profile, especially its massive rural and Micro, Small and Medium Enterprise (MSME) base. Therefore, the solutions adapted for the green transition in India must cater to its unique circumstances, reflecting the nation's distinct aspirations and challenges. India's demographic composition and economic structure are markedly different from those in the Global North. The Economic Survey of India 2022–23 notes that nearly 65% of our population lives in rural areas (Press Information Bureau, 2023). This demographic reality necessitates a dual approach that focuses not only on urban industrial transformation but also on rural sustainability and modernisation.

The key to India's green transition lies in leveraging our human capital (which is substantial, given our more than half-billion-strong labour force) and our rich natural resources base in a manner that is environmentally sustainable and socially equitable. In addition to a significant finite resource base, India's vast topographic diversity and size offer immense potential for harnessing solar, hydro, and wind energy. Therefore, integrating renewable energy sources is vital, considering India's renewable energy capacity (including nuclear) stood at 176.49 Gigawatts (GW) constituting about 43% of its total energy capacity as of 2023 (Manohar, 2023). India's renewable energy capacity is projected to reach 500 GW by 2030, per the Union Ministry of New and Renewable Energy, with rural areas contributing significantly (Press Trust of India, 2023). Speaking specifically about solar capacity, as of end-2023, India has installed over 72 GW, a substantial portion of which is in rural regions (DD News, 2023). However, the focus should be on more than just integration- also on maintaining these renewable energy infrastructures. As highlighted by Chaurey and Le (2022), maintaining rural infrastructure is vital not only for the success of state and business-led programs but also for two additional key reasons. Firstly, it catalyses local economic growth by providing maintenance training and creating regular employment opportunities for job seekers. Secondly, it actively involves local communities in the green economy by normalising the use of renewable energy in these areas. The combination of these three outcomes – successful integration and maintenance of renewable energy sources, stimulation of local economies, and community involvement in the green economy – collectively eases the transition to green energy. This approach is rooted in and expands from India's rural base, making the transition more organic and inclusive.

Our rural base presents not only a challenge but also significant opportunities. It is worth noting that according to data by the Indian Chamber of Commerce and Bain & Company, the rural economy made a substantial contribution of approximately 50% to the entire Gross Domestic Product (GDP) of the nation during the period of 2019-2020 (Jain, 2022). Moreover, this sector also serves as a significant source of employment, engaging approximately 350 million individuals, which accounts for approximately 68% of the total workforce. In the past five years, the rural ecosystem has had an annual growth rate of approximately 10% per annum (p.a.), indicating significant potential for further expansion. To realise a holistic green transition, Indian businesses must strategically harness the potential of the rural sector by addressing its environmental, economic, and social dimensions. This involves integrating green technologies and practices in agriculture, a sector that employs 42% of India's workforce according to the Periodic Labour Force Survey (Damodaran, 2023). The promotion of sustainable farming practices is crucial in this regard. For instance, the area under organic farming certification process in India has expanded to 10.17 million hectares (5.39 million hectares of which is cultivable land) as of 2023, indicating a significant shift towards more environmentally friendly agricultural methods (Agricultural and Processed Food Products Export Development Authority, 2023). This shift towards sustainable practices sets the stage for adopting more advanced techniques like precision agriculture. This method optimises crop yields and farm management through the use of advanced sensor technologies and analytical tools (Singh *et al.*, 2020). Globally embraced, precision agriculture enhances production efficiency, reduces labour, and manages resources like fertilisers and irrigation more effectively. Central to this approach is the extensive use of data to fine-tune the use of agricultural resources, leading to improvements in both the quantity and quality of crop yields. Measures like this can significantly enhance productivity, with studies suggesting that sustainable agricultural practices, in developing countries, can increase crop yields by up to 79% while reducing environmental impacts (Pretty *et al.*, 2006).

Promoting rural entrepreneurship and SMEs focused on green products and services is another crucial area. This not only creates employment opportunities but also facilitates the dissemination of green technologies at the grassroots level. The Pradhan Mantri MUDRA Yojana (PMMY) has been instrumental in supporting this initiative, disbursing loans to over 41 crore beneficiaries, many of whom are in rural areas, as of April 2023 (The Hindu, 2023). These initiatives can be leveraged to bolster green rural enterprises. Empowering rural communities, particularly women and marginalised groups, through education and skill development in sustainable practices is essential. The role of micro, small and medium enterprises (MSMEs), which form the backbone of the Indian economy, also cannot be understated. MSMEs contribute around 30% to India's GDP, employ about 110 million people, and contribute 49% to our exports (Ahuja *et al.*, 2023). Recent data released by the government paints a worrisome picture of the Micro, Small, and Medium Enterprises (MSME) sector in India, with a reported closure of over 10,000 MSMEs in the fiscal year 2022–23 (Ahuja *et al.*, 2023). This development raises significant concerns about the sector's stability and health. Further exacerbating these challenges is the increasing incidence of climate-induced heat stress, which places an additional burden on the workforce. The repercussions of such environmental risks are far-reaching, impacting not only the physical infrastructure and operations but also leading to financial difficulties, job losses, and consequent migration. The role of MSMEs in bridging economic disparities is well-recognized, making their transition to sustainable and climate-resilient practices a critical component of India's journey towards equitable and environmentally sustainable development. Notably, the MSME sector significantly contributes to greenhouse gas emissions, with an annual output of approximately 110 million tonnes of carbon dioxide. This level of emissions is on par with the energy consumption equivalent to about 50 million metric tonnes of oil each year, emanating from 200 energy-intensive manufacturing clusters across the nation (Goel *et al.*, 2022). Such a substantial environmental impact underscores the need for a strategic shift in the sector's operational practices. To facilitate this transition, it is imperative that these businesses receive adequate support through policy measures and incentives that promote sustainable practices. This includes providing access to green financing, an area that is currently in its developmental stages in India but is showing signs of growth. For instance, the issuance of green bonds in India had reached USD 21 billion in early 2023, indicating a positive trend towards environmentally focused financial instruments (Hussain & Dill, 2023). These measures are crucial in ensuring that the MSME sector not only thrives but also contributes positively to the country's commitment to reducing its carbon footprint and achieving sustainable development goals.

In urban areas, the focus should be on nudging businesses to contribute towards building smart, sustainable cities. With over 34% of India's population living in metropolitan and peri-urban areas, the development of sustainable urban infrastructure becomes imperative (Press Information Bureau, 2023). This includes initiatives like the Smart Cities Mission, which aims to develop 100 smart cities nationwide, focusing on sustainable and inclusive urban development. India's residential market witnessed a remarkable surge in 2022–23, with a 36% increase, setting a record for the year (Outlook Money, 2023). By the year 2030, India is projected to become the world's leading consumer of cement, a testament to its rapid urbanisation and construction growth. Currently, the construction sector is accountable for 40% of carbon emissions in India a significant environmental concern (Kuchimanchi, 2023). The industry is also characterised by its extensive use of resources, including water and energy, and is a major generator of large-scale waste. For a country experiencing rapid urbanisation like India, these factors present a substantial environmental challenge. Consequently, green businesses real estate sector holds the potential to be a pivotal force in achieving the global objective of limiting temperature rise to 1.5 degrees Celsius (Kuchimanchi, 2023). Construction offers the greatest opportunity for greenhouse gas mitigation at the lowest capital investment. Research indicates that green buildings can lead to substantial savings, reducing energy consumption by up to 30% and water usage by 50% while cutting maintenance costs by approximately 25% (Abdullah, 2022). By embracing sustainable design, construction, and operational practices, it is possible to develop buildings that are not only climate-resilient but also efficient in water usage, optimal in energy use, conserving natural resources, and minimising waste generation. This approach is crucial for India as it navigates the complexities of urban development while striving to meet its environmental and sustainability goals. The burgeoning middle class, estimated to grow to a total of 715 million people by 2030, can be a significant driver of change by adopting sustainable lifestyles and supporting green businesses in urban centres (Shukla, 2023). The reason that this demographic shift is significant is that it presents a substantial market for green products and services, potentially driving the demand for sustainable solutions.

STRATEGISING FOR BHARAT

For businesses to transition to sustainable practices, the first step is recognising the limited nature of the Earth's resources. Companies must evaluate their operations to ensure that short-term profits are not achieved at the expense of long-term environmental damage. Setting scientifically backed targets for nature, climate, and pollution is essential. Responding to the urgent appeals from international organisations like the United Nations' Intergovernmental Panel on Climate Change and the World Economic Forum, Indian businesses are intensifying their initiatives to diminish their carbon footprint. This strategic shift involves a gradual transition from reliance on traditional fossil fuels, including coal, oil, and natural gas, to embracing cleaner energy sources, notably renewables and green hydrogen. Significant challenges towards strategising for green transition in businesses exist, however, particularly in the context of identifying and addressing critical areas within their value chains and potential technological solutions. This difficulty often stems from a lack of comprehensive baseline greenhouse gas inventories encompassing Scope 1, 2, and most importantly Scope 3 emissions (Singal, 2022). Additionally, securing low-cost financing for these emerging and clean technologies remains a constraint. Furthermore, the initial investment required for clean technologies is high due to their emerging nature, limited scalability in the short term, and the underdevelopment of supporting ecosystems. The focus on research and development (R&D) in this field is not as robust as needed, and there is a noticeable scarcity of skilled professionals specialised in these emerging technologies. Policy inconsistencies also pose a challenge, affecting the visibility that is crucial for the adoption of capital-intensive clean technologies. Another significant hurdle is the gradual phasing down of coal-based power plants, which currently constitute over 60% of India's power supply mix (Ministry of Coal, 2023). Considering India's substantial energy requirements and the direct and indirect jobs tied to the coal industry, transitioning away from coal-based power will be a prolonged process.

In line with India's goal to derive 50% of its energy requirements from non-fossil fuel sources by 2030, a significant surge in new investments is anticipated. It is projected that green investments will reach around INR 36.5 lakh crore between the fiscal years 2024 and 2030. This figure marks a substantial increase from the estimated INR 7.2 lakh crore invested over the fiscal years 2017–2023 (Master, 2023). The primary focus of these investments will be in the power sector, encompassing the development of power grids and distribution networks, the installation of smart meters, and the establishment of transportation and hydrogen infrastructure. Many Indian industries had already committed to emission reduction goals, with over 89 corporates committing to science-based emission reduction targets by mid-2022 (Aggarwal *et al.*, 2023). Additionally, 400 Indian companies have joined the UN Global Compact, committing to universal sustainability principles (Andersen, 2021). Ensuring that suppliers and trading partners also adhere to these standards is crucial for a comprehensive approach to sustainability. India's journey towards a green economy reflects its diverse and multifaceted population, necessitating a unified effort across all societal sectors. Embracing its unique challenges and capitalising on its strengths, India is poised not only to achieve its green transition but also to become a role model for other developing nations. This transition aligns with the globally recognised necessity to reduce our collective carbon footprint. Significant research has been channelled into developing alternative energy sources, automotive innovations, and waste management methods. However, a critical aspect often overlooked is the enhancement of current operations to minimise their emission impact. In this context, the role of Business Process Management (BPM) technology becomes pivotal. With its focus on understanding, modelling, and refining business processes for optimisation, BPM is a crucial starting point in this endeavour. The application of process modelling technology transcends traditional business processes, extending to optimising manufacturing and other tangible processes. This approach is integral to India's strategy for a green transition, as it combines technological advancement with a holistic view of societal and economic change. Therefore, the importance of business process augmentation cannot be understated in the domain of maximising environmental benefits.

India's vast population of 1.3 billion, which accounts for 18% of the world's population, occupies only 2.4% of the world's land area. This demographic and spatial reality highlights the urgency of the nation's resource limitations. As our nation endeavours to attain economic growth commensurate with its expanding population, we are compelled to address resource scarcity. Adopting a model of development that is positive, inclusive, and environmentally sustainable could be the solution. The circular economy, characterised by its restorative and regenerative design, offers a viable path forward. Distinct from the traditional 'take-make-dispose' linear paradigm, a circular economy emphasises principles such as reducing, reusing, recycling, refurbishing, and remanufacturing. This model not only promotes the reuse of materials, thereby mitigating environmental degradation but also the judicious utilisation of products nearing the end of their useful lives. This strategy is especially relevant for products with significant environmental impacts, such as plastics and electronic appliances. Nonetheless, the current situation is fraught with obstacles. For instance, according to a report by the Central Pollution Control Board (CPCB, 2018), India generates approximately 25,940 tonnes of plastic waste daily, of which only 90% is recyclable, but less than $1/10^{th}$ of that is actually recycled. The remaining waste frequently ends up in landfills, water bodies, and the wider environment, exacerbating pollution and endangering marine life. Additionally, e-waste is a growing concern. According to the Global E-waste Monitor, India produced over 3.2 million tonnes of e-waste in 2019, placing it third in the world. However, only about 5% of this waste is recycled formally, with the remainder being informally processed or discarded, which has hazardous environmental and health consequences (Bhatt, 2023). Rapid urbanisation, escalating environmental challenges, and looming climate change threats increase the urgency for India to adopt a circular economy. By adopting this model, India can significantly reduce its reliance on natural resources, resulting in substantial annual economic benefits. In addition, the circular economy can reduce urban congestion and pollution, which has a multiplier effect on the economy of the nation. The overarching objective is to increase resource efficiency, reduce existing resource consumption, and foster innovative business models in order to propel India towards self-sufficiency.

At COP26, India announced its ambition to become a net-zero emitter by 2070- an important milestone in the fight against climate change. Despite low per-capita emissions (1.8 tons CO2), India is the third-largest emitter globally, emitting a net 2.9 gigatons of carbon dioxide equivalent every year as of 2019 (Gupta *et al.*, 2022). The bulk of these emissions (about 70%) are driven by six sectors: power, steel, automotive, aviation, cement, and agriculture. This indicates the need for a targeted decarbonisation policy focused on the top emitters. Three main technologies can aid us in this fight against anthropogenic climate change: green hydrogen; carbon capture, usage, and storage (CCUS); natural climate solutions; and material circularity. These four can enable India to potentially create 287 gigatons of carbon space for the entire world. This amounts to almost half the global carbon budget for an even chance at limiting warming to 1.5°C (Gupta *et al.*, 2022). The current pace of emissions intensity reduction is insufficient for India's emissions curve to bend with the expected growth outlook. If policies are set in place to create the right signals within this decade, then India could amplify the positive externalities of the same. According to a report by McKinsey & Company (Gupta *et al.*, 2022), India's transition from thermal power to renewables is expected to save a cumulative USD 1.7 trillion in foreign exchange, which may otherwise be spent on energy imports until 2070. In addition, India will be able to build itself right the first time, minimising asset stranding. If India can start manufacturing newer technologies, it has the potential to be a world leader in batteries, electrolysers, green steel, and other areas.

LEARNING FROM SUCCESS

India stands at a pivotal juncture, possessing a unique opportunity to significantly contribute to the United Nations' vision of inclusive and sustainable industrial development (ISID). Leading this charge are several Indian companies that have embraced sustainable practices. The Tata Group, for instance, has been pioneering the implementation of circular economy principles, for the previous half-a-decade with a focus on sustainable packaging and converting waste into fertiliser (Tata Sustainability Group, 2018). Similarly, ITC's E-Choupal initiative has revolutionised the supply chain in agriculture, creating more efficiency and addressing key challenges (Das, 2023). The Godrej Group has made notable strides with its green construction projects, achieving significant reductions in greenhouse gas emissions, and enhancing the use of renewable energy. In the realm of sustainable mobility, the

Mahindra Group has been notable in making impactful contributions by manufacturing electric vehicles (EVs).

This movement towards sustainability is not limited to large corporations. Numerous young entrepreneurs in India are also making waves with eco-business models and a "sustainability first" approach. In addition to newer entrepreneurs, our focus must be on transitioning pre-established smaller firms. Ultimately, Small and Medium Enterprises (SMEs), which form a substantial part of India's economy and workforce, are instrumental in achieving the Sustainable Development Goals. Government initiatives like "Zero Defect, Zero Effect" are instrumental in nurturing a sustainable business ecosystem, demonstrating India's commitment to a greener and more sustainable future. India's progress in the sector has also been internationally recognised and awarded. The Integrated Domestic Energy Systems (IDES) initiative in rural Bihar has been felicitated by international institutions as an extremely powerful model. This innovative model aims to provide energy security to low-income households, improving their incomes, education, and health. The IDES skilfully combines an enhanced cookstove with a solar PV-based lighting solution, offering customisation through various cooking energy options to meet individual household needs at a minimal additional cost (The Energy Resources Institute, 2015).

IDES involves women-run community organisations in every step of the energy delivery value chain, from need analysis and system design to demand aggregation, supply chain management, and after-sales service. This comprehensive approach ensures faster adoption and better alignment with the community's needs. Women, forming self-help groups, are taking on decision-making roles, granting loans, and managing credit repayment cycles. The impact of IDES is significant; it has reduced rural families' dependence on fossil fuels and fuel wood, thereby decreasing greenhouse gas emissions and enhancing environmental conservation. Moreover, IDES empowers rural women to lead their communities in eradicating poverty and promoting activities that enhance income while reducing vulnerability to climate change. With the introduction of IDES, these women are now channelling their time and efforts into more productive, livelihood-generating activities. Currently, IDES has reached over 10,000 households in one district and is expanding to reach 25,000 households across nine districts (United Nations Framework Convention on Climate Change, 2023). The long-term goal is to reach 10 million rural households. The high adoption rate of IDES demonstrates its potential to fill the demand-supply gap with cleaner energy sources, addressing climate change and exploring consumer responses to solar energy in rural areas.

In addition to the very important social impact space, green ventures have also become increasingly more profitable. India's green business economy landscape has witnessed a significant surge in enterprises integrating environmental and societal benefits with financial gains. In addition to achieving their sustainability objectives, these enterprises ensure their commercial success by generating consistent revenue streams. These innovative businesses not only contribute to India's sustainability but also set a precedent. Their success stories inspire aspiring entrepreneurs in India to establish businesses that are not only profitable but also environmentally conscious and prepared for the future. Listed below are some Indian start-ups that are capitalising on the opportunities presented by the emerging green economy:

1. Waste Ventures India, a pioneering for-profit social enterprise located in Telangana, is at the forefront of transforming solid waste management practices. This innovative organisation has committed to achieving a remarkable 90% reduction in waste for communities and offices, thereby significantly minimising their carbon footprint. The enterprise's research and development team has developed a scientific approach to managing organic waste, effectively eliminating pests and odours. Through their efforts, Waste Ventures India actively encourages recycling, composting, and other environmentally sustainable practices within local communities by efficiently handling ground waste. Since its establishment in 2013, Waste Ventures India has made a substantial impact on the environment by diverting over three thousand tonnes of waste away from Indian landfills, demonstrating a successful model of waste management that combines environmental responsibility with innovative business practices (Waste Ventures India, 2022).
2. Nexus Power, an enterprising start-up, is at the cutting edge of technology, utilising advanced nanotechnology to manufacture biodegradable batteries for electric vehicles, innovatively crafted from crop residue. This process involves converting unburned crop waste, a major source of air pollution, into rechargeable energy cells through a specialised extraction technique. These energy cells are subsequently integrated into battery packs designed for electric vehicles. Notably, these battery packs are enhanced with Internet of Things (IoT) and Artificial Intelligence (AI) capabilities, representing a significant leap in the field of sustainable energy and smart technology. Nexus Power's approach not only addresses the issue of air pollution caused by crop burning but also contributes to the advancement of eco-friendly transportation solutions (Nexus Power, 2023).
3. Founded in 2016 and based in Gurugram, Zunroof Solar is a home-tech company that has carved a niche in the domain of residential solar rooftops. They provide solar energy solutions that are seamlessly integrated with IoT smart energy technologies. Boasting an impressive portfolio, Zunroof has successfully completed over 10,000 solar rooftop installations and has designed 30,000 systems across various regions of India. This extensive reach has reportedly culminated in substantial savings for their clients, amounting to USD 6.1 million (approximately INR 50 crore) in electricity costs. Zunroof's operational footprint extends across more than seventy-five cities in twelve states, and their work in the

sector has garnered the attention of notable investors, including the Godrej Alliance (Zunroof Solar, 2023).

4. Phool.co, a visionary start-up, has pioneered a unique approach to flower recycling technology, focusing on converting floral waste into charcoal-free luxury fragrance products. This enterprise actively collects floral waste from temples and mosques across Uttar Pradesh, effectively preventing the daily disposal of approximately 7,600 kilograms of flowers and 97 kilograms of harmful chemicals into rivers. Through an inventive process, rural women's self-help groups play a crucial role in this eco-friendly initiative, transforming the collected floral waste into organic fertilisers and incense sticks. This not only aids in environmental conservation by reducing river pollution but also empowers rural women by involving them in sustainable economic activities (PHOOL, 2023).

CONCLUSION

To expedite India's decarbonization effectively, it is imperative for all stakeholders to collaborate and take immediate action. The government's role is crucial in providing policy and regulatory support to render projects across various sectors economically feasible. This support could manifest in various forms, such as offering incentives for the adoption of new green technologies. This could be achieved by balancing taxation policies, streamlining regulatory processes for the authorization and installation of new power and grid infrastructures, and creating market demand for higher-cost green materials like steel. Additionally, fostering support for the localization of green manufacturing is essential. Equally important is ensuring a just transition that mitigates adverse impacts on low-income households. The implementation of these actions needs to be strategically sequenced to prevent potential issues such as energy shortages, price hikes, and disorderliness in the transition process. Achieving significant technological advancements in this realm will necessitate sustained investment from both public and private sectors. Moreover, a willingness to embrace new technologies among business leaders and policymakers is critical. This includes adopting long-duration storage technologies to harness the seasonality of renewable energy sources, advancing fuel cell technology, and enhancing recycling technologies. Such comprehensive and coordinated efforts are vital for India's journey towards a sustainable and low-carbon future.

REFERENCES

Abdullah, A. (2022, September 2). Building Green Homes: Planet over Profit. The Hindu. https://www.thehindu.com/real-estate/planet-green-buildings-homes-construction-building-environment-eco-friendly-materials/article65487348.ece

Aggarwal, V., Prasad, B., Santhosh, A., Rustagi, V. and Makol, N. (2023). Net Zero Roadmap for Corporates in India. World Wildlife Fund India and Bridge to India. https://wwfin.awsassets.panda.org/downloads/net_zero_roadmap_for_corporates___wwf_india.pdf

Agricultural and Processed Food Products Export Development Authority. (2023). National Programme for Organic Production. https://apeda.gov.in/apedawebsite/organic/organic_products.htm

Ahuja, B., Chakraborty, A. and Venkataraman, V. (2023). Greening of msmes key in India's journey towards climate-resilience. Down To Earth. https://www.downtoearth.org.in/blog/climate-change/greening-of-msmes-key-in-india-s-journey-towards-climate-resilience-88404

Andersen, I. (2021, November 28). The business of Sustainability: Opportunities for India. Commonwealth Business Communications. https://commonwealthbc.com/2021/11/22/the-business-of-sustainability-opportunities-for-india/

Bhatt, A. (2023, February 10). How the e-waste you produce is providing poor children with a dangerous living. Deutsche Welle. https://indianexpress.com/article/explained/explained-health/how-the-e-waste-you-produce-is-providing-poor-children-with-a-dangerous-living-8435127/

Central Pollution Control Board (CPCB) (2018). Life Cycle Assessment (LCA) Study of Plastics Packaging Products. https://www.cpcb.nic.in/uploads/plasticwaste/LCA_Report_15.05.2018.pdf

Chaurey, R. and Le, D.T. (2022, August 18). Infrastructure Maintenance and rural economic activity: Evidence from India. *Journal of Public Economics.* https://www.sciencedirect.com/science/article/abs/pii/S004727272200127X

Damodaran, H. (2023, March 7). What India's labour force and national income data tell us about jobs shifting from agriculture. The Indian Express. https://indianexpress.com/article/explained/explained-economics/explained-economics-agriculture-and-employment-8480945/

Das, S. (2023, April 16). ITC to expand climate smart initiative to a million farmers. Industry News | The Financial Express. https://www.financialexpress.com/business/industry-itc-to-expand-climate-smart-initiative-to-a-million-farmers-3049495/

DD News (2023). India surpasses 72.02 GW in solar power capacity, driving renewable energy transition. https://ddnews.gov.in/national/india-surpasses-7202-gw-solar-power-capacity-driving-renewable-energy-transition

The Energy Resources Institute (2015). Technology: Integrated Domestic Energy Systems. LaBL, TERI. http://labl.teriin.org/blog-detail.php?id=2

Goel, S., Biswas, D.A., Banerjee, S. and Kedia, S. (2022). Financing Low Carbon Transition in India's MSME Sector. The Energy and Resources Institute. https://www.teriin.org/sites/default/files/2022-10/Financing_Low_Carbon_Tranistion_for_India_MSME_Sector.pdf

Gupta, R., Malik, D., Sankhe, S. and Unni, N. (2022, October 27). Decarbonising india: Charting a pathway for sustainable growth. McKinsey & Company. https://www.mckinsey.com/capabilities/sustainability/our-insights/decarbonising-india-charting-a-path way-for-sustainable-growth

The Hindu (2023, April 8). Banks sanction □23.2 lakh crore to about 41 crore beneficiaries under Mudra Yojana. https://www.thehindu.com/business/banks-sanction-232-lakh-crore-to-about-41-crore-beneficiaries-under-mudra-yojana/article66713167.ece

Hussain, F.I. and Dill, H. (2023). India incorporates green bonds into its climate finance strategy. World Bank Blogs. https://blogs.worldbank.org/climatechange/india-incorporates-green-bonds-its-climate-finance-strategy

Jain, P. (2022, March 2). Innovation in India's Rural Economy. Bain & Company. https://www.bain.com/insights/innovation-in-indias-rural-economy/

Kuchimanchi, S. (2023, June 14). What will it take to build Green in urban India? *India Development Review.* https://idronline.org/article/climate-emergency/what-will-it-take-to-build-green-in-urban-india/

Manohar, A. (2023). Renewable energy in India – Indian power industry investment. in India: Investment Opportunities in the Pow... https://www.investindia.gov.in/sector/renewable-energy

Master, P. (2023, October 13). The green shift: India embraces challenges, takes concerted action for a low-carbon future – ET energy world. Energy World, Economic Times. https://energy.economictimes.indiatimes.com/news/renewable/the-green-shift-india-embraces-challenges-takes-concerted-action-for-a-low-carbon-future/104406216

Ministry of Coal (2023). Major Statistics: Coal – Indian Energy Choice. Ministry of Coal, Government of India. https://coal.nic.in/en/major-statistics/coal-indian-energy-choice

Nexus Power (2023). Technology. Nexus. https://nexuspower.in/technology.html

Outlook Money. (2023). Indian residential real estate market hits record sales in FY23, says Anarock Group. Outlook Magazine. https://www.outlookindia.com/business/indian-residential-real-estate-market-hits-record-sales-in-fy23-says-report-news-286448

PHOOL.CO (2023). The journey of an incense store- Our Story. https://phool.co/pages/our-story

Press Information Bureau. (2023). Economic survey highlights thrust on Rural Development. https://pib.gov.in/PressReleasePage.aspx?PRID=1894901

Press Trust of India. (2023). India to achieve 500 GW renewables target before 2030 deadline: RK Singh. The Economic Times. https://economictimes.indiatimes.com/industry/renewables/india-to-achieve-500-gw-renewables-target-before-2030-deadline-rk-singh/articleshow/103936965.cms

Pretty, J.N., Noble, A.D., Bossio, D.A., Dixon, J., Bragg, R.E., de Vries, F.W.T.P. and Morison, J.I. (2006). Resource-conserving agriculture increases yields in developing countries. Environmental Science and Technology. https://www.researchgate.net/publication/7206194_Resource-Conserving_Agriculture_Increases_Yields_in_Developing_Countries

Scott, M. (2023, October 18). The 100 most sustainable companies of 2023. Corporate Knights. https://www.corporateknights.com/rankings/global-100-rankings/2023-global-100-rankings/2023-global-100-most-sustainable-companies/

Shukla, R. (2023). The Rise of India's Middle Class: Gearing Up For a Billion-Plus Middle Class by 2047. People's Research on India's Consumer Economy.

Singal, N. (2022, December 6). India's Elusive Net Zero target: Reducing Scope 3 emissions by companies may be key. Business Today. https://www.businesstoday.in/magazine/bt500-indias-most-valuable-companies/story/focus-on-reducing-scope-3-emissions-by-companies-might-help-india-achieve-net-zero-targets-355353-2022-12-06

Singh, P., Pandey, P.C., Petropoulos, G.P., Pavlides, A., Srivastava, P.K., Koutsias, N., Deng, K.A.K. and Bao, Y. (2020, August 7). Hyperspectral remote sensing in precision agriculture: Present status, Challenges, and future trends. Hyperspectral Remote Sensing. https://www.sciencedirect.com/science/article/abs/pii/B9780081028940000097

Tata Sustainability Group (2018). Closing the Loop- The Circular Economy in Action. https://www.tatasustainability.com/pdfs/Highlights/TheCircularEconomyInAction.pdf

Torkington, S. (2023). We're on the brink of a "polycrisis" – how worried should we be? World Economic Forum. https://www.weforum.org/agenda/2023/01/polycrisis-global-risks-report-cost-of-living/

United Nations Framework Convention on Climate Change. (2023). Green Business Opportunities – India. Unfccc.int. https://unfccc.int/climate-action/momentum-for-change/activity-database/green-business-opportunities

Waste Ventures india. (2022, June 1). About Us – Waste Ventures india. Waste Ventures. https://wasteventures.com/about-us/

ZunRoof Solar. (2023). Zunroof solar – About Us. ZunRoof. https://www.zunroof.com/about

Author Index